The Arnold and Caroline Rose Monograph Series
of the American Sociological Association

Working daughters of Hong Kong

Filial piety or power in the family?

Other books in the series

Working daughters of Hong Kong

Filial piety or power in the family?

Janet W. Salaff
Department of Sociology
University of Toronto

with a Foreword by Kingsley Davis

Cambridge University Press
Cambridge
London   New York   New Rochelle
Melbourne   Sydney

Published by the Press Syndicate of the University of Cambridge
The Pitt Building, Trumpington Street, Cambridge CB2 1RP
32 East 57th Street, New York, NY 10022, USA
296 Beaconsfield Parade, Middle Park, Melbourne 3206, Australia

First published 1981

Printed in the United States of America

Typeset by KeieL Enterprises, North Bergen, N.J.
Printed and bound by The Murray Printing Co., Westford, Mass.

Library of Congress Cataloging in Publication Data

Salaff, Janet W
Working daughters of Hong Kong.
(The Arnold and Caroline Rose monograph series in sociology)
Includes bibliographical references and index.
1. Young women – Employment – Hongkong. 2. Young
women – Hongkong. 3. Family – Hongkong. 4. Hongkong –
Social conditions. I. Title. II. Series: Arnold and
Caroline Rose monograph series in sociology.
HD6055.6.H85S24   331.3'44'095125   80-23909
ISBN 0 521 23679 7 hard covers
ISBN 0 521 28148 2 paperback

To Steve and Shana

In a traditional bridal lament from a Hakka village in Hong Kong, a bride bewails the lack of family recognition for her toil:

> From the first month your daughter began to work –
> Worked until the winter;
> Never before did venerable father
> So much as calculate a wage.
> This morning your daughter's hand
> Seizes the abacus;
> Father was never scrupulous
> In reckoning my wage.
> Your daughter would count little more than a dime
> To be sufficient wage;
> But one dollar and some
> That would be fair!
>
> – C. F. Blake,
> "Death and abuse in marriage laments"

Contents

Figures and tables

Figures

Tables

Foreword

At a time when much of social science consists of fitting equations to data, it is refreshing to read a social scientist's account of the lives of actual people. Janet Salaff, a well-known sociologist and specialist on China, has studied the history of twenty-eight young unmarried working women in Hong Kong, and in this volume she has given us not only her conclusions but also the full stories of ten of the women. The reader can thus identify with these individuals, seeing in their experience and through their eyes how work, education, family, friendship, and marriage interact as their lives unfold, and can gain unique insight into the clash between traditional Chinese familism and the individualistic industrialism of a modern city.

The author's acquaintance with eighteen of the young women began in volunteer evening classes in English, which she taught for Hong Kong factory workers in 1973; the other ten were selected in various ways to secure representation of additional occupations. Her contact with the young women, whose average age in 1973 was 19, was prolonged and deepened by visits to their homes, acquaintance with their friends, and discussions with parents, siblings, and suitors. This participant observation, maintained over the years, has enabled her to depict each woman in her milieu in a totally realistic but focused manner. The result is not the smooth but involved type of character study that a novelist would portray, nor yet the symptomatic case study that a social worker or psychiatrist would provide, but rather a dynamic biographical analysis of how the lives of women are shaped by traditional institutions and changing conditions. The author is of course aided by her knowledge of the theoretical literature on social change and her outstanding knowledge of Chinese society.

All of the twenty-eight women who form the focus of the study belong to refugee families, mostly from the neighboring province of Kwangtung. Coming mostly from small towns or rural areas, these families are characterized by exceptionally strong bonds. Hong Kong, however, although composed mainly of refugees, is a huge city of five million people living at an average density of some 12,000 per square mile. Short of resources, including water, land, and energy, the colony must depend solely on the skills and work of its people in the cruelest of all markets, the international market in textiles, manufactures, and finance. Its wages have to be extremely competitive, even for Asia; otherwise it could not live. This necessity has been reinforced in large part by the hundreds of thousands of refugees pouring into the city, whose advent has been due to conditions they find intolerable in the People's Republic of China rather than to attractive conditions in the city. The immigrants have accepted the low wages that Hong Kong employers must pay in order to remain competitive on the international market, and they have been reasonably content with the reluctance of the colonial administration to provide costly government services. In the eyes of those who worship economic development, Hong Kong has been a marvelous success story, but no one can pretend that it has become a paradise.

Strewn with human tragedy is the conflict between stubborn familism and the exigencies of the modern great city. Across the border, on the mainland, the adversary of familism is Marxism, and it has not won a complete victory in the majority of China that is still rural; in Hong Kong the enemy is simply the bustling impersonality of a huge city. In the absence of a frontal attack on family institutions, the city's influence is insidious and ambivalent. Ultimately it may undermine familism more in its own milieu than communism does in a rural milieu, but in the meantime the struggle is by no means one-sided. By its very competitiveness and impersonality, the city throws people back on the nuclear family as a haven. And the tenacity with which each family behaves as a unit, planning and sacrificing for vertical mobility years and even generations ahead, is amazing. Accordingly, the fact that all of the author's twenty-eight young women work, and that this work is located outside the home and paid for individually, does not "emancipate" them. Although their families are large (nineteen of the respondents grew up in families of five or more children) and are cooped up in unbelievably crowded quarters, the young women do not rent a place for themselves, as they could do, but rather all live with their families. Although legally entitled to spend their money as they wish, they all contribute three-fourths or more of their wages to the family – not only to help with general household expenses but to meet the personal wants of other family members, such as the educational expenses of younger siblings. Being daughters, they are not usually given much say in family decisions, even when these involve spending money they have contributed; and they are not themselves the objects of much family investment, because when they marry, they will join their husband's family. The daughters, who often start work at ages 13 to 15, must therefore contribute to the education of the sons, and in crowded Hong Kong, where education is financed mainly by families, this investment can be substantial.

Can it be, then, that the most powerful familism in the world (the Chinese variety) can withstand the corrosion of the big city and thus refute conventional theory? At first blush, the vivid portrayals of dutiful daughters might suggest a positive answer, but the author does not give that interpretation. It is by delving into the aspirations and emotions of these young women that she finds the harbingers of future change. She seems to view the present circumstances as a phase in the readjustment of the family to the city – a phase in which the family utilizes for its own purposes the new opportunities presented by the city but in so doing prepares the ground for its own weakening. For instance, as long as the daughters are submissive and turn over most of their wages to the family, their work outside the home reinforces rather than undermines the family unit; but the daughters are well aware that the money they give the family they cannot spend on themselves, that it is unfair for a male in the family to decide arbitrarily how their wages should be spent, that when they marry they will simply be subjected to another male authority, and that their own education (and hence their own advancement) is being sacrificed in favor of their brothers' education. Given this awareness, it seems unlikely that these women will instill the same amount of docility in the next generation, their own daughters. Since the wages of an unmarried girl now go mainly to her parents, the parents are motivated to have her postpone marriage until a late age, and she herself often feels an obligation or a preference to do so. But marital postponement means more education and sophistication before marriage, and also more self-selection of marital partner, none of which contributes to wifely submission after marriage or to the subjugation of the daughters who will be born.

Actually, statistical measures of family change show that "defamilization" is proceeding rapidly in Hong Kong. Fertility, which was extremely high during the 1950s and early 1960s as the rural refugees streamed in, has fallen dramatically. In seven years, between 1969 and 1976, the total fertility rate dropped by 33%, and it is now lower than it is in some European countries. The rapid rise in the average age at marriage has given Hong Kong a very European distribution by marital status. For instance, despite the large surplus of males in the young adult ages (a surplus that would normally lead to a high proportion of married women), the percentage of Hong Kong women ages 20–24 who in 1971 had never married was 68% compared to 36% in the United States. At ages 25–29, 20% of Hong Kong females had never married, compared to only 12% in the United States. This is a revolutionary change compared to the early marriage pattern in precommunist Kwangtung, and it signifies not only a further reduction in fertility but a future reduced propensity ever to marry, a higher level of female education, and a greater equality in marriage when marriage occurs. It will not be long, it seems, until the familism by which China lived for so many centuries will be reduced to the attenuated family structure so familiar in the West. In this transition, the generation now coming into adulthood bears the main burden of the change. No one has given a better account of how that burden looks from the standpoint of the female participants than Janet Salaff in the present volume. She is to be congratulated for her insight, commitment, and ingenuity. She has made a fascinating contribution to the literature on social change.

Kingsley Davis

University of Southern California
November 1980

Preface

My study of the power of the Chinese family to direct its working youth's material contribution to the family within the burgeoning Hong Kong industrial economy embraced twenty-eight employed young working- and middle-class Hong Kong women. I gathered data on these women from 1971 to 1976 during five field trips, encompassing 16 months in the colony. My most intensive session of interviewing and participant observation occurred in 1973. To obtain complete portraits of these women as workers and daughters I combined intensive, in-depth, open-ended interviews with a sharing of experiences in factories, in the women's homes, and during their leisure-time activities. I stayed overnight in the homes of three women in the book. Friends, family members, and relatives were auxiliary contacts who amplified respondents' own testimonies. I spoke with the women's parents, sisters, and friends on all occasions possible.

I sought the personal interpretation of each woman's responsibilities, hopes, and frustrations in the workplace and in the family. In these sensitive areas, the woman's candor in disclosing her feelings and attitudes depended above all upon our mutual rapport. I was gratified not only at the candidness of our interviews but the trust that developed between us, which enabled me in many cases to join in the women's social activities. This participant-observation style of investigation, coupled with direct discussions, brought the woman's behavior into much closer focus than close-ended verbal interview protocols.

My relationships with the group of Hong Kong working daughters introduced in this book spanned 6 years of my life. Our engagements were punctuated by intervals of separation, during which I sought to clarify the issues that would become most problematic as their lives unfolded. I decided rather early that the most suitable form for my research would be a panel study, in which a population of individuals is contacted and interviewed over an extended period of time. As my field visits continued, I naturally went through my own series of social role changes: from being childless to early motherhood to a mother with an older child. These personal changes placed me in a different role relationship with my working daughters of this book, their families, and friends. In 1971, as a young married woman not yet a mother and unaccompanied by my husband, my position was reasonably close to that of my unmarried women respondents and I could easily adapt to their roles and activities. However, as a new mother in 1973 I found that my role had altered, and that it had become easier to interact with additional members of the respondents' families, including their mothers and married siblings, on the common ground of motherhood and a shared concern for children.

I was a nursing mother when my 7-month-old daughter Shana and I arrived in Hong Kong in January, 1973. She accompanied me on many visits for nearly 9 months, watching over my shoulder from her snug backpack. At first it did not occur to me that Shana's presence would greatly affect my investigations, but I soon realized that a child could be an asset. My Hong Kong Chinese friends and acquaintances were absorbed with small children and lavished much affection on Shana. Shana's presence in the homes of my respondents indicated my acceptance and appreciation of their everyday milieu, and they responded with a gratifying willingness to share their views and aspirations. Their homes provided a kind of extended family environment for both of us, without which I would have found it difficult to carry out my work. Shana was a universal stimulus to discussions on child care and motherhood expectations and provided me with considerable insight into the way my respondents' families raised children.

The evening English classes I taught to factory workers provided my initial entry into the women's milieu. Organized by religious and social service agencies for working-class youths who had terminated their education at primary and lower-middle school levels, these inexpensive, semiweekly classes offered no recognized language training but functioned rather like clubs. The young people enrolled voluntarily, but they were typical of Hong Kong youths, because by attending evening classes organized by European and Chinese social workers they were partaking of an extremely common self-improvement activity for young people of their age and social situation. The women, whose average age was 19 in 1973, were at liberty to join the class primarily because there were no longer baby sisters or brothers who required nurturing care and the junior siblings were old enough to do household chores.

An assessment of the continuity and change of the family in industrialized settings as brought about by women's work must analyze the two
main features of the woman's position: her job and her family structure.
My evening class sample was thus informed by a series of quotas. I
taught three evening classes, each of which drew its students from a
range of working-class occupations and income levels, and I approached
eighteen of the women students, all of whom agreed to participate in
this study. The remaining ten women were contacted through a variety
of ways to comprise: 1) the occupations held most frequently by young
women in Hong Kong (factory work, sales, service, semiprofessional),
2) the size of firm in which they toiled (large and medium factory,
small workshop), 3) its capital mix (multinational branch plant, domestic capital, family business), 4) family structure (father present or resident elsewhere; mother the sole, primary, or secondary wife [concu-
bine]; mother employed or a homemaker), 5) sibling order (respondent
is the eldest, middle, or youngest daughter in the family), and 6) education (respondent completed primary, secondary, or college education).

I collected material for all twenty-eight women concerning their
several areas of experience of family structure, education, peer group,
and work, and these materials are presented for each case included in
this volume. The life histories of the interviewees are arranged according to their occupations when I was interviewing them. The arrangement of material by respondent's vocation is necessary to address the
stress of some writers on the disruptive experience of work, the technology of the workplace, and entry into the market economy, which
are said to alter the relationship of the worker to her family. Each employed daughter reacts to her social environment, with its shared societal precepts, norms, and values, but her particular constellation and
life course vary. Thus, in addition to those realms of her life she holds
in common with the others, for each woman I also elaborate on the
specific socially derived experiences that create her identity. Together
the shared and distinctive biographical nuances form the basis of each
life presented in the book.

The women in the book are real people, and only the names are
fictitious. I am still in contact with a number of the working girls of
this study, some of whom have married and started families of their
own, while others remain single and in the workforce. The conclusions I
reached in the course of participant observation and interviewing are
borne out by the subsequent life experiences of them all.

In Chapter 1 I define the concept of the centripetal family, discuss its historical origins and development in the Chinese polity, and demonstrate that the competitive and factional nature of contemporary Hong Kong society supports the continuation, in modified form, of centripetal family structures. With this social history material as background, my ten Hong Kong working daughters are presented in Chapters 2 through 5, where they are grouped according to occupational categories: factory workers, office employees, and service-sector personnel. In conclusion, Chapter 6 develops an overall picture of the position of women in family and society and assesses the impact of employment on the status of women in a centripetal family regime. For this purpose I introduce material from all twenty-eight working women interviewees. Although the effects of industrial employment resonate throughout their lives, nevertheless strong bonds of loyalty and obligation to family are sustained for all twenty-eight daughters.

This study of the effects of industrialization upon Chinese family and society would not have been possible without the assistance of numerous people. I owe my friend Leung Kei-kit a debt of gratitude for her sympathetic and talented assistance during and after the research was completed. As is always the case with studies based on field work, I owe a special debt to the women who participated so enthusiastically and willingly. The Universities Service Centre in Hong Kong provided a helpful and friendly setting for my writing, and special thanks go to Stella Wong, my daughter's "adopted" mother and administrative assistant at the Centre.

The study was funded largely by a grant from the Program in Support of Legal and Social Science Research on Population Policy, sponsored by the Ford and Rockefeller Foundations. The International Studies Programme at the University of Toronto also provided helpful financial aid in the initial stages of the project. I wish to thank these programs not only for their support but also for their flexibility, which allows the results to take the present form.

In Hong Kong the generous assistance of members of the Department of Census and Vital Statistics deserves special mention. Kenneth Topley and Bernard Williams unstintingly assisted me by providing unpublished census tabulations that greatly contributed to the validity of this type of research.

Several people who have commented on earlier drafts have helped clarify the issues and their expression. For the effort they put into their comments, I am very grateful to Gordon Bennett, Steve Berkowitz,

Richard Bilsborrow, Fred Blake, Jerome Ch'en, Rik Davidson, Norma Diamond, Wolfram Eberhard, Bernard Farber, Edward Friedman, Margaret Greenfield, John W. Lewis, Angus McDonald, Raymon Myers, Andrew Nathan, Eleanor Rawski, Edward Rhoads, Al Richmond, Paul Rosenblatt, Mark Selden, James Sheridan, Mary Sheridan, Ned Shorter, Jetse Sprey, Allen Sutterfield, Louise Tilly, Pru Tracey, Lillian Weitzner, Martin K. Whyte, Roxanne Witke, Marilyn Young, and the anonymous reviewers from the Arnold Rose Monograph Series of the American Sociological Association.

I appreciate the assistance provided me in preparation of the graphics by members of the Department of Geography, Chinese University of Hong Kong; the Department of Geography, Hong Kong University; the Hong Kong Housing Authority; and Jenny Wilcox, Geoff Matthews, and Chris Grounds, Department of Geography, University of Toronto. Fred Salaff gave his time and talent to preparation of the photographic essay.

I would like to record my great debt to Irene Taeuber, who sadly did not live to see the final outcome of the kind of work she encouraged.

Finally, my warmest appreciation is given to my husband Steve, whose sympathetic encouragement, support, and talented ear made completion of this work possible.

Janet W. Salaff

Toronto
November 1980

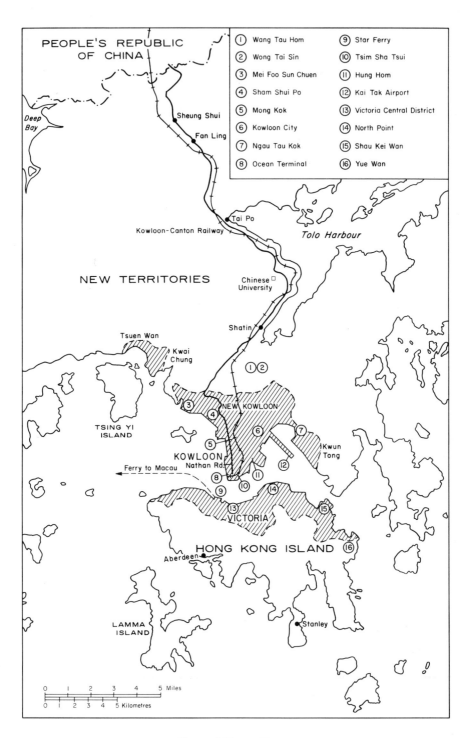

Map of Hong Kong

Introduction

In this book the impact of industrialization upon family relationships and the fabric of society is illustrated through the lives of ten Hong Kong working daughters. The literature on modernization and the family, and in particular the debate on the liberation of women wage workers, are reviewed in this introduction, but the reader who wishes to enter the Hong Kong lives directly should begin with the socioeconomic background in Chapter 1.

Throughout the manufacturing centers of the developing world, country and city girls toil on assembly lines and at piecework labor. Although their opportunities and motives for a work career are varied, their employment outside the home invariably affects family life, and sociologists are increasingly concerned with one central question: Does female industrial employment tear apart long-standing family hierarchies of authority, responsibility, and obligation, or do working women remain essentially subordinated to their families? In this book I assess the impact of women's factory, office, and service-sector employment on their family bonds in a metropolis that has experienced particularly rapid economic growth since the 1960s: the British crown colony of Hong Kong.

Urban Hong Kong has been subject to British sovereignty for almost a century. Since World War II it has become an industrial city of over four and a half million persons. Less than 4% of the population is employed in agriculture and rural industries, and thus Hong Kong is atypical of most developing nations, with their preponderance of cultivators. Moreover, Hong Kong is enveloped by a peculiar atmosphere of political, economic, and social uncertainty generated by the impending expiration of Great Britain's lease from China of the New Territories, Hong Kong's sizable internal hinterland.

Despite Hong Kong's singularities, this industrial colony offers a useful natural laboratory for evaluating the relationship between rapid industrialization and traditional culture and their effects on contempo-

1

rary family structure. Since the economies and social institutions of today's developing nations depend, to one degree or another, on global markets, Hong Kong's export-driven industrialization is prototypical of socioeconomic growth patterns along the Pacific Rim, where young women constitute a pool of relatively inexpensive labor that, throughout the area, is steadily drawn into factories from South Korea to Taiwan, the Philippines, Singapore, Malaysia, and Thailand (AMPO, 1977; Arrigo, in preparation; Diamond, 1976; Kung, 1976, in preparation; Mintz, 1977; Snow, 1977). Once primarily agrarian, these areas are increasingly characterized by rapidly expanding industries and institutions, such as export-processing zones that bind them to the global capitalist economy.

Rapid industrialization has occurred, in different places, since the beginning of the 1700s and for over a century has stimulated critical analysis and theories about the impact of industrial production on social bonds (Nisbet, 1970). Several late-nineteenth- and early-twentieth-century investigators focused specifically on women's participation in England's mills and workshops to illustrate industry's disruption of sacrosanct family roles. The scattering of young members of the once-cohesive family economy to factories, the consequent attenuation of parental authority and profound alteration of moral codes, rising infant mortality, illegitimacy, and other dramatic effects were attributed to the entry of women into industry (Collier, 1965; Engels, 1973; Hammond and Hammond, 1966; Pinchbeck, 1969).

Contemporary social scientists who observe the developing nations against the backdrop of such pessimistic nineteenth-century Western European views still grapple with many challenging problems raised by the increased economic contributions of women and the possible liberating effects of their wage labor on women's domestic standing. The thrust of analysis less frequently assumes the destructive impact of industrialization and more frequently idolizes the freeing powers of technology upon family roles. Both the earlier concerns over disruption and the present individuating interpretations emphasize the powerful impact of industrial production upon the social fabric. Better understanding of these past and present dynamics depends on the extent to which women's wages and extrafamilial contacts become opening wedges for the renegotiation of their position in the family.

Although writers agree on the pervasiveness of socioeconomic change attendant upon industrialization, two relatively distinct approaches to its force govern contemporary concept formation in this field. One group of writers, the "disjunctive theorists," holds that women's work drives a wedge between women and their families by providing income and experiences in the world outside the home. Factory work seems wonderful in its ability to break apart long-standing kinship structures, free young people from parental vigilance and control, and provide young people with opportunities to develop a life apart from their families, in particular with their age peers (Aries, 1965). Accordingly, the assembly-line organization of production competes with parentally directed household labor in which pre-industrial women formerly participated, thereby undermining parental authority (Smelser, 1959). The factory can be considered a school for modernity because it presents an objective standard of productivity, strict requirement of profitability, models of efficiency (exemplified by engineers, technicians, and skilled workers and reinforced by a system of rewards and punishments), strict planning, regimens, and rules. Thus the factory trains its employees in new approaches toward humanity, nature, time, and the social order. These new modes of orientation center on the individual, who is the focus for the systems of payment, reward, and punishment; and the newly enforced time sense and hierarchy of authority. Generally, individual workers learn to put themselves and what they need ahead of demands of the social group (Inkeles and Smith, 1974; Miller, 1976). Accordingly, as soon as women move from family toil into factories, they obtain rights, power, and authority consistent with their newly acquired economic worth (Blood and Wolf, 1960; Goode, 1963).

These disjunctivist views suggest that modern industry has even greater behavioral implications for contemporary family life than the relatively small factories of the late-nineteenth and early-twentieth century had. The first factories, workshops, and stores in which women and men toiled – with their associated paternalistic managerial ideologies – have been replaced by the large-scale industrial organizations of advanced capitalism (Bendix, 1957). These enterprises enter the contemporary developing nations in search of labor in the form of transnational corporations, and their domination over the local economy magnifies the impact of the industrial order several fold. Transnational corporations are not only larger than local capitalist enterprises, but in late-developed nations, as in Hong Kong, they operate according to monopoly capitalist market principles, rarely introduce paternalistic management styles, and consequently attenuate vestiges of kin relations that so often are a concomitant of indigenous capitalism. The disjunctive school of modernization expects the contemporary forms of industry to crush the social organization of the inherited host society even more thoroughly than occurred under conditions of early capitalist industrialization.

According to disjunctivist theory, modern industry not only cleaves asunder the economic and organizational underpinnings of family control but also undermines traditional attitudes of respect toward the family, which loses long-standing legitimacy. The separation of factory girls from their families of origin is strengthened by the spirit of modern capitalism, the "wish to be free" (Weinstein and Platt, 1969). Edward Shorter (1972, 1975) postulated that beginning in the late nineteenth century, the rise of the market nexus and wage labor led to individualism and differentiation, to fundamental changes in male-female relations, and to a large-scale change in family systems. At the root of these transformations was, eventually, "the desire to find personal happiness, to commence on that long voyage of personal development and self-discovery that constitutes the Inner Search . . ." (1975: 259). Employed women, freed from past restrictive social bonds, were ready and able to embark upon this search. As a result, illegitimacy increased, the birth rate dropped, the age of marriage fluctuated, and neolocal households took root and spread widely. A qualitatively new, individually based social structure emerged.

Shorter's general propositions regarding the progression from the nineteenth-century market economy to individualism, freely formed romantic attachments, and the eventual rupture of organic village life and family economic units are shared by other students of modernization in contemporary transitional developing societies. Shorter's focus upon technology as a trigger for value change finds a ready audience among the disjunctive modernization theorists. Well before Shorter, they emphasized industrialization as an uprooting process in which the forces of individualism and autonomy versus group orientation, achievement versus ascriptive orientation, and husband-wife egalitarianism versus patriarchal authoritarianism epitomize the tension and conflict between modern and traditional society (Levy, 1970; Miller, 1976; Parsons, 1951).

The mass media contribute integrally to the modernization process in shaping the attitudes of developing peoples, according to disjunctive theorists. Western-derived television, in particular, and its advertising, has the power to transform viewers' long-standing, culturally rooted attitudes, replacing them with adulation for the consumer economy, a glorified picture of the Western nuclear middle-class family, and other attitudes and information, thereby ineluctibly drawing the passive viewer into the modern consumer economy. Although their impact upon the Third World's behavior and attitudes still needs further study, the media's opponents and proponents maintain that the media have a great potential to uproot the populace around the globe from its inherited way of life (Ewen, 1976; Lerner, 1958, 1967; McLuhan, 1966; Mander, 1978).

The hypothesis of societal convergence is closely related to the thesis of the uprooting powers of modern industry. Propounded by Inkeles (1960), Kerr et al. (1960), Miller (1976), and Wertheim (1965), this perspective maintains that industrialization gives rise to closely comparable institutions and attitudes across cultures, among which is the modern nuclear family institution. According to convergence theory, families in such widely divergent societies as the European, African, and Asian should all eventually experience relatively similar changes under the impact of industrial organization and the mass media (Goode, 1963). Convergence theory, like disjunctive concepts, posits that industrialization manifests itself in a polarity between the individual and the group and maintains, moreover, that this polarity can be found worldwide.

There is another approach, however. In contrast to the disjunctivist/convergence theorists' stress on the uprooting power of industrial work organization and accompanying values across time and space, studies of family strategies in the early stages of industrialization have demonstrated the continued force of family-based norms, values, and sanctions. The view that parents' authority over their offspring is inevitably and uniformly destroyed by industrialization is especially surprising when considered in light of such studies on the family economy in late-nineteenth- and early-twentieth-century Europe and North America. Tilly and Scott's (1978) empirical work on the family economies of English and French urbanites demonstrated that working offspring continued to place their income at the family's disposal. The family was transformed from a pre-industrial unit, in which domestic necessities like food, clothing, and furnishings were manufactured by women at home and possessed what Seccombe (1974) after Marx called "use value," to a family wage economy in which all earners voluntarily deposited their cash into the central family fund. Parents gave a great deal of overt attention to enforcing the family wage economy, but they also were found to direct the social life of young people, albeit more discreetly than before. Thus the family remained the dominant unit of reference for unmarried working women, whose labor power was a disposable family resource from one generation to the next.[1]

The findings of Tilly and Scott and others[2] have been echoed in primary investigations of family strategies in contemporary late-developing economies, which also demonstrate the continuation of family-based earning units. Key features of the Third World urban centers are an absence of jobs for married women and the predominance and expansion of women's jobs, occurring mainly in the unskilled manufacturing labor force. In economies like that of Brazil, "working-class families appear to be surviving by following a policy of multiple wage-earning, which drives both men and women into the labor force at an early age" (Safa, 1978:7).

If the family could retain its hold over its wage-earning offspring in societies where loosely organized kindred prevailed, as in Europe, New England, or Brazil, a society like China, with a more tightly organized corporate kinship group and where the virtues of family loyalty were supported by the state and educational system, should have enabled even greater continuity of family control over working offspring. In the terms used by Tilly and Scott (1978), the family wage economy must have continued among working-class families as a fundamental strategy of family survival and self-upgrading.

No matter what the findings for European-originated societies, considerable research on the transformation of the family in Taiwan under the impact of industrialization indicates the still-pervasive extent of parental authority over the disposable income of the children. The Taiwanese wage economies studied by Arrigo (in preparation), Kung (1976, in preparation), and Marsh (1968) draw upon the earnings of all children but in particular single out the working daughters' wages as the mainstay of the family budget. Jobs are available for young, unskilled women, and their earnings enable their younger brothers to obtain the higher level of schooling needed to move ahead in the industrializing order. These studies and others found that parents retain control not only over their offsprings' earnings but also their friendships and romantic alliances (Schak, 1974).

In studying the effects of industrialization on social structure through the lives of Asian working women, my research led me to conclusions congruent with those of the continuative historians: The labor power of working daughters is a resource essentially controlled by their families. I reached this conclusion by entering into and sharing directly and immediately the eventful lives of the women. I found convincing evidence of organic continuity in family goals even under the turbulent and externally disruptive conditions of war, the revolution in China, and the laissez faire colonial industrialization. My struggle to understand why the Chinese working-class family is so powerful led me away from views of societal convergence and directly to the concept of a centripetal family regime and its determination by an overarching institutional framework. The centripetal family perspective is essential to the comprehension of the dynamic impact of the industrial order on Hong Kong life.

The factional polity and the centripetal family

Hong Kong Chinese family goals are shaped by the political, economic, and cultural institutions of the colony. The political systems of southeastern China before 1949 and contemporary Hong Kong can be characterized by the term *factional*. The family sociologist Bernard Farber (1975) introduced the concept of factionalism to refer to polities that legitimize and promote the pursuit of particularistic and exclusive kin interests. (Here *factionalism* does not refer to political party politics or the dynamics of bureaucratic organizations.)[3]

Factionalism is generated in many polities when structural properties of social groups separate them sociologically, if not in the geographic sense. Kinship, ethnicity, and culture are used by people to organize and gain control over access to scarce resources. Groups encompass people who share important cultural traits and exclude those who do not manifest the same traits. Such groups are thus characterized by overlapping bonds of friendship, kinship, language, and residence. Members participate wholeheartedly in such associations, and group solidarity is much enhanced. However, relations between units that do not share particularistic traits, each of which attracts a different clientele, are often contentious and disruptive, and this results in factionalism. The internal cohesion of units with overlapping roles will increase as a result of disputes with outsiders, and occasions for conflict may be pursued by group leaders in order to obtain total involvement of members and heighten internal control[4] (Coser, 1964).

Farber employs the equally suggestive expression *centripetal family* to describe the family that operates in such a factional regime. In the centripetal form, the family becomes a power base to manipulate other institutions. Families consequently stratify the community while endeavoring to develop their own power and wealth. A centripetal family gáthers in its forces by demanding the primary loyalty of its members and mobilizing their labor power, political, and psychological allegiances on behalf of kinsmen. The centripetal norms and values aid families in their competition against other kin groups for scarce resources.

Factional social structures are found in pre-state African tribes, in villages of the Swiss Alps, and in certain immigrant North American communities, and families of these communities are all considered centripetal by their chroniclers (Cole, 1973; Farber, 1975; Paige, 1973; Tavuchis, 1968). Thus the centripetal family regime is not limited to China, but Farber's construct compels our attention to the structural underpinnings of Hong Kong family lives.

The two main practices of the Chinese family that compel members to center their loyalty on the family and kinship units are partible inheritance, in which all sons hold equal claim to the property of their forebears, and ancestor worship. According to the system of partible inheritance in force in pre-1949 China, all sons could work the family land until division of family property (usually after the death of the father), after which sons could remain on their shares of family land. Migration to the city for nonagricultural employment did not vitiate a son's claim to his ancestral land, and thus his ties to the family group were sustained over time and great distances. A common household budget accompanied this form of property management and inheritance (see Cole, 1973, for a European example).

The partible inheritance regime gave rise to secular expectations and claims for assistance by local families who shared a recognized common heritage. This "generalized" form of reciprocal assistance entailed an exchange of gifts, labor, and material aid that need not be repaid immediately, and indeed it was repaid over the course of decades, if not generations (see Sahlins, 1965).

In industrial Hong Kong today, partible inheritance remains customary (see Chapter 1). Lacking property, however, it is necessary for proletarian families to enter the labor force. Male heads of households cannot earn enough to support a family, and comprehensive welfare provisions are lacking; consequently, poor families are thrown back upon their kin to obtain short- and long-term economic assistance. The resulting form of domestic cooperation for economic survival and betterment is the family wage economy. All Hong Kong sons expect to benefit equally from the family wage economy through family subsidization of their education or inheritance of a father's craft, skill, or trade, as is consistent with the heritage of partible inheritance. Daughters do not share in the jural estate, but they are educated and provided with a dowry to the extent permitted by family circumstances. Like partible inheritance, ongoing reciprocity with the family's circles of kin and assorted helpers is also upheld in Hong Kong.

Ancestor worship has intensified attachment to the soil and community where the ancestors were buried and worshipped and promoted concern that sons be well educated to further the family name and build upon its resources. Families emigrated from China to Hong Kong, Southeast Asia, or even North America and remained recognized members of their village and descent group. Fathers conferred membership in their lineage to their sons who were born overseas, and their sons in turn passed membership on to their sons. In Hong Kong today parents still venerate their forebears, expect support from their sons in their old age, and prefer to reside with married sons. Families must thus bear one or two sons for economic and religious reasons. The cultural/religious complex of ancestral veneration is an important determinant of family authority relations in Hong Kong.

I contend that Hong Kong society takes a factional form and the Chinese family maintains a centripetal regime, and that the life courses of Hong Kong working women were formed by time-honored centripetal family norms. Consequently, working women accede to ongoing family control of their wages, as is expected of all dutiful daughters in Chinese families. The factionalism of Hong Kong society and the centripetal features of the Chinese family regime are analyzed historically in Chapter 1 and illustrated descriptively in the chapters that follow.

In contrast to factional societies comprised of exclusive groups with overlapping bonds are societies that feature cross-cutting roles. Farber (1975) calls "communal" those polities in which the state, powerful social classes, and professional and other interest groups promote educational, business, military, and political organizations that ideally and legitimately recruit members from a universe of all family, ethnic, and religious groups. Organizational members affiliate with a multiplicity of cultural circles, and consequently the multiple group affiliations of individuals produce a skein of commitments that traverse society. The diversified interests held by people do not harden into fundamental cleavages between groups. Such cross-cutting groups are loosely organized associations in which members participate segmentally and not with their total psyches. Social stability is thus more likely to obtain under such circumstances than when units are characterized by overlapping bonds (Coser, 1964: 76–9; Paige, 1973).

In a "communal" polity where cross-cutting ties prevail, families are structurally unable to marshal their forces exclusively to promote kin interests, and indeed the advancement of particularistic family goals is considered illegitimate in such a polity. The correlative term *centrifugal family* describes the kin group that propels members outward into the wider socioeconomy to lend their talents to the instrumental goals of broader societal institutions and organizations. In the centrifugal family form, family goals are subordinated when they conflict with those of other institutions, and the family loses its capacity as a power base. Table 1 summarizes the features of the centripetal and centrifugal families.

In the conclusion I reassess the dichotomy of factional society/centripetal family versus communal society/centrifugal family in the discussion of the future of the family and the position of women in the Hong Kong Chinese family. Chinese women cannot attenuate their subordination to family control by means of wage labor alone. Rather, only when the entire panoply of factional institutions is replaced by communal institutions and the centripetal family takes a centrifugal form can a measure of equality between sons and daughters be obtained.

Changes in women's status
There are several means to assess the improvement of the female estate in the family and community, and in this study family cycle changes were taken into account. The lives of Hong Kong working daughters from childhood through young adulthood revealed no dramatic changes that imbalanced long-standing patterns of parental influence and authority, attesting to the continuation of women's subordinate status in industrial society. Historically, unmarried Chinese daugh-

Table 1. *Characteristics of centripetal and centrifugal kinship organization*

Structural arrangement	Centripetal form	Centrifugal form
Property rights		
Inheritance patterns	Partible inheritance favored	Nonfamilial inheritance favored
Type of reciprocity	Generalized reciprocities	Specific reciprocities
Relation to community structure		
Stratification	Use of family as a means for stratifying community (endeavor of the family is to heighten power and wealth collectively)	Use of family to diffuse power and wealth throughout territory
Family ideology	Religion and culture establish single paradigm of loyalty to family	Plurality of family paradigms prevalent
Relation to other institutions	Family as a power base to manipulate other institutions (e.g., government)	Subordination of family norms that may conflict with those of other institutions
Social order	Factionalism prevails between groups, and conflict disrupts the social order	Intergroup relations stable, accommodation is possible

Source: Adapted from Farber (1975:877).

ters were subordinated to elders in their homes, and young married women were likewise beholden to the families into which they married. Women anticipated that when their own sons married and ultimately bore grandsons to further the family line, and they became the oldest generation in the home, they would gain ascendancy. As their star reached its zenith, the matriarchs could at last manage the household budget and contemplate retirement from active household labor and drudgery. (The elderly poor, however, could never fully withdraw from productive labor; see Friedman, in preparation.)

Elevation of women's station as a result of their wage-earning opportunities must be reflected in long-term improvement of their position, but the lives presented in this volume reveal little evidence of such enhancement of their value. However, the case studies do lead me to conclude that opportunities for unmarried working daughters have expanded in four main areas: marriage choice, the utilization of personal earnings, peer-group activities, and affections and prestige within the family of orientation. All of these areas of opportunity were considered meaningful by my subjects and attested to changes in their position as their families adapted to the industrial economy. Nevertheless, the elimination of constraints in these areas is necessarily temporary and limited to the life-cycle stage before marriage; these greater opportunities are not transmitted to the next phase of family building. Because working daughters cannot invest their hard-earned wages (as, for example, older women in Taiwan invest in credit associations or become money lenders), they do not secure access to funds for their next stage as married women.

The expansion of opportunities for women is both temporary and circumscribed due to the family form. The centripetal family, which limits the access of women to productive property and the fruits of joint labor and excludes them from domestic decision-making councils, renders Chinese women economically subjected to the patriliny. The inability of women to invest their wages in order to gain control over capital is intimately linked with the position of women in the family economy. Davin (1964:4) argues convincingly that women cannot gain real power in the family until they break their bonds of economic dependence, and the anchoring of the centripetal family in Hong Kong signifies that conditions for women have not improved decisively in the colony.

Of great interest to me as an observer and participant in the lives of the women reported upon is their obvious enthusiasm for their augmented opportunities as unmarried daughters. The women's stress upon their options and their downplaying of the costs involved in the maintenance of work and family roles is integral to their daily routine and character. Underlying the young women's sense of value in their position in the family is, first, the continuous involvement in a family routine in which their position is clearly prescribed, despite the considerable changes that have occurred in industrializing Hong Kong. Recent work on age-graded societies indicates that where the transition to adulthood is delineated explicitly, there is less youth-adult antagonism than where adult status is unpredictable and depends upon power of adults to provide young people with the economic and political perquisites of adulthood (Foner and Kertzer, 1978). The lives of working daughters in Hong Kong, with their admixture of change and continuity, are marked by their feelings of well-being and pride in their family contribution. A second source of the women's sense of widened opportunity is their choice of groups with whom they compare their lots. Reference group theory establishes that people assess their personal and social gains by gauging their situations against those of significant counterparts (Kemper, 1968; Runciman, 1972). Maturing in a highly sex-segregated society, where women's status is defined separately from that of men, my respondents looked to their mothers and elder sisters as behavioral prototypes. They never contrasted their status with that of their brothers, and in comparison to older siblings and generations of women, they considered their own conditions much improved.

However, women in Hong Kong, although having experienced measurable life-cycle improvements in certain opportunities (higher education, wage-paying jobs), have not been rapidly equalizing with men. In fact, the gap between men and women in education, employment, and earnings remains nearly as wide today as in the past. Hence, although the women's subjective feelings of progress are understandable, qualitative amelioration of their standing with respect to men and to their position in the centripetal family is as yet unrealized (Safilios-Rothschild, 1972).

1. Modern times in a colonialized Chinese city

When the plane descends to Hong Kong's Tak Airport, the magnificent Repulse Bay surrounded by bare, brown sugarloaf mountains comes immediately into view. Pink and white villas on the hills gleam in colorful contrast to the deep blue-green waters below, and graceful sailboats and stolid brown junks can be spotted in the distance. Then the plane screams over rows upon rows of barracklike public housing interspersed with factories, reminding the traveler that Hong Kong is one of the world's most densely populated cities, a major trade and financial center of Southeast Asia, and the locale of a newly implanted modern industry. The plane lands adjacent to the beautiful harbor, the home of boat-dwelling fishermen as well as dock workers descended from militants in the 1920s' labor battles against British imperialism. This book focuses upon the young women factory, office, and service workers who were raised in the city-state and whose labor has transformed Hong Kong into a major exporter of light industrial goods and Asia's commercial and tourist beacon.

The complex political, economic, and social institutions of the Hong Kong governing infrastructure and industrial bureaucracy blend paradoxically with strong personal relationships among the people — their most powerful resource. The everyday reality of the populace starts with the centralized family economy that mobilizes the energies and loyalties of the working daughters and sons.

Hong Kong: land and people

A British crown colony on the southeast coast of Kwangtung province, the present political unit of Hong Kong was entirely Chinese territory until 1842, and today 98% of Hong Kong's four and a half million inhabitants are of Chinese descent. After waging a series of wars with China, Britain wrested away the island of Victoria and the peninsula of Kowloon and took a 99-year lease on the New Territories, which expires in 1997. Under international law, the New Territories will then be incorporated into China. With the present rapid opening of China to the capitalist world, Hong Kong's traditional entrepôt role for the Chinese market is likely to be enhanced during the coming years, but no firm policy on the exercise of its rights over the colony has yet been articulated by Peking.

In 1971 Hong Kong's urban populace lived in three distinct districts, each with its own characteristic business and residential pattern. Victoria's Central District, the original British base, remains the commercial and administrative heart of the city. Among the numerous heavily populated subdistricts of Victoria, those mentioned in this book include North Point, to the northeast, with its mixed housing, commercial, and entertainment developments, and Shau Kei Wan, a suburb with reclamations from the bay, resettlement estates, and factories (see map). The Star Ferry plies Hong Kong's fine natural harbor between Victoria and the isthmus of Kowloon. Old Kowloon consists of Tsim Sha Tsui, a magnetic tourist focus based on hotel, restaurant, bar, and shopping complexes geared to the wants of customers from all lands. Mong Kok, another central business district that caters to working-class Chinese needs, lies along Nathan Road, the main north-south thoroughfare of Kowloon, and entry to the rapidly growing New Territories. To the west and northeast are densely populated, working-class districts that include Sham Shui Po and Hung Hom.

New Kowloon (Ngau Tau Kok and Kwun Tong) gained its population and industrial dominance when modern light industry and large apartment blocks were constructed in the mid-1960s. In 1971 this area accounted for 36% of Hong Kong's population and 62% of the industrial employed (Leeming, 1977:7). Respondents of the present study live in all three Hong Kong districts – Victoria, Old Kowloon, and New Kowloon – and many have labored in the large factories situated in Kwun Tong industrial town. Some still toil there, but others now work in smaller factories and workshops in Sham Shui Po and in hotels, restaurants, and offices in Tsim Sha Tsui and Victoria's Central District.

The geography and land-use patterns demonstrate that Chinese commercial intercourse is based on an intricate scheme of interpersonal relations. The exclusive kinship ties of New Territories' walled villages are carried over to the market towns that serve these areas, where shops and streets are divided according to native place of origin and ethnolinguistic group. In Old Kowloon, communally linked occupations include Hakka rattan weavers in Sham Shui Po and Ch'iu-chao woodcarvers in Tsim Sha Tsui (Baker, 1968; Blake, personal communication; Cooper, 1980; Young, 1974).

In the formative commercial center of Sheung Wan, Victoria, clusters of businesses in closely related import-export food trades occupy a specific geographic locality because even today they depend heavily on partnerships among relatives, business contacts with old friends, and other forms of personal contact. In more recently developed commercial areas there are also many specialist locations: bars in Wan Chai, bookstores in Mong Kok, fashion clothing on Nathan Road. Such geographical clusters of enterprises of related trades are, according to an urban geographer, less a collection of similar businesses than a network of personal contacts (Leeming, 1977:52–3). The dense network of overlapping relationships in the small business community dictates familial concern with the maintenance of a variety of particularistic bonds.

The colonial political framework

Colonial rule forces families to generate their own reliable personal networks for protection and advancement. British colonial polity is authoritarian and has fostered a compliant Chinese leadership to represent and control the populace while curtailing mass political expression. The colonial machinery suppresses the power of local groups that could disturb the orderly operation of an economy that rests upon a propitious investment climate, although periodically there are explosive outbreaks against colonial authorities (as in 1966 and 1967) (Freedman, 1966:5; Miners, 1975).

A highly centralized administrative machinery has evolved that rests atop a pyramid of loosely knit socioeconomic groups that have been permitted considerable domestic initiative, although never enough to contest for political power. All fundamental policies are formulated by the Commonwealth Office in London, which appoints the colonial administration headed by the governor, who in turn chooses his official and unofficial advisers from men of industry and finance. The Chinese "unofficials" head charitable organizations and meet in social clubs, and there is considerable intermarriage among their families (Endacott, 1964; Rear, 1971:73, 123–39).

Although the Chinese population is barred from holding central political office, the regime provides advisory channels for local leaders to influence policies. Organized pressure groups attempt to influence government decisions without ever seeking to exercise the formal powers of government (Emerson, 1937:390; Miners, 1975:ch. 17). There are as well important Chinese benevolent associations: the Tung Wah group of hospitals, the *kaifong* (street or residential welfare associations); the Po Leung Kok society for orphaned girls; district, trade, and clansmen associations; and rural committees that represent New Territories villages to the district officers of the Hong Kong government. Most of such benevolent associations are cleaved along speech or native lines, but a few like the Tung Wah group and *kaifong* span a broad spectrum of Chinese interests.

The authorities sanction local groups to varying degrees: The government may encourage their formation (e.g., the *kaifong*) or withhold permission to register. The government may underwrite the expenses (e.g., rural committees), and it may read and honor petitions by leaders requesting a redress of grievances on behalf of association members. The government thus has become a major source of material benefits and advancement for the most powerful local Chinese leaders, who are appointed as magistrates and to numerous advisory posts and thereby obtain colonywide standing. Middle-level Chinese leaders, such as *kaifong* chairmen, spend time and their own funds in government-permitted or encouraged associations. They handle health service administration, family reconciliation tribunals, and represent shopkeepers' needs to the political authorities, and their expenditure of time and money is understood by their local constituency as concern for the welfare of their group (Endacott, 1964:229; Lethbridge, 1978; Wong, 1972).

The government thus provides resources and access to colonial officials, which rebounds to the status of local Chinese leadership. In return, the Chinese heads of associations are expected to provide information and advice on popular sentiments, convey Government House policy to their clientele, and cooperate in local administration: in short, to ensure the compliance of the governed (cf. Epstein's study of Rhodesia, 1958; Selznick, 1952:135). This relatively passive or indirect rule permitted the local leader to promote his own sectional constituency in competition with others. However, when the first postwar large-scale political outburst (over an increase in ferry fares, 1966) caught the government unawares, a more active approach to political control was initiated (the city district officer scheme). Nonetheless, the basic premises of top-down, essentially nonparticipatory rule remain in force (King, 1975; Miners, 1975:141-3; Wong, 1972).

The lower levels of the civil service (8% of the employed populace in 1973) provide an outlet for participation of educated Chinese in government administration. However, the administration of government policies cannot be construed as political participation, since the top posts are still manned by British expatriate officials. Educated Chinese youth are co-opted by recruitment into the lower cogs of colonial machinery (Rear, 1971; Wong, 1973a). The propertied groups and professionals (1% of the populace) elect one-half the members of the Urban Council, whose powers do not extend much beyond the control of hawkers, the operation of parks and recreational facilities, and the naming of streets (Hoadley, 1974).

None of the factory or shop women I interviewed in my study, and none of their family members, has ever qualified to vote. The Hong Kong labor movement is fragmented, and there are no large-scale youth movements or consumers' rights groups. Perpetuation of the existing colonial system is predicated on the absence of openly contending political activity.

The electronic media are not permitted to criticize the government, and Radio Hong Kong is a government department, whose basic function is to mold public opinion in favor of government policies. Printed journalism partisan to the People's Republic of China and also to Taiwan is disseminated by presses, and there are pro-Peking and pro-Taipei cinema industries. Unions, schools, and benevolent associations of each faction also coexist in Hong Kong, yet each allegiance group speaks primarily to its own constituency, and there is little mixing with the unaffiliated population. This hermetic isolation of viewpoints discourages political inquiry and is functionally necessary to prevent open clashes between Left and Right or between the Left and the government (Hoadley, 1970; Wong, 1970-1). Not only is party politics illegitimate, but the general population lacks a clear conception of political differences between regimes and social interests.

As Mann (1970) pointed out, a flow of media data that are never generalized to an abstract set of propositions and therefore not formalized into an ideology may actually inhibit the understanding of the structural underpinnings of society and interfere with the formation of political convictions and social action (cf. Mander, 1978). As long as there is no meaningful political mobilization, the popular classes will continue to participate in voluntary associations largely along family and ethnolinguistic lines.

The advent of industrial capitalism

The colony added to its long-standing functions as commercial-financial entrepôt and a key British military outpost east of Suez the role of industrial manufacturer after the Chinese Revolution ended in 1949. A wave of refugees from the social changes wrought by Liberation came to the colony with industrial and managerial skills and capital for the opportunity to continue their entrepreneurial way of life. Hong Kong first pursued the manufacture of textiles, which its commercial facilities were able to market in North American and European centers. In the late 1960s transnational corporations increasingly sought Hong Kong's cheap, disciplined, and non-unionized labor power for the production at low cost of goods that require no lengthy job training, particularly in the growth industry of electronics. Hong Kong thereby became the best-known example of an "industrial colony" (Boxer, 1961:ch.4; Chou, 1966; Owen, 1971; Szczpanik, 1958).

Chinese capitalists remain overwhelmingly in control of the colony's manufacturing facilities. Retaining their familist and ethnolinguistic connections throughout, the immigrant Chinese bourgeoisie organized their investment capital from among familiar districts and industrial circles of prerevolutionary China. Although the traditional recruitment patterns of personal networks remain intact for capital formation, they became anachronistic for labor-force recruitment with the advent of large-scale factories and the open labor market in the 1960s. Hong Kong's total dependence upon the requirements and possibilities of the capitalist world market (90% of the manufactured output goes overseas) means that few local employers can afford to link themselves paternalistically to workers whom they would regard as superfluous at a time of retrenchment (Djau, 1976; England and Rear, 1975:47, ch. 3). Foreign capital in the shape of transnational corporations also makes no commitment to employ its mostly unorganized local staff over the long term.

Women's labor has been central to such an export-dependent economy, beginning with the labor-intensive textiles and garment machining in the 1950s. As the industrial sector expanded, young women joined the labor force in significant numbers, resulting in their full employment today.[1] The proportion of all factory operatives in the economy rose to almost 50% in 1971, and more than half of the factory labor force was women, a proportion greatly in excess of that anywhere in the region. The Hong Kong government describes tourism as the colony's second largest revenue earner: The proportion of women workers in the closely related services industry rose to over 30% in 1971. The proportion of women workers in the third-ranking commercial sector was 25%. The "second industrial revolution" has not yet swept Hong Kong, and despite the actual numbers and proportions of women in clerical and sales occupations (14% of the female labor force in 1971; in 1961, 10%), the majority of the labor force performs value-added manufacturing work (Census and Statistics Department, 1961:Table 143; 1971a:Table 1; 1971b:Tables 6.6.2, 31).

The key role of women workers in Hong Kong industry is due to their relatively low wage levels. In 1977 hourly rated electronics assemblers earned $23 (H.K.) per day ($4.60 U.S.). A daily rated sewing machine operator earned $22 and a piece-rated operator earned $32 (H.K.) ($4.47 and $6.40 U.S., respectively) in registered industries (Department of Labour, 1978:58–9, Table 5D).[2]

In addition, the labor of minimally trained female workers is easily replaceable, and young women are assumed by management and the Department of Labour to be indifferent to long-term job security. Women workers are concentrated in industries in the colony's manufacturing economy within which the volume and especially the nature of overseas demand fluctuates most strongly: textiles, garments, and shoes; plastics; metalware; and electrical appliances and electronics (Department of Labour, 1972–3: Table 1b). During the short-lived boom enjoyed by the Hong Kong wig industry, for example, the industry expanded from several thousand employees in the late 1960s to a mid-1970 peak of 478 factories that hired 39,000 women; but by June, 1973, there were only 160 wig manufacturing factories and fewer than 8,000 workers. Under such circumstances women workers cannot expect long-term employment in one factory and must accept as part of their work-force contract frequent shifts in job category and workplace, if not also in wage scale. The portraits of Mae, Suyin, Wai-gun

(Chapter 2) and Sa-li (Chapter 3) suggest that the effects of such occupational impermanence on the lives of Hong workers are substantial.

Garment workers' wages depend on the specific pattern and type of materials that pass through their sewing machines, so that the workers' income varies considerably and the fixing of the workers' income is subject to arbitrary management decisions. When a firm introduces a seasonal pattern that is especially difficult to sew, its workers may decide to try their luck in a competing company. Piecework and repetitive tasks render workers easily replaceable, and the unsteady position of women in the job structure renders them prime candidates for short-term employment.

Transnational manufacturers are committed to preventing the organization of their Asian work force.[3] The Hong Kong government shares manufacturers' fears that in the contemporary capitalist world economic configuration, higher wages would drive capital out of the colony and into newer, low-wage sources in the Pacific region. Thus the government nominally adopts a neutral stance in labor-management questions, but collective bargaining and strike legislation favor management.

The Hong Kong Federation of Trade Unions, politically aligned with the mainland, endorses the industrial system in Hong Kong. The second trade union center, the Trade Union Congress, has been regarded as pro-Taiwan. Workers in trades and industries are prevented from forming large, multitrade unions by the Trade Union Ordinance (Cap. 332:17–23). The ordinance, by permitting a minimum of seven people to form and register a union, encourages proliferation of small unions; general unions are illegal (Djau, 1976:120). Of the 165,000 female employees registered in 1974 in the textile, wearing apparel, and leather industries, these two labor centers organized a scant 13,000 workers. The textile and garment workers' unions are small and compete with one another politically, and the resulting absence of a single coordinating voice in labor has until now limited the benefits brought to women by their union membership. In electronics assembly enterprises in 1974, there were only 260 members among 68,000 workers. The number of strikes increased in the early 1970s, although these were short (England and Rear, 1975:279; Registrar of Trade Unions, 1975:Tables 1,2).

All of the factory women with whom I came into contact matured in the factory system without joining a trade union, and the only one who was a union member did not join until her tenth year of factory work.

These women's lack of trade union participation was not due to the lack of worker consciousness, as the cases of Wai-gun and Ming show. Young women workers in Hong Kong industry suffer from the absence of a seniority system, dependable piecework wage norms, grievance procedures, and above all a wage scale that brings them close to financial independence. Such remunerative patterns are sought with varying degrees of success by trade union movements in the Organization for Economic Cooperation and Development and other capitalist states. In Hong Kong the politically determined absence of effective unionism in the extensive light industrial sector, hotels, and service industries limits the workers' commitment to the individual firm.

Hong Kong women do not have access to a ladder of increasingly better paid job categories. This is due to Hong Kong's station on the "global assembly line" in electronics and other mass production, high technology industries. The initial research and development and testing phases of this transnational assembly line are concentrated in the metropolis, whereas the repetitive, mass-produced operations are carried out largely by young female hands offshore along the Pacific Rim or elsewhere in lesser-developed country orbits. Furthermore, locally capitalized textile firms producing low-cost garments for mass markets do not require highly trained operatives, so the bulk of the textile industry also fails to provide significant job advancement possibilities for its work force, 80% of which is women. In the flourishing textile industry of 1967, 28% of the men but only 3% of the women were technicians or skilled workers. Conditions for women's advancement were even more limited in the electronics industry (Department of Labour, 1967:321–35, 1969; Wong, 1973b:20).

Fewer employment opportunities for work-force promotion for women exist than for men because of prevailing definitions of a woman's place. During 1967 and 1971–6 I carried out seven interviews of Labour Department officials as well as Western and Chinese electronics and textiles factory managers for their various employment practices regarding women workers. I asked each of these men why so many young women were employed in these particular sectors. The standard responses were "Women have nimble fingers and keen eyesight." "The girls are willing to work hard for long hours at piecework occupations in order to boost their take-home pay." This strong commitment "raises our productivity and profits." The outcome of factory management's and government officials' presumption that women are forever dependent upon their families and that they will not remain in the labor force after marriage is a low individual wage and lack of job training – an inevitable fulfillment of their presumption.

Seventeen of the women in this study worked at one time in manufacturing; fourteen were still so occupied in 1973. Ten of the seventeen began in their early teens with the California-based Fairchild Semiconductor, Ltd., of Kwung Tong, for a 2-year average stint, then moved to other industries. Fourteen of the interviewees who had worked in manufacturing had tried their hands at the garment sector at some time during their careers, where the employer spectrum included Shanghainese and other Chinese capitalists. The women who attained the white-collar and service categories were generally in the employ of foreign capitalists in entertainment, service, and missionary-welfare occupations. Such conditions of employment in today's Hong Kong are not conducive to allegiance and commitment, and the family roles of women remain their most salient status.

The standard of living

The indicators of Hong Kong's economic growth are strikingly high: the per capita gross domestic product increased from $14 in 1948 dollars to $500 in 1966 dollars and $791 in 1971 dollars.[4] The average real daily wage in industry and services increased by more than 50% from March, 1964, to the midpoint of my interviewing (March, 1973), and went on rising at a slightly decelerated pace through 1977 (Department of Labour, 1973, 1977:Table 5C).

Despite these advertisements of progress, the Hong Kong household head still does not command sufficient wages to support a family. Large families improve their standard of living primarily by sending all available labor onto the market, and strive continually to increase the ratio of wage workers to dependents. The offspring begotten by the influx of mainland refugees at the start of the 1950s began entering factory occupations in the mid-1960s, and this demographic surge made rising family prosperity possible. Consumer goods expenditures were directly proportional to the age of the household head and length of family residence in resettlement estate dwellings, according to a 1968 survey. The study also found that in 30% of all households, one or more children age 14 or under worked full- or part-time for a wage (Hopkins, 1969:7; Owen, 1971:153). Thus older, longer-established Hong Kong households are more likely to have their teen and young adult offspring contributing to the family income.

Government support for social services and security is minimal. Since unemployment insurance has never been instituted, unemployed workers must somehow secure new jobs, thereby contributing to the emphasis on personal, familistic, kin, and ethnolinguistic connections. The colonial government has not adopted the International Labor Organization Convention (No. 102) on Social Security, which calls for medical care, protection from suspension of earnings due to inability to obtain suitable employment, old age benefits, employment injury benefits, provision of wages due to losses for pregnancy and childbirth, and benefits for survivors of deceased breadwinners (ILO, 1966). Existing minimal legislation on wages, hours, and labor conditions is inadequately enforced by an understaffed inspectorate[5] (Leung, 1973; Porter, 1975; Yeung, 1973).

As in any industrial society, many families live below the poverty level (Hong Kong Council of Social Service, 1967). Public assistance is required for these people, but until the late 1960s the Hong Kong government, supported by the business community, declined to introduce comprehensive welfare and social security measures. Missionary charities stepped into the breach and were especially active in working-class squatter areas and resettlement estates. Through the 1950s Christian service groups constructed cottage area housing and schools and paid pupils' school fees. In the 1960s, missionaries added youth centers to their projects and, in the 1970s, organized communities for "self-help." Some of the best-known examples are the Baptist Hospital on Argyle Street, the Aberdeen Floating Clinic for boat dwellers, the Gee Hip (Church of Christ in China) Technical School, and the Lutheran Church World Service Kwun Tong Industrial Training Centre. Charity and volunteer services are members of the Council of Social Service, which is subsidized and thereby controlled by the government (see the story of Ming, Chapter 5).

The Hong Kong government, committed to improving the quality, availability, and regularity of the industrial labor force, does allocate limited funds for a variety of social benefits, without which social unrest would seriously affect the economic status quo. The major direct social investment by the colonial government includes staple food and small allowances for the poverty stricken and destitute, neighborhood clinics and public hospital care, public housing, and primary education.

Government clinics and hospitals, although they are seriously under-staffed, manage to provide low-cost treatment and prophylaxis of major diseases endemic to Southeast Asia. The general population also avails itself of the private hospitals of the Tung Wah and other benevo-lent groups, but most do without the services of family physicians, dentists, and other preventive medical care that have become accept-able in the developed countries.

Government-built and financed public housing comprises several types, the most impressive form being the resettlement estate, a sub-city of multi-block units, each block housing thousands of residents. Their erection was forced upon the government, which was faced with a million and a quarter refugees from revolutionary China, who arrived in the colony from 1945 to 1950, and scores of thousands of others who have been crossing legally and illegally ever since (Hambro, 1955:148). The people (squatters) seized the land upon which they set makeshift dwellings. There were fire and flood hazards, drug trafficking, and crime; local and regional gangs quickly organized the communities and resisted colonial control. As Dwyer (1971) and Hopkins (1971) show, the im-mense housing estates were cheaply and rapidly constructed by the alarmed government, and the financial success of this experiment en-couraged its continuation until over twenty had been erected in various parts of the colony. Forty percent of the metropolitan populace in 1979 lived in government-built or government-financed housing proj-ects, which England and Rear (1975) argue enable working families to survive on their inadequate wage packets and provide a ready labor force for manufacturers who locate nearby.

In the 1970s, the government expanded its social services and welfare schemes and budgeted increasing sums for primary and secondary school education (fee reduction and fee remissions, financial aid to the elderly, upgraded rooms in older public housing accommodations). Toward the close of the decade, the able-bodied unemployed were granted public assistance for the first time. The Social Welfare Depart-ment met the increased problems of crime and delinquency with seven community centers in resettlement estates that aim toward "mutual adjustments of individuals and their social environment." The department further implemented programs of family life education to "improve the quality of family life . . . so that the individual is made a happy being whose healthy personality is ready to serve his communi-ty" (Social Welfare Department, n.d.).

Even when taken together, however, government and parochial assistance are far from comprehensive. Whereas 60% of the Gross Domestic Product went for government expenditures in the United Kingdom from 1966 to 1972, the figure for its main colony was a scant 13% (Miners, 1975:104–5). This wide gap, with its negative effect on social welfare and transfer payments, was caused by the colonial government's undiluted free enterprise policies and lower tax base, and the absence of any programmatic commitment to advancement of social welfare by organized opposition. Family wages still provide all the necessities, but by underwriting housing and health needs, government investment in services subsidizes employers and frees families from subsistence concerns to invest in education for their future.

Education

Education is a central constituent in the nation-building process. Modernization theorists and development strategists argue that primary and secondary schools serve to blend diverse ethnic groups into a national unit and transmit a historic civilization and national value system, before which the circumscribed horizons of village culture are expected to yield. Moreover, education fuses different channels of inherited opportunity into a single achievement-oriented ladder to jobs. The system for providing the fundamental technical knowledge underpinning its industrial and commercial needs has by now been implanted in Hong Kong. However, in the peculiar circumstances of this colonial city-state with a politically wide-open future, the education system has never seriously attempted to mold a unified Hong Kong spirit and shuns the teaching of the society and culture of contemporary China. The school system is thus unable to attract youths to a broader, colonywide framework of values and institutions that could compete with the demands of the family economy and traditions.

Primary education is nearly universal in Hong Kong today. Most of the women studied in this volume, ages 20 to 24 in 1971, received some primary schooling in government-operated and subsidized structures, and half of them continued to lower-middle school. This achievement contrasts favorably with their mothers, ages 40 to 44 in 1971, half of whom received no schooling at all (Table 2).

The government has long preferred to finance the colony's postprimary education through the factional network, and secondary educa-

Table 2. *Educational attainment for two generations in 1971, by sex (in percent)*

	Female		Male	
Educational attainment	20–24	40–44	20–24	40–44
No schooling, kindergarten, private tutor	6.7	52.4	4.0	22.5
(Some) Primary	44.5	35.3	38.0	51.8
(Some) Secondary	43.2	10.4	49.7	21.0
Postsecondary and higher	5.7	1.9	8.2	4.7
Totals	100.1	100.0	99.9	100.0

Figures do not total 100% due to rounding.
Source: Hong Kong Census for 1971.

tion is pursued in a wide variety of community-operated institutions (Mills, 1942:496–8). These are schools operated by each Christian mission and an assortment of neighborhood, clan, and other native associations, party-affiliated schools (mainland-connected "patriotic" schools and several that retain allegiance to Taiwan), schools run as outright business ventures, Cantonese- and Mandarin-based schools. In the majority of these schools, English is the language of instruction. Schools within this heterogeneous mixture compete intensely for government aid, wealthy Chinese and overseas patrons, and academic philanthropies.

The populace has heightened its interest in secondary education in quest of improved employment opportunities. There is keen competition among employers for the more highly qualified school graduates. The professions and semiprofessions demand higher standards of entry, which leads to interprofessional competition for the still-limited pool of postsecondary labor power. Secondary school administrations rival to recruit the better-prepared students, whose examination performances and university entrances redound to the prestige and benefit of their institutions. Government bursaries and allocation of secondary school and university places are eligible solely for those with high scores on the colonywide Secondary School Entrance and Certification of Education Examinations (Ross, 1976; Rowe, 1966).

Even in this economy, which thrives on semi-skilled, unorganized labor, there are clearly opportunities for skilled and educated labor, and white-collar jobs are attractive. Thus great thirst for postprimary education pervades the colony today. In the past, when under half of the youths matriculated secondary school, they naturally seized the best jobs. Now, as in most industrializing countries with burgeoning secondary school pupils, the link between diploma and salary is bound to weaken.[6] Many others may boast roughly equivalent achievement, but only the small minority of pupils fortunate enough to matriculate from the highest-ranked middle schools have a chance at select occupations. College graduates in 1971 obtained starting salaries approximately three times greater than those who graduated from middle school and entered directly into the work force, a triple magnification of incentive that exceeds even corresponding ratios in the United States, United Kingdom, other Western countries.[7] Despite absolute limits on university expansion and the consequent bottleneck in the postsecondary entrance stream, parents are tenaciously adhering to this route of family advancement.

In 1973 over 62% of the primary school graduates failed to win government support in public or aided secondary schools, but the families of one-half of this number nevertheless underwrote their secondary school attendance cost (UMELCO, 1974). Tuition fees in denominational secondary schools averaged $150 annually in 1969 (Cheong, 1969). This sum, the entire monthly budget for many poor families, failed to deter working-class parents from reducing personal consumption in order to place their sons and daughters in these highly reputed centers. Although Chinese families voice Confucian precepts of literary moral education for its own good, only the specific economic constellation of Hing Kong today, with its stringent competition for limited university and professional slots, demands this allegiance to secondary school commitment.

Even if there were a coherent set of civic values for Hong Kong, the decentralization of schools would inhibit the transmission of these "national" values through formal educational channels. The colonial government has not fostered programs to win youth through the school system for serious civic consciousness and attainments. It is true that age grading and the opportunities provided by impartially administered examinations give rise to a youth subculture of achievement-oriented, hard-working teenagers with an academic esprit de corps, but the status quo paternalism of colonial government and its allied educationalists effectively confine the big population of young scholars to a parochial education climate. Without a vibrant educational system, the means to integrate youths into centrifugal structures and values are completely lacking.

Demographic background

The Hong Kong population rose sharply from its World War II low of under half a million people to two million in 1951 and four million in 1971 (Podmore, 1971). Fertility was high after the war: 39.7 per 1,000 people in 1956, declining through the 1960s to 17.7 per 1,000 in 1976. Because of public health measures, the crude death rate also dropped from 7.4 (1956) to 5.1 (1976) per 1,000 people (infant mortality was 60.9 per 1,000 live births in 1956; 14.3 in 1976). These demographic parameters created a large under-14 years of age population, whose proportion increased from 25% in 1931 to 42% in 1961 and then decreased to 35% in 1971, but the contemporary Hong Kong populace is still relatively young.

Completed families are large due to past high fertility. Hong Kong women born between 1927 and 1931 and ages 40 to 44 in 1971 (the age of the mothers in my study) averaged more than 4.3 births, and 46% had borne five or more children, most of whom survived (Census and Statistics Department, 1971a:Table 4; 1971b:Table 16). The families in this study are sizable: Nineteen respondents grew up in families of five or more children. A substantial proportion of households are headed by women: 22% of married women ages 35 to 39 headed households in 1966 (Census and Statistics Department, 1966:Table 24). One-third of my respondents lacked fathers who lived at home, a result of mortality, desertion, male emigration, and the custom of concubinage.

Hong Kong's women and men marry relatively late. In 1964, 49% of females ages 20 to 24 were unmarried, whereas a decade later 68% of this age group had not yet married. In 1961, 86% and, in 1971, 90% of the young men in the same age bracket were still unmarried (Census and Statistics Department, 1961:Table 145; 1971a:Table 2). Succeeding chapters develop the hypothesis that a strong reason for the long-term trend upward in the female marriage age is the increasing availability of unskilled urban factory labor for young women, brought about by Third World industrialization (Salaff, 1976a). There is variation in marriage by the occupation of the partners. The highest proportion of women who marry before age 19 are the menial and semi-skilled workers and domestic and office servants; the small group of professional women delays marriage longest. The case studies in this volume suggest that age at marriage is related to the length of education required for the bride's and groom's jobs (Table 3).

The totality of these demographic indicators reveals that the life experiences of my respondents are radically different from those of their mothers. The average young woman expects to complete her education, to work, to marry, and to bear children at an increasingly older age than her mother. At the same time, the number of years during which she bears children and raises them to school entry age is a full 20 years less than the corresponding statistics of her mother. As a result, she will have more time for the improvement of the quality of her family life, for directing her children's education, and for making other efforts to elevate the status of her family.

Heritage of the centripetal family

The tradition of the Chinese political economy

All of the women of whom I write in this book grew up in Hong Kong, but their parents came from villages, towns, and cities of Kwangtung province, southeastern China, whose linguistic particularities and social structures shaped Hong Kong family and community patterns. The traditional Chinese family was centripetal and self-reliant. The centralizing character was fostered by Chinese economic conditions, political institutions, and social values. In the late nineteenth century, and especially during the republican era of the twentieth century, those conditions, institutions, and values changed in ways that intensified the always latent factional character of Chinese society, and thus more than ever nourished the inward-turning tendencies of the Chinese family. The following detail may contribute to an understanding of the parental background of my respondents.

The Kwangtung people engaged in rice farming, which required intensive cultivation of small plots and villages situated on higher rises to preserve the flat, productive land for irrigated paddies; this encouraged nucleated village settlements. Villages included well-organized single and plural lineages and those of mixed surnames with poorly developed lineage structures. In this pre-industrial economy, formal contractual

Table 3. *Age at marriage by selected occupations, Hong Kong, 1970–1, as proportion of 5-year cohorts*

Age	Menial/ semi-skilled workers; domestic and office servants	Skilled operatives	Clerical and sales workers	Managerial and working proprietors	Lower ranks of disciplinary services, minor supervisory staff	Artists, technicians	Professionals and technologists	Supervisory staff	Government officials	None	Average
Brides											
15–19	15.8	6.2	6.4	1.7	3.5	3.2	2.1	9.5	–	15.5	13.0
20–24	61.2	62.1	64.9	39.2	59.2	48.5	45.5	58.0	44.4	41.0	54.9
25–29	14.8	16.6	22.4	24.3	23.9	34.8	36.7	24.3	40.0	12.0	17.5
30–34	3.4	3.3	4.2	9.9	5.0	8.8	10.0	4.0	11.1	7.1	5.1
35+	4.8	11.8	2.1	24.9	8.4	4.7	5.7	4.2	4.2	24.4	9.5
Total number	6,209	15,656	7,213	181	201	2,561	1,117	276	45	13,983	47,442[a]
Grooms											
15–19	2.2	1.4	–	–	1.6	–	–	–	–	6.4	1.3
20–24	24.5	23.0	26.1	13.6	38.8	24.4	12.4	23.2	12.0	31.8	23.3
25–29	29.0	36.4	34.6	24.9	32.9	37.3	40.0	37.1	41.8	12.2	33.6
30–34	20.6	22.8	21.1	21.0	16.4	22.7	29.5	22.4	29.6	3.6	21.7
35+	23.7	16.4	18.2	40.5	10.3	15.6	18.1	17.3	14.8	46.0	21.1
Total number	6,724	18,609	8,602	4,850	2,256	2,091	1,902	1,632	122	641	47,429[b]

A dash signifies less than 0.1%.

[a]Three unskilled laborers and one worker whose occupation is unclassifiable have not been included in tabulations.

[b]Sixteen unskilled laborers have not been included in tabulations.

Source: Hong Kong Government, unpublished Marriage Registration Data, 1970, 1971.

legal ties were supplemented by social bonds of reciprocal expectation, which provided reliable economic coworkers and partners. Such expectations were formed by kinship, marriage, fictive kin ties, reciprocal mutual aid, and sentiment (Belshaw, 1965; Fei, 1975; Fried, 1953; Jamieson, 1970; Pasternak, 1972; Polanyi, 1957; Young, 1974).

Economic development was extremely uneven in the province. By the late 1920s only the major delta cities — Canton, Hong Kong, and Swatow – had experienced the rapid growth of native and foreign industry. However, commercialization was slowly penetrating the countryside. Occupationally, the Kwangtung people were among the first in China to enter industrialization through the textile industry and treaty port commerce. An estimated 33% of Kwangtung village families engaged in nonfarming occupations in the 1930s (Yang, 1959:5). The considerable interest the families in my book evinced in trade had a forerunner in their provincial homeland. In the cities, mercantile families likewise depended upon their interpersonal connections with affines and agnates, family, native place, and local reputation to start and operate enterprises, transport goods, and trade (Ho, 1966; Jones, 1972; McElderry, 1976).

The polity was based on indirect rule, the state operating through representatives of local groups organized along particularistic lines. Citizens had none of the franchise rights that emerged in Western countries and Japan. In Kwangtung, overpopulation, competition for land, and a diversity of subcultures contributed to the history of inter-ethnic wars, lineage feuding, the rise of secret societies, and alternative forms of local power. The breakdown of national control in the late Ch'ing and early republic gave rise to peasant rebellions, warlordism, and an intensification of factional politics at the party and local levels.[8] The individual, who could look for little support in production, administration, and social services from the national or provincial capitals, or even from his own county seat in the best of times, struck a variety of patron-client relationships for security more than before (cf. Jacobs, 1979:256–7; Powell, 1970; Scott, 1972). The need for strong and well-led families was intensified in China, and these families continue as remnants in present-day Hong Kong.

In the absence of the dominant lineage group that supports the nuclear family in economic and political endeavors, fathers will seek patrons of slightly superior resources who share a surname, county of origin, or dialect. This is indeed the case with the fathers of Chin-yiu and Mae, who worked closely with fellow countrymen and relatives. Young (1974) has extensively researched this tendency in the market town of Yuen Long in the New Territories.

It is necessary to appreciate the extreme importance that Kwangtung people attach to their linguistic differences. Speakers of Cantonese (itself subdivided by mutually unintelligible subdialects), Hokkienese, Ch'iu-chao, and Hakka follow patterns of cultural, social, and settlement exclusiveness (Blake, in press; Cohen, 1968; Sparks, 1976). Intense local loyalties that focus on minute subcultural differences of each group play a major part in the marriage alliances of the women in this study, which include members of the main speech groups of Kwangtung province.

Family formation

The political-economic relationships necessary for families to operate in the pre-modern society and binding agnatic and affinal relatives, neighbors, and friends were accompanied by an "open" marriage pattern that expanded family networks. Marriage was universal, and divorce and remarriage, rare (Barclay et al., 1976:610; Fei, 1975:59–60).[9] The marriage age for brides averaged 17.0 to 18.0 years but was rising in the cities.

Since the emphasis of marriage was on furtherance of the family economy and the ancestral line, marriages were arranged and negotiated by the families of the betrothed. Westernization had begun to affect the arranged marriage system among the urban elite, but in rural areas men and women worked apart, and coeducation had not been widely introduced; hence ruralites lacked opportunities to mingle with members of the opposite sex.[10] Nevertheless, as the sociologist Goode (1959) pointed out, the authority of family conventions was preserved when the partners consented to or conceivably initiated their unions.

Surname exogamy predominated and people tended to marry within their same speech group. Marriage patterns varied with village composition: in multi-surname villages in which lineage organizations were sizable and highly developed, descent groups competed for use of local resources. Their daughters married some distance from the community, thereby cementing personal contacts. Where lineages were poorly organized and small, village families of diverse surnames were likely to cooperate in exploiting the environment, and a woman often married within the community in which she grew up or a short distance from her natal home (Blake, in press; Diamond, 1969; Freedman, 1958; Pasternak, 1972:62; Treudley, 1974:153). Most newlyweds joined the household of the bridegroom's family (patrilocal residence), but many households later divided. However, even where families divided the hearth (the symbol of the household) and separated budgets, they continued to exchange labor and provide mutual assistance. This exchange of services is a feature of Hong Kong families today.

The groom's family was obligated to pay a bride price, out of which the banquet and all or part of the dowry were paid for. The dowry returned with the bride in the form of furniture, bedding, and clothing, which contributed to the formation of the new family (Fei, 1975:110; Parish and Whyte, 1978:180–2). The dowry was considered the woman's property, and was not under normal circumstances absorbed into the household economy (Shiga, 1978:118).[11] In no case did the departing daughter take land or inheritance rights with her. Marriage was an important occasion in that it maintained social status and reaffirmed reciprocity, as it does today in Hong Kong. Parents saved for 5 or more years for wedding expenses, the size of which was guided by custom and the market rate. Guests at the banquet contributed to its costs, and in return were entertained with a feast. "There is an exchange, so that the money spent on the ceremony is used not merely for a display of wealth, but brings returns of both a social and material nature" (Fei, 1975:256).

A Chinese male might marry one wife in accordance with these arrangements, and he might also take a concubine, which Kulp (1966:151) refers to as a clear case of purchase. Drawn from poorer classes, the concubine was accorded a minor place in family affairs, but the same property system that applied to the wife's sons held for her sons. The mothers of several of my respondents are concubines, referred to as "secondary wives," and one respondent's mother is the legal wife of her father, who resides in Singapore with his secondary wife.

Despite the close dependence of villagers upon reciprocal assistance from others, a farm family mainly had to depend on its own members. Family economic goals and closely related ancestral religious beliefs led to the older generation's desire that their children bear sons. Nevertheless, the typical farm family had a "moderate level of fertility" (Barclay et al., 1976:613), and the average completed family size was five to six children (Salaff, 1972).

Socialization

Contemporary comparative psychologists have found that in low-surplus societies based on regular tending of crops and constant care of farm animals, children customarily are rigorously trained to be completely obedient and responsive to commands and concerned for the well-being of siblings and other family members (Barry et al., 1959). Chinese parents used various methods to instill in their children the values of frugality, hard work, and compliance to the group. Such socialization was a unifying component of the self-sufficient centripetal family system, in which members needed above all to pool all available labor.

The upbringing of sons and daughters differed almost from birth. The father-son bond was the most important relationship in the family. The father trained his sons and saw that they married, and sons were expected to defer to their father, provide him with male descendents, support him in his old age, and worship his spirit after his death. Fathers were relatively strict with their sons.

The mother, lacking rights, property, or legal claim to her sons, compensated in human terms and favored her sons, functioning as the "kind one of the house" (Lang, 1946:247). In her work on the "uterine family," Wolf (1970, 1972) described how the close bonds between mother and son are based less upon agnatic family codes and more upon her close nurturance and caregiving. The uterine connection is still the prime source of security through the woman's life in Hong Kong families (see also Chodorow, 1978; Slater, 1968). The case studies in this volume evidence the close ties of sentiment that bolster the religious value of sons and the economic and political necessity of bearing sons for security through women's lives. These ties that bind put considerable pressure on sons to marry in accordance with the wishes of Mother and to bear grandsons to perpetuate the filial bond.

The mother's treatment of girls was traditionally less nurturing than that of her sons. She viewed daughters as poor long-term investments for emotional energy and instruction in all but rudimentary tasks, since daughters eventually marry and contribute their skills to another family, but she sought maximum returns from them while they were young. Moreover, mothers were marked by their own earlier subordination before and after marriage and were expected by the patriarchy to perpetuate this unbalanced treatment of females. When the household reached maturity, the mother hoped finally to obtain status, respect, and a measure of personal power.

Family roles and obligations

The family head was a male who represented the household in all contractual matters with other families and outsiders and made key decisions on family work schedules, sources of income, and expenditures. Patrilineal and patrilocal family patterns lent continuity and leadership to the economic enterprise, and this combination of delegated leadership and cooperation by all members was the key to the economic family (Myers, 1975). A woman learned from a very early age that her life would be determined by the fate of its economic unit and that the future of the family economy depended on forthcoming contributions from her and all of her siblings.

Women's roles in the household economy were shaped by the nature of production, notably the spatial contiguity of home and workplace, intrinsic to interrelated farm and handicraft labor. A woman's vigorous input to family consumption was an essential part of the household economy (Kulp, 1966:252-3; Yang, 1959). All women were assigned domestic chores. The mode of production, which changed little over the centuries, gave rise to a tradition of women's role in the home economy. Although men helped with chopping, carrying, and using firewood, and fetched water from wells or streams, domestic tasks were consigned to women. Male participation in marketing chores in South China varied with the village, from sites in which marketing was mainly a male preserve to villages wherein each spouse purchased particular items (Lang, 1946; Parish and Whyte, 1978:205; Treudley, 1974:44, 69, 138-9).

Although women did not alone direct the level and pattern of family consumption, their consumer activities were calculated to enhance the capital accumulation of the family enterprise. Especially at the early stages of foundation of the family farm or shop, it was important for women to be thrifty and make items that they later might prefer to purchase. In the fields and in the family home, the assistance of neighbors was required, because no household had sufficient members to cater the weddings, birthdays, wakes, and feasts to the gods and goddesses that dotted the peasant calendar. Those families who provided assistance for the feasts were usually engaged in ongoing cooperation more directly related to subsistence (Pasternak, 1972:64).

Although the farmstead's needs consumed considerable time and energy, many women worked in agriculture as well as handicrafts and contributed greatly to family earnings. In southeast China, where there was a high demand for manual labor due to extensive irrigation, the weeding and transplanting of the rice crop, and population density, women's labor amounted to 30% of the total family farm work (Boserup, 1970:27-35; Buck, 1978:292). Women's productive roles were important, and in some villages they received wages and retained their income from sideline activities (Cohen, 1976; Fei, 1975:65-6). Berkner (1972:149) explained that what was most crucial for Western Europe was not that at the time of inheritance the children obtained a share of movables (dowry, furniture, livestock) but whether the land was divided. Nowhere in China, the world's biggest agricultural society, could women inherit land. This helps explain their lowly status within the nuclear and economic families despite their productive routine, and their exclusion from societal and religious functions.

When women were responsible for enlarging family resources, power did not accrue to them, but nonetheless they increased their influence within the existing family economy. Lang (1946) likened family government to a political entity, whose rules could range from the absolute monarch who governed alone without consulting anyone and decided how the family enterprise was to be conducted to families in which the father's rule was tempered by nominal consultation. The latter form of modified absolutism was most prevalent in Lang's researches and in Treudley's (1974:144) study of a Szechuan market town. Treudley emphasized that shopkeepers' wives, who minded the family store as well as raised and sold farm animals, used their wages to pay for food and the children's education, and thereby became family decision makers. Buck found that where women's agricultural input was relatively great, their families demanded a higher bride price (Parish and Whyte, 1978:181).

During the economic blockade of World War II by the Japanese and the central government against the Communist North China anti-Japanese base areas, women turned to a former female occupation that had fallen into disuse: weaving and spinning cloth. Initially opposed by family members, who objected to the loss of the young weavers' labor in the household, this leap upward in the productive process eventually raised women's self-esteem and commanded new respect in their families for their additional material contribution to family income (Belden, 1970:315-6; Croll, 1978:204-5; Crook and

Crook, 1959:67–9; Sheridan, in preparation). These studies support the view that women's participation in rice cultivation and various forms of handicrafts brought about measurable improvements in their lives within the centripetal family but in no way shook the foundation of this deeply rooted Chinese institution.

Commercial and factory occupations before 1949

Women's nonagricultural occupations were linked to their sex and procreation roles and to work that they might learn from other women that did not demand capital, schooling, or apprenticeship and that was close to the home or family enterprises. The proportion of women workers engaged on their own account in nonfamily endeavors before 1949 was only 7% of all commercial workers (Liu and Yeh, 1965:182, 188). In Chung Ho Ch'ang, Szechuan, women were small-scale traders, and 85% of kindred workers in shops were women, but only 2% of the 263 market town shops were managed entirely by women (Fei, 1975: 45, 48; Treudley, 1974:56, 135, 148–50).

Women first made a breakthrough in nonagricultural labor when the growth of Chinese- and foreign-owned light industries during and after World War I created new openings for impoverished urban and peasant women. In Shanghai, textiles comprised about one-third of all factories, and a substantial proportion of workers were women. An industrial survey carried out in twenty-eight cities and nine provinces in 1938 concluded that 45% of the nearly one million industrial workers were women. Factory workers in Shanghai in the 1930s, like those in Hong Kong today, were young and unmarried (T'ien, 1968: 180; Wales, 1951:19, 1954–5).

Writers on commerce and industry have concluded that women's employment was responsible for measurable improvements in their lives in the following main areas: marriage choice, the right to some fruits of their labor, geographic mobility, social life, and recognition of their contribution to their natal home. First, marriage was affected most dramatically by paid labor among the silk weavers in Shun-te county, Kwangtung province. Young women who labored from the third quarter of the nineteenth century through the 1930s earned high wages for the time, much of which they remitted to their families. Intent on remaining at their looms throughout their productive years, the young Shun-te weavers exchanged vows of celibacy with one another and formed Buddhist-inspired residential "sisterhoods." These workers exercised a certain working-class militancy, and when their wage demands were not met by the management they conducted strikes. Bolstered by their benevolent sororities, spinsters joined in marketing, worship at temples and shrines, and attendance at operas and folk festivals. Remittance of their wages to their homes was the condition set by the community for toleration of their challenge to marital institutions (Howard and Buswell, 1925; Sankar, in preparation; Smedley, 1978; Topley, 1975).

In contrast to the marriage-resisting spinsters, the typical treaty port worker in Shanghai was an unmarried girl who would work until she married – she was not expected to choose work as an alternative to married life. However, working women were likely to postpone marriage as a way of perpetuating their earning years, which they enjoyed. In his study of employed daughters in the fifty families of a Shanghai farming suburb, circa 1930, Herbert Lamson found that in exchange for the substantial financial contribution that these new proletarian women made to the household, their parents allowed more personal freedom in such decisions as choice of marriage partner, the right to delay marriage, and a chance to participate in factory-based peer groups (Lamson, 1931:1072-4). Lang (1946:263) also linked the girls' employment to late marriage.

Second, Chinese women who resided at home generally gave their entire paycheck to their parents and received back a fixed sum as a personal allowance, and women who resided in dormitories usually reserved even more to spend on sundry items and amusements before they gave their money to their parents. All women financed their outings and purchases with their earnings (Lamson, 1931; Lang, 1946: 264; Wales, 1951). These pre-war laboring women benefited from their wages, but since there were no outlets for investing their funds to ensure fiscal refunds, their salaries did not provide economic power.

Third, Lamson (1931) and Lang (1946) found that Shanghai women of the 1930s were pleased at being able to travel, if only to the city where they were to work. Fourth, workers in the wartime industry that was moved from Shanghai to Kunming, Yunnan, especially welcomed the opportunity to build peer relations on and off the job. Restraint was the watchword in their dealings with family adults, but with friends these women could share confidences in a relationship free from the hierarchical expectations of the centripetal family. All twelve roommates in one cell of a factory dormitory invented an elaborate surrogate, fictive kinship network and embellished this make-believe family for many months. Others paired off into dyads of sworn sisters and patronage relationships well known in Chinese folk literature. These "family" relationships not only gave the women emotional support but also accustomed them to working (T'ien, 1968:186–7).

Finally, in all surveys referred to, women's wages made a sizable contribution to their families' economies. Lang (1946:262–3) found those peasant women who worked in factories in the city of Wusih were often the major cash earners, and elsewhere urban women earned from one-third to two-fifths of the family income. "The childhood of the poor does not last long," pronounced Lang (1946:259). Young girls were able to find work in textile factories, and if it was economically impossible for more than one child to be educated, the son was certain to be chosen. Sisters then supported their brothers' schooling by going out to work (Lamson, 1930).

Some women workers lacked choice in their economic input to the families. In areas distant from the cities, fathers handed over their daughters to employment contractors without full understanding of the contract terms. Contract laborers were indentured servants and lacked the pocket money to leave the factory dormitory before their contract ended (Ch'en, 1920). Most young women, however, contributed their earnings to the family willingly. They were not in a position to earmark their wages for specific uses and were expected to repay with labor and goods the accumulated "cost" of their upbringing (Lang, 1946:264–5). Even if a daughter's factory wage was a relatively insignificant contribution to the family budget, she at least relieved her family of the burden of her personal support.

Lamson (1931), Lang (1946:150, 264), and others found that despite the girls' removal from the family dwelling, the closer bonds forged by their economic contribution led, if anything, to better treatment of them when they were home. In most cases the proletarian women asked relatively little in return for their financial contributions, but did expect to receive respect from their elders and were on the whole gratified by their say in such matters as education of siblings and their own futures.

Comparisons

Studies on Chinese working women in the new industrial labor force since 1949 in Taiwan also have demonstrated that women's wage labor could only go so far in changing their position in the centripetal family. In contemporary Taiwan, which has economic parallels with Hong Kong and republican-era China, the trend toward young women's prominence in the light manufacturing labor force has taken firm hold.[12] Taiwan factory workers are unmarried women fresh out of school who work for a limited period and then leave the factory upon their marriage. But factory-sponsored outings widen women's options to select their own mate, and they postpone marriage in the interim (Kung, in preparation). Like the earlier generations of Chinese working women, Taiwan women give much of their wages to their family, "to repay the cost of their upbringing" (Arrigo, in preparation; Kung, in preparation; Marsh, 1968). With the remainder they purchase clothing and enjoy picnics, skating parties, movies, and other peer outings. Married women in contemporary Taiwan are known to invest in loan societies, but this practice is uncommon among the younger women comprising the new wave of factory workers. Various forms of night school are their sole means for transforming bank balances into permanent personal gain (Kung, 1976, in preparation). The hunger of my Hong Kong working women subjects for further education is one of the main characteristics of their lives as well, as seen in the following chapters. Like their earlier Shanghai counterparts, Taiwan women workers express pleasure at being able to transfer to other factories to gain slightly better wages and a variety of work experiences (Kung, in preparation). They work out of necessity, but they also feel gratified at being filial daughters by means of their family income-augmenting possibilities.

Kung and Arrigo hold that the long-standing Taiwan family patterns cannot be overturned by such temporally limited factors as a daughter's biweekly financial contribution. According to Kung (1976, in preparation), the family holds claim to women's labor and therefore grants few meaningful concessions to toiling daughters. Arrigo (in preparation) described economic and political controls, which limit the earning power of Taiwanese working women and render them lifelong dependents upon their husbands and families. Arrigo's respondents thus have failed to gain ascendance in their family relationships, despite daily toil.

In contrast, Lang (1946) and Lamson (1931), who observed village and treaty port Chinese women factory laborers in the 1930s, emphasized the gains of proletarian women over their rural counterparts. Through interviews with working women, Lang glimpsed the reluctance of families to permit women to assume family council and decision-making roles in the patriliny, which she attributed to "cultural lag": the delay in remolding family structure to accord with new economic realities. Lang's sensitive reportage of women's increased personal stature flowed from her interactionist perspective. However, Lang's optimistic hope that wage labor would erode the bonds fettering proletarian women followed equally from her microscopic view, and she underestimated the power of the Chinese family to absorb the wage-earning contribution of its working daughters.

My study demonstrates that Hong Kong working daughters must, in addition to the unrelenting demands of their families, contend with large-scale economic, political, and social institutions. My approach is both interactionist and structuralist, and I take into account the peer-group activities of the Hong Kong women and their own views of their status in the hopes of providing a more balanced picture of the continuities of the traditional family and the relative freedoms that working women can gain therein.

The Hong Kong family

The solidary family that calls forth the resources and energies of its working members is both a product of the Chinese society before 1949, described in the previous paragraphs, and the demands of the contemporary Hong Kong colonial system. Administrative modernization and industrialization have modified considerably the structure and form of the centripetal family, which lacks land and the means of production upon which wider alliances with kinsmen could be based. Since industrial society takes primary responsibility for the provision of education, health care, and vocational training for its members, these too are rarely family functions today. The material basis for self-groupings of families has thus disappeared.

However, the family must turn to itself for economic survival and eventual well-being. A combination of low wages, which force two or more family members into the job market, and rock bottom governmental social service commitments frequently creates the conditions of desperation that drive families back onto their own resources. A necessity for survival, the family wage economy is also a precondition for cherished aspirations for future advancement in the class structure. Social restrictions, which in other capitalist societies might somewhat curtail the economic aggrandizement of individuals and their family units (high taxes, partial nationalization measures) are absent; so even families with no hope of acquiring property or the means of commodity production entertain hope of advancement through the concerted efforts of family members. The population at large banks primarily on the educational system as its path to success, and salaries and wages of earning adults are pooled to meet the not inconsiderable educational expenses of the advancing younger members. Even Hong Kong emigrants remit substantial proportions of their overseas earnings to underwrite family livelihood and advancement in the colony, where household budgets are generally managed in common (Lam, in preparation; Watson, 1975).

Closely interwoven with the centripetal family form, codes of partible inheritance are still normative, if not legal, in the New Territories villages (Baker, 1968; Evans, 1973). Bourgeois families with productive property also pass their assets along the male line and reserve the capital to launch sons in their own or in the family business. Those without property apply family savings differentially to ensure the future of the sons through education. Although daughters may be educated when family income permits, the quality is usually inferior, as this study shows.

The Hong Kong family of today, for the same reasons as its Chinese predecessors, promotes relations of mutual indebtedness with a broad sphere of acquaintances. In the large New Territories market town of Yuen Long, villagers establish relations of *kan-ch'ing*, involving regular assistance and mutual interaction, benevolent patron-client relations, and fictive kin relationships related to Father's birthplace (Young, 1974:57-60, 82-3). As my case histories show, wedding and ceremonial banquets, which certify the credit-worthiness of my respondents' families in their matrix of social and economic allies, continue to be important.

As in the past, marriage is universal and divorce infrequent, which ensures that offspring gain a family role. It is a long-established tradition that the Hong Kong ethnolinguistic groups marry endogamously: In 1970 two-thirds or more of non-Cantonese Chinese speakers married within their speech groups (Census and Statistics Department, 1970-2). Dialect group endogamy reflects the continuation of competing discrete groupings and strengthes communal cleavages between Hong Kong families.

Agnate priority is evident in the patrifocal marriage pattern. Since an estimated one-third of young adult couples (with one member between ages 35 and 39 in 1968) lacked any parents in Hong Kong, and the price of housing precludes extending a family for all but the upper-middle class, the average Hong Kong household does not span three generations (Mitchell, 1972b). However, one study of the New Territories middle-class residential complex of Mei Foo Sun Chuen found paternal relatives who purchased adjoining residences, shared meals, exchanged child care, and visited frequently (Rosen, 1978). In the following case studies it becomes clear that men are loyal to their fathers' families from birth and until their fathers' dying years must heed his commands. Girls are trained from childhood in self-control and responsibility and to serve their families while they mature (Mitchell and Lo, 1968). Girls must transfer their loyalties to the family of their eventual groom, and wives invariably defer to their husbands' wishes. Individuals have scope to maneuver mainly within these family scriptures.

Summary: the conditions fostering the centripetal family

The centripetal family, characterized by the drawing inward of family resources and creation of long-term interpersonal links, was determined by the partible inheritance system and the religious attachment to the male-centered ancestral system, which bonded young men to their families of origin and women to their families of procreation after marriage. This family form was further fostered by the decentralized, authoritarian polity in pre-war China which, as in Hong Kong today, permitted the poor no legitimate access to power. The pre-industrial economy also encouraged forging of bonds to obtain cooperation from people outside the immediate family.

Change in the centripetal family form presupposes the establishment of a central political structure with institutions that will reward the populace for expending its energies toward fulfillment of societal goals. A social security system with guaranteed assistance in old age and other times of need and a universal education system to recruit members into wider societal institutions are preconditions to an alternative family form. The proletarianization of the family and deprivation of productive property as a main source of subsistence will further contribute to family change. However, without family reforms directed against ancestral and patrilineal continuity, the centripetal family is likely to remain, although possibly in a modified form.

The centripetal family persists in contemporary Hong Kong, which fulfills few of these political, economic, and ideological conditions. Cultural lag and cultural renewal through continual immigration from Kwangtung province are not alone responsible for family strength (Gutman, 1976). The particular features of the political and economic systems encourage inward-drawing family actions for security and survival; the family structure is modified to meet the new industrial environment, and its core features remain intact.

2. Introducing three factory workers

Hong Kong industry consists of small, medium, and large factories. The small factories are scattered widely throughout the colony, but there are concentrations in old urban districts of Kowloon – Sam Po Kong, Sham Shui Po, and Mong Kok. Most large and medium-size factories, which appeared in the 1960s, after the central core of Kowloon and Victoria (Hong Kong Island) were already densely packed, sought land in previously uninhabited areas where Kowloon joins the New Territories, notably in Tsuen Wan and Kwun Tong. Bulldozers, followed by black-garbed Hakka women laborers, baskets hanging from their shoulder poles, scooped the red earth from the hillsides, flattened mountains, and filled in the sea for the new factories.

Because they are located some distance from the offices, shops, hotels, and residences of the downtown Kowloon (Tsim Sha Tsui) district, a visitor must deliberately seek out these large factories. The districts of the large-scale factories differ sharply in appearance from the multipurpose residential, office, hotel, and shopping areas that give Tsim Sha Tsui and Victoria their distinct charm. Tsim Sha Tsui streets are lively with sights, smells, and color that attract the wanderer's senses, whereas the factory areas overwhelm the visitor with the single-dimensional impression of grayness. The dull, monotonic sound of textile machinery matches the monochronic gray, punctuated by the screams of jets as they wing their way overhead toward Kai Tak Airport. Where fabric is printed in Ngau Tau Kok, the acrid smell of formaldehyde masks all other senses. In neighboring Kwun Tong, gray buildings and pedestrian bridges arch over wide, treeless streets and contrast with blue waters of the nearby bay, the blue skies, and white summer heat shimmering off the buildings and sidewalks, but there is little natural or man-made beauty in the environment.

The factory districts become enlivened solely by their people. When shifts change, young, colorfully dressed factory workers descend from company buses and, shielding their eyes from the bright sun with their purses, swarm through the gates to work. A few minutes later, other young women emerge from the electronics or garment factories, crowd around the waiting pushcarts of food vendors to purchase sweet, salty, or pickled Chinese delicacies or ice cream, then board the company buses homeward.

On several occasions I visited the workplaces of my friends and interviewees. The arrangements to visit the small or medium-size garment factories that were managed by the Chinese were a simple matter. No one complained when I strolled through the factory doors unannounced into the work areas on the arm of one of the workers after the lunch break. In these shops a familylike atmosphere prevailed, and after my introduction to the boss or the section leader, I was invited to sit and chat with the workers and share their hot tea or water. In contrast, in the larger, more strictly managed factories of the transnational corporations, and in those few Chinese-owned enterprises that prided themselves on their high-quality garments, a well-regulated work pace was exacted. It was impossible to walk in with one of the line workers or to chat at random with them while they toiled. I gained entry to such factories by means of formal introductions to management, usually via government intermediaries. Such differences in management style stimulated my curiosity and led me to pursue the differences, if any, in the impact of multinational and local Chinese managerial authority patterns and ideologies upon the women workers. I was to find, however, that although the management ideology and work atmosphere of small shops and large factories differed in many ways, they were similar in their impact upon the women workers' life-styles and family roles.

This chapter examines how involvement in contemporary factory wage labor affects a woman's obligations to her family. Modern industrial society demands the sale of labor to industry. The pre-modern family economy, however, promoted the continuity of the family as a unit, toward which all members contributed their work. According to some writers, women who work for a wage in modern industry are likely to use their individual earning ability to bargain for freedom from family obligations in favor of their own individual goals. In addition, the large size of modern factories and machine-based work groups, which are organized in rational form based upon technology without heed to personal ties among workers, attenuate the allegiances of workers to their families.

The final disjunctive factor of the contemporary market economy is the mass media, which cross international cultural and geographic boundaries and instantaneously intrude into such exotic areas as Hong Kong with splashy advertisements inspired by Hollywood and pop culture. The media attached to the transnational corporations penetrate new markets, wielding advertising slogans designed to create local receptivity for factory-made consumer goods among the young people newly employed in local factories. The molders of the "Pepsi generation" invite local youths to enter the cash economy, work where they wish, date freely, marry a mate who attracts them, and, most of all, buy what they fancy. In short: On all fronts youths are being urged to make economic decisions independently of their families.

To determine the degree of disjunctive impact of these features of contemporary industrial life, we can look at the lives of Mae, Waigun, and Suyin, women who were in their early 20s in 1973 who worked in factories for most of their teenage and young adult years. All three came from large working-class families in which they were eldest or second daughters. These women experienced considerable social pressure to contribute to the operation of the family, and especially to the family wage economy. The different personalities of each provided alternative ways of reconciling family obligations and the nonfamilial opportunities that were easily available through work experiences. That the three Hong Kong daughters introduced in this chapter made the important and necessary reconciliation to the family needs, however, there is no doubt.

Mae: dutiful second daughter

Mae Goh was 22 in 1973. Her solid build, her hair fixed in an outdated, ear-length coif, tightly curled, her broad face with its calm, serious demeanor, and the plain, conservative gaberdine pants and knit skirts and tops she wore gave her the look of a hardworking, no-frills woman. This impression was appropriate, because Mae was a pivotal contributor to her family economy. Mae singlemindedly devoted herself to her family, and she derived her self-esteem from this care and attention.

The Goh household consisted of Father, Mother, and six siblings. Father was a low-paid clerk and First Brother was a delivery boy for a well-known retail comprador firm in Hong Kong. Mae and First Sister, Hua, were factory workers. The three youngest children, all sons, were students in 1973. The Goh family aspired to upgrade itself economically by drawing upon the wages of the three eldest children, and in so doing advance the education and hence the careers of the three youngest. Although ambitious for a working-class family, those plans were attainable as long as no unforeseen crisis occurred to weaken the family earning power. All family members had become keenly aware of the importance of coordinating their working efforts and pooling their individual earnings. Self-upgrading the household by multiple wage earning was the Goh family's strategy that had long guided Mae's behavior.

Home

Mae was a Ch'iu-chaonese born in a village near the port city Swatow, northeast of Hong Kong in Kwangtung province. Father brought his mother and younger brother along with Hua and Mae with him to Hong Kong on a fishing boat in 1951. The Hong Kong government lacked the facilities to receive the incoming wave of refugees from the newly founded People's Republic, and families like the Gohs initially had to manage with rudimentary, makeshift accommodations. Upon their arrival, the Gohs purchased an overpriced, ramshackle squatter's hut from a petty entrepreneur who had nailed it together from old crates. The squatter huts were crammed together on a Kowloon mountainside, which teemed with impoverished refugees. Within months their hut was badly burned by a fire that swept the squatter complex, and although the Goh family escaped unscathed, they had no other recourse but construction of a second shack similar to the one they had evacuated. Eventually the community was provided with a pump with running water, one communal outhouse for every 100 families, and cement walkways. Primary schools were built in the neighborhood by missionary societies, but few other community services were available in the squatter area, which the government considered temporary (Hopkins, 1971:278–95).

In fact, the Gohs remained in this squatter area for nearly a decade, during which three sons were born, before the family was finally resettled in two rooms in Lok Fu resettlement estate, where the sixth, and last, child was born. Government-built resettlement estates were a relatively inexpensive form of housing for the Goh family, but their facilities were rudimentary. Their two 10′ by 12′ rooms, standard for the time, were allotted on the basis of 24 square feet per adult (6' by 4'), and they had a nine-member household. Children were allocated only one-half of the "adult" space, so resettlement estate families had to curtail the physical movement and indoor play of their youngsters. Simple home industries like plastic flower assembling and piecework sewing were permitted in the rooms. Shops, schools, churches, a playground, and even factories were contained in the basements and on the rooftops of the Gohs' block of flats. This older estate in which Mae lived lacked indoor plumbing and water taps and private kitchens. The outdoor balcony was the sole walkway on each floor. Here the Goh family cooked, stored water, hung clothes, washed children, and socialized with the neighbors. There was a common stall-type toilet on every floor, laundering and bathing areas, as well as a common water spigot, where the family filled its water jars.

One of the Gohs' rooms was partitioned into three sleeping areas: the first for the two elder girls and Grandmother, the second for the three eldest brothers, and the third for the parents and youngest child. The other room served as their living room and contained a long sideboard that held a matching tea service, a large Kewpie doll, and a telephone. A wall of the room was dominated by the 23-inch television set. A refrigerator was placed against the second wall, and the sewing machine took up yet another wall. The dining table, which filled the central floor space, doubled as the evening study area for the boys. Calendars advertising the fishing gear sold at Father's workplace adorned the walls.

By the 1970s, the Goh family could afford a more spacious flat and was put on a waiting list for a government-built low-cost housing unit. But Mae was relatively satisfied with her estate apartment, despite its obvious shortcomings, because of its proximity to her place of work. She explained, "Living here is quite convenient. We have the market just downstairs, and transportation to work is easy. The only bad thing about this place is security. Just the other day a restaurant on the next block was robbed of sixteen hundred dollars, and not long before that a fellow was robbed in the staircase. Also, there are a lot of peeping toms here. The management installed doors on the toilet stalls only a few months ago. Before that, it was really horrible. There was no privacy at all. And they still haven't done anything about the bathing area yet. A friend of mine had to scream for help not long ago when she was bathing – someone was peeping at her. Now I have to go early to bathe, when there aren't too many people hanging around the bathing area. Also, it's very dangerous to walk around the estate very late, and so I usually try to get back before eleven. If I come home after that, then I ask Mother to be my guard."

The Goh family tolerated these cramped, difficult accommodations because they were a decided improvement over the squatter shacks in which they had lived for many years. Also, this future-focused family concentrated its meager funds on the younger children's education and preferred not to squander its money on housing, which apart from short-term comfort promised few returns on the family investment (Topley, 1969). Nevertheless, the need for space and physical security were increasingly pervasive concerns, and by this time the Gohs could afford to search the private housing market for a modest alternative to the older resettlement estate apartment. While waiting for a government-financed low-cost housing apartment, the Gohs rented an inexpensive two-room flat in the Kowloon Walled City, a district not far from their estate home. Several of the Goh family members moved to the Walled City and others remained in the estate rooms, which began to seem comparatively spacious.

Parents

Mrs. Goh was a large-boned, rather stout woman, broad shouldered and easygoing. Her childhood was spent in a village near the city of Swatow, and like all of the mothers in my sample she matured during the economic depression and the turbulent years of China's war with Japan and the civil war. Mrs. Goh never attended school and at age 18 entered an arranged marriage with a neighboring villager whose father was a trader in small wares. After two children were born, the Gohs emigrated by sea to Hong Kong. At first, Mr. Goh's mother shared a squatter home with the family, but she and Mrs. Goh were continually at loggerheads, and the older woman finally moved to a one-half room resettlement estate apartment nearby.

Mrs. Goh was required to cook, sew clothes, shop daily for food bargains in the open-air market, and take the youngest child to and from the nearby kindergarten, so she never had time to undertake employment outside the home. Her main diversions were chatting with her neighbors and watching television, and she gained pleasure from being with her family. Mrs. Goh never attended the cinema because she was not able to understand either the Mandarin dialect of contemporary Hong Kong films or the Chinese subtitles. At home, however, Mr. Goh cleared away the table and washed the supper dinner dishes so that Mother could view her favorite television soap opera after dinner.

Observing her children develop and doing her best for them was a source of fulfillment for this dedicated mother. Mrs. Goh made it clear to me that she was distressed by the large size of her family and revealed that she originally had wished to have fewer children. She had taken herbal contraceptive formulas in an effort to prevent her sixth birth. Later she blamed herself for the consequences: "My youngest son has been in the hospital several times, and as you see he has no appetite. Mother-in-law says that the child is sickly because of the herbal medicines that I drank." Mother's attempt at rudimentary birth control indicated that she never ceased attempting to control her life, although the action she took was not effective.

A slightly built man, Mr. Goh had a broad face, and Mae proudly pointed out their physical resemblances: "Many times I've been walking down the street and people have stopped me to ask, 'Are you Goh's daughter?' We look so much alike!" Father clerked behind the counter in a small Ch'iu-chao trading firm that exported Chinese fishing nets to Ch'iu-chao traders in Thailand and Singapore. He dressed neatly in a white shirt and gray slacks, in contrast to the blue or black garb of the manual workers. Father's status on the job was low, and as jack-of-all-trades (or, as he put it, a "many-kick-foot") he was required to toil long hours and sometimes all night as counterman, stockboy, and watchman.

This was Father's first steady work in Hong Kong, and he had remained at the same firm for over 20 years. The manager spoke the same Ch'iu-chao dialect, and Father felt loyal to the firm. When Father first obtained this position he earned only $40 a month, and after 20 years (with annual raises of $4), his income reached $120, a probable ceiling. Father's earnings would soon be topped by the wages of his sons, who would, he fervently hoped, do much better than he in the world of work. By "better" he meant higher wages and shorter hours in a steady white-collar position. A modest man, Father had never complained to his manager about his low pay. Hua and Mae both wished that Father could find a position with improved wages and hours, but they realized that it was impossible for a man his age to change his line of work. The girls loyally insisted that the firm did not pay Father his worth, and they endeavored to make up for it by contributing their earnings to the family. Although Eldest Son had already taken a job as a delivery boy in a grocery store, paying somewhat less than Father's job but with shorter hours, hopes were pinned on Second Son, who would be promoted through technical college by dint of the family's efforts and who would vindicate Father's expectations.

Education

Such an expectation was realistic because neighborhood schools were accessible to working-class children residing in the resettlement estate. The Gohs obtained small sums of money from missionary societies to pay the school fees and sent all six children to school. Each successive child attended a bit longer, paving the way psychologically and socially for the improved schooling of the next-younger sibling.

The primary school that the sisters and brothers attended enjoyed a modest reputation. It was a private missionary school, with a curriculum oriented toward the Secondary School Entrance Examination taken by all Hong Kong primary graduates. The pupils were taught in vernacular Cantonese, but Mandarin was the medium of written exercises, which the pupils rarely learned to proficiency. Mae's parents chose the school because of its proximity to home, low tuition fees, and the fair-minded reputation of its principal, a missionary who was outspokenly critical of the political and economic conditions that Hong Kong working-class people endured. "It's a good school. It's close, too. The headmistress is a good person who's done a lot for people like us," commented Mae.

Hua left school after primary 2 to work in a light bulb factory at 20¢ per day, but Mae completed primary 6 before going out to work. Mae proudly included her graduation from primary school among her major accomplishments. First Brother, the third child, obtained 3 years of secondary schooling, after which he held several jobs, including factory worker and delivery boy. The family pinned its economic hopes upon the fourth child, who was studying to enter a postsecondary technical institute, and the fifth, a form II pupil (the second year of secondary school. The sixth was still in primary school.

The two sisters deeply regretted their inadequate education, which they attempted to remedy by attending night school after work. At great physical cost and with few tangible results, Mae sat in a crowded classroom every night vainly attempting to absorb the rudiments of English grammar and a few facts of European history. She recalled, "Hua and I rushed right to school from work. We never had time to eat dinner. I used to buy a bread roll and eat it when the teacher turned his head to write on the blackboard. It was really tiring! But I enjoyed it because that's where I met my best friend I-ling, as well as A-li and some other friends. Although we have all dropped out of class by now, we still keep up our friendships."

Mae then enrolled in part-time English lessons at the Caritas (Catholic) Youth Centre, where we first met in 1973, and various other classes as well – folk singing, European cooking, and social dancing. At the end of 1974 she re-enrolled in nightly classes, favored by Mother as a means to improve her job opportunities. However, Mae candidly admitted that such an evening school, which provided no recognized certificate for its graduates, would not greatly elevate her job options, and she continued mainly to make more friends and for the contact with organized knowledge.

Mae and Hua ended their formal schooling for self-proclaimed "economic reasons," but the reasons for which their parents sent them to work were based on conventional definitions of the elder daughters' obligations. The family's undoubted need for cash, coupled with norms limiting women's education and the ease of factory employment for young girls, made inevitable the sacrifice of their further education in favor of the family's economic needs. Nevertheless, the girls' education as far as primary level should be viewed as an assertion of a woman's right to learn. Hua and Mae themselves saw it that way. Secondary education was psychologically and sociologically remote for working-class girls of their age at the time. The sisters learned to read whereas their mother had not, and their formal education, however limited, distinctly increased their employment and social opportunities.

Because school provided extrafamilial experiences, it had a lasting value beyond the formal curriculum. Mae and Hua came into contact with other women their age, and their participation in the age-graded classes stimulated a consciousness of the common bond that unites youth. They also became aware of their ability to achieve on their own apart from their family, which paved the way for their assumption of continued responsibility for their own friendships, leisure-time activities, and jobs after leaving school.

Mae at work

In both large factories and small workshops, all of Mae's jobs consisted of repetitive operations: electronics assembling, seaming garments, and fusing the seams of plastic bags. Mae found small workshops preferable to larger factories because the personal proximity of the workshop owner meant he was aware of and could appreciate Mae's hard work on his behalf. Mae responded best to such personal calls upon her effort.

Mae invited me to visit one place of work, a small plastic bag factory in a narrow, two-floor tenement building within earshot of the busy Kai Tak Airport, with neither heating for the damp winter air nor air conditioning for the intense summer heat. The plastic bags were printed on the first floor, and Mae and three other women cut the bags to size and seamed three edges in the loft. They worked from a fifty-pound roll of plastic, unwinding it by hand, pulling one end under the arm of a machine that resembled an electric paper cutter; then the electrified arm dropped and seamed a bag. These actions took a few seconds but could not be mechanized because one machine could not handle the many sizes and shapes of bags, and as Mae further remarked, "We girls are cheaper than machines." Mae was paid on a piecework basis, $1 for 1,000 plastic bags, which represented 2 hours of seaming at a fast pace. She preferred piecework because of the flexible working hours and the lure of higher earnings than on a fixed wage. However, Mae earned at most $19–$20 for a 6-day week in 1973.

Before joining this workshop in 1973, Mae had tried her hand at several other jobs typically performed by women. In 1970 she left a relatively low-paying electronics factory for a slightly better wage in a plastic bag factory, where she learned the shortcuts from her sister Hua, who was already employed there. Mae quit that factory because a defective automatic machine she had been using to seam the bags emitted electric shocks and she burned her hand. The management refused to repair it, blaming Mae for handling the machine poorly. Mae commented, "After I left, my replacement received such a serious shock that she was sent to the hospital, and only then did the management send someone to fix the machine." Soon after that, Mae attended an evening class where she learned wig assembly. She paid $18 for the class, but shortly after she had acquired the skill, the artificial hair industry collapsed.

In 1973 alone, Mae worked in three separate establishments. Attracted by the promise of 2¢ more per 1,000 plastic bags (for 2 hours of work), Mae phoned in "sick" to the shop I visited and tried out another workshop that offered higher pay. However, the manager of the new workshop broke his word and reduced the wage to the cheaper rate prevailing on the labor market. Conceding that they had lost the dispute with the management, almost all of the women who worked there left for other shops, and Mae joined them, returning to the first plastic bag plant. But she was soon laid off due to a shortage of plastic materials, which the manufacturers imported from Japan but whose local supply was temporarily being hoarded by larger factories. For several weeks Mae worked only a few hours a day in her workshop, supplementing that with work in a larger factory with an adequate supply of materials. A few months later, the small workshop suddenly closed its door when the owner absconded with the funds. Mae turned to another type of work altogether: seaming garments.

Mae did not undertake these job changes lightly, because they were costly in time and money lost. On her first day in the plastic bag workshop that I visited Mae earned only $1.60 because she had not yet learned how to use that particular seaming machine. On her second day there she earned $2.40. "Still too low!" she complained – she was aiming for the $3.50-per-day wage that was her usual ceiling. Mae did not find the transportation to the new shop convenient either, and she walked a round trip of 70 minutes between home and work to save 8¢ bus fare each way.

Mae attributed her poor and irregular working conditions, the frequent layoffs, and lack of work security to the personalities of the employers operating in the competitive economic situation in Hong Kong. Her naïveté of the local employment situation was grounded in a basic incomprehension of the international capitalist division of labor and Hong Kong's dependent role in this division of labor. Accordingly, Mae stated the reason that the manager would not pay her the extra 2¢ per 1,000 bags was his "stinginess," whereas the next manager was "all right." Though he had laid off the workers without pay or warning when he ran out of materials, this was "not his fault," but was due to the "competition among workshops for plastics." Mae was not critical of the government, and she rarely read newspapers. Regarding a then-current teachers' strike, Mae said vaguely, "It's hard to know who is right, the government or the teachers."

Mae was unaware of the location of the export markets for the products she manufactured. She showed me a large yellow plastic bag she had finished on which was written, "Have a safe Hallowe'en, from your Esso dealer," embossed with a picture of a witch riding a broomstick. She did not know what Hallowe'en was. I thought it ironic that Mae had lost one of her jobs in a dispute over 2¢ for 2 hours of work, and yet the bags she seamed had so little value that they were to be given away with the purchase of a tank of gas. Mae thought her firm also finished bags for Mexico, "because the words look like Spanish." (It seemed more likely to me that the bags bore the emblem of a chic boutique in New Haven or Chicago.)

Despite her shallow understanding of Hong Kong exporting practices, Mae manifested an undirected but vital response to her poor working conditions in her willingness to change jobs. Although her frequent job shifts were reflex responses to work problems, from which Mae fled instead of altering, she at least demonstrated an active rather than passive stance. Hua, in contrast, was considerably less resourceful and remained in one factory for over 10 years. "I have considered changing jobs," Hua said, "but I don't know any other trade. Also, I'm different from Mae, who changes jobs frequently. It's not worth it! You'll just have to change again later."

Mae felt responsible for her family's economic station. Very close to her parents emotionally, Mae willingly subordinated her personal goals to their view of family needs. She saw very few contradictions between her personal work ambitions and the economic needs of her family. Mae had no personal work goals, but she would labor as hard on their behalf as she could. For that reason, it was not easy to discuss with Mae her "future career ambitions," a somewhat abstract concept that suggested a freedom of choice between work and marriage or between careers that she did not feel empowered to make. Whenever I raised this topic, Mae responded that she intended to do "the usual thing" expected of young women – to work, see her brothers through school, then marry and continue working until her own children arrived.

In this context, Mae's work goals were limited to the realistically attainable paycheck, friendly coworkers, and time for leisure. Elder sisters worked not only to improve their family's economic situation but also to attain a greater sense of independence and to spend small sums of money on themselves. They were relatively satisfied with their paychecks because they were an improvement over the recent past. Hua recalled that at age ten she earned only 20¢ daily in a light bulb factory, and even then the employer did not even pay all of her pitifully low wages. "The management sometimes delayed paying me because I was under age and too afraid to complain, until Mother would go and raise hell." Although consumer prices were considerably lower then (Hua paid only 10¢ for a meal and 2¢ for bus fare), the Goh family considered itself worse off in those days. On the contrary, Mae's 1973 daily wage of close to $3.50 was a decided improvement, even with the rise in prices. This decade-long gradual wage increase committed workers like these two women to tedious factory jobs because they helped alleviate family poverty and want.

The widening of the family's horizons that followed its solution of the critical problems of shelter and hunger committed the offspring to work even longer for the common good. The stagnation of real wages from 1972 to 1974 further strengthened the girls' commitment to work, because they were still expected to elevate their family's living standards.

Improvement of the young women's work situations was discouraged by the family, the international division of labor (with Hong Kong workers performing labor-intensive, low-skilled manufacturing work), and the educational system. The Goh family encouraged daughters to study only when the training did not interfere with their current earning power. Although some of Mae's friends preferred jobs in which they learned new skills, few such jobs were available, and since most women were enjoined to remit their wages weekly, they invariably abandoned ideas of job training and upgrading in favor of higher-paying piecework machining. As a result, these two sisters and their friends were fixed in a work routine at an early age, and they could acquire other skills only at the fringe of their working routines, in evening school. Their brothers, however, who were expected to contribute significantly to their parents' support, even after marriage, were more likely to undertake low-paying apprenticeships for several years or to remain in school longer, to ensure themselves better prospects for the future. Although an employed married daughter still contributes small sums from her wage packet to her own parents, she is not obliged to do so. This gives rise to the relative lack of concern for the daughter's future career opportunities, a carryover from the patriarchal traditions of Chinese culture, which severely restricted those young women's chances for remunerative work after marriage.

Mae disliked her work but had no future job plans. Mae believed that the only kind of job advancement for a woman was to study sewing and tailoring skills in evening class and then leave the factory to become a tailor. Her friend I-ling did just that, but Mae rejected that idea. "What other kind of job could I have?" she asked rhetorically. "I don't know how to do anything else, and I don't like to sew!" Mae held a conventional notion of women's proper sphere. Pointing to the man who ran the machine that painted the logo on the plastic bags, Mae said, "Only men do that. Of course it's better paying than seaming work, but your hands get dirty when you handle that equipment." After the small plastics workshop closed its doors, Mae turned to garment manufacturing despite her distaste for sewing.

The truncation of Mae's ambitions was consistent with the limited employment opportunities available in Hong Kong. For example, in the electronics industry, Mae's first job setting, the transnational corporations assign only a narrow spectrum of labor-intensive assembly jobs to their Hong Kong plants. But the reasons for the limited career mobility in factories and shops were little fathomed by Mae or Hua. The educational system encouraged neither an understanding of the international political economy in which Hong Kong was situated nor the necessary technical training for women in those highly skilled factory jobs that did exist. Nor did the factory ever train Mae for its supervisory or management posts, which were filled by male graduates of technical institutes, and these technical colleges would not accept students like Mae and her friends with only primary school education. Some of Mae's peers attended private evening school in English, hoping to improve their service girls' qualifications, but the classes were for the most part poorly taught.

However, a few factory women were selected as "lead girls." Two of Mae's friends, A-li and Kitty, advanced to such positions. At first both hesitated, doubting their ability to direct others, but ultimately A-li took the job. The second firmly rejected the position of section leader, stating, "I was afraid that when I had 'm.c.' [menstrual cramps] I would not be able to work or give orders," thereby revealing her agreement with the prevailing dictum that "anatomy is destiny." Thus, feelings of self-limitation and lack of social support, rooted in their subordinate position in the family, the workplace, and the educational system, undermined the determination of Mae and other women to compete for the few opportunities for advancement open to factory hands.

Neither Mae nor her elder sister Hua compared their jobs unfavorably with those of their brothers, since they felt that men and women "naturally" held different types of jobs. Instead, they contrasted their work experiences with those of women of their social class in earlier generations. In so doing they realized that opportunities to work had broadened considerably compared to even the recent past. The speed of economic change was exemplified by the fact that Mae's mother had never worked outside the home whereas her daughters held semi-skilled factory jobs. Hua had remained for years at an unsatisfying job in the plastic bag workshop, whereas Mae, 2 years her junior, more easily transferred from one factory to another. The generational comparison that Mae made was thus rooted in reality. The increased importance of single-sex peer groups further underlined the young woman's identification with other women like herself and suggested the inevitable contrast with women older and younger than herself.

Family relationships

Mae's paid labor input to the family economy was a continuation of her earlier unpaid work at home. It was assumed that the elder children in large families would take responsibility for everyday tasks, and Mae and Hua fulfilled this expectation. Many jobs fell to them before they were adolescents, because of their mother's busy involvement with toddlers and infants. Hua and Mae hauled water daily and cooked, cleaned house, and washed clothes.

After they joined the paid labor force, the two sisters continued to view their primary goal in working as the elevation of their family's living standard. Even though Mae's earnings varied with her frequent changes of employer and the length of her work week, she generally contributed close to three-quarters of her wages to her family. Mae and Hua accounted for over two-fifths of the family income in 1973, a relatively high proportion, because their father earned so little (see Figure 2 in the Conclusion).

Hua and Mae clearly understood the centrality of their earnings, which helped the family purchase essentials: rent and food for the entire family, medical expenses, and education for the younger children. Rent for public housing was low, but utilities (including telephone) were expensive. Food comprised a substantial portion of their budget. Sociologists usually interpret a high proportion of family budget spent upon food as a trait of poverty, but there was little doubt that the Gohs' meals greatly improved in substance and appeal as their income enlarged. They could afford meat or fish daily, to eat out as a group in restaurants one or more Sundays a month, and occasionally to bring cooked food from stalls to eat at home.

Mae and Hua visited private physicians for minor ailments and they purchased Chinese herbal medicines when ill. The two sisters' income also enabled the Gohs to pay for Second Brother's education when he failed to qualify for a government scholarship. As the family income rose with several members working, more consumer goods were purchased. The television set, electric rice cooker, electric fan, small refrigerator, and sewing machine were all considered necessities in Hong Kong and could normally only be purchased by means of the children's additions to the family wage. Thus, according to Mae, her family came to enjoy a relatively comfortable existence only when there were more workers than dependents. "Then," Mae said with obvious satisfaction, "our family was finally on its feet!"

For a family of daughters, this relatively comfortable life was necessarily of limited duration. Several years before Hua became engaged to Lam Bing in 1973, some of her income had been put aside for her dowry, and when Hua married at age 25, she could no longer contribute to the family budget. Mae's earnings became even more important than before (see Table 4 in the Conclusion).

Mother and Father took the daughters' income for granted, and the two sisters had little say about how their earnings were spent. Mae recommended that her younger brother attend her old primary school, and since her parents had little experience with educational institutions, they followed her advice. This did not signify their acceptance of a decision-making role for Mae. Nevertheless, Mae felt that her income contribution to the family did not go totally unrecognized, because she gained more freedom in her personal life. As long as she made the expected contribution to the family budget, Mae was freed for peer relationships of her own choosing, and thus she attained her goals in work: time to spend in activities with her friends. Mae legitimately withheld a part of her earnings for her own clothes and for outings with friends, such as Sunday tea and movies, which she could afford only when she was employed full-time.

Mae shared her mother's opinions about the importance of enlarging the family wage, and hence there were few conflicts over the money Mae spent on herself. She gave an example: "I had to go to a wedding banquet and had to pay night school fees at the same time. So I talked it over with my mother. I said, 'To be a *person,* which, after all, reflects upon the family, I must give money at the banquet. Furthermore, my schooling might be beneficial to me in getting jobs in the future.' Mother agreed that both expenses were reasonable, and so we agreed that I would give less money to the family for several weeks." Indeed, Mae could recall only one recent conflict with Mother over expenses. She wished to consult a Chinese herbal doctor about her cold, and her mother protested at the extra cost. But because Mae herself considered it a reasonable use of her earnings, she saw the herbalist anyway and paid for it herself.

Although Mae remitted most of her money to her family, she spent her leisure time as she wished. After she entered the labor force she performed little housework. Her mother did most of it, and even her younger brothers helped out. Mae was at liberty to spend her spare time visiting friends, attending courses, and going on outings. But Mother found it unthinkable that Mae might ever move away from home and rent a room by herself, if only because of the drop in family income this would entail. In agreement with her mother's viewpoint, Mae never seriously entertained such an option.

Although the sisters gained little authority in the family through their wage contribution, they gained considerable status as "good daughters" from that contribution and increased their sphere of freedom. Mae valued that enlarged personal sphere highly, especially when she contrasted her position to that of women of earlier generations, who had lower status and considerably fewer personal options.

Peers

Young people form a substantial and visible part of Hong Kong life. Adolescents comprise a large sector of the population, and organizations like schools, factories, and clubs that draw members from teenagers and young adults thereby promote interaction among youths. Consequently, Hong Kong youths have many experiences in common and are aware of their status in society. After leaving primary school, where Mae and Hua first participated in meaningful activities with others their age, the sisters entered large factories with other girls also recruited from school. Ever since, the two sisters have worked side by side with other women of their age, and they freely turned to peers for assistance with job-related problems (Chaney et al., 1973:45, Table 2.25).

Friends helped the sisters locate work; Mae herself was an important link in the job information network. One evening during the wage dispute with the manager of the plastics workshop, I arrived at Mae's home to find her on the phone. A friend and former coworker had just phoned the name of a newly opened workshop that was hiring women to seam plastic bags. Next, several of her current coworkers telephoned to receive that information. This situation was not unique to Mae, and her friends also kept in touch with their former workmates at picnic reunions or on the phone to exchange job intelligence. The express purpose of such reunions was social but expanding channels of information was also important.

When I spent a day in Mae's workshop, the informal assistance she afforded her workmates was obvious. Mae twice stopped her plastic bag seaming to help two women next to her push and lift the 50-pound roll of plastic to their benches. The cooperation of two or three workers was not only necessary to perform mechanical tasks but it was also the means of learning the job, and in fact Hua had taught Mae to seam the bags. "Otherwise I'd go too slowly while I was learning and wouldn't earn much," Mae explained. She did not appear to begrudge the time such cooperation cost her, all the more striking given the rapid pace at which she resumed her piecework seaming, perhaps because she anticipated a future need for the assistance of workmates herself. (Other studies that describe women's assistance to each other in learning new work skills include Langer, 1972; Richardson, 1972.)

Work is just one identity-forming activity, and becoming an adult in Hong Kong involves learning many more social roles. Mae and her sister, having taken on heavy obligations at an early age, lacked an opportunity to enjoy an "irresponsible adolescence" during which they could test out adult roles. This testing is especially important in a society like Hong Kong that is undergoing rapid social change, because youths cannot learn all their expected behavior from adults (Davis, 1940). Friends teach each other about clothes, dating, Western films, picnics, and work opportunities. And youths look to the work setting for friends.

Mae's oldest friends were former workmates. Her photo album contained three major sets of pictures, of which friends from work were and important part. One group of pictures showed three girls posing in different settings. The more recent of these were wedding photos. Mae explained that the three girls had been employed in the large plastic factory where Hua and Mae worked, and all five became fast friends. She asked me excitedly, "Do you recognize me? This is my sister, and that is a friend who married two years ago. She has a baby now. That other woman married just last year. Now we hardly meet. Actually, our 'group' has only three who are unmarried, and pretty soon my sister will marry, too. Then the only other maidens left will be me and the other girl in the picture." Mae pointed to a young woman in the snapshot who she called Kitty. Mae and Kitty went out together to film shows and teahouses and visited me at my apartment for lunch. When the other women married, Mae rarely saw them, and she and Kitty became inseparable.

Mae relied upon formal recreational groups for new experiences. The youth activities sponsored by missionary and other welfare associations enabled young workers like Mae to make the transition to a youth-oriented culture with many links to the West. The missionary societies set out to provide "something constructive" for young Hong Kong working people with spare time and money.[1] Their Western-originated peer activities filled the cultural vacuum.

Mae joined those activities with enthusiasm and was a responsible leader of her peer group just as she was a leader at home or in the workshop. Whenever an outing was planned, invariably it was Mae who compiled the list of participants and collected money from them. She arranged for each person to make or purchase food for the parties of my English class. When I return to Hong Kong for brief visits, it is Mae who I phone in order to contact the other former language class members, their sisters, and friends.

The Hong Kong way of life is also influenced by the mass media. A decade ago the media barely reached the working girls, but their presence has since become pervasive. Like other Hong Kong youths, Mae saw films almost once a week, watched television several hours a day, and read fashion and movie magazines frequently (Allen, 1970:31; Lee, 1969). What is the message of the media for Mae and her friends? When flown across the ocean do products and behavior that portray Western centrifugal society directly influence the centripetal Hong Kong way of life?

Studies of the media's impact upon North American viewers' behavior find, first of all, that people are likely to be influenced personally by ads if the product or advertised behavior counters no important social norm. A related consideration is that when persons who are important in the viewer's milieu (what sociologists call reference groups) use or advertise the product, the viewer will be more likely to adopt it (Klapper, 1960; Lazarsfeld, 1968). Advertisers, well aware of this phenomenon, deliberately associate consumer products in their commercials with images of powerful people and opinion leaders to suggest that viewers can become just as powerful if they simply buy the goods (Berger, 1972; McLuhan, 1966).

Accordingly, Mae and her family are likely eventually to adopt the consumer goods they view on television but are not likely to accept the human relationships portrayed in the media, because only the former accord with the fundamental norms of Hong Kong society. For most of the women in Mae's milieu, the purchase of goods is limited chiefly by the amount of money available. Thus the most visible impact of the media was in the areas of fashion and entertainment, to which there was little parental opposition. As long as they had some money, Mae and her friends purchased clothes or records that were advertised.

The marriage and family relationships viewed in films made and influenced by Hollywood contained elements of behavior congruent with family norms, such as dating patterns, the wedding dress, and honeymoons. Hong Kong youths were encouraged by the media to date, and those who did not know the modern customs and codes of dating could learn from the movies or press. For several years one local magazine, *Lover (Ai-lü)*, gained popularity by capitalizing on this phenomenon. Many of the articles and letters to the editor concerned the meaning and cultivation of "love," and local starlets depicted the new marriage style in the magazine's pages. *Lover* thus profitably assumed the role of sounding board and contemporary authority on dating and boy-girl dilemmas faced by young working women.

The cinema presented various complex dating situations and solved them in Western fashion. The dilemmas presented in such films surrounding the institution of romantic love captivated Mae and her friends. Their favorite films were *Love Story, The Graduate, The Young Ones* (a Taiwan film), and a Hong Kong film from the 1960s, *The Prince and the Maid*. The plots of these films featured a couple in love whose marriage was opposed by their parents. The films showed that love triumphed over parental objections based on status, but the successful romance ended in the death of the bride (except in *The Grad-*

uate.) Mae and her friends identified emotionally with the celluloid couples' love affairs and thought it tragic when the brides died.

However, the impact of the cinema upon Mae's behavior was limited by the fundamental differences between the styles of courtship and marriage portrayed on the screen and Hong Kong family norms. Hua was introduced by friends to a young man she liked well enough to marry, but their relationship was successfully opposed by her parents. In this situation Mae sided with the parents and not with "romantic love." Thus there was no opposition to these young women's adoption of clothes, grooming styles, and consumer goods that they saw on the screen. Such consumer goods countered few fundamental family norms. However, when it came to matrimony, the media-portrayed family dramas that advanced the children's right to act as independent individuals when choosing a mate fell on hostile ground.

The mass media are also especially effective when there are conflicting expectations among the groups that comprise the viewers' social environment. If people with contradictory social roles wish to reduce the discomfort or even pain caused by competing demands upon them, and if a product or behavior is presented by the media as the means to resolve such role dilemmas, then such media can become very persuasive (Klapper, 1960; Lazarsfeld, 1968).

Superficial media portrayals of family life and Western marriage that omit much of the reality and portray only the gloss may possibly encourage young Hong Kong women in their conflicts with the older generation. Asked about the discrepancy that remains, however, between their vicarious enjoyment of love matches in Western films and their reluctance to counter their parents' opinions, A-li, a friend of Mae, explained, "Oh, we think that the Western way is really the best! We really want to learn how they do it, even if we ourselves can't always follow that way just yet." The women adopt Western marriage values as portrayed by the media only if their families support them. Perhaps when the conflict of social opinion regarding their expected behavior intensifies even further, Mae, A-li, and other friends will adopt the centrifugal marriage pattern of the media programs.

Dating and marriage

Mae did not have a boyfriend and rarely met eligible bachelors at work. This did not distress her, however. She once dated a man she met through friends in the factory. She recalled, "The fellow did not phone me after that one time, so I guess he didn't want to keep up the relationship. Anyway, I'm too young to marry!"

When the time did come to marry Mae did not want Mother to arrange the match. Mae told of the way Mother interceded in Elder Sister's marriage plans: "The person Hua is marrying is her second boyfriend. She met the first one on her own through a factory friend. Mother didn't like him and called him a 'teddy boy.'"

"Was he really a 'teddy boy' in your opinion?" I asked Mae.

"Well, he looked a bit like one, but the main problem was that he was not Ch'iu-chao. And so Mother arranged a marriage with Lam Bing, a Ch'iu-chao like us. Mother and Hua visited someone's home to meet Lam Bing. He answered a few questions, but both he and my sister were too shy to say much."

Lam Bing turned out to be a low income earner. "With the baby coming they have lots of money troubles. As for me, I prefer to accept complete responsibility for my choice, otherwise later I might blame mother!"

Mae intended to marry a person with whom she was "compatible." Having participated in peer activities for several years, she valued the kind of marriage in which her husband would hold similar ideas and would be as much a companion to her as her friends had been. Since Mae and her parents saw things in much the same way, however, she did not exclude the possibility that a man introduced to her would become compatible. Compatibility could develop given enough time.

Mae's accommodation to members of the older generation did not extend to living with them after marriage. Mae and Hua both recalled Mother's long dispute with Paternal Grandmother, which was only resolved when the old lady was provided with her own quarters. Mae explained it this way, "Despite the fact that Mother is very easygoing in nature, Grandmother was too conservative. There was no real ill will between them, but they always argued over their different ideas." That instance of generational conflict was impressed deeply upon the two sisters and they swore not to live with their own future mothers-in-law.

When Hua married in late 1973, she and Lam Bing first rented a small room near her mother-in-law's residence. Lam Bing stressed the limits of his obligation to his mother: "We need not live together. So long as we give my mother the first choice of living near her, as opposed to living near my wife's mother, that's enough. Neither side wishes to do more than that. We don't really get along, and Mother herself wishes to preserve her independence."

When the Lam's first child was born, Bing's face-saving attitude could no longer be maintained. A relative was sorely needed to care for their baby so that both parents could work. Mrs. Goh was willing to take over care of the child and so the couple moved into the Gohs' Lok Fu resettlement estate apartment with Mother. At that point there were too many people in the Lok Fu flat, and Mae obligingly went to live with her aunt and uncle in their resettlement estate apartment. Finding that their small flat was still overcrowded, Mae's parents rented a two-room apartment in a nearby tenement in a district known as Kowloon Walled City, where rents were cheap.

Domestic arrangements for the Goh family

March, 1973
A. Mother, Father, and six children live in two rooms in Lok Fu resettlement estate, Kowloon. Hua, the eldest daughter (age 25), is engaged to Lam Bing.
B. Father's brother and his wife and children live in another resettlement estate. Their child occasionally comes to spend the night with the Goh family, and the Goh children often stay with them.

September, 1973
A. Mother, Father, and five children live in the same resettlement estate.
B. No change.
C. Hua has married, and she and Lam Bing rent a room in an apartment on Hong Kong Island. Hua is pregnant.
D. Lam Bing's mother lives near the Lams with her brother's family. Mother Lam eats with her brother's family and assists them with child care.

September. 1975
A. Residence unchanged, but now Hua's baby stays with Mother Goh. Mae has moved out.
B. Mae moves to the resettlement estate room of her aunt and uncle.
C. Hua and Lam Bing live during the week in their rented room. On weekends the couple returns to the Gohs' Kowloon resettlement estate rooms to be with their child.
D. No change.

September, 1976

A. The Goh family (Father, Mother, Mae, and four brothers) moves into a private two-room tenement flat in Kowloon Walled City. Mother continues to care for Hua's child.

B. Mae moves out of her uncle's place, back to her family.

C. Hua, Lam Bing, and paternal grandmother Goh live in the Lok Fu resettlement estate rooms vacated by the Goh family.

D. No change.

After Hua married and had a child, Mae's earnings were more important than ever, and Mother was apprehensive about her possible marriage. Mae had anticipated gaining such centrality in the family wage-earning unit, and so at the time of her sister's engagement she emphasized to me her plans to remain single until Second Brother completed his schooling and went to work: "Mother said I can marry whomever I wish, but even after I find someone I must postpone the marriage for several years. With Elder Sister married, we can't afford to lose another income just now!"

Realizing that her marriage was an event that concerned the family as a whole, Mae did not worry about being without a boyfriend. At the age of 22, she was not yet considered an "old maid." Because her parents and peers understood that Mae was meeting family obligations, and because those obligations were equally incumbent upon Mae's friends, little pressure was exerted to find a spouse. Mae's relative unconcern over being single was also related to the eventual possibility of arranging a marriage should she approach age 30 with no prospect in sight. At our last meeting, however, she was not yet considering this eventuality. She gained status from meeting her family obligations and she enjoyed opportunities to interact with friends. Neither would be possible if she were to marry.

Summary

As second daughter in a family of six children who were growing up while the family was in straitened circumstances, Mae was trained to put her family's definition of its economic needs before her own desires. The theme of Mae's life was that she not only accommodated the needs of her family but realized her own desire to enjoy peer-group experiences. Both were possible through Mae's factory employment. Her duties to her family did not prevent Mae from enjoying peer activities, and her loyal fulfillment of her family's expectations gave her more independence to pursue friendships.

Suyin: bachelor working girl

Suyin Yuen operated sewing machines in small garment assembly workshops and carried the heaviest economic burden in her family. Two-thirds of Father's $150 monthly wage as a cashier-clerk in a Chinese herbal apothecary was given to Mother, an unskilled illiterate factory worker who was his secondary wife, and a small amount went to the family of his primary wife. Father resided, as was traditional for the staff of small Chinese retail outlets, in a bedroom at the rear of the store. Over 60 years old in 1971 when I met Suyin, Father had received some schooling in Kwangtung province, where he was taught the "Four Classics" (Confucius, Mencius, and other ancient texts) and commercial arithmetic, including accounting and the use of the abacus. The Chinese pharmacopoeia is deeply rooted in ancient philosophy and lore, and as an apothecary clerk who shared bed and board with similarly traditional workmates, Father held firmly to custom. He extrolled the virtues of sons and demeaned his daughters.

Suyin's training and character were molded by the stringent economic demands upon her. All of my respondents suffered the denigration of women embodied in the structure of the Chinese centripetal family. Suyin's identity was shaped more than any of the daughters in this study by her active confrontation with a deprecatory father.

Suyin's family

Suyin entered my cosmopolitan English class in June, 1971, a proud and assertive 18-year-old. Despite the differences in our ages, she guided me when we traveled through bustling Hong Kong. Suyin met conventional beauty standards for an attractive face and shapely build, and she moved confidently. Suyin frequently patronized a hairdresser, fashion boutiques on Nathan Road and in Mong Kok, Jean's East outlets in Tsim Sha Tsui, and when looking for bargains, the pushcart vendors of factory seconds on Argyle Street. Even though the appearance of most other workers suffered after a day's toil at the sewing table, Suyin would be ready to join me by 6 p.m. at the clothes-conscious Cellar Bar in the downtown President Hotel.

The Yuens emigrated to Hong Kong from Swatow around 1973. My-rae Yuen and her two baby girls, Suyin and Yeuk-yin, took up residence in a squatter's shack, from which they were resettled to their present dwelling in the late 1950s. Father, who like other emigrants lacked personal possessions, worked as a clerk while his first wife resided in a small Mong Kok tenement apartment with First Son, who paid the rent.

Suyin resided with her mother and five young siblings in one and a half 10′ by 12′ second-floor rooms in the Wang Tau Hom resettlement estate on Broadcast Drive in Kowloon City. Second Sister, Yeuk-yin, 18 months Suyin's junior, and quite unfinished compared with Eldest Sister, was also a seamstress, and during my visit was employed at the sewing machine alongside Suyin. Although not a shy person, Yeuk-yin had difficulty maintaining a conversation. She hesitated in my presence to articulate her thoughts and depended upon Suyin for confirmation of her ideas. Third Sister, Lai-yin, a form III student, was an agreeable, pleasant young adolescent, who obediently kept house and cared for the three youngest boys. These cheerful lads, ages 12, 9½, and 7, attended neighborhood primary schools.

Father's primary wife, a half-blind woman in her 60s who was already growing senile, lived with her 40-year-old son by Father and his wife (who operated a garment workshop and was the employer of Suyin and Yeuk-yin for 4 years, 1971–1974). Female offspring of concubines may feel bitter when their father's primary wife adopts the traditional view that they were better born male. Suyin expressed what seemed to be a long-standing resentment at the nonacceptance of her gender in the primary branch of the family with the uncompassionate taunt, "That woman is quite pitiful, isn't she?" There was also a great distance between Suyin and Elder Brother, as expressed in her quip, "He's almost forty; that's old enough to be my father!" I never heard Suyin speak further about Elder Brother, and she apparently saw little of him. However, at the time of our meetings in 1973, Suyin's workbench adjoined that of his wife.

My-rae was a lively, warm woman, whose smile invariably beemed in welcome and who was never too exhausted after a long day's work to shop for bargains at neighborhood street stalls and then rush home to entertain visitors. My-rae met Father in her home town in Kwangsi province, some 600 miles distant, and he perceived the benefits of a match with a local woman who could manage his Kwangsi interests. Suyin explained how Mother happened to accept an older married man: "Mother's home town was way off in Kwangsi province. Father came from Swatow. In those olden days what did people know? Women were glad to marry anyone who made a living at his business. Father did not reveal to Mother that he had already a wife in Swatow, until after their marriage. The damage had already been done and it would have been useless for her to struggle. So she resigned herself to being his 'small wife.'"

Suyin's acerbity is explained perhaps by Father's resentment that My-rae's firstborn was a female. Suyin did not attribute Mother's concubinage to the inferior social class standing of the maternal grand-parents, and indeed Suyin exonerated Mother's family for calculating-ly bargaining away their daughter. In Suyin's version, Father had taken unfair advantage of Mother. "Father wanted sons and he was bitterly disappointed when we three girls came first. He cheered up when three boys came along at the end." Suyin accented this statement with a defiant toss of her head, as if to say, "I don't care. Girls are good!"

Lacking much-needed paternal affection, Suyin sought especially to win the esteem and love of her male peers. The intensity of her quest seemed to be directly related to Father's rejection of his three daughters. From 1971 to 1976, the entire period of my interviewing for this book, Suyin continued to prevent me from meeting Father, despite the fact that she introduced me freely and with pride and pleasure to many other relatives. When I therefore directly requested a meeting with Father, Suyin evaded my request. "Him? I'm afraid that will be very difficult. He only comes for a short while."

In order to accommodate the seven family members in their small, four-bunk bedroom, Mother normally slept with her youngest son. However, on Father's regular bimonthly conjugal visits to the Yuen apartment, Suyin and Second Sister vacated their bunk and moved their bedrolls to the living-room bench. The three lads took over their bunk, enabling Father and Mother to share the upper one.

Some Chinese men who have taken a second wife are able to live with her family. Suyin complained, however, "Father is absent so much and when he does come he brings only forty dollars with him, I tell Mother that since he does so little on our behalf, she should close the door on him, but she won't listen."

Mother in fact did not share Suyin's bleak view of Father's actions and attitudes. Even Suyin was forced to admit that her parents felt affection for each other. My-rae accompanied Father on a group holiday in Malaysia and Singapore in the spring of 1973 and they were planning a similar low-budget excursion to Japan for 1974. These two tours were organized for economy-minded vacationers by a Hong Kong travel bureau that books a block of seats on Cathay Pacific (CP) Air and reserves hotel accommodations in a CP hotel for the tourist trade. Day excursions are conducted in Singapore to Tiger Balm Garden and the Botanic Garden and to an offshore recreational park. *Dim sum* ("little hearts," small pastry snacks) lunches and evening banquets are provided. Most popular with the Hong Kong set perhaps are the protracted mahjong sessions that they organize in their hotel rooms each evening. Although I saw no evidence that My-rae played the game, the mothers of other working girls (Syut-wa and Shu-pui) were certainly addicted to mahjong and they reportedly rarely left their hotel rooms during the tours they took. Upon returning from Singapore, My-rae gaily showed me her souvenir photo album featuring snapshots of her excursion.

Although they made Mother happy, Suyin criticized the expense of these holidays. "My parents should save their money for the education of all three boys instead." Concerned to lead the family, Suyin hoped for the entry of each son to secondary school and sought to budget somehow for the stiff fees that this would entail.

Since the combined wages of Suyin and Yeuk-yin tripled that of Mother, and overshadowed Father's contribution even more, the daughters accounted for over two-thirds of the family income. Suyin did not totally dedicate her earning power to Mother and her siblings, and occasionally, without consulting Mother, she appropriated as much as one-quarter of her monthly paycheck to finance her own pleasure. Her economic behavior thus differed from that of Mae and Wai-gun, who for 5 years or more rebated more than 80% of their paycheck to their similarly impoverished large families. Suyin was bent on spending her money for apparel and cosmetics. She attempted to adorn herself in current fashion to gain the approbation and love of her male companions and admiring glances from other women. Most important, Suyin seemed to feel that she could overcome the accumulated sadness of her weak relationship with Father and win his approval by embellishing herself in fashionable attire.

Before Suyin and I embarked upon a shopping trip to Tsim Sha Tsui boutiques, she first opened the door of her bedroom wardrobe and reached into the deep pocket of her winter coat to remove a small wad of $50 and $100 (H.K.) ($10 and $20, U.S.). This was a stouter cache than the bankrolls sequestered by other working-class daughters of my acquaintance. It would have taken Suyin several months to accumulate such a sum, which may have been her Lunar New Year bonus. This and similar spells of boutique hopping still did not detract from Suyin's remitting the usual two-thirds or more of her salary to the family budget.

Suyin was proud that her wages sponsored Third Sister Lai-yin's successful entry into secondary school. In addition, Suyin underwrote financially the marketing of the family's groceries and further showed her rank by dispatching her younger brothers on expeditions to the tuck shops in the basement of the resettlement estate, where they regularly purchased roasted peanuts and soda pop for family snacking. Thus, in the family, Suyin sought to assume the mantle of the missing father.

The Yuen family acknowledged Suyin's aspirations by designating her to represent them at wedding banquets and various family functions. "I attend these affairs because I'm the one who knows what's going on in the family!" Suyin asserted proudly. Suyin was the link between her nuclear family and their five or six close relatives in Hong Kong. Sister-in-law frequently invited Suyin to visit for tea and family conversation after work.

Essential to the role of a Hong Kong matron is the maintenance of visiting relationships with relatives, and I asked My-rae if she had much opportunity to visit her kin. "How can I?" Mother complained, "My job takes too much time."

"What about Sunday?" I ventured.

"Who will do the laundry, clean the house and cook the evening meal if I go out on Sundays?" My-rae countered.

On Sunday, Third Sister was excused from domestic duties and Mother was obliged to perform them because Suyin and Yeuk-yin were the major wage earners and could not be required to help in the home cooking and cleaning. Suyin vowed that she would never permit her life to be so limited to the home.

When I asked her how she shared decision making with My-rae, Suyin responded, "Mother does not rule me. I have too much power for that."

I suggested that her power stemmed from her large income contribution to the family. She didn't think so. Like all the other working daughters I studied, Suyin's financial contribution was a familial obligation she was required to fulfill by deep-seated norms and mores. Suyin believed that, beyond all material factors, the force of her personality shaped her guiding role in the family. Although the absence of a strong paternal hand in the Yuen household caused material and emotional hardships, it may have given Suyin more decision-making opportunities and freed her from male restrictions.

Suyin boasted that she exercised much more domestic authority than most other first- or secondborn working daughters. Suyin deplored the fact that all older Chinese men commonly make the important family decisions while their wives carry out the men's wishes. She gestured in defiance to all oppressive males: "It's always like that with the older generation. It was even worse in our grandparents' day. Back then the women had to abide by all the Confucian rules."

"What would you do if you were in the position of those wives?" I asked her.

"I'd fight! I'd never let them boss me around like that!"

"How can you tell if the man you are dating is the kind of person who would after marriage treat women as equals?"

"I'll find one. If they are kind I can feel it, but if a man is too bossy, I can tell it right away."

Suyin was, in fact, consulted by My-rae (acting for herself and at times for Father) on all decisions involving the siblings. For example Mother became pregnant in 1974 and Suyin remarked, "Women in our neighborhood always talk about cheap and safe abortions in Canton. Yeuk-yin and I advised Mother to go there and have one right away. She called Father and told him our view, and can you imagine? He actually tried to stop her. I'll bet he still wanted more sons, as if three isn't enough already. Mother listened to us and not to Father and drew upon her savings to pay for the two-day trip across the border and back. So Father had to accept our decision."

Suyin reacted to the weak father bond with a fighting spirit, which determined her position in the household and colored the rest of her personal life. In her everyday actions Suyin appeared always to be struggling against her birth as an offspring of a subordinate, and hence inferior-status, wife. As a female child, Suyin could not attract the love and affection of a man like Father, and her resentment at this loss of what must be seen as a human birthright was a major theme of her emotional life.

Evenings with the Yuens

The apartment shared by the seven Yuen family members was among the cleanest of the more than thirty working-class homes I visited in Hong Kong. The cement walls were freshly whitewashed and the beige linoleumed floors were scrubbed daily by the older sons. The major room, 10' by 12', contained a long, straightbacked iron-wood seat (which doubled as a spare bed) and a glass-paneled cupboard filled with dishes, pots, and an array of medicine bottles, each labled with a formula from the Chinese materia medica. The portable television set and the table on which it stood supported pictures of Suyin and no other family member. A sliding, gaily patterned cloth curtain separated the outer room from the interior bedroom chamber, which barely accommodated a pair of double bunk beds, curtained for privacy, and Suyin's wardrobe. Suyin's presence dominated both rooms: framed photographs on the television table, on the cupboard, her Kewpie doll (a gift from a boyfriend), the wardrobe crammed with her clothing. The other children and Mother used a single barrel for their clothes chest. Suyin treated the home as a place for her personal display, a form of extroversion unequaled by any other working daughters of my study.

The Yuens were sociable, and neighbors often dropped in on them. Except on Sunday, the cooking chores were ably borne by Third Sister. When I visited Hong Kong families at their homes, I usually brought with me my daughter Shana, who celebrated her first birthday in Hong Kong in 1973. One weekday evening I arrived with Shana at 6 p.m. for dinner to find Third Sister chatting on the balcony and Mother preparing the dinner. A fire had broken out in My-rae's factory, and the management sent the employees home and shut down the plant. At the market on her way home, My-rae had made a special purchase of the best fish available. I overheard her say to her neighbor, "This fish costs a dollar and twenty cents, but it's still cheaper than eating chicken." My-rae was unskilled in its preparation, however, and sought the assistance of her neighbor. Lai-yin returned to the wok, tasted each dish as it simmered, and from her domestic wisdom advised My-rae to add more soy sauce to the fish and lengthen the cooking time of the bean curd.

That night as usual the two breadwinning daughters Suyin and Yeuk-yin performed little housework. Suyin instead assumed the hostess role and oversaw proper food service. For the occasion she removed from a holder mounted under the dining-room window the family's prized set of plastic chopsticks engraved with a dragon and phoenix. Suyin issued a steady stream of commands to the three boys, who were engrossed in a favorite melodramatic television serial on youth and family life in Hong Kong resettlement estates. At one point, when the youngest lad spoke what sounded like a criticism of Suyin's conduct that evening, she rebuked him at once with the command, "Shut up and do as I tell you!"

The entire family enjoyed viewing television throughout the meal. Suyin shuddered in embarrassment each time an embrace or other form of physical closeness was enacted by the courting couples. Mother used the drama as an opportunity to discuss morals for Suyin's dating behavior and the peer-group activities of her children. My-rae commented sarcastically about the character who played around with men, "Just like Suyin." She added, "This is a good year for weddings!" with side glances at her eldest daughter.

Nervously polite, My-rae consumed little food during dinner, but when the others had completed their meal, she gathered together the serving dishes, scraped the contents of each into her bowl, and ate them with the airy moral that "food must not be wasted." After she swallowed the last portion of fish remnants from the platter, My-rae walked to the cupboard and removed a bottle of Five Snakes Wine from its niche among the Chinese native medicinal preparations and poured out a small glass. "People say that this wine is good for me and so I drink a glass every day," she commented to me as she sipped the beverage.

Lai-yin and My-rae cleared the dishes and then First Son pushed aside the table, swept half of the floor, and passed the broom to Second Son, who swept the other half. "It's a division of labor," First Son reported, "I do one-half and he does the rest." The boy then marched out to the hall tap and returned with a bucket of water and washed the linoleum floor. Third Son chimed in gleefully, "I'm not big enough and I haven't learned how to wash the floor yet," whereupon he resumed his television viewing. The boys pulled back the dining table and placed their school books upon it in preparation for their nightly tutoring in English grammar and mathematics. Lai-yin was the only sister who had studied English and the burden of coaching the boys for their examinations fell to her, along with the domestic household maintenance.

A middle-age neighboring housewife from the busy floor entered the sitting room to join the company, followed by another housewife, who carried with her a dish of cooked diced yams. She offered this after-dinner repast to all of us, but only the first neighbor partook. When her evening chores at the wash basin were completed and she had exchanged pleasantries with the two newcomers, My-rae sought the company of her favorite god daughter, the 15-month-old infant next door. My-rae saw the little girl in the evenings and on the weekend, taking with her gifts of toys and food. After her godparenting mission was completed, My-rae returned with arms outstretched in quest of Shana, whom she lifted heartily and carried four doors down the hall to join a clatch of housewives in conversation. She proudly displayed her Caucasian guest to them and won admiring comments. Meanwhile Suyin and I were chatting with a couple of young adult neighbors who had strolled into the Yuens' apartment – Chun-yon, who clerked in his father's small light bulb factory, and an airline receptionist.

The same timetable and division of labor were observed on my subsequent visits with the Yuens. Suyin and Yeuk-yin were not as a rule assigned domestic duties. Most days after she returned from school, Third Sister did the marketing, cooked the dinner, and washed dishes before tutoring the younger boys. Mother and Father timed their Singapore journey to coincide with Third Sister's Easter vacation from secondary school, and while Suyin partied after work and on weekends, Lai-yin assumed full charge of the household. During this vacation, Third Sister cooked on her two-burner gas stove, not only for the six Yuen children, but even for Suyin's spring evening dinner parties of four or more guests.

Suyin's work

Suyin's primary school was located in the basement of a resettlement estate block near her home. At age 12 she left this school to work in a small neighborhood factory producing light bulbs. A $25 wage appeared at that time adequate for a month of 30 working days. Suyin got her job by tagging along behind 13-year-old Chun-yon on his way to the factory one morning. She claimed proudly, "I found that job myself, without help from the grownups!" After 1 year in the light bulb workshop, Suyin shifted to a better position as a sewing machine operator in a garment factory, where she was taught rudimentary machine operations. She became a semi-skilled seamstress and has spent her working life at this occupation.

Suyin's pay increased over the decade, even relative to rising prices, until in late 1974 she took home $130 per month before overtime. There is no ladder of regular promotion to positions above lead seamstress in the Hong Kong garment industry, and Suyin, whose ambition did not even extend to this head assemblist position, expressed no desire to advance her job category. Suyin's largest wage was earned in 1971, the year she assembled wigs for the fashion industry.

When the unstable wig industry slumped in 1972-3, Suyin and Second Sister took employment in the workshop operated by their stepsister-in-law, the wife of Father's first son. Sister-in-law had installed her workshop in the sizable living room of their comparatively spacious four-room flat in a Mong Kok tenement, where she had long been a resident. It was there the two sisters stitched brassieres on sewing machines for domestic retailing by small independent proprietors. The living-room workshop was staffed by at most three sewing machine operators, while Sister-in-law hand-sheared the cotton fabrics to the stitching patterns. The flat-rate salary of each sister somewhat exceeded the monthly average of pieceworkers in the colony's garment trade. The pace of toil was less hurried, and working hours were more flexible than in a larger garment factory. When orders were short, or when Sister-in-law failed to keep ahead of the stitchers, the girls were paid for a full day but were dismissed early. The job was also more varied than assembly-line operation, and Suyin had the opportunity to master more complex sewing tasks. Moreover, Suyin was sent from time to time to visit potential new retail outlets in quest of increased distribution and sales.

I benefited from the family spirit in the workshop when Suyin on several midafternoons invited me to visit there with Shana for a cup of tea, a snack, and relaxed conversation. Sister-in-law's 9-month-old daughter was positioned in the center of the workshop in a walking chair, which was fastened to the leg of the cutting table with a 2-foot strip of cloth to prevent her from straying. The infant was then taken out of her chair so that she and Shana could play freely together on the cutting room floor with bits of cloth given to them. Work temporarily ceased while we seated ourselves at a low end table between the workbench and the living-room couch to sip warm puree of red bean soup. We conversed about life in the Yuen family and Suyin's social calendar, after which Suyin and Yeuk-yin were permitted to quit work early and take me to their home for dinner.

Although Sister-in-law's workshop afforded relatively steady and high wages to the semi-skilled seamstresses and more opportunities to learn trade skills than did most larger garment factories in the colony, I nevertheless noted certain disadvantages to Suyin's family work environment. Although a paid holiday is observed in Hong Kong on the occasion of the Ch'ing Ming festival (homage paying to the graves of ancestors), Sister-in-law denied this grace to the girls because, according to Suyin, "she knows that none of Father's ancestors is buried here." After 6 years of operation in her living room, strenuous competition from other small manufacturers sapped Sister-in-law's will and forced her to cease operations. Before she was totally worn out, Sister-in-law wanted to teach the entire repertoire of garment assembly skills to Suyin and Yeuk-yin in the hope that they might carry on her trademark. But the girls lacked the drive and ambition to take over the business. In response to my queries at the time of collapse, Suyin replied: "It would take Sister-in-law a whole week to teach me to run all the machines, and I would have to learn at least forty styles and patterns from her. It's too difficult. I don't know how to cut or to carry accounts. It'll be really troublesome if I lose money. Anyway, I'm getting tired of sitting at my sewing machine for eight hours a day."

Yeuk-yin nodded her agreement. "It's too much trouble to learn the business, so we might as well work somewhere else."

Indeed, within 2 weeks the sisters were employed, albeit at a somewhat lower wage, seaming brassieres in a medium-size plant. By choosing this course of least commitment, the sisters lost employment stability, and within 6 months they found themselves stitching brassieres in a smaller workshop.

Hong Kong factory women like Suyin and Yeuk-yin rated the workplaces principally by the wages they offered, and although a congenial factory peer group was welcome, it seldom determined completely place of employment among the Hong Kong women proletariat. If one workshop exhausted its order book, or if other establishments offered better pay, the girls might simply shift employers. When Suyin invited me to visit her at the small shop where she took a position after the demise of Sister-in-law's enterprise, I noted the friendly rapport she had established with the girls busy at her seaming table. Nevertheless, business there slumped and a few weeks later she received me at still another small factory.

Suyin seamed deftly and was unconcerned about such defects as raveled edges or mismatched components. When I visited Suyin at one of her workshops, I heard her remark offhandedly to the owner: "Didn't you just tell me that the strap of this bra should be eleven inches long? Well, it says here on the instructions you gave me last week that the length must be twelve inches. Eleven inches or twelve inches, the strap can be adjusted anyway so it's all the same, isn't it!" Then without waiting for the reply of the owner, she resumed her rapid seaming. Perhaps because the workshop could not afford to tear out many yards of stitching, the owner did not pursue Suyin on this occasion. The other factory workers in my sample displayed more care for the quality of their work and wished they could exercise more control over their finished output. Occasionally, when their work was not up to standard (as in the case of Mae's defective seaming machine and the contention-ridden section of Wai-gun's brassiere factory), these women expressed considerable frustration and consternation.

The limited horizons in the garment industry allowed few attainable work aspirations. During a conversation about employment prospects with several of my English instruction pupils, I asked each in turn, "What is your ideal job?"

Suyin replied vacantly, "Never thought about it."

"All right, do you have friends with an ideal job?"

Suyin's unadorned response was, "All their jobs are about the same as mine."

Each of Suyin's hopes for betterment seemed based on a chimera. Suyin was unwilling to invest much effort to attain her goals for a financial breakthrough, and her limited aspirations were manifest after her wages peaked in the wig industry. Thus Suyin's refusal to shoulder Sister-in-law's workshop testified to the weakness of her competitive business drive. Stimulated by advertisements and promotional gimmicks on handbills from brand-name firms that rarely proved profitable, Suyin was attracted to speculative, flashy ventures that promised quick returns. Several cosmetics companies offered their neighborhood marketing franchise to young people with independent business aspirations. In May, 1975, Suyin paid $25 for a course in facial cosmetics application, and in a joint venture with Chun-yon, her neighbor in the resettlement estate, she purchased the basic makeup kit for $50. They obtained the right to sell the company's cosmetics for a share of the profit, but Suyin approached only her friends, and since she gave away more than she sold, the venture was short lived.

Suyin next considered joining a publishing venture with Man-hon, a young man who proposed to found a cultural magazine dedicated to the revival of the vernacular Chinese arts in Hong Kong. In the absence of encouragement for indigenous theater, crafts, or fine arts, such a magizine could never win a large audience. Suyin was intrigued by the entrepreneurial possibilities of an avant-garde business venture but had not seriously considered the prospects for such a magazine, nor did my questioning elicit from Suyin any definition of Chinese folk culture itself.

"What share of the work will you carry out in the magazine?" I queried.

"I don't know. Maybe typing, recepitionist, telephone operator, or even reporter. I'd love to interview some famous pop artists and film stars."

Despite her annoyance at this line of questioning, I persisted: "Have you ever written anything before?"

"No, but my partner said he'd teach me, and I'll learn as we go along."

Not unexpectedly, this well-intentioned project proved highly unfeasible.

With her limited education and lack of family contacts, repetitive factory assembly labor was the only work Suyin could reasonably expect to get. Such work never leads to adequate financial or personal recompense. Suyin sought an active and exciting dating life, which she interspersed with flights of fancy to transcend both her limited past and the tedium of her rank-and-file present. In her quest for a strong male consort to help her achieve a lucky break, she appeared to be looking for a kindly and worldly-wise surrogate father, who would care enough to discover her latent talents and skills and direct her future life course.

Peers and dating

Beset by pressures of family and workplace, Suyin lived vicariously through cinema, television, and movie-magazine portrayals of Hollywood heroes and heroines who drifted magically into glamorous liaisons with those of the opposite sex. One afternoon my two Sinology graduate student roommates and a pair of their colleagues, all of whom were film afficionados, returned from a cinema matinee performance of *Last Tango in Paris* with Marlon Brando. Suyin was visiting me at the time and the discussion in our apartment turned to film personalities. I asked her, "What kind of movies have you seen lately?"

"All kinds, American, British, and some Mandarin also. But I go mainly to see the stars and not the type of movie."

"Who are your favorite performers, then?"

"I like pretty starlets, who dress well and charm the men. Jane Fonda and Sophia Loren really send me. Last year I enjoyed Jane Fonda's *They Shoot Horses, Don't They?* And now I've just seen her in *Klute.* She's really good, isn't she? I cut my hair just the way she did in the film."

"What about actors?"

"My favorites are tough, manly heroes. I like Omar Sharif's beautiful eyes. Such a handsome man!"

Suyin delved into the details of Omar Sharif's early films (*Lawrence of Arabia, Dr. Zhivago, Funny Girl*) and his sideline as an Arabic and international contract bridge master.

For Suyin, cinema attendance was both a comfortable dating venue and an occasion to identify with starlets whose attractiveness was attested to by their many beaux. She acquired pointers on fashion, cosmetics, poise, and other commonly accepted perquisites of media charm. In preference to such then-current controversial and difficult films as *Last Tango in Paris* and *Scenes from a Marriage,* Suyin (like Mae and A-li) chose more complacent offerings, such as *The Graduate* and *Love Story.* After we heard Suyin's commentary, my roommates began a critique of *Last Tango in Paris.* Suyin was prompted by their favorable analysis to retort, "I don't know what you mean by an art film, but sex movies make me uncomfortable. It's so embarrassing, especially if I were to attend such a movie with a fellow."

Suyin's criteria for male companionship were personal sophistication, the wherewithal to entertain her in comfort, and the ability to converse smoothly. Although she claimed to be seeking a charming knight errant, until 1976 Suyin had not narrowed her choice and strove to exploit the potentials of several attractive male admirers.

Suyin, who possessed little formal education and could not converse on abstract topics, was ill at ease in the company of college men. Although intrigued by the prospect, she had not dated university students so far. Her mistrust of intellectuals notwithstanding, her quest for worthwhile male companionship led Suyin to inquire of me testily: "Wouldn't you think a student is risky and may change his mind about a girl by the time he gets ready to graduate? A student is supported by his family to enter the professions, but there are so few good jobs in Hong Kong, how can I know whether a college boy actually will become a success? I hear that boys at New Asia College are snobbish, but the Chung Chi men are nicer and more straightforward. Do you think that's true? You see, one of my friends dated a boy from New Asia College, but she was hurt when he dropped her without explanation, and I'm wondering if they will all be like that."

Our conversation must have given Suyin encouragement, because she asked Kit, my research assistant and herself a Chinese University student, for introductions to third-year students there. Kit, however, chose to do no more than note Suyin's request in her interview logbook.

Referring to the mate she was determined somehow to win, Suyin observed: "Men who have already started their working lives and who treat me well before marriage will continue to care for me afterwards. I know what an honest man should be like, and that type of person will remain kind and considerate even afterwards."

Suyin's views on marriage and dating in a society where premarital relationships are by convention restricted to one-person relationships are portrayed in a series of interpersonal encounters with other young adults. The first episode began one evening in July, when Suyin and I arrived at a rendezvous she had arranged for us with two young factory technicians near the box office of a large Mong Kok cinema. As we approached the theater, we noticed the young men, shifting their feet nervously. After offhand words of greeting, during which she cast her glance up and down the street, Suyin spotted the arrival of two 19-year-olds, dressed like most Hong Kong working girls of the time in stacked heels and miniskirts. With a broad smile, Suyin introduced them to the two young men. She had recruited them moments earlier as substitutes because she had impulsively decided to execute more ambitious plans for the evening. Taking our leave of this unwitting, blindly paired foursome, Suyin and I proceeded to our second rendezvous in a nearby soda bar, where four other Chinese awaited us: two well-dressed businessmen, a young women companion of one of them, and a civil servant, whose English was the best and who was to be my escort. From this bistro we walked along Nathan Road to a Mandarin nightclub featuring a Marache band, a strobe light show, and a Chinese balladeer for an evening of drinking and dancing. Suyin had tardily, but accurately, realized that night life in this urbane company was bound to be more exciting than a cinema date with two sincere, but unelegant, factory workers.

A second incident further reveals Suyin's talent for hastily enmeshing herself and others in situations that she soon came to regret. One sunday, Suyin, Yeuk-yin, and two young men on an impulse boarded the afternoon Macau ferry, carrying with them only small change and vague ideas of the possibilities for spending a constructive half-day in the nearby Sino-Lusitanian enclave. Macau's best-known tourist pastimes are gambling in the more than ten thriving casinos and at a canine racetrack, sightseeing at the marina, and attending a noted annual auto rally. Possessing neither the means nor the sophistication to test the casinos or the greyhounds, Suyin's entourage was content to stroll the narrow cobbled streets and enjoy a trishaw ride along the tree-lined thoroughfare until dark. By midnight their effervescence was spent. "We couldn't find a comfortable place to go inside and rest. Everytime we went into a casino lobby just to sit down, one of the bouncers threw us out. So we had to walk around all night long."

When at Sunday noon Suyin had belatedly informed My-rae about this venture, Mother's reaction was predictably negative. "But Yeuk-yin and I were paying our share so Mother was unable to prevent the journey. Who could have known that Sister and I would catch cold from the long chilly night outdoors, so in the end Mother was really mad because she had to pay five dollars for a doctor!" She continued, "The boys who came to Macau are average types. My date is only a year older than I, and still naïve about many things. He's always talking about love, and reveals all his plans to me. He claims that he is ready to wait four years until marriage, but I'm not taken in."

Suyin at this time was more partial to Poon, a young technician in an air conditioning firm who treated her generously and was big-hearted. "Mother warned me that he would be jealous if I told him about Macau. But I want to be honest, and so I tell one fellow that there are others. Poon didn't act jealous to me. He phoned me on Monday morning at work and when told that I was at home in bed with a cold, he came over in the evening to pay me a sympathy visit. Look, he brought me this tooled leather belt, too. That at least was a fine ending to my Macau weekend. Poon's earnings are good: over two hundred dollars a month and he's going to get raises. I prefer technicians to clerks because technicians can earn more if they're clever."

Her companions of Sunday and Monday by no means exhausted Suyin's repertoire. A factory technician who she met at a party invited her the following Sunday to photograph the scenery and each other in Hong Kong's municipal botanic garden and aviary. Afterward they walked 20 minutes before stopping at an outdoor hawker's stall for a snack of soft drinks and cakes. Suyin commented, "Maybe you're wondering about his choice of eating place. I certainly prefer elegant restaurants. But this happened just once and I would be disappointed if he made a habit of it. He told me that this stall during the week is patronized by properly dressed girls from nearby big offices and common laborers from construction sites alike. There is a spirit of equality at this particular setup. That's an example of how a good talker like him can reveal interesting aspects of a simple cafe, and I think I'll go out with him again."

On another occasion Suyin told me that she had been invited to join a Saturday afternoon beach outing organized by the office mates of a boyfriend who was employed by a Western trading firm. This young clerk phoned Suyin early that Saturday morning to cancel his invitation. He apparently explained to Suyin that he had just discovered that no other young women would attend the beach party and she would therefore be bored. The prospect displeased her less than it did the young man. Laughing, Suyin told me, "He's selfish! He was afraid that his office mates would all compete for me." She nevertheless accepted his explanation and he took her to lunch at a sandwich bar, and afterward they strolled for half an hour in Moss Park. This story once again suggested to me that Suyin sought whenever possible to demonstrate her personal worth by surrounding herself with a coterie of young and attractive male admirers, a wish that flowed in part from her desire to compensate for a lifetime of paternal neglect.

Suyin seriously considered marrying a barber who, at age 32, was already the proprietor of a hair salon. "His mother really liked me and wanted us to marry that same year," Suyin said with a self-satisfied air. "You see, his younger brother had already married, and the family thought that he was getting 'old.' Chinese parents are like that when it comes to an eldest son and especially their determination for a first grandson. I liked the affection and respect that his family showered upon him as the first son, but the haste with which his family attempted to set the wedding date made Mother uneasy, because she needed my earning power for another several years. I'd never marry a man who didn't get along with Mother," she said, explaining her rejection of this promising union. Most important, she preferred to marry a companionable man.

"He must stand and cut for ten hours a day at least, even on weekends. That means I would have little time to share with him at home alone. I don't care for that prospect at all. I'd like to continue my night life with my husband. He finally became engaged to a manicurist. That's a good solution, because they can work in the shop together."

Suyin had other opportunities to marry, and Man-hon, a young factory technician in our English class, was seriously pursuing her. The sole son of a widowed domestic servant, Man-hon had already purchased a working-class apartment in which his mother installed the family ancestral altar to prepare for his early marriage and for her grandmother role. This young man capably hosted our Sunday afternoon English class reunions in his new apartment. When he learned that I preferred natural foods to soda pop and sweets, he thoughtfully purchased on each occasion vegetarian dumplings and plain pastries. Suyin snickered at such maladroit party fare. It was during these gatherings that Man-hon recruited Suyin to assist him in producing his cultural magazine.

Suyin became infatuated instead with another fellow English student, an equally sincere but better-dressed, middle-class clerk at Butterfield and Swire, one of the colony's major trading organizations. She was impressed by his adept management of our class journeys to the beach on Sundays, when our party of twenty or more competed for scarce bus, car, and boat transportation on crowded arteries with other pleasure seekers heading toward the beaches and outlying islands. He was a confident, jaunty fellow, with a lively sense of humor, and generous with lifts in his old car. Suyin appeared to enjoy dating him, but when he showed a clear preference for another, more sedate young seamstress, Suyin was forced to the realization that "maybe he was jealous and angry when I continued to date other fellows. Probably he's also looking for the traditional submissive type of woman anyway. But what can I do? I can't change and become like that." Because he held an enviable job and belonged to a more refined social class than Suyin's other beaux, this clerk was able to court a woman who could focus her sole attention on him. Suyin's unconventional dating behavior distanced her from his family and those of the other better-positioned young men in her circle.

My-rae was anxious to restrain Suyin's dating and for her to settle down to steady income earnings and an eventual marriage upward. In 1971, when Suyin was only 18, her parents attempted through Father's emigrant kinsmen in London to match their eldest daughter with a proprietor of a Cantonese restaurant. Suyin's response was, "I didn't like that idea. You know the saying, 'A person might have money, but no love.' I'm certainly not willing to settle down at the cash register of a restaurant for the rest of my life."

Despite Suyin's rejection of old-fashioned matchmaking, she was trained from childhood to elevate family needs above purely personal fulfillment. Although she could become engaged, Chinese family convention could not countenance her marriage until Third Sister successfully completed her middle-school course and secured respectable employment. Only then could the family budget sustain the loss of Suyin's substantial income contribution. Third Sister's matriculation from form V was a matter of only 3 to 4 years, during which she would continue to contribute her domestic labor in the Yuen household and tutor the young lads. Although this family obligation set well-defined duties and bounds for Suyin, it impressed few hardships upon her because Suyin enjoyed bachelor life and wanted to prolong it as long as possible. Suyin was determined to experience social life to the fullest because she realized that her husband would have the prerogative to curtail or cancel her afternoons and evenings about town.

I was visiting the Yuens one sweltering midsummer afternoon when the young housewife from the apartment two doors away called, complaining that she had been home all day with her baby, even though there was a park and a pool on the neighboring estate. She told us that she had once enjoyed swimming with companions, but since her marriage her husband's family prohibited her from bringing her child to this pool. "They're afraid their only grandson will catch a cold in the water. I think it's ridiculous, but I have no say." Her taxi-driver husband worked long hours behind the wheel and was rarely able to accompany her to the pool or beach. Suyin winked knowingly at me and later commented, "Chinese men always take their women before marriage to the beach, bowling, or other places, but notice how he's leaving her alone now. So that's one reason I don't like the idea of early marriage."

Suyin felt that 25 would be the ideal marriage age, but that 26 or 27 was getting "too old." Suyin told me that a low-cost travel wedding (modest ceremony, no exchange of gifts, and travel to an offshore resort for a honeymoon) would for her equal a more conventional reception and banquet costing several thousand dollars. In the eyes of Mother and Father, however, the eldest daughter needed to give face to the family and provide excitement for its members with a proper wedding partner and elaborate wedding spectacle. Although Suyin tenaciously affirmed that Father had little power within the family, the effective dominance of his ideas on her marriage and wedding ceremony belied this supposition.

To broaden my views on the images of marriage and conjugality cherished by Hong Kong young working daughters, I sought Suyin's opinion on courtship and engagement, the employment of young wives, and the possibility of divorce. Suyin's views on marriage were of special interest since she, more than any other working daughter in this book, cultivated and enjoyed night life and a limited period of bachelor freedom.

Suyin explained why none of the young women of her acquaintance lived with their fiancés before their marrying. "We Chinese enter marriage not for sex alone, but mainly for bearing children and continuing the family line. Living together is understandable only if there is a special reason, such as the refusal of the parents to approve the marriage. But if the parents agree initially, then there is no point to their living together and they might as well marry to begin with. Otherwise, if the girl becomes pregnant, then the couple must marry anyway and instead of this complication, it's better that they marry at the outset. Since marriage is a permanent family affair, I don't know anyone who has divorced, although people frequently separate. Foreigners take divorce more lightly."

"Does that mean you'd be afraid to marry a foreigner?" I asked. "Well, I'd certainly hesitate," she replied.

I wondered how long Suyin would continue employment after marriage and childbirth. "I'll keep working so long as the costs of child care aren't too high. If a day nursery is going to take up half my income, I'd prefer to stay at home with the child myself." She was uneasy about the less expensive custom of hiring an elderly babysitter. "So many grannies are minding babies now," she said and gestured to both neighboring apartments. "They haven't got the know-how or the energy to instruct the child." She reminded me of her own painful situation, where both My-rae and First Wife could claim the three girls and three boys as their children. "It's not good to have two different women in charge of a family of children. They don't treat the children evenhandedly. Substitute mothers for many hours every day confuses the children, too."

When Suyin passed her 22nd birthday, she became ready to settle down and she was within a 2-year engagement of her desired marriage age. She began thinking more seriously about a permanent attachment and found a young factory technician who was attentive to her . After my summer, 1976, return visit to the ten working daughters of this book, Suyin brought her intended with her to Kai Tak Airport to bid me farewell. This was my first glimpse of the couple. In the airport lounge she beamed as she handed me a small bouquet of flowers and told me, without announcing a marriage plan, that they cared deeply for each other and that they would be happy together.

Summary

Suyin toiled in factories from the age of 12 for her family's sake and gave most of her wages to Mother. As the eldest of six siblings in a household with a wandering father, Suyin's input to family earnings had to be substantial from the outset. Suyin met conventional family expectations of the dutiful income earner, but bent tradition in her pursuit of greater status for herself in the family and by despising and denigrating Father. In exchange for her income contribution, Suyin obtained a leadership role in the family and came close to becoming its key decision maker. Suyin attempted to ally with My-rae in numerous disputes with Father. Resenting the low regard he long displayed for her, Suyin justified her actions by protesting that Father had been unfair to My-rae and the siblings as well.

In her quest for the good things in life, Suyin maintained a far wider social life and dated more frequently than any of the other working women of her age group in my sample. She attempted both to surround herself with a coterie of worldly, admiring males and to win the attention of a kind and caring suitor. She expected her male friends to show their regard for her by purchasing elegant food and drink and by arranging good-quality entertainment. Ultimately, she hoped to marry a man who was personally attractive, economically secure, and generously protective. Suyin's dating profile was shaped less by pointers from Hollywood (in which she nevertheless maintained an avid interest) than by a deep need to compensate for the absence of paternal love and the psychological and economic insecurity in which she was raised. Since Suyin conformed to the Hong Kong family expectations of the older daughters as major rice bowl providers, her mother and siblings accepted her active social life, and Suyin postponed marrying both as a means of continuing support for the family and of enjoying a variety of male companions.

Despite her intention to enter a close and companionate marriage, Suyin knew that in her culture marriage is an affair of the wider family. Soon after her wedding she would be obliged to bear children, and she planned to postpone marriage until she was personally and economically ready for motherhood. Until her marriage partner materialized, Suyin periodically transferred her affection from one friend to another, as if she were searching for the elusive relationship that Father could never bestow upon Mother or herself.

Wai-gun: family obligations prevail

Wai-gun's history was shaped by her leading position as the eldest in a line of seven brothers and sisters in an impoverished family. Her contribution to the family economy was central. As with the other working women, family structure and domestic economic pressure forged a conscientious and capable working-class daughter. Nevertheless, no woman's personality is completely conditioned by such structural factors, and since all working women have unique identities formed from various adventitious and socially determined forces, I sought for the personal aspirations and limitations underlying Wai-gun's life. She firmly believed that existence held out some purpose beyond that of obtaining and using material goods. Although Wai-gun could not quite articulate to me her goals and purposes in life, she never hesitated to seek for answers. During the time I knew her, Wai-gun deepened her search and enlarged her individual exploration of her Chinese cultural roots into a political search for the direction and forces of broader social change.

Home and parents

Wai-gun's family came from mountainous Tai-shan county, Kwang-tung province, some 90 miles from Hong Kong, where agriculture pre-vails. Partly because of its geographic isolation, Taishanese peasants speak a Cantonese dialect that is not readily comprehended by fellow Cantonese. Tai-shan is populous and has been a departing point for North America-bound Chinese emigrants since the end of the nine-teenth century.

Wai-gun's family lived in an apartment in the huge Wong Tai Sin re-settlement estate complex (population 97,000). A single resettlement estate room, 10' by 12', housed all seven children and two adults of Wai-gun's family. A cotton curtain subdivided the room into a window-less inner area, which contained a pair of bunk beds wide enough to sleep two people on each level, and a bureau. The outer area nearest the door and balcony was a bedroom/livingroom with another double bunk bed, a cluster of shelves with a family shrine and some accumu-lated objects that had gathered dust for years, a television set, and a small refrigerator for bottled drinks. The phone rested on the television. The telephone was installed in 1973, much later than in other neigh-boring households, a reflection of the family's poverty. The few re-maining belongings were stacked on other wooden shelves built into the wall beneath the ceiling, which unfortunately impeded the circula-tion of fresh air. To combat the stifling summer heat, an overburdened electric fan, also newly purchased, revolved wearily from the ceiling. There were two windows in the outer room facing the courtyard, but fluorescent lights mounted on the ceiling were the only source of interior lighting.

Mother, age 42, had always been employed, but her health was de-teriorating, making continued labor more difficult for her. When the children were small, she assembled plastic ornaments at home for a small Chinese company, straining late at night under the dim fluo-rescent lights. She blamed this work for "ruining my eyesight and health." When her lastborn was old enough to remain at home unattended, she took a better-paying factory job in a Chinese company cutting metal into pieces for kettles and cups, which did not require good eyesight. "It's not a complicated job. The task is easy to learn and clean, although quite arduous," she explained. Mother was often tired and ate foods valued for their nutritional properties, such as liver, gall bladders, and snake meat in winter, and consumed much ginger, in an effort to bolster her rundown condition.

While Mother was away at work, the children kept house, cooked their meals, and prepared the family dinner. Mother said, "It's not very good for the children, you know. They are left unsupervised, but what can I do?" She shrugged her shoulders to express the futility of a working woman like herself attempting to discipline and control her offspring. Providing a philosophical justification for her laissez faire style of child rearing, she continued, "I am a relaxed mother. I just let my children grow up as they are. 'Heaven broght them and heaven will take care of them,'" she quoted a Chinese proverb. She breast-fed each child until the age of 2, when she introduced the standard fare of rice, vegetables, and meat. Mother remarked that although nowadays Hong Kong mothers couldn't be bothered nursing their children, she thought it was a good practice. "Don't force children to eat solid food," she counseled me about my own daughter, born in 1972. "If they don't want it, let them be. Force feeding will give them indigestion or something worse."

Although she had left the countryside almost two decades earlier, Mother still considered herself an illiterate woman of the soil. She lacked the means to generalize her urban experiences and, in her view, factory work in no way broadened her life. After sweating 9 hours in the factory, she returned home immediately, rarely having the time to visit relatives and friends.

Mother was frustrated by the conditions in her factory. Once, when her hand was cut during work, she reported the injury to the foreman, only to be summarily sent home without pay (a violation of the Hong Kong industrial compensation ordinance). She justified her subsequent passivity this way: "It doesn't do any good to report such treatment higher up. Shop floor managers speak with 'two mouths,' one to the workers and one to their superiors. Powerful officials will pay no attention to an illiterate woman like me." She alluded in her speech to the character for official (官), formed from two "mouths" (口).

Father worked an exhausting shift in a factory that manufactured cast-iron weights. He was paid by the piece and could set his own schedule. Although piecework has the advantage of permitting a strong worker to wrestle for a greater income by extraordinary exertion, it penalizes the weak. In 1972 Father underwent an operation for a cancer of the liver, in which half his liver and his gall bladder were removed. Care in the government public hospital was free, but his factory did not pay sick leave and there is no government compensation in Hong Kong. Father never again drew a full day's wage, which meant that the earnings of his children became even more important than before.

After his hospitalization, Father's strong personality dominated the family scene just as it had before. A blunt man, he spoke his mind to anyone who would listen. In his view, everyone in Hong Kong was out for himself, so it was useless to organize the workers, because under such conditions "they could never get together!" He spoke in favor of piecework wages, which enabled an eager worker like his former self to move ahead. Father dominated most family decision making, from the education of the children to the choice of everyday household purchases, including the television set, which represented the combined labor for 3 weeks of Father, Mother, and Wai-gun.

Despite his verbal bluster and pronouncements on the importance of each person acting for himself, Father had a low sense of self-worth, which he judged by his pocketbook. He often commented that the "real successes" in his family were those who left Tai-shan for Canada and "made a fortune there." "But of course my relatives are only distant cousins," he added quickly. "Otherwise they would have helped us out, and I wouldn't remain such a flop!" Financial aid from well-to-do relatives was Father's sole hope for betterment. He spurned any strategy that would collectively benefit his entire social stratum.

Father's paramount role in the family and his outspoken, egotistic views influenced his offspring's thinking on Hong Kong society. Wai-gun acquired her father's essentially defensive verbal adroitness, but she fortunately was spared his self-centered pessimism. This is probably because, as a woman, she did not measure herself and her achievements in strictly economic terms. In addition, she had somewhere obtained more idealistic goals, and she held onto them through the years of difficulty and impoverishment endured by the family.

Family relations

From the time she began outwork alongside her mother at age 12, through her acceptance of her parents' decision that she withdraw from school at age 13, to the assumption at around age 20 of her role as a principal contributor to the household budget, Wai-gun served the family dutifully as eldest daughter. Her response to my queries on her feelings on having sacrificed her chances for education and independence was, "Well, I am part of the family, too. I must share responsibility for running it!"

Wai-gun would have blushed in denial, but her attitude of eager contribution to the family through great personal sacrifice reminded me of the "big-foot" weavers of the Kwangtung silk industry described by Smedley (1978), who proudly made great contributions to their family. Wai-gun's altruistic attitude was consistent with the suggestions in life histories and folk tales of heroic women that, despite being taught they did not belong to their natal family, they unconsciously desired to be considered as intimate members. Could it not be that the working daughter is in part motivated to earn money and contribute her wages to her home in order to gradually but perceptively plant her roots deeper and become a more appreciated member of her family, if only for the short period until she marries? I had not seen this subject of the daughter's unconscious desire to belong to the natal family analyzed, and it certainly violates the classic strictures of the centuries-old Confucian Chinese family, which was founded on the precept that women were not members of the patriarchal unit. However, Wai-gun's conscious desire to help her family is consistent on an unconscious level with the objective structure of the patriarchal family reality. When for a short time as an unmarried factory girl Wai-gun became a wage-earning member, she must have realized that finally she had the chance to be better accepted by her family because of her wage-earning input. Thus I am reminded of the epigram attributed to Jung, "No noble, well grown tree ever disowned its dark roots, for it grows not only upwards but downwards as well." This statement connotes an image of an unequal balance between two families: the husband's family, acceptable and hence well lit in the sunlight, versus the wife's family, strongly rooted but submerged and maintained out of view.

For several years, Wai-gun's contribution to the family income was sizable: In early 1973 she earned around $80–$100 per month, or 28% of the family income. After her 15-year-old brother began employment as a delivery boy on a 7-Up truck – his first job out of middle school, which netted him less than Wai-gun made in mid-1973 – this share dropped to a still-substantial 22%. Further entries into the work force followed 2 years later. The frequent economic crises that arose from the illness of her parents gave Wai-gun's stable earnings particular importance. Despite this, Wai-gun seldom was consulted by her authoritarian father: "Purchases? Schooling and jobs for the younger ones? Father is really obstinate and makes these decisions. He says that my mother is "just a peasant woman" who doesn't know how to shop for goods. Father selected the television set, but it turned out to be a lemon! So, now we just grin and suffer his purchases. Even though I put money into them, I don't choose them."

Wai-gun's central economic role in the family did not confer the right to a voice in the family's long-term affairs. She did not know how much Father earned, for example. But her role gave her a clearer perspective for following and judging its inner dynamics. Despite her father's decision-making monopoly, Wai-gun felt she could weigh his actions on her own scale and did not have to take him as seriously as in the past. If the consequences of his decision making were tragicomical, as in the case of the faulty television set, she could chuckle from an emotional distance.

Work also gave Wai-gun the right to spend up to $15 every fortnight on personal needs. For her July birthday, her mother gave her $2 to buy whipped cream cake and barbeque pork for the whole family, and she also spent $4 of her own money on a new blouse and shoes, her main summer clothes purchases. There were traditional elements to the fête as well. On her birthday, Wai-gun had to burn incense at the ancestors' altar and bow low to them, and also to her parents, thanking them their gift of life. Nobody "congratulated" the child who had the birthday. At dinner they ate long noodles shaped in a pyramid, which is symbolic of long life.

Wai-gun felt completely free to pass her spare time as she chose, which was mainly with friends, and she performed very few domestic chores. Household chores were done by her siblings: Eldest Brother hauled water – "He is the coolie of the family," I was informed amid peals of laughter; two younger sisters washed the dishes; the younger brothers had no tasks. Father did more housework than Wai-gun, since he increasingly took time off from his job because of ill health. Father purchased food for the family and for Mother's, Ying-gun's, and Wai-gun's lunch boxes, and he prepared dinner on evenings when Mother worked overtime. The help Father provided at home was noteworthy to the neighbors. One Saturday afternoon, as Father was squatting on the family's verandah in the housing development tenement walkway, peeling ginger for a favorite chicken dish, a friend of his jested in passing: "You look like you are giving birth!" Father's vegetable-peeling posture (the squatting "childbirth position") is common in the East, and ginger is the main ingredient in a soup Chinese prepare to nourish postpartum mothers. The pun kidded him for performing "female" kitchen chores. Father told me that he had learned to cook in his native village but that "young people nowadays generally don't know how to do anything useful."

Wai-gun's sibling relationships illustrated the rapidity of life-style change within a single generation. She was very close to First Brother, 2 years younger than she, and they frequently went places together and took each other's photograph. One Lunar New Year's eve they set up a stall at a local night market and sold neckties. On another occasion they went to films together. Yet Wai-gun and her sister Ying-gun, the third child in the family and 5 years her junior, were never very close, in part because their age gap created substantially different experiences and outlooks. Ying-gun dropped out of school at around age 12, even though at the time the family wanted her to continue. She took up an assemblist job at the Fairchild Semiconductor plant. She preferred the "independence" gained from employment, and although as a learner her earnings were too meager to be of much help to the family, she did support herself while living at home and spent her pocket money on recreation and clothing. In her group of friends, clothes were important symbols, and she had a large wardrobe of bell-bottom trousers and stacked shoes. Wai-gun was openly critical of Ying-gun's decision to leave school and her considerable expenditures on clothing and dating. She quipped sarcastically about her sister's clothes even as Ying-gun was ironing and hemming them in preparation for a date. In much the same way that Mother's scorn of Wai-gun's expenditures on Chinese culture was of no avail, Wai-gun ultimately resigned herself to the carefree spending of the younger sister's generation. It was not legitimate for Wai-gun to express openly irritation over her sizable contribution to the family purse, but her purchase of the Chinese lute and folk music lessons, to which her parents objected, and her reproach of Ying-gun's spending habits reminded them all of the opportunities that this eldest daughter had sacrificed for her family.

Education

Wai-gun attended a rooftop primary school run by the government in her resettlement estate complex. To encourage attendance, schools like this one accept all youngsters from surrounding districts, regardless of aptitude or achievement. There is no entrance examination, and as a rule all pupils graduate from one grade to the next to make a place for the newcomers. The schools are crowded, with an average of forty-five children per "room" on the fenced-in roof, and classes are held in two shifts, from 8 a.m. to 1 p.m. and from 1:30 p.m. to 6:30 p.m. For these reasons, government-run primary schools have a low standing in the community and are generally believed to be less rigorous than missionary or other private schools catering to the higher income levels, which require entrance examinations and maintain better pupil-teacher ratios.

Wai-gun characterized the teaching style as the "stuffed duck" method. Pupils were crammed with facts, like grain is force-fed to Peking ducks, so they can pass the Secondary School Entrance Examination. Rote education repelled her, and she willingly accepted Father's decision that she drop out after graduating from primary 6 at age 13. Given her family's impoverished financial circumstances and need for her earnings, however small, Wai-gun felt grateful for even that much schooling. In mid-1960s' Hong Kong, it was the norm for working-class children to leave the educational stream before it took them very far into the secondary curriculum. In her last year at primary school, Wai-gun had already limited her study time in order to assemble plastic flowers with Mother.

"My brother went to school longer, because he's a boy. With only a primary school education, it was easier for a girl to get a job than for a boy. He has the responsibility to rear his own family in the future, and further education is more important to him than to me."

"But women certainly work after marriage," I said.

"Yes, I know that large numbers of women are now working, but these numbers were very much less six years ago. Anyway, a woman's job is second to a man's even now," she replied.

The same factory job that Wai-gun obtained as a primary school dropout and that was considered a good spot for a daughter was seen as a dead end for a son, who needed further schooling because he would eventually have to support his own wife and children.

"How did you feel about quitting school?" I asked Wai-gun.

"Well," she replied, "I am part of the family, too, and since two of us cannot attend secondary school in the same year, they especially need my labor now that brother is advancing in secondary school."

Later, however, she came to regret deeply her lost schooling and tried to recoup the deficit during 8 long years of night school, when she nearly completed form V. All the children attended the same government primary school. Elder Brother's Anglo-Chinese Secondary School, operated by the Church of Christ of China, had a good reputation. His school fees were contributed by a Canadian family under the International Children's Association. Wai-gun, more than anyone in the family, had the aptitude and drive to continue schooling, and it was ironic that although she dropped out to support her family so that Elder Brother could receive secondary schooling, he preferred to play soccer and basketball and to earn a living. He left his studies for a job as a delivery boy that paid little more than Wai-gun's job.

By 1974, the two eldest children were contributing their wages to the family, and the parents fervently hoped that the five younger children would complete secondary school. Second Sister Ying-gun was next in line for secondary school but was not a strong student. Like other upward-bound pupils attuned to the examination system, Ying-gun chose to repeat primary 6 in a fruitless effort to obtain a government bursary by bettering her score on the Secondary School Entrance Examination, and then she left school altogether. According to Wai-gun, Second Sister should have persevered despite her low grades, because the family would have stepped in to meet the tuition fees of between $15 and $20 a month; instead Ying-gun, too, preferred to enter a factory. Her desires were fostered by the traditional presumption that women have far fewer career prospects than men. In contemporary industrial Hong Kong, Ying-gun's interest in continuing her education was completely undermined by the availability of assembly-line wage labor for 13-year-olds (child labor in the Hong Kong statutes).

Second Sister was strongly attracted by the commodity consumption of mainstream youth culture, and work provided money for her to enjoy clothes, the cinema, and popular music. By centering their main hopes on Eldest Son, the parents had paid little attention to Ying-gun's study habits, and when the opportunity for choice was left to her, Second Sister's leaving school was understandable. The quest of young people for tangible, short-term gain at the cost of longer-term and seemingly vaguer opportunities will only cease when companies find it unprofitable to employ school dropouts and the government institutes universal compulsory public education through secondary school. The opening up of jobs for older, educated women would also have a salutary effect on this process.

Wai-gun's passionate interest in learning continued after she left primary school. For many years she took evening classes in European history, English literature, and liberal arts subjects, all of which were taught in English, but she lacked the time to do homework, and her grades were barely passing. Because her school was run for profit, it encouraged all the pupils to re-enroll year after year and advanced them no matter how they performed on the tests. I once looked at Wai-gun's history book and grammar texts and found them quite difficult. The text was copied from one used in Britain and oriented to the GCE examinations there with few adaptions to Hong Kong culture. For example, students were told to write a composition about snow, sleet, and frost.

Wai-gun saw learning as a broadly defined, dynamic experience extending from the classroom into society, a perspective that she somehow retained through all her years of banal schooling. In 1976 Wai-gun finally lost interest in acquiring the elusive diploma and, without renouncing her idealistic view of the importance of learning, dropped out of evening school forever. Her creative energy was beginning to flow in channels better suited to her character and aspirations.

Work

Although Wai-gun's career was limited by her leaving school, her educational level, like that of most in her age group, was much superior to that of her mother and the older generations of women. This gave women of Wai-gun's age a competitive edge in employment, and Wai-gun obtained a factory job at age 13. Her continued efforts to improve her skills suggested an attention to job mobility and personal improvement that was also lacking in her mother's generation.

By the time I met her, Wai-gun had held four jobs, beginning with home plastic flower assembly, at age 12, followed the next year by garment sewing in a small workshop. She then joined numerous other 14-year-old girls on the assembly line at the United States–owned Fairchild Semiconductor, Ltd., in Kwun Tong, piecing together electronic circuits. After this, she seamed brassieres in a large West German-owned undergarment factory, Triumph Co. Her dislike of the piecework system there was unusual for a young and potentially fast worker, but it stemmed from more than her individual situation. Wai-gun recognized that piecework discouraged solidarity among workers by creating a breach between the younger, stronger ones and their less dynamic, older workmates. Piecework automatically weeded out older women workers, like her mother, whose health was run down by family and work tasks until declining earnings forced them to quit. Wai-gun further objected to the control such method of pay gave the employer. Her company set an unofficial maximum wage of $5 per day. When an experienced worker mastered shortcuts that enabled her to attain this maximum, the management reduced the value of each piece, thereby keeping wages well below the ceiling. Employing a "scientific management" approach (timing the girls' motions with a stopwatch and blueprinting for economy their physical workflow), the foreman often arbitrarily and without notice changed the piece rates. In Wai-gun's words, "In our factory, employer-worker relations are awful. There is a German woman walking around the room all the time. When she sits in front of you clocking your speed, it makes you really nervous. They also 'pick stones from eggs' and find tiny faults in our work. We pretend not to understand English. When they speak to us we pay no attention. If they hand us work to redo, we just put it aside, and make repairs only when the stitching is really poor."

Wai-gun also found this job dissatisfying because the fast assembly-line pace and rigid work rules forbade conversation. She especially disliked sitting at the sewing machine all day. "You can't even go to the washroom, except at your break. We must take our lunch sitting at the bench," she complained. On the other hand, Wai-gun had this to say: "I don't have to think about the work while I do it. I can think about other things instead!" This and the much-needed paycheck accounted for her acquiescence to the deadening routine of factory work.

However, certain management actions that they felt were particularly unfair occasionally triggered workers' expressions of pent-up resentment. Wai-gun described a 1-day sit-down strike in her factory to protest the management's decreasing the piecework rate without informing the workers. The factory was not unionized, but a spontaneous feeling of ill will spread through the shop. People whispered the plan as they passed by each other's workbench. Everyone took part except the well-paid section of workers who operated the multipurpose sewing machines. The management was forced to raise the wages by a few percent. Wai-gun exclaimed, however, "It was only a gesture! After that they returned to their old habit of cutting the workers' wages without informing them." Once the decrease amounted to $1 in a single day.

"This shows that the bosses are very smart. They know how to drag the issue out until our workers' 'organization' disintegrates."

Wai-gun also complained to me about compulsory overtime to meet shipment deadlines. One day, the foreman asked her section to work overtime. She wanted to refuse for a variety of reasons: She would have to be absent from evening school, overtime work did not receive higher rates of pay, she would miss the company bus and would have to pay her own carfare home, and she would have an inadequate dinner because she could not afford a proper restaurant meal. But at the end of the 5:30 workday, the factory exits were locked and barred; she could not leave without the foreman's consent. Fearing reprisals, Wai-gun did not pursue the matter.

This was not an isolated incident. In July, 1971, women workers in a Hong Kong wig factory brought suit against the owners over a similar issue. They were dismissed when they objected to forced overtime, and they sued for the pay owed them. The owner unsuccessfully argued against the suit, claiming they would not have had to work overtime if they had been better, faster workers to begin with ("Wig factory-girls win $8670 in damages," 1971).

Wai-gun also worked in the Fairchild Semiconductor plant with over 1,000 workers, assembling components of microcircuits for aerospace products. Years before, in another context, I had interviewed a Stanford Business School–trained American official of the factory. He told me that his company practiced enlightened business management in the United States and had learned to get what they wanted by working with, not against, the union. But they had located part of their operations in Hong Kong to save labor costs, and he could not permit workers to organize for fear wages would increase; the advent of the union would cost him his job, he claimed.

Wai-gun, who saw the interests of workers as being opposed to those of management, joined a spontaneous strike in 1970 by the unorganized workers in the Fairchild Semiconductor plant (England and Rear, 1975; Lutz and Snow, 1971). The dispute concerned differential pay rates for shift work, an accepted North American practice, but one that was considered unfair by the workers on the day shift. Wai-gun recalled, "The management was really unfair. People should get the same pay for the same work. Most of us joined out of solidarity. Who wants to work while everyone is on strike? People would hate you!

"The strike failed, probably because we were not united enough. For one thing, we didn't know each other too well beforehand. For another, the leaders were too weak. We elected them just because they were the most vocal, but they were too excitable and lost their tempers during negotiations, giving management the impression that we were immature and naïve. Management knows ours is not complicated work and that new workers can be trained easily. So they fired those of us who had worked ourselves to the highest wage ceiling, without giving us the required one month's notice or one month's extra wage. They summoned us to the office to do it, and let us wait for three hours in a cold air-conditioned room without sending anyone to talk to us. It was a damned frigid way to lose a strike."

Wai-gun's untutored and instinctive identification with the sporadic worker protests in the factories in which she worked reflected not only a passionate commitment to social betterment but also latent leadership potential. She probably could have been a capable section leader, which would have given her a more skilled, and hence not only more secure but more satisfying, position. But despite Wai-gun's clear interpersonal skills on the factory floor, she was reluctant to seek promotion from the ranks of assemblers to that of section head by currying favor with the foreman. To her, the slight pay rise was not worth the increased responsibility and estrangement from her workmates. She spoke of playing up (*p'ai ma p'i*, "pat the horse's rump"), which has the negative connotation of apple polishing. Any peer group member who strives for the blessing of authority rather than for informal prestige and popularity is bound to evoke hostility from peers. The members of the factory group with whom Wai-gun worked considered themselves peers to a certain extent, enough so that those who broke ranks to accept a promotion feared being shunned. Conversely, workers felt obliged to support spontaneous strikes and fellow workers' protests.

Advancement also meant special training to become a better seamstress than the rest, because the lead girl had to perform all the tasks in order to teach them to others. This was particularly difficult in the garment trade, where new types of clothing are introduced every season. In Wai-gun's line of work alone there were new backless, strapless, and transparent dresses that required their own matching brassieres, and the style of stitching changed in each instance.

"I learned to use a single-needle sewing machine when I first started working in a smaller factory. Now I have been operating one for two years. There is a slight chance of being transferred to a two- or three-

needle multipurpose machine, but the management is not interested
in providing the necessary training, unless I seek promotion, and only
wants us to work as fast as possible on the existing machine."

Wai-gun's reluctance to aim for the position of section leader was
not due to limited personal vision or idealization of the role of a factory worker. When pressed she revealed a cherished hope of qualifying
as a nursery or kindergarten teacher. She had already applied unsuccessfully for several posts. For example, she applied for a job teaching 4-
and 5-year-olds in the basement kindergarten attached to a church in
the Shep Kip Mei resettlement estate. The school had over 250 working-class children from the neighborhood and was run in two half-day
shifts. The teachers had all taken the several-month-long government
course and obtained a certificate, and Wai-gun would not have qualified
for that course. Night school credits were not recognized by the government or professional associations as equivalent to courses taken in the
accredited day schools, which prevented employed economically poor
students from translating their after-work education into occupational
advancement. Wai-gun's goal was beyond reach of her connections and
credentials at the time, but her inspiration to envision a totally new
type of job suggested her confidence in the possibility of radical change
on the individual level. A chimera for a factory worker some years
earlier, Wai-gun's ambition had by 1973 become less unrealistic. Deep
changes were continuously, although not always visibly, taking place in
Hong Kong society which, when they were understood by factory
workers, were seen as positive. This attitude may be contrasted with the
fears of socioeconomic change said to be held by traditional Chinese
women.

Although Wai-gun felt that workers were exploited by capitalists, she
was pessimistic about the long-term prospects for uniting the proletariat,
and as we have seen she attributed the collapse of the Fairchild strike
in the first instance to subjective divisions among the workers. She felt
that the workers' position would remain low even under socialist rule
or, as she put it, "even if the color of the colony is changed," referring
to the ever-present expectation that someday sovereignty would revert
to the People's Republic. Wai-gun's limited faith in the possibilities of
organizing flowed partly from Mother's passivity and Father's individualism and partly from the dearth of militant unionism in the new
industrial sector, which effectively nullified the workers' discontent. Yet
Wai-gun's social vision was slowly widening and her views were open to

change. Compared to Mother, who was totally helpless and who did not protest her loss of pay due to a work-related accident, Wai-gun was at least outspoken and potentially more effective. Nor did she, like Father, confine her criticism to the workers for failure to organize but traced the divisions among them to management tactics and to the imbalance of power in the factory and government.

Her example revealed an emerging, if still undirected, awareness of the necessity of the workers to unite to improve conditions. As long as she lacked a deeper perspective on the role of her factory cohort in the domestic and international economy, however, Wai-gun coped with her experiences largely as an individual and family member.

Peers

Like most other working daughters of my study, Wai-gun engaged in recreational activities and joined evening and weekend classes as a means of locating like-minded friends and broadening her skills. Peers provided a psychological counterweight to her formidable family obligations and this, too, was true for the other women. The chance to confide without fear of being criticized as self-centered or unfilial and the freedom to engage in activities without regard for the family rules of hierarchical deference were attractive to Wai-gun. But Wai-gun, of all my subjects, was most attracted to activities that involved her cultural heritage and appealed to her self-identification as a Chinese. The search for one's national roots was understandably difficult in culturally undernourished and politically dismaying Hong Kong, but Wai-gun followed her populist bent for many years and assembled a group of other young people who shared this interest.

Wai-gun and her best friend Shing-wa joined a folk art class at a large, four-story, well-funded YWCA branch that had significant community outreach in a neighboring estate. Their cultural interests were as close as their workplace attitudes. Both were at one time employed on the Fairchild Semiconductor assembly line, although they had not yet met each other, and both had participated in the 1970 strike.

Wai-gun and Shing-wa teamed up with a young unmarried man named Kung-ngai, about age 25, who lived in the same apartment block as Wai-gun. He was mainland-born, and his family resided in China. He rented the half-room apartment from friends of his who had moved elsewhere. The apartment was located four doors from Wai-gun's family's apartment, with the entrance on the same side of the corridor. Wai-gun had made his acquaintance gradually over the course of the years. His apartment was simply arranged, with a bunk bed and a table, some cooking utensils, and a shrine on the top shelf of a cupboard. There was no television, radio, refrigerator, or phone, unlike the apartments of married couples and families.

The trio exchanged rings and swore to become "blood brothers and sisters." "This is a fictive kinship relationship of solidarity that was common in traditional China," I was told by Wai-gun. Kung-ngai shared his intellectual interests with Wai-gun, taught her calligraphy, and bought her every issue of a monthly journal, *Hong Kong 'Seventies,* which was critical of the Hong Kong establishment and published by the highbrow newspaper *Ming-Pao.* Kung-ngai was not a union member, and he looked askance at the avowedly politically oriented Hong Kong unions.

"Brother" had invited a friend of his, Chen-kwok, to share his half-room on a voluntary basis. No rent exchanged hands. The friend's father was an Overseas Chinese in the Philippines, and his mother was a cleaning lady who lived in the factory dormitory where she worked. It was not uncommon for male friends to share a domicile. I do not know how Kung-ngai and Chen-kwok first met, but they shared many intellectual interests, and Chen-kwok was of the same questioning persuasion reflected in the *Hong Kong 'Seventies* journal. Occasionally Kung-ngai, Wai-gun, Shing-wa, and Chen-kwok could be found reading and discussing issues of interest to them in the evening after work or on the weekends.

In spite of her heavy schedule of work and family obligations, Wai-gun kept up an amazing roster of activities. One evening, while she and I were strolling in Victoria Park, Wai-gun showed me the rink where she and Shing-wa often roller skated. Later, while we sipped tea on the terrace overlooking the park's 50-meter outdoor swimming pool, she mentioned that she also was learning to swim. Wai-gun's dedication to fitness was not unique – two other working women in my study swam in their Urban Council–operated pool in their resettlement estates at 7 a.m. before going to factory jobs. They found the pool crowded even then.

"I attend lessons after work three times a week for an hour. We have to rush like mad to get to the pool at six-thirty, because traffic jams slow down our bus. I hope to pass the test with my class in two weeks, and then go on to the next class. The program is run by the Urban Council and it's free."

I then asked Wai-gun about her other activities. Wai-gun ticked them off on her fingers. "English at night school – but I am stopping next month until the fall because I need the time to study Mandarin – folk dancing and singing and theater. We write and perform our own plays. My 'brother' plays the Chinese flute, but he discourages me from learning because it's not 'feminine,'" she said, wrinkling her mouth to demonstrate how awkward it looked.

Wai-gun's parents did not overtly oppose her friendships, classes, and outings, but they harbored reservations, and so she often kept her pursuits a secret. For example, her parents had objected to her $40 purchase of a Chinese lute, the *p'i p'a*, and to lessons at $14 per month. For the parents, any "outside" activity had to be an investment, and learning the lute would not advance Wai-gun economically. Wai-gun borrowed money from "Brother" and purchased the lute despite their objections. She stored it at Kung-ngai's apartment and also practiced it there. But her parents still quarreled with her over the expense of the lessons. Their lukewarm receptivity to Wai-gun's keen pursuit of Chinese culture was obvious. Wai-gun fetched the lute and brought it to her room to play for me. She sat on a straight chair in the front room, while her mother leaned out to watch from the lower bunk bed and her father squatted on a low stool. As Wai-gun demonstrated the lute to me, her mother accompanied with a counterpoint of sarcastic comments, like "That little thing is so expensive, but if it broke, the wood in it would not even be sufficient to make a fire to cook a meal!"

Wai-gun defied them in buying the musical instrument, and she kept part of her wages for lessons because she had decided, based on her assessment of the family economic trajectory, that when her next two siblings entered the work force and with her parents also working her family could finally make do with less of her money. She felt she certainly deserved the lute after having contributed dutifully for so many years to the family. She added, a bit wistfully, "I will never really become a good player, however, because I began too late. When I would have really benefited from the lessons a few years earlier, I could not purchase them because of my duty to the family."

She also defied her mother by going on an overnight camping trip with five friends in the New Territories, where they slept overnight in a tent. "Boys and girls together, you don't know what will happen!"

her mother whined to me. Wai-gun went anyway and eventually, after the fact, Mother resigned herself to it and gave Wai-gun permission to attend a second outing sponsored by the YWCA in a camp. Indeed, Wai-gun's parents grumbled whenever her social activities cost money or included contact with young men, although both were obviously beyond their control. Since this dutiful eldest child never reneged on her family obligations, I sensed that their protests were more for a show of dogged propriety than from a conviction of curtailing Wai-gun's behavior.

Wai-gun also looked to the cinema for direction. Whereas other Hong Kong girls I knew preferred romantic, escapist Hollywood (dubbed Cantonese) and Taiwan (Mandarin) films, Wai-gun sought out social commentary films. Chaplin's *Modern Times* played to a full house in Hong Kong for weeks. This Hollywood classic, popular in the West for its trenchant condemnation of the assembly-line inhumanity, appealed to Hong Kong audiences for the relief it presented, through humor, of severe pressures in (primarily Western-owned) industry. When Wai-gun took me to see it, she remarked on the similarity of her own work environment to the one enacted by Chaplin: "My boss should get together with that one and compare notes on how to get more out of the workers!" Nevertheless, in a consumer-oriented society where political change is not the current agenda, such a critical film had little impact upon the audience beyond the cathartic relief of tension through laughter.

It was not only social/cultural magazines and the cinema that united Wai-gun with her generation. Her peers also shared a political heritage different from that of their parents. As refugees who fled the mass campaigns of China, which frequently involved people at all levels, Father and Mother rejected political action to attain their goals. Wai-gun's father in particular was one of the most self-seeking fathers I knew in Hong Kong. Undereducated, without property, and disenfranchised, Father counseled his children to avoid political movements and unions. Although Wai-gun and other youths of refugee parents maturing in Hong Kong had grown up in the colony and had no recollection of life in China, many of them were keenly engaged in a search for their Chinese identity. Wai-gun naturally reflected upon her cultural and political ties with her homeland, and in 1971 she took the first step toward commitment by joining a protest against the Japanese claim to the Tiao Yu Tai Islands, disputed by both Peking and Taipei.

Wai-gun's folk singing club sang "patriotic" songs to support the demonstrators.

Wai-gun was acutely sensitive to the injustices she saw around her. Since in neither her work group nor her cultural circles were such matters discussed and she was not widely read or politically organized, Wai-gun lacked an analysis of the root causes of social problems. She thus had no alternative prescription for social change other than cultural renovation, and her peer group and its cultural activities became, next to her family, Wai-gun's source of meaning in life.

The difficulty of dredging up and breathing life into Chinese learning and traditions in intellectually moribund Hong Kong, where fewer and fewer cultural practices remained and the Chinese heritage was crumbling, were apparent to Wai-gun. Such observations perhaps heightened her feelings that although culture was becoming paramount for her, it was futile to see in it a panacea for Hong Kong.

Wai-gun's visits to the People's Republic of China were another crucial step in her search for roots. On her first trip in 1974 her parents brought her to visit relatives, but much to her parents' discomfort she was more interested in posing political questions to her village relations – especially regarding the role of young people. At first her parents' flight from their Chinese roots gave her pause, but she like other Hong Kong youths was magnetically attracted to China, and in 1975 Wai-gun visited China with Shing-wa and without her parents. Although she perceived the difficulties that Hong Kong-residing Chinese had in adjusting to life in China, Wai-gun was one of the few working daughters I knew who unequivocally supported the reversion of Hong Kong to China in 1997. All of the working daughters were highly constrained by their family obligations and work responsibilities and all sought relief from those duties in various ways (Western cinema excursions, picnics, other jaunts with friends). Wai-gun, however, searched with her companions for the cultural roots that had been overgrown by the industrialist capitalist system in which they were raised.

Wai-gun shared with other Hong Kong working girls an attraction to a congenial peer group both as an end in itself and as support for the steps that could be taken jointly toward adulthood. Wai-gun knew that her peers did not have access to sufficient resources to provide an institutional base to offset the domination of her life by the family economy, but peers were her sole relief from the familiar and economic constraints enmeshing her. Wai-gun considered her family structure constricting and dreamt of moving away from home. She was straining not only for a physical but a psychological space of her own. Our conversation returned to this topic many times. One evening Wai-gun, her sworn sister Shing-wa, myself, and my Cantonese assistant, a sociology student at the Chinese University of Hong Kong, were strolling in Victoria Park. Wai-gun asked where my assistant lived, and upon hearing she shared quarters with friends, Wai-gun and Shing-wa said in one voice, "We wish we could do that too. That is wonderful!"

Wai-gun went on wistfully about her wish to live alone: "We have so many people in our room. Do you have your own room at home? Your own bed? You have only two in a room! In a big family like ours, only when Eldest Daughter, First Son, and Second Daughter move out will my family's place be the right size!" Wai-gun spoke of a woman in her drama class who was trying to move away from home. "Naturally her mother wouldn't allow it," she ended emphatically.

Shing-wa contributed her own views to Wai-gun's, who nodded her assent. Shing-wa dreamt of having a 10′ by 8′ room of her own where she could put her things neatly together without their being "messed up" by the nieces and nephews who resided in the apartment of relatives where she was presently quartered. Instead, she had only the bed on which she slept. "I can't have a minute of quiet to myself," she affirmed.

"Have you thought of moving out?" I asked her.

"Yes, but it's very difficult to do! As a single girl, where can I move to? *You* tell me how to live alone! Furthermore, unless you are really sure you can make it yourself, it's very unwise to move out and then move back again. As we always say, 'A good horse doesn't turn its head to eat the grass behind.'"

Single working-class girls as a rule did not live apart from their parents and were most fearful to attempt it. Leaving home signified to Wai-gun and Shing-wa a break with the family rather than an approved-of search for independence. Most parents believed that their daughters' incomes belonged entirely to the family, and they looked askance at the girls paying rent unnecessarily. Their objections extended even further than this, however; in the parents' minds the family system of control was associated with living under one roof. Girls who moved away from their families would be unfilial. In my observation, daughters were able to obtain greater opportunities for peer activities and freedom by remaining at home.

It might be thought that Wai-gun and her friends would seek a marriage partner in order to pursue independence, given their tight family demands and their fledgling efforts to discover themselves and work out their identities. Even though she was emotionally prepared for adult relationships with the opposite sex, marriage was not feasible for Wai-gun until she fully discharged her specific economic obligations to her family. Furthermore, as Wai-gun and her contemporaries were aware, marriage, however desirable on other grounds, would entail even greater subordination to a new family unit, that of the husband.

Dating and marriage

On principle, Mother wanted Wai-gun to marry someone from Tai-shan county, and she got busy arranging this when Wai-gun was only 17.

"Mother wants me to marry for money. She wanted to fix me up with a Taishanese who lives in America so I could later bring in the rest of my brothers and sisters to study. Mother would have arranged it through friends and relatives."

"What do you think of this arrangement?" I asked.

"There would be many practical difficulties. Maybe we'd have money, but maybe not. Many Chinese in the United States are shop-keepers, and that means I'd be working in the shop all day long, and that's a difficult life! Even though the man Mother found might claim that he had a high-paying job, he might not have such a job at all! You can't really check uo on his house and friends from her. I have a friend who entered an arranged marriage like that a few years back, but I don't know if it worked out. If she wasn't happy she wouldn't dare admit that she made a bad choice! Anyway, money isn't everything."

In certain cases, the arrangements would involve finding a reliable nosy relative or friend who knew many people or a professional match-maker who could collect the names of eligible bachelors, the former as a favor, the latter for pay. The names, photographs, and qualifications, including testimonies from relatives, would be presented to Mother, who would select from among them and show the candidates' material to Father, and then to Wai-gun. Such an arrangement might have had a chance of success in the small town/village setting where reputations were well known or knowable, but there were fewer likelihoods of success in an industrialized society that spanned the seas. Wai-gun made it clear from the outset that she was not prepared to go along.

Mother realized that her eldest daughter's wage packet would remain substantial for some years to come and, despite her ambition to achieve even greater family material success through Wai-gun's marriage to a North American Taishanese, was enough of a realist to realize the formidable obstacles standing in the way of such a long-distance marriage. Father was also willing to gamble his daughter to improve the whole family, in addition to his efforts to radically improve the family fortune at one stroke through his Tai-shan relatives. But when both his daughter and his wife pulled back from such a gamble, Father went along with their decisions.

When she was 18, Wai-gun became enamored of Chen-kwok, the roommate of "Brother," Kung-ngai, who was an active participant in the magazine-reading and Chinese-culture circle revolving around sworn brother. Chen-kwok was a warehouseman of cloth and he earned a modest wage, a little more than Wai-gun's, although his work was steadier and he had a greater chance of promotion. Most important to Wai-gun was their common experience and viewpoints.

"Chen-kwok is my first boyfriend. Chen-kwok is intelligent, thoughtful, and decisive, and fits my marriage standards. While I also know how to make up my mind, I do not want to have to make all the crucial decisions. His salary is not too bad. But most important, Chen-kwok is someone with whom I can have serious talks, someone who is not Westernized, and who likes things Chinese."

The wish to share common experiences with a spouse, which pervades the yough culture as a whole, directly contradicted the style of marriage in her parents' generation, in which companionship was secondary. Their long working hours allowed Wai-gun's parents little time together. Besides, Father had labeled Mother a peasant woman, effectively denying her the status of equal partner. Whereas Mother accepted this inequality, Wai-gun would not. She rejected the sort of marriage where a wife would work long hours behind the counter of a family store, because "sharing interests" meant much more to her than common labor in a family business. "Sharing" meant not only joint decision making but also having cultural and political interests and friends in common throughout the marriage.

Wai-gun enumerated other features of an ideal marriage partner. Her prospective mate Chen-kwok was 4 or 5 years her senior, an age gap that accommodated their similar peer interests and also gave him an edge in maturity and experience. However, there was one critical difference in their backgrounds. The young man's family originated in southern Fukien province, in contrast to Wai-gun's Taishanese roots in southern Kwangtung province. The dialects and traditional cultures were correspondingly different. Although this was no obstacle to the young couple, who had grown up in the common culture of Cantonese-speaking Hong Kong, Wai-gun's mother openly objected to the match for this particular reason. Chen-kwok's father also objected for similar reasons. Although Wai-gun's Father never voiced his opinions regarding Chen-kwok and Wai-gun's relationship, I am sure that this headstrong man, who proudly quoted his Taishanese ancestry at every turn, shared Mother's suspicion of people of other ethnolinguistic groups, especially if they were not wealthy.

Wai-gun and Chen-kwok disagreed over the type of wedding to hold. Whereas Chen-kwok wanted to satisfy his family's wish to stage a lavish banquet for friends and relatives, which runs to thousands of dollars, Wai-gun preferred a simple ceremony at the marriage registry preceded by an exchange of small cakes and followed by a honeymoon. For such a travel wedding, no banquet is required. Wai-gun faced opposition from everyone over this matter. Her mother insisted that a banquet was necessary. The family would lose face if their eldest child was not married in style.

"Mother doesn't want me to have the travel wedding. She prefers the feast because she's conservative. Without it people would gossip about us, saying that we are stingy and didn't want to invite friends. A travel wedding is a bit like running away from home. They'd say that Chen-kwok and I are avoiding social recognition of the marriage."

Despite her views regarding the wedding ceremony, Wai-gun was no rebel in regard to the marriage itself. She planned to be respectful and obedient to her future mother-in-law, who was "getting old" at 52. Chen-kwok's mother was eager for him to marry. Parents save a long time for such moments, and Chen-kwok's mother had just made a down payment on a small two-bedroom apartment in a crowded Hong Kong district where the three of them would reside, in anticipation of the event.

"Yes, I do expect to live there with my mother-in-law," Wai-gun explained. "We get along quite well, although of course we are very polite to each other at present."

After her marriage, Wai-gun expected to continue working as long as possible, but she hoped for early motherhood, "We Chinese marry because we want to bear the future generation. If there's any financial reason not to have children right away, then we just don't get married right then, because we're afraid that birth control might interfere with having children. Probably I'll have two or three and then take pills or get my tubes cut. We Chinese are afraid to follow you Westerners and use birth control before we have children, just in case something goes wrong and we lose our fertility."

Wai-gun's mistrust of the pill was common among my respondents in Hong Kong, as well as among those Chinese women I interviewed in Singapore (Salaff, in preparation). The reasoning of Wai-gun and her friends was that having children, especially sons, was essential for a woman to be accepted into her newly established family. Traditionally, the woman was blamed if she did not carry forward the ancestral line of her husband. Young married women were apt to follow their in-laws' advice and experience, thus taking no modern chemical concoction like the pill until they had given birth to that son. If they did take the pill and then did not have a son, they would be blamed for having interfered with nature. Contemporary media reports on the harmful side effects of the pill further helped to justify these women's avoidance of it and of modern contraceptives in general.

Wai-gun did not expect her mother-in-law to help with the housework. "It would not be right. She's of the older generation, and *we* have to help her. However, Chen-kwok will pitch in to help in the house."

Wai-gun anticipated that these obligations would require her to abandon most of her peer activities. Wai-gun did not expect her husband and mother-in-law to tolerate her continued peer activities, which would signify to them that she was not accepting the marital obligations of child care and housework: "I will regret having to give up these activities with my friends. I'd like to postpone marriage for a while because of this. But in exchange, I will gain many other interests to share with my husband."

Wai-gun's remark on postponing the marriage was prophetic, because a serious interfamily rift developed over the timing of the nuptials. As the eldest child and only son, Chen-kwok was expected to marry immediately and to present his mother with a grandson. Wai-gun's family might have swallowed their objections to a Fukien partner if the marriage could have been delayed several years. The reasons for this demand were again pecuniary: As long as she stayed engaged but unmarried, Wai-gun would have continued to swell the family purse.

It is common in Hong Kong for courting couples in their late teens or early 20s to become engaged and then continue in their respective occupations for several years in order to contribute financially to their families. Most of the engagements contracted among my twenty-eight working girls and their siblings exceeded 12 months, and some continued for more than 5 years. In these cases the working daughters invariably maintained economic contributions of well over half of their wages to the family's budget. Therefore, Wai-gun believed that she could for 2 or 3 more years retain Chen-kwok's devotion while satisfying her family's need for the wages. Furthermore, she believed that Chen-kwok's commitment to her was strong enough to withstand the family's demand that he marry in short order.

"Mother has told me that she wants me to marry in my mid-twenties. That's three or four years from now. She may not care for Chen-kwok, but I mustn't wait too long, otherwise she might be stuck with an old maid!

Chen-kwok's mother tried to schedule the match within the year by promising to underwrite both the banquet and a travel wedding that the couple desired. Like Wai-gun, Chen-kwok realized that his mother's offer would give rise to obligations later. Wai-gun put it this way: "Later, if Chen-kwok and I come in conflict with his mother over family issues, she will try to argue, 'Do as I suggest. After all, I paid for your wedding.' " Moreover, this projected expenditure would not materially benefit Wai-gun's household. As far as Wai-gun's parents were concerned, therefore, the sweeteners proffered on her fiancé's side could not possibly balance 3 years of continued income from their working daughter. And Wai-gun, used to seeing family matters through the eyes of her parents, had to acknowledge the merits of their position.

The affection and esteem bonding Wai-gun and Chen-kwok were not strong enough to withstand the intense and single-tracked pressures of their respective families. Wai-gun obeyed her parents' strictures to delay marriage and rebuffed the bid of Chen-kwok's mother for an early wedding, and Chen-kwok accepted his own elders' plans for him. Chen-kwok's parents managed through relatives a match for him with a young woman in a village neighboring his father's home town in Fukien. Chen-kwok was dispatched to his father's relatives, who arranged an elaborate ceremony uniting him with his newfound bride. A few days after his village wedding, Chen-kwok bid farewell to her and returned to his home and job in Kowloon. (The bride remained with Chen-kwok's elderly grandparents because she lacked emigration papers and was needed to perform the important tasks of caring for the elderly generation still in the village and maintaining Chen-kwok's ancestral home.)

This abrupt turn of events crushed Wai-gun, who shouldered part of the blame for her sorrow because she had permitted herself an engagement to a man her parents fundamentally disapproved of. Because she accepted this level of responsibility and from birth was trained that parental judgment is wise, Wai-gun never seemed to display anger at her parents or even feelings of disappointment and bitterness over her rejection by Chen-kwok.

Mother failed to share Wai-gun's sorrow, saying "I told you so" and exuding triumph at her confirmation that the Fukienese were impatient and unreliable in family affairs. I was not aware that anyone in Wai-gun's family except perhaps Elder Brother and Second Sister secretly commiserated with her.

Wai-gun stopped seeing her former friends, who like most Hong Kong youths considered engagements generally binding and regarded Wai-gun as a failure in her main role in life. Shing-wa alone remained loyal, but she had her own budding romance and had little time for Wai-gun. Even more damaging to Wai-gun was the demise of her ideal of a marriage by choice. As a consequence of losing her friends, Wai-gun hesitated to visit her former haunts for fear of being embarrassed by running into Chen-kwok or even Kung-ngai, who was inevitably identified with Chen-kwok.

Wai-gun's mind was in a turmoil, and the only solution she could think of was to leave home. Wai-gun desperately considered trying to obtain factory work in Singapore but was realistic enough to set it aside because she lacked the training to become a lead girl, the only job for which garment factories were recruiting Hong Kong workers. As for Chen-kwok, he was able to continue his main family roles and obligations and, as I was to learn later, sought out opportunities to continue the relationship with Wai-gun.

Did Wai-gun's match founder on new or old grounds? I asked myself. New elements in the affair were Wai-gun's willingness to oppose her mother on the issues of cultural background and wedding banquet. Wai-gun was marrying because she judged her young man worthy, not because her parents had deemed him suitable. In these respects, the match was appropriate to Hong Kong contemporary life.

But this broken romance certainly contained many traditional features. Wai-gun and Chen-kwok had long been trained to a sense of family obligation, which they both ranked higher than a love marriage. In my opinion, as narrow-minded as Wai-gun's mother and father may have been about Chen-kwok's ancestry, this was not the prime consideration in her parents' opposition to her early wedding. Rather, Mother knew that she and Father were in poor health and unable to earn much, and Mother's insistence that Wai-gun delay marriage more than likely was due to her foreboding that the family's fortunes would gradually worsen when her illness and that of her husband progressed.

Wai-gun herself realized that by marrying and hence withdrawing her income from the family at that point she would dash all hopes of her younger sisters and brothers receiving higher education. Eventually, then, it was the family appeal to her economic obligations that swayed Wai-gun to postpone and thereby nullify the prospects of the match. And it was because of his obligations to continue the family line that her fiancé turned to his mother rather than to Wai-gun.

The resolution of this love dilemma by tradition, wherein the parents' wishes won out over the wishes of the young couple, bore striking resemblances to Chinese marriage tragedies of classical and popular literature. In Wai-gun's case, however, the old and new were inextricably mixed. Long-standing features of family life (the obedience of the eldest daughter to her family) were evoked in the service of new family goals. Those were the raised expectations that daughters would contribute to the family economy until the family had achieved a more comfortable life.

Ultimately, Wai-gun had to choose between her peers and her family over the issue of marriage versus maintenance of the family cycle. If her family's economic position had gradually improved, as had been anticipated before the seriousness of her parents' illnesses became apparent, then Wai-gun might not have had to choose so definitively between her fiancé and her family. But such was not the case. The failure of the family wage economy posed the issue clearly and the romantic impulses that Wai-gun felt succumbed in the struggle.

The family cycle runs its course: summary

Wai-gun was constricted by her family's straitened economic status, her sibling position, the personalities of her parents, and the two siblings next in line. Ill health dealt a devastating blow to this impoverished family, as it does in all societies lacking comprehensive medical care benefits. Even in the best of times, as during her adolescence, the parents' poorly remunerated work barely kept the family afloat. From her early teens Wai-gun was responsible for maintaining an unbroken economic input to the family, and her training, and the centripetal norms that fostered it, were so thorough that despite numerous inducements, she never reneged on her obligations.

A fleeting period of family good fortune did occur when wage earners outnumbered dependents. Wai-gun was 18 and her teenage siblings were 16 and 13 years old. Wai-gun then had the greatest opportunity to enjoy a partly free adolescence. She was able to afford music lessons, spend money on outings, and more deeply explore the cultural heritage of China's historic civilization through art, music, and literature.

Regrettably, Wai-gun's family could not savor their modicum of prosperity. The parents' recurrent and ultimately fatal illnesses submerged the family deep in poverty soon after Wai-gun reached early adulthood. Although I knew that he was not faring well, I was stunned to learn from Wai-gun when I revisited Hong Kong in the summer of 1976, hoping once again to experience the warmth of her family life, that Father had passed away from liver cancer in 1975. Mother's health steadily worsened until she, too, lay on her deathbed, when I paid my final visit. Mother died later that year. The long-term illnesses and early demise of the parental breadwinners taxed the family unit severely, and its coherence began to dissolve. The unusual disarray of the family apartment reflected this – the children were working and nursing their ill mother in shifts and lacked the time and will to keep the household in any semblance of order. Wai-gun naturally took over in an effort to keep her brothers and sisters together, and she organized a new household division of labor, in which each brother and sister received an assignment: work, attend school in day or night sessions, and nurse Mother at other times.

Wai-gun arranged for Father's burial. Their relatives gave only the minimum assistance; his brother did the necessary paperwork and visited various clan and other benevolent associations to raise the money for the coffin, but "they asked for cab fare and money for lunch to do even that. None of our relatives helped us out financially at all," she remarked in a feeble, dispirited voice. Father's brother did not attend the funeral, and only the immediate family saw him buried in their kinsmen's Chai Wan gravesite. At her side, however, was none other than Chen-kwok, whom she still saw occasionally and who was able to give her moral support.

The third child, Ying-gun, married when she had not quite reached age 18. Her Cantonese husband obtained employment in Western Europe through his relatives, and the two left Hong Kong, leaving their infant child in the care of the husband's family and separating themselves from the family altogether. The fourth and fifth, both girls, were pressed into caring and tending roles. The two youngest boys continued their schooling.

When Wai-gun took leadership of the family, the other areas of her life were transformed. She was forced to terminate her evening classes, lacking the time and spirit to continue. Whereas Father's outspokenly negative views on political participation and trade union organizing had once dampened Wai-gun's ardor for entering the political arena, she was able after his death to develop her own thinking and transferred her commitment from schooling to a garment workers' union affiliated with the "patriotic" Federation of Trade Unions. In 1976 she found there a completely new set of friends who were innocent of any involvement with her shattered peer group and engagement. Wai-gun was thrilled that the union lionized traditional Chinese folk culture and she attended folk dances and songfests in the union hall itself. The union addressed the problem of industrial exploitation in Hong Kong with more self-confidence than the individualistic and essentially defensive stance of the loosely organized cultural revival groups. Even though the Hong Kong working class does not now call for fundamental social change in the colony, it is inconceivable that Wai-gun could ever before have identified herself with such a potentially revolutionary organization.

Summary: a comparison

The work lives of Mae, Wai-gun, and Suyin were spent mainly in light manufacturing for export. They put in long hours for relatively low wages and their job tenure was uncertain, but the availability of work was a certainty. They had little hope of advancement to improved positions. Their conditions of work were not completely uniform, however, and different management ideologies were associated with workplaces of different sizes and nationalities. Wai-gun toiled at assembly operations in large plants that applied few normative or ideological inducements paternalistically for workers to understand or adopt management perspectives. Mae worked in small shops in which paternalistic controls over the work force were activated, and Suyin's shop itself was operated by a member of her family, who drew upon family ties to commit her to the enterprise.

These variations in management ideologies were limited to market conditions that were determined by Hong Kong's role in the international division of labor. Hong Kong is a locality where relatively skilled, inexpensive labor is available, and profit maximization is the key to firm survival; profits are valued more than personal relationships, even in paternalistic firms. The work setting reinforced prevailing Hong Kong definitions of acceptable jobs for women, because factory duties did not compete with women's identification with family roles. The jobs these three held did not provide enough security, pay, or meaningful experiences to compete with their dedication to the family.

The pressures to conform to family needs led these women directly into the labor force. Sheer poverty necessitated their working to ameliorate the family's subsistence-level income. There were differences in family earnings of the trio, not primarily due to their fathers' job, because fathers experienced little improvement in salary or authority throughout their work cycles. Rather, family earnings differed because the household head was absent, economically. Wai-gun's family was most impoverished. Mae's household budget was the fullest of the three – Wai-gun's and Suyin's fathers put little into the household income because of illness and separation, respectively.

The accumulation of wage earners was the key to the family economic station. Each of the three families expected to and did experience some improvement in their household finances that was generally consistent with the family cycle. As the children entered their wage-earning adolescent years, the number of earners exceeded dependents and family finances invariably improved.

Because the crucial feature of family income was the family cycle, the daughter's ordinal sibling position determined the family demands upon her. The eldest daughter invariably matured at a time when there were few workers and many dependents; hence her contribution to the family was especially heavy, and she was expected to meet its demands without shirking. In contrast, a young sibling found life less exacting, as long as the eldest daughter fulfilled her expected role. Thus, should an unforeseen setback to the family fortunes occur, as happened in Wai-gun's family, the youngest daughter was not always prepared to meet the renewed demands upon her.

The overall level of economic prosperity in Hong Kong was shifting as these daughters grew up and this further contributed to their experiences. For example, when these three were young girls in the 1960s, the limited economic surplus available not only in their families but in society circumscribed their opportunities for higher education or Anglo-Chinese schooling, necessary for job mobility.

The subordinate position of women in the Hong Kong family further limited their opportunities. If they had been sons, despite the limited opportunities available to people of their social class for education or jobs, they would have had a different set of options. They might have gone to school longer or been trained for a job that would eventually pay a higher wage, as would a skilled job.

Nevertheless, their work itself opened opportunities – by providing pocket money, experiences, and friends – and freed these Hong Kong daughters from household tasks for leisure activities for their own enjoyment. Each had her own approach to work and peers. Each in her own way enjoyed her work and sought to do a good job at it. Mae designated interpersonal experiences at the workplace as most important. She helped her co-workers at the job and maintained a group of friends whose link was their work. Wai-gun searched for her roots as a Chinese. She viewed organizing for social change as having more of an impact on workers' lives than the informal networks of friends, which Mae viewed as an end in itself. Suyin was least interested in her work and downplayed activities with her coworkers in pursuit of her own pleasures.

All three peers found solutions to existential problems in daily life, such as job selection, dating, and clothes, as well as to more abstract tensions and contradictions engendered by relationships at the workplace or in the family. Suyin's peers provided her superficial solutions to her daily frustrations by advocating consumerism. Wai-gun's peers provided solutions of active engagement with the political order.

Peers did not completely replace demands of their families upon these three. When peer activities and the core areas of family economics and bearing the next generation conflicted, family needs prevailed. Thus, Wai-gun could not marry out of her ethnoliguistic group, nor could she marry while her family needed her income. Nevertheless, if family needs prevailed, it was also obvious that they did not circumscribe women's lives in the same complete fashion that they had in traditional China. It was the admixture of obligations to family, opportunities for work, and friendships that, by providing women with a broader range of alternatives than that of following the more limited patterns of their grandmothers, mothers, or elder sisters, characterized the experience of growing up in contemporary Hong Kong. Family demands have thus become more circumscribed than for women growing up in rural China. Industrial Hong Kong today gives some space for the manifestation of different styles of association and different goals of young women.

In sum, however different their personal styles may have been, they nevertheless affected their contribution to the family very little in the core areas. Each woman reconciled her obligations to her family with the pull of nonfamilial opportunities in a different manner, yet each did so in favor of the family.

3. Women in the service sector

Every year hundreds of thousands of tourists visit Hong Kong from all parts of the world, making tourism the colony's second largest industry.[1] Their main activity is shopping in the arcades of downtown Kowloon (Tsim Sha Tsui) and Victoria (Hong Kong Island), which have been built for the tastes and needs of the typical 3-day visitor. The most modern and grandiose of these is the Ocean Terminal, situated at the communications hub of Tsim Sha Tsui. Ocean-going passenger vessels can dock alongside the terminal to discharge passengers directly into glittering tiers of shops, restaurants, and art galleries. An internal arcade of the Ocean Terminal links it to another shopping concourse adjoining the large, luxurious Hong Kong Hotel and the Ocean Movie Theatre. A short stroll through the crowded Star Ferry Concourse fronting the terminals brings the visitor to a large China arts and crafts department store offering a wide range of artifacts and antiques from the People's Republic. The concourse serves as a bustling conduit for the tightly packed throngs of workers who ride the Star Ferry to and from offices and other places of business in the island's Central District. At the gate of the Star Ferry crossing, vendors hawk prolific Chinese vernacular press and newspapers from all over the world, usually available the day after publication.

The Tsim Sha Tsui (Hung Hom) terminus of the Hong Kong–Canton Railway empties swarms of travelers at all hours from the New Territories into the Ocean Terminal–Star Ferry hub and twice a day carries Hong Kong passengers north to Sam Chun, the gateway to China's Kwangtung province. The nature of these China-bound travelers depends upon the season. Executives of transnational corporations the world over sojourn biannually in Hong Kong where, after sampling its commercial and tourist attractions, they board a train (there is no air service yet) for the Canton spring and autumn trade fairs. At the Lunar New Year, in contrast, long queues of black-garbed working-class Hong Kong residents board the railway toting old valises filled with used

123

clothing, antibiotics, and Chinese herbal remedies, all scarce in China, which they will hand over to their relatives. En route they wear several layers of clothing, even in sweltering weather, but they invariably return wearing just one suit and shouldering wooden carrying poles. Suspended from these are large clay cooking pots, empty wicker thermos jugs, bottles of peanut oil, and a squawking chicken or two, all of which are cheaper "across the way." These overburdened passengers must hire porters for the ferry crossing and rickshaw drivers or taxis to take them home, and I have often wondered just how much money they save in the end by these purchases.

The Ocean Terminal is a city in miniature, consisting of three concourses crammed with shops, large Chinese and Western restaurants and coffee bars, and nightclubs offering discotheques, Mandarin dance music, and floor shows of Chinese entertainers and acrobats. The terminal remains open well past midnight every day of the year to serve the tourists bedded at the nearby luxury hotels. Hong Kong's European residents also shop at the Ocean Terminal for Western-made products, "guaranteed" tailor-made clothes, and other luxury items. Well-dressed Chinese families stroll and window-shop in the terminal's glass-lined arcades and sip soda and munch cake at the centrally located Maxim's coffee shop. Families of all stations shop at stores selling mass-produced Western clothing, like Dodwells, which markets Marks and Spencer's products, and Swindons' Bookstore, where poetry and murder mysteries from Europe rub jackets with a splendid array of books on China for tourists and scholars alike.

Chinese intellectuals young and old gather at the attractive Café do Brasil, easily accessible along the corridor that joins the Ocean Terminal to the Ocean Centre. Salesmen frequently meet their customers at the small but well-polished Café, one of the few places where, in addition to afficionados of coffee and conversation, weary shoppers and salespersons can while away an unhurried hour over a simple brew. (I was told that the Café's Portuguese owner does not make a profit and operates his retreat solely for personal enjoyment, but this is improbable anywhere in Hong Kong.)

Several of my Chinese factory worker friends and interviewees visited the Ocean Terminal to window-shop along its corridors and even patronized the Chinese nightclub restaurants for weddings or special dates. The majority, however, purchased necessities much more cheaply in the lanes and alleys of Hong Kong's Chinese neighborhoods and never set foot in the Ocean Terminal, although they used its front entrance to rendezvous with friends on Sunday for picnics and movies, as did most active youths.

Male sales clerks in the shops of the Ocean Terminal and the other fashionable arcades dress well in tailor-made suits and speak fluent and persuasive English. They serve behind the counter for 10 or more hours a day (Chaney, 1971). Girls are more often found as clerks at Dodwells and other major department stores, where their hours are somewhat shorter, but sales commissions are not paid. They speak serviceable English, and by working in the Ocean Terminal and the major hotel complex they are situated in the center of the bustling tourist industry.

Choi-hung (Rainbow), Sa-li, and Ci-li held jobs that brought them into direct contact with overseas tourists and Hong Kong expatriates. Rainbow was a waitress at the Café do Brasil, and Sa-li served coffee at the Hong Kong Hotel next door. Ci-li was a day servant in the homes of Western businessmen and consular officals. The fathers of Rainbow and Ci-li were petty bourgeois– an artisan and a shopkeeper– and Sa-li's father was a waiter. All three of these young women were able to enroll in Anglo-Chinese secondary schools, where they learned English, but only Ci-li, whose family earned the highest income of the three, completed her schooling as far as form V (grade 11 in U.S. high school). Rainbow and Sa-li both began their work careers in factories; after that they were personally and occupationally on the move, although their service employment stood no higher than the status level of their families. Ci-li adopted middle-class values of achievement and saving money for social mobility, whereas Rainbow chose and was strongly influenced by a work milieu permeated by cash transactions, the pop and entertainment media, and the creed of new generational independence.

The jobs held by these service girls distinguished them from the factory proletariat introduced in Chapter 2. Not only was their formal education better and their English more proficient, but they were more highly paid and interacted substantively with Westerners. Their jobs depended on the skills and poise they could muster to attend customers and residents from abroad, whereas factory workers have few opportunities to meet Westerners face-to-face. Factory girls may be attracted by the mass media and inspired by European and North American consumption patterns, but they seldom encounter anyone in the social marketplace whose life-style is depicted in these media. In sociological terms, the factory girls have no meaningful reference groups of opinion leaders who would support an outright adoption of Western behavior (Katz and Lazarsfeld, 1964; Klapper, 1960).

The service girls are influenced even more directly than are the factory workers in their work, home, and leisure habits by the international capitalist economy and the patterns of consumption and culture with which it has saturated Hong Kong. Their jobs not only depend upon the buoyancy of the world economy, which in general determines the volume of tourists and the cash they spend, but they are also strongly keyed to the superstructural norms and values of a commercial and colonial entrepôt.

These three girls who served contrasting clienteles differed significantly. Theorists who suggest the inexorable destruction of the fabric of traditional society by industrialization affirm that jobs shape social identity. If we apply that view to those three women, Rainbow, whose Café do Brasil was frequented by youths, and who was closest of the three service girls to the Western milieu, would be the most affected by contemporary Western youth mores. Ci-li, employed in established middle-class homes, would then be influenced by more staid and permanent bourgeois values, and Sa-li, who worked in an ultramodern hotel but did not mingle with guests, would have been the least influenced by their values. Furthermore, if work environment determines personal identity in such a linear way, this trio, far more than their blue-collar peers, would have perceived (in degrees varying with their Western exposure) the attractions and need for independence from the family. In effect, they would have more likely identified closely with a youth culture advocating independence, spontaneity, and depreciating family obligations than would have the factory women.

Of the three women, only Rainbow was determined to escape family bonds, which she postponed until she had completed her designated input to the family as befitting her position in it. She did not succeed. The lives of all three are far more complex than can be encompassed in the singular wish for freedom, and the causes of their strivings are more varied than predicted by the disjunctive theory of the family-shattering impact of industry. The continuative view demonstrates that work milieu does not condition life-style in any elementary way. People are initially attracted to their place of work for many reasons, and in two of these three women's family backgrounds we already see evidence of the tourist industry. (Rainbow's father manufactured tourist artifacts, and Sa-li owed her position at the Hong Kong Hotel in Tsim Sha Tsui to her brother, a waiter there.)

Ingham (1970) studied British industrial settings that ranged from assembly-line machinery to small craft shop and described substantial differences in workers' attitudes toward those work settings. Contrasting attitudes toward authority, autonomy in work, coworkers, and the craft prevailed in these varied work areas, suggesting that a filtering or selection process occurs wherein workers move in and out of different work settings. If satisfied, they try to remain in a particular type of workplace and, if dissatisfied, quickly leave for another, more compatible, position. Ingham's findings that workers' attitudes precede their job setting cast further serious doubt upon the disjunctive theoretical position. The implications of those findings for the Hong Kong service girls are that work pace and technology cannot be singled out as the major factors that unilaterally determine changes in workers' lives; the workers themselves exercise some choice in selection of a job with a particular work milieu. Thus those women workers who are keenly interested in a modern workplace will choose that sort of work setting, whereas those who do not care to cater to the consumer culture will leave for a more conventional work environment.

Modern work culture further affects the lives of women toilers in varying ways according to their levels of education, language stream, and such domestic factors as birth order, number of wage earners in the family, and even personality. These and other heterogeneous factors must be taken into account when we examine the ways that the service sector ideology of self-fulfillment affects aspirations in the choices and outcomes of peers, dating, and marriage.

Finally, it is important to note that the freedom putatively available to the youths who manage to break from their families under the influence of independently earned wages and the individualist ideology pervading the marketplace is not supported by the social institutions that govern the lives of working-class women. The force of such an ideology cannot in the sociological and political senses be very deep or long lasting, and it turns out that the families remain recognizably centripetal as they adjust, reincorporate, and ultimately prevail over the unsettling effects of the worlds of entertainment, sales, and services.

Introducing Rainbow

Taking the picturesque name from the popular Hollywood version of the *Wizard of Oz,* Choi-hung called herself Rainbow. As is conventional in Anglo-Chinese education, Choi-hung was dubbed with a Christian name (Rachel) by a secondary school teacher. Most Chinese girls keep these first names, but some later reject them as alien and readopt their original Chinese names. Equally uninspired by traditional Chinese culture and staid Christianity, Choi-hung borrowed hers from an American film.

At the age of almost 18, Rainbow quit secondary school in 1973 to become a head waitress at the Café do Brasil. She was the most Western-looking Hong Kong girl I knew, and on our first outing together she donned boys' sneakers and blue jeans with ragged bottoms instead of the modish, bell-bottomed Apple Jeans her friends were purchasing in the Jeans-East Boutique in Tsim Sha Tsui. Her hair was shoulder length, and her grooming and demeanor suited her place of work. Rainbow's English slang put her reasonably at ease with Anglo-Saxon men. Underlying her adoption of a symbolically Western couture were the profound tensions in Rainbow's life: the responsibilities to the family in and for which she had been reared versus a long-standing concern to maximize her own personal living and growth space and individually paced way of life. Rainbow was the only Hong Kong woman I knew who was willing to take decisive steps to attain her personal dreams, even if it meant separation from her family, despite their continued need for her assistance. She did so in a particular way that reemphasized the reciprocal relationship she had with her family: She asserted that because she had already repaid to them the debt she had for her upbringing, she then had the right to strike out on her own. The concept that all persons have the birthright to select their own path in life is not part of Hong Kong Chinese upbringing and education, and no working woman I met, Rainbow included, believed that she had no family obligations whatsoever.

Home

Rainbow was the firstborn of five children from Father's second marriage. Father's primary wife lived in another part of Hong Kong with her 40-year-old son and his family. Because she had a son to support her, the first wife received no regular allowance from Father, although she received the customary "red packets" of gaily wrapped silver coins and gifts at the major yearly festivals.

Father was an ivory carver whose workshop filled one of the three ninth-floor apartment rooms in a mixed lower-middle working-class residential and factory area situated between North Point and Shau Kei Wan. The walk-up flat was built in 1964, during one of Hong

Kong's prolonged water shortages, and since seawater was used in construction, the pitted and cracked cement walls were unstable. Several other dwellings erected during the seawater period have collapsed, and this one looked three times its age. Nevertheless the family was glad to relocate there from its previous squatter shack on a Shau Kei Wan hillside. Because of the absence of an elevator, the family paid only $40 a month rent for their bedroom, kitchen, bath, and living room/workroom suite.

Railroad flats lined the main stairwell of Rainbow's narrow tenement. The front door opened into a dingy bedroom, with double bunk beds on the opposite wall. If there were windows in this room, they admitted so little light that I could make out only the outlines of the furniture, and I had to rely on a naked overhead light bulb to illuminate the way. To the left was a bright corner with three genuine windows, to which the visitor was at once drawn. Two workbenches were fitted into the corner nooks, one used by Rainbow's father and the other by her 16-year-old brother. Suspended next to the window was a bird cage, and a rooster strutted up and down the corridor and hens clucked from their coop under the kitchen sink. A dog and several cats rounded out the domestic menagerie.

A venerable craft

On my first visit, Father returned at 10 a.m. from breakfast in a teahouse toting the caged bird, which he had taken there for fresh air and admiration. Father was cheerful and outgoing, and on my second visit he invited me to attend his 60th birthday party banquet the following evening. Although I ate their simple lunches on many subsequent occasions, my work schedule unfortunately did not permit me to attend this banquet. But father announced with great pleasure that at a nearby restaurant, six tables of guests, about sixty people total, would come to pay their respects. When a man is 60 years old and has lived through a full cycle of the Chinese calendar, his family generally holds a special celebration. At 60, Father was attaining longevity, wisdom, and a new social standing in the community. His primary wife, first son and daughter born to this union, along with his grandchildren would be in attendance. Other relatives and business clients were also included in the gala occasion. They would bring gifts and scrolls. Before the war they would have kowtowed to this venerable man, but now a simple nod of recognition suffices.

Father was keen to tell me of his life as an ivory craftsman, which he began as an apprentice in Canton: "Nowadays, young people don't have the patience to apprentice for five years, like I did. They usually train for only three years and then consider themselves journeymen."

Father executed the designs and trained his children to help him carry out the simple, routine jobs, done on machines requiring little manual dexterity, such as ivory burnishing. At the time of my 1973 visit, only his first wife's son practiced ivory carving as a trade; the rest of the children devoted their spare time to working with Father. But Father's eyesight was already failing, and soon either his children or someone else would need to shoulder his work. Father was loath to seek outside successors and, moreover, this would be difficult to accomplish.

"Have you taught other people the trade?" I asked.

"Yes, I trained several who have all become *si-fu* [masters] . I haven't instructed anyone in the past few years, though, because nobody wants to learn."

Father therefore considered his sons to be the only possible inheritors of his trade, his suppliers, and his clientele. Because Rainbow was female, she was not the one to carry on Father's handicrafts, of which the family was so rightfully proud. Nor was she looked to as the family breadwinner after Father could no longer carry on his trade. Instead of training this capable eldest daughter in the intricate skills of design, carving, and fine finishing of the pieces, Father treated Rainbow as an extra hand to perform rough work under his supervision.

Some workers took jobs home from other ivory-carving establishments and were paid by the piece, but Father characteristically preferred to purchase the stock himself and sell the finished work to tourist outlets. Some of the sales took place in arcades like those of the Ocean Terminal and the tourist hotels.

"This way I can have more control over what I do, and I don't have to sweat frantically to complete work on someone else's schedule. I rarely carve large pieces, because the initial investment has become too big, and sales prospects are difficult. I make many snuff bottles like these," he said, cradling a small bottle in his palm. "First, I design and carve out the model, and then let my sons and daughter do the filing down. I invest about five or six dollars in materials for a snuff bottle one-half palm size, and require a day to finish it. We can sell such a piece to a Tsim Sha Tsui tourist shop for about eighteen dollars, which means that we earn about ten dollars per piece."

This sum slightly exceeded the daily wage of a piece-rated skilled male factory worker in basic industry.

Father's business worsened in the early 1970s because of the steep rise in the price of ivory and the cost of living. He explained that Hong Kong craftsmen could not compete with carvers from China, whose products were "cheaper and better." He claimed further that "China buys ivory form South Africa in large shipments, which boosts the price of this commodity in Hong Kong. China's craftsmen are also better trained, and they have no worries about feeding their family, quite unlike us in Hong Kong."

Speculating about future employment in the occupation, he continued, "As a matter of fact many workers have returned to China because of better working conditions there."

"Do you also want to return?" I asked.

"No, I couldn't adjust to life there. In Hong Kong I visit the teahouse several times a day, but in China I could only go once a day. There are so many things that I have gotten used to in Hong Kong that simply aren't available in China."

At first Father insisted that ivory carving would never die out in Hong Kong because it commanded a market separate from those of China. But then he immediately appeared to contradict himself: "Before Nixon went to China, Chinese exports to many countries were restricted, while Hong Kong enjoyed freer overseas markets. Now that Chinese handicrafts, sell everywhere, more people will buy from the mainland instead of Hong Kong."

It is unlikely, however, that any individual can assess the future of Hong Kong artisanship and the market for traditional crafts, and this must have worried Father. Yet at his age he had to insist that not only his eldest son, who was trained when the trade was flourishing, but also his younger sons help in his workshop, and he coached them gradually to take over all duties from him. Thus, he uneasily recognized that he was tying Rainbow's brothers to a career with uncertain prospects. But Rainbow's family could never expect to survive unless several members of the younger generation carved diligently alongside Father.

Home and family

Mother had long worked outside the home in unskilled jobs in garment workshops, such as snipping threads from garments before they were pressed by a more skilled worker. When Rainbow was young, Mother worked a full 9-hour workday, 7 days a week. As first daughter, Rainbow was saddled with sizable family responsibilities; consequently she intermittently left school for 6 months at a time to keep house and care for the younger children. Rainbow hauled water, washed and dried clothes, chopped wood for the cookstove, and prepared meals. "I could barely reach the pole to hang up the clothes," she recalled. Until age 12 she would return for a semester in school, only to drop out again. Then Father taught Rainbow to burnish ivory, and she joined him at the workbench while younger sisters assumed the major housework burdens. As a result of her patchy schooling, Rainbow at age 12 was several years behind her age group.

In Rainbow's home, the unique characteristics of all the family members were visible. Sixteen-year-old brother worked on ivory by the light of the window after school. His tools occupied one side of the workbench and his books (*The Old Man and the Sea* and several Japanese novels in Chinese translation) claimed the other half. A thoughtful lad, he liked to climb the hill behind home and play melodies on his flute while he gazed out over the horizon. Brother was ranked quite low academically in his class in an Anglo-Chinese secondary school, perhaps because he preferred reading novels and other self-assigned material to the rote memorization of texts, which is a hallmark of Hong Kong education.

Mother was taciturn and ventured only a quiet "Hello" when I entered the home and a polite apology for not serving "enough good food" at the luncheon I shared with the family. On this occasion she helped herself to a slice of delicatessen-bought roast pork, egg custard from her own breeding hens, and stir-fried green beans, then removed her rice bowl from the table, slid away on her stool, and finished dinner facing the wall as if she were silently quarreling with Father. Her wooden demeanor never became animated in my presence, unlike many other women I met socially. Mother never engaged in conversation with me, nor was she interested in demonstrating her cooking skills like the mothers of Ju-chen, Mae, I-ling, and others were proud to do. Perhaps she seldom cooked, since Father regularly returned from his morning walk with buns or other edibles from the teahouse or delicatessen. Rainbow confirmed my impression that Mother was much less social than Father and a rather despondent woman.

Rainbow had always behaved autonomously and revealed that she had never been afraid of adults, even when she was small, and was prepared to quarrel and even fight with her elders. "I'm like Mother.

We both argue with people, and sometimes shout at them. Several years ago, Mother even moved away from home for a while after a dispute with Father."

Rainbow also shared the stubborn independence of Father, whom she did not hesitate to confront when the occasion demanded. Rainbow did not openly resent helping her family until at adolescence she learned to identify and protect her own interests. Father tried to block her from attending secondary school for reasons not fully clear to me, but related to his real or imagined need for her to work full-time in the shop. Father saw no way that his daughter's higher education could help her carve ivory, and his horizons were limited to the family artisan enterprise. The labor power of this eldest daughter was far more useful to him in the short run than a better-educated Rainbow would be in the future.

When Rainbow was 14 and still responsible for the care of the three youngest, she decided to risk a bitter clash with Father by enrolling in a secondary school, and when he remained predictably adamant, she left home with the three siblings in her immediate care. She set up house in a vacant squatter's hut on the Shau Kei Wan hillside where her family had been squatters and where she still knew the neighbors. She proceeded to enroll in morning classes, and her charges were watched by a neighbor. Each afternoon she sent the children to primary school while she trudged off to work a 9-hour factory shift to support her brood. This lasted 6 months, during which Mother visited the hut regularly but concealed its location from Father. She reported to him the children's well-being but, not being skilled at negotiation, Mother could not bring together the strong-minded father-daughter pair. Father could not bear having his family so divided, and eventually having his family together under one roof became more important than sticking to his original dictum that girls should not be educated. When Father's will was finally broken by Rainbow's daring maneuver, "He begged us to come home," she recalled proudly. After her return home and resumption of schooling, Rainbow guarded her own interests even more vigorously, and at my suggestion that family needs could again be assigned priority over her own, she quickly retorted, "I have *already* repaid the costs of my upbringing to my family!

Rainbow's independence was also manifested in her resistance to the compulsory religious training at the English language missionary secondary school she attended. Denominational institutions offered many inducements for their students' conversion, and Christian stu-

dents had a greater likelihood of receiving scholarships to upper-
and postsecondary schools, obtaining employment in mission-related
organizations, and participating in a plethora of church-based youth
groups. Rainbow turned her back on all these opportunities. "No, I
didn't convert, because I'm strong!" she boasted. She left school –
not over theology, but because she was not "really scholarly" and was
more interested in earning money. She felt that it was right and proper
for her 16-year-old brother to continue school even if his grades weren't
high, because he, in contrast, had the "aptitude." By succumbing to the
temptation to earn money and leave school, Rainbow made the choice
endorsed by her parents, who would be the major benefactors of this
decision. This sacrifice of the daughter's long-range chances in favor of
short-term gains for the family and especially the brothers typified
the narrow range of opportunities of Hong Kong elder daughters.

"In spite of all our quarrels, I love my family and I enjoy living at
home," Rainbow countered when her coworkers and friends asked her
to move out and live with them. There was still a communication gap
separating Rainbow from Father and Mother, but she nonetheless
preferred the home environment, partly since Father became more
understanding of her and less severe and demanding. "Maybe it is advancing age that has changed him," she reflected. "He's much more
tolerant and accepting of me now." Father must have realized that
only by turning a blind eye to Rainbow's social life and dating and private banking of part of her income would he keep his eldest daughter
home.

Working in a coffee shop

Rainbow's first job after leaving secondary school was as a waitress in
the Café do Brasil. There were only three young women working at the
Café, and the one with the most seniority automatically became headwaitress, a position Rainbow eventually attained.

The petite Café do Brasil, located in the Ocean Terminal, Kowloon's
star tourist and shopping attraction, served coffee, fruit juice, cakes,
and pastry, but not the wide range of snacks available in other coffee
shops. The Café offered fragrant, freshly roasted and brewed Brazilian-
blend coffee, ranked by some the tastiest in town. Other coffee shops,
with larger kitchens and tables, sold soft drinks, ice cream, light snacks
of spaghetti, omelets, chicken, and hamburgers, plus the obligatory egg
rolls and fried rice. In this coffee shop, already a minor institution in
Hong Kong, friendly liaisons and business appointments took place, and

the emphasis was on subdued discussion rather than food consumption. To its Chinese clientele, the Café offered an alternative meeting place to the small noodle shops and teahouses specializing in *congee* (rice porridge) and *dim sum* ("little hearts" or small pastry snacks), where patrons were required to vacate the table as soon as the meal was consumed.

Rainbow worked from 9:30 to 5:00, with six weekdays off per month. Her work consisted of time-consuming coffee preparation, which required lugging heavy sacks of beans from the storage room behind the kitchen nook to the grinding machine at the counter, grinding the coffee for the day, brewing the coffee to order in individual small glass pots, cutting and serving the prepared cakes with the coffee, and billing the customers. It was not complicated work and her work days were not overly long, although she was always on her feet.

As headwaitress, Rainbow earned about $160 per month in basic salary and tips. With her seniority, she received 50% more of the tips than the other waitresses. Nevertheless, she professed to dislike her work. Switching from Cantonese to English, she emphatically declared, "This is a lousy job!" She resented in particular having to walk around pouring refills when another waitress would present the customer with the bill. Rainbow was not uncomfortable that customers might assume that the second cup was free and be shocked at the extra charge, but she disliked work that she considered undignified. "Sometimes I carry those coffee-bean bags from storage to the grinding machine at the counter. They weigh over one hundred pounds. Then I must walk around, pot in hand, like I am modeling something!" She was annoyed by the paternalism of the Portuguese manager, who required petty services from the other waitresses (taking his broken shoes to be repaired or fetching his daughter's clothing purchases from the Ocean Terminal shops). One of her workmates left the job because she saw the Café as a hangout for young men prowling for women, but Rainbow did not find this in itself objectionable.

"My dislike of the Café is not caused so much by the customers. It's not a costly place. Teddy boys hang out there, but if I were working in a more expensive spot it would be much worse. The more expensive the place, the more complicated it is. All those pimps and fat cats patronize high-priced restaurants and not the Café."

Rainbow worked primarily for the wage, and because her tips flowed from pleasantries to the patrons, she chatted smilingly with the middle-class Chinese and overseas habitués of the Café. Her tips afforded her some independence from Father, to whom she never disclosed her precise income. In fact, she donated $60 to her family each month and deposited the tips. She also developed a life-style to suit the milieu and further her independent spirit.

Rainbow knew she could not stay on at the Café do Brasil. She was almost 20 in 1974 and restaurants preferred to employ teenagers. She explained the difficulties of older women finding work. The main reasons she remained at the Café through 1974 was her inability to land a better-paying job. She had already saved $400, and when she succeeded in saving $200 more, she promised herself a year or so of traveling, not realizing that the sum saved would cover 1 month – not 1 year – abroad. When she first discussed her plans with me in mid-1973, she expected to visit a boyfriend in England. This plan was never realized. By June of the following year she was thinking of traveling through Southeast Asia with girlfriend employees at Ocean Terminal shops and nearby restaurants and bars. Two months later, however, she was considering marriage.

Father had only an inkling of Rainbow's plans, but he disapproved of what he knew. She was once more prepared to defy him, stating emphatically, "I have already given much of my life to my family, and my money as well! Now I want to live for myself!" Using English for emphasis, her voice rose with excitement, "Anyway, youth must be *free!*" She finally left the Café in late 1974 and lived at home on her savings. Under the impression that Rainbow had been temporarily laid off (a common occurrence in Hong Kong), her family did not complain of her temporary withdrawal of support from the budget. At the time, it was hard to predict whether she would resume work elsewhere or instead embark upon one of the trips about which she had long been dreaming, because she herself had not chosen between work or an escapade. She was certain only that "I need to enjoy myself and rest for a while before I decide anything."

Peer relations

Greatly influenced by the fashionable atmosphere of their workplaces, Rainbow and her coworkers spent much of their wages on clothing, which they sometimes purchased at fancy boutiques. Although they wore uniforms in the Café, the latest fashions were anticipated and admired in their circle.

The family relations of these shop girls were also affected by the values prevailing in the work and leisure environments. Rainbow's workmates were even less closely tied to their families than she was, and a number had already moved away away from home to share rented rooms. As Rainbow explained, "Their parents can't do anything to prevent this, because the girls are old enough to look after themselves."

It may appear unremarkable that waitresses in a big city rent rooms together, but the factory workers I knew did not believe that attaining the age of 20 necessarily merited physical separation and personal independence from the family. Instead, factory girls generally moved directly from one tightly knit family to another through marriage. Although their peer-group activities (evening classes, weekend parties, beach outings, picnics) helped them consolidate a separate identity, they engaged in these pursuits while living at home. I have since wondered whether the service women were decisively influenced by the working atmosphere or whether they entertained strong ideas of independence at an early date, which led them to the cafés and department store counters, which in turn reinforced their earlier direction. There is no way of knowing for certain, but Rainbow manifested her independence before starting at the Café and then strengthened it with her wage packet and new contacts. She did not join her coworkers for lunch at restaurants but instead economized by bringing her own lunch to work. This resulted in good-natured but nonetheless stinging taunts of "stingy" and "anti-social." She said in her off-handed manner, with a shrug, "I have my own goals and I do what I think is good for me. I don't care about them and their criticisms."

I met several of Rainbow's friends on one of our beach outings in 1974. Most worked in bars and nightclubs, and some were also models and entertainers. They interacted easily with the non-Chinese men they met at work. They conversed about the relative merits of the phonograph that one Western fellow who was present had just purchased. They discussed the modeling engagements of another man. One woman had just recently changed her job, and the discussion then turned to nightclubs and the various atmospheres and humorous incidents that had arisen between the boss and the girls.

Rainbow's friends spoke up-to-date English slang and dressed in a style acceptable only to non-Chinese. For example, they wore bikinis purchased in a tourist boutique rather than the more modest two-piece bathing suits sold in Chinese stores near their homes. Although they dressed "in fashion," however, they exhibited none of the modish languor often seen in sportier and wealthier circles of Hong Kong girls. And although they adorned their bikini outfits with silver bangles and Indian bead necklaces, they played catch with beach balls and tossed sand at each other vigorously with the same healthy abandon as the factory girls. After swimming, they decked themselves out in floor-length dirndl skirts and semitransparent Indian muslin shirts without bras. (Wai-gun would have goggled at this costume – she wore at least two pieces of underwear even in the hottest weather.)

Despite the substantial amounts of money they spent on clothing, Rainbow and her beach-outing companions still contributed to their families. Their expensive life-styles, when combined with the cut from their wages taken by their families, left them perpetually dissatisfied over the wages from ordinary factory and clerical jobs. Thus it was understandable when some of them were eventually attracted to the better-paying jobs in the hundreds of bars catering mainly to tourists, including, at one time, scores of thousands of U.S. servicemen sent to Hong Kong for rest and recreation during the Vietnam war. To the uninitiated, these bars may all seem the same, as they seemed to me from their garish, glittering exteriors, until Rainbow's friends assured me otherwise. "For example, some owners think they possess you," one said, "and I would hate to work in such places." She introduced me to her companion, a young Australian photographer who she had met in the bar, and pointed out that some bars would have tried to prevent her from dating him outside working hours.

Rainbow also dated men who she met at the Café. Her most recent boyfriend was a man whose work temporarily took him to South Korea but whose family, of mixed Portuguese and Chinese ancestry, lived in Hong Kong. She told me that she was "engaged" to him and proudly showed me his photos and one of his letters from Korea. "He loves me," she stated as simply and romantically as any North American teenager. She wanted to marry him when she turned 20, but her father was ignorant of this plan. Father had originally opposed her dating at all. He not only opposed girls' dating, but also feared that when Rainbow married she would withdraw her income from the family. When Father realized she was dating a non-Chinese, he relented by urging her to marry a nice Chinese boy and settle down. Rainbow explained that Father preferred her to marry at a young and more controllable age rather than risk her marrying out of the family and its culture altogether.

Rainbow believed in the powers of romantic love. She was trying to find a young gallant to transport her out of the narrow confines of family-centered Hong Kong life to the wider world of travel, exploration, and adventure. For a dissatisfied but untrained girl in the service sector, marriage seemed almost the sole alternative to the bar-girl circuit. However, Rainbow's plans were not clear, and she had not decided upon her next step (another job? travel? marriage?) when we parted in 1974.

A centrifugal woman bows to centripetal social expectations

Rainbow struggled to evade the demands of her family by responding to promises of love, affection, and nurturance. In the second major escapade of her youth, she again took off from her father's tutelage. But this time, unlike the first, she was not prepared to return. In 1975 she followed her heart, withdrew her savings from the bank, and attached herself to her boyfriend. They lived together in South Korea for a year, but this was only a passing conceit. He was reassigned to Hong Kong, and when they returned home, Rainbow was pregnant.

They married, and Rainbow moved into her husband's family home, joining his married brother and sister-in-law. The wheel of material demands and obligations turned for Rainbow just as for most young mothers, even those who yearned just as passionately to avoid the treadmill of responsibilities. There were no household conveniences, and Rainbow washed all the diapers by hand. She awoke at night when her son fretted, prepared all meals for her husband, and since her Chinese mother-in-law often played mahjong outside the home, Rainbow was also burdened with cooking chores for the entire family.

Rainbow sighed complainingly as she recollected her experiences during the year and a half since we had met last: "I wish I hadn't run off with him, because life as a mother is so hard compared with that of a coffee shop waitress." But then she smiled down at her chubby, healthy-looking boy trying to inch off her armchair onto the rug to practice crawling. "Well, he's a wonderful baby boy!" she acknowledged, revealing both warm maternal feelings and the awareness that frivolity was at an end.

Summary

No other working-class woman manifested so clear and forceful a desire to break away from family cares and had actually carried out this action two times. I wondered where this remarkable trait of Rainbow's originated. Was her position in the Café do Brasil chiefly responsible for fostering, or at least furthering, this determination? As we became closer friends from 1973 to 1975 and I learned the context of her quest for latitude, I realized that she had grown to have much in common with Father long before she gained a foothold at the Ocean Terminal.

Father, being independent and headstrong, preferred to run his own shop rather than work for others. Rainbow, like Father, not only earned a better wage by servicing tourist customers but she came to believe that the best opportunities would arise from aspects of the tourist life-style. Her instruction at an English-language secondary school, although incomplete, made her even more receptive to Western ideas, although Rainbow disputed the missionary educators as strongly as she did the paternalism of Father. When Rainbow entered a job that introduced her to many like-minded friends in the entertainment and service trades, she found that they spent their leisure time in conspicuous consumption of such items as clothes, jewelry, and popular music. Rainbow's job setting and her close personal friends stimulated her to think of her individual needs as gratifiable and worth attending to. Rainbow's close contact with Westerners actually confirmed her in the family artisan heritage of fierce pride and independence.

Rainbow was obviously juggling the tensions she felt between her obligations to her family and to herself. She acknowledged the legitimacy of the debt that, in her eyes, she had fully paid to her family and justified her late adolescent breakaway by citing the time and energy she lavished on them during her teens. This duality was quite unusual among the women interviewed. The most modern person I met, Rainbow was the only one who had turned around the terms of the centripetal family and was now due some form of reciprocation. But the exception proves the rule, and while trying to pull away from her family obligations, Rainbow used the framework of these necessary and inevitable obligations to justify her independence as a young adult. In the end, she followed through with her independent goals in the face of parental disapproval, a remarkable testimony to her strength of character and the encouragement of her peers and work environment. Girlfriends alone cannot come to the rescue of a Hong Kong married woman, and once having absconded, Rainbow no longer had the workplace and wage to support and strengthen her resolve to keep clear of family bonds.

Sa-li: waitress and youngest daughter

Sa-li Wong, age 24, worked as a waitress in the busy coffee shop at the large Hong Kong Hotel, a stopover for businessmen and tourists situated near the Ocean Terminal. In the spring of 1973, two of Sa-li's brothers served as waiters in the dining rooms of major hotels, and a brother-in-law drove a tourist bus. Father was also a hotel service employee before he died of cancer in 1972. Even after Father's death, the employment of four family members in the tourist industry was providing the Wongs with a measure of economic security.

Sa-li and her twin sister were Mother's fourth- and fifthborn. The Wong family could not afford to feed five young mouths, and Sa-li's twin was adopted by Mother's childless sister, who nurtured and educated her as if she were her own child. Sa-li thus grew up the youngest in the Wong household. The two eldest siblings had begun families of their own, and Second Brother also planned to marry in September, 1973.

An attractive young woman, Sa-li wore a pageboy haircut, swept back from her face with a pastel ribbon. Sa-li's demure smile matched her soft hairdo and understated manner. Although often quiet, Sa-li at times sparkled vivaciously and related amusing anecdotes with verve and humor. The mild manners of the brothers and sisters offset the edginess of Mother, a homemaker for most of her married life. A chain smoker, Mother spoke and took her meals at a rapid-fire pace and looked forward to regular afternoon mahjong parties.

Sa-li's life offers useful insights into the domestic and interpersonal demands made upon a youngest daughter who grew up in the 1960s, before the nominal improvement in popular living standards. Sa-li was a steady financial contributor to the household, and her income was especially useful in helping the Wongs accumulate more than $2,000 for Second Brother's impending wedding. Since marriage among the Chinese entails a realignment of persons and households, Sa-li's balanced, accommodating personality helped work out a modus vivendi between the old and new members of the Wong household.

Home and the family rift

The Wong family dwelt in one room of a postwar two-story tenement building on Haiphong Road in downtown Kowloon. They shared a lavatory and bath with three other tenants. The Wongs occupied a brightly lit front room; the middle area served as a shoemaker's workshop during the day and the rear was occupied by another tenant family. The Wongs' room was partitioned into two half-rooms, and on those infrequent evenings when the entire family dined together, they waited until the cobbler and his assistant departed and then set up their collapsible table and large, round, metal tabletop on the floor of his shop.

The inner chamber of the Wong's quarter served as a living room/bedroom in which Mother, Sa-li, and Second Brother slept. Mother and daughters observed the chief Buddhist religious ceremonies at the temples for goddesses at home, and a large altar to Kwan-Yin, Goddess of Mercy and Compassion, with a stand for candles and incense, adorned one wall of their compartment. This room contained a double bunk bed and a folding camp cot. A 23-inch television set was placed beneath the altar. A somewhat tidier front compartment was occupied by Elder Brother, Sister-in-law, and their children, ages 4 and 1. This nook contained a single bunk bed, where Mother and Son slept on the bottom and Father on the top, and a folding crib for the baby girl. A large chest of drawers topped with wedding photos and a full-size refrigerator occupied one corner. The presence of another television set revealed that the two subunits gathered separately for television, and indeed I soon learned of the deep split between them.

First Sister lived with her husband and child in a new-style flat in the Ngau Tau Kok resettlement estate, 1 hour by bus from Haiphong Road. This apartment was awarded to the Wong family by the Resettlement Department around 1970, when their former Kowloon tenement abode was demolished. Father felt, however, that Ngau Tau Kok was too far from the Peninsula and Miramar hotels where he and his two sons were then working, and so he let the new flat to First Sister's family and took the Haiphong Road quarters.

Under the usual condition of patrilocal residence, the classic dispute in the Chinese family takes place between each new daughter-in-law and the mother of the home, who expects at least one son to remain with her to contribute his earnings and support her in old age. In addition to the competition between the youths and the elders over the apportionment of First Son's economic contribution and his loyalties (along with those of First Grandson), the rift at the Wongs' was widened by personality differences. Elder Brother had found his wife independently, and married for love, despite Mother's wish to select the marital partners of her children to ensure that all new family members would accept her management of the home. Although Elder Brother was diffident, his wife was as sharp tongued and opinionated as Mother, who criticized First Daughter-in-law's lack of filiality at length.

"I could tell even before their wedding that Daughter-in-law was no good, but I didn't say anything directly to my son, because in Hong Kong today youth like to choose freely. But once or twice I hinted to him that I wasn't happy about his choice. When he told her that they ought to rent the vacant apartment next door to us, so he could be near his job at the Miramar Hotel, she replied, 'What? So close to your mother and father?' This proved to me that even in those days she didn't want to be good to us. Daughter-in-law was raised by her aunt, who was not badly off and had no children of her own. She was probably spoiled at that time. She started school late and didn't do too well. When she finished she soon married my son, and never had to work hard. That made matters worse.

"First Son is really a fine husband. He doesn't smoke, drink, or gamble. He listens obediently to everything his wife says, and tells her everything, even though he reveals very little to me, his own mother. Daughter-in-law is stubborn and won't take my advice on how to raise the grandchildren. She doesn't feed the children as often as she should. She lets the children wear open-necked clothes in winter, and they catch cold in the neck. The children may even get pneumonia if this keeps on. But I'm trying to avoid quarrels, and so I just let her do whatever she wants. Whether she cooks or not, whether she dresses her children properly or not, whether she feeds them these new drugs when they are sick or uses my Chinese herbal medicines, I won't make a sound."

Mother thought she was generous to Daughter-in-law by not openly criticizing her, but nevertheless commented obliquely to all hearers on First Daughter-in-law's faults. Sa-li shared and amplified on Mother's view.

"First Sister-in-law is stupid and lazy. She didn't study well in school. Although she finished the fifth year of secondary school, she doesn't know any English, and her Chinese language isn't too good either. She never had the experience of working before marriage, and she can't cook or take proper care of children."

Daughter-in-law and Mother first feuded over the costs of the wedding banquet. Indeed, quarrels over the size and scope of the nuptial celebration are common in Hong Kong, since the affines frequently desire to enlarge the affair and the groom's family, which must meet the expense, tries to economize. Sa-li speculated that "since Sister-in-law never brought home any earnings to her parents, they demanded a lot of money from the groom."

Mother amplified: "They wanted over twenty tables of guests [at ten guests per table] for their own side of the family at the wedding feast, and four hundred catties [about 500 pounds] of sliced vanilla layer cake for the guests. And then, just one day before the wedding, the mother of my daughter-in-law told us that the menu we planned was inferior, and that her family had decided to stage their wedding dinner separately. She even asked for cash to finance the replacement dinner! Our invitation cards had of course been mailed, saying that the two families would host the dinner jointly. So my husband and son had to rush to the printers to prepare new invitation cards, and then stayed up all night to address them. We decided to hand the cards to our guests at the front door of the banquet hall, because it was too late to deliver them."

Sa-li added, "Father was working in the Peninsula Hotel at the time, and we invited some of his workmates and superiors from the hotel to the wedding, including some Europeans. Then there were a number of businessmen and shopowners our family got to know over the years. So, our twelve-course banquet wasn't going to be too bad!"

Mother concluded: "Actually the mother of my daughter-in-law was just trying to find an excuse to give us trouble. She's very fussy person and changes her mind all the time about everything. First Son really hates her now, and refuses to visit his wife's family!"

Elder Sister did not share the critical opinions of Mother and Sa-li and timidly attempted to mediate between them and Sister-in-law. When I first visited the apartment, the two sisters-in-law were wearing blouses of the same pattern, which they had purchased on a joint shopping expedition. Elder Sister was uncomfortable when mother began to denigrate Sister-in-law and interjected: "Why don't you leave her alone! She knows what she wants for her children."

When First Daughter-in law herself protested at the sullying of her reputation, the onus for starting a quarrel inevitably fell upon her. Because of the strained relationships between family units, each keep apart as much as possible in the cramped quarters. The children did not observe the unspoken boundary and hence became the focus of arguments as they wandered freely from one compartment to the next. During one of my visits the 5-year-old grandson entered the main room to play and Mother threw him a series of comments like "Pull up your pants properly!" "Don't touch that dish of food!" "That picture is not for you to play with!" Meanwhile, Eldest Daughter-in-law remained on her own side of the partition and refused to be drawn into the quarrel. When she later took her two children out for a walk, she pointedly bid goodbye only to Elder Sister and not to Mother, who likewise ignored the trio's exit.

Four years after Eldest Son, Second Son was born, and 4 years later Eldest Daughter was born. Eldest Daughter married after Eldest Son to a friendly, personable, recent refugee from Kwangtung province. He was employed as a tourist van driver for a Tsim Sha Tsui hotel travel agency and earned in addition to an average working-class wage a substantial commission from store owners to whom he brought shopping parties of overseas tourists.

Son-in-law was brought by relatives to Hong Kong and his parents remained in their village in China. Son-in-law remitted a monthly pension to his parents, but apart from possibly one or two home visits, these funds were his only contact with them. Mother Wong was able to obtain the full compliance of Eldest Daughter and Son-in-law, and her relationship with them was cordial. Mother explained to me. "We've certainly had our problems with Elder Son's choice of a wife and their wedding, but the marriage of my duaghter went off much more smoothly. After all, Son-in-law is practically alone here in Hong Kong. There was no one at all to save money for his wedding, and so I had to be satisfied with a small affair. There are no in-law conflicts for Eldest Daughter. Since I made a good impression on him at the beginning, Son-in-law has been much more cooperative than Eldest Daughter-in-law."

Second Brother's bride, a native of the Wongs' home county Pan-yü, was chosen for him by Mother through a trusted intermediary, whose roots were also in this county. This woman was a regular hand at Mother's mahjong table, and one day Mother took her out for tea and explained to her that since Second Brother was nearing 30 and First Sister had already married, it was time that a bride be found for him. The mahjong partner told Mother that in the Poon family there was a modest 22-year-old daughter who would be able to get along with in-laws after marriage, and she arranged for an introduction of the Wongs to the Poons.

Sa-li explained to me, "It is only 6 months since Mother's friend introduced Second Brother to his fiancé. Ordinarily they would date a year or more to get to know each other better before their marriage, but Mother is impatient for another grandson. That's the reason for the rush."

Mother assured me, "I can tell from talking to her and her family that Second Daughter-in-law will turn out all right. We've already settled the date and location of the banquet." Mother budgeted $2,610 for the following components of the ceremony: a twenty-two-table restaurant dinner, twelve tables for the bride's side and ten tables for the groom's family ($1,760); 400 pounds of wedding cake ($600); barbeque pork for members of the Poon family ($50); and pocket money for distribution to the bride's family, wrapped in red paper packets ($50).

Mother revealed proudly to me that she was able to economize the number of tables originally requested by Mrs. Poon by one, on the grounds that thirteen is an unlucky number. Mother explained that the family had deposited more than half of Second Son's wages for the past several years in anticipation of this event.

The marriage of Second Son provided Mother with the opportunity to detach herself from First Daughter-in-law. Eldest Son vacated the Haiphong Road apartment and took his wife to a modern flat some distance away. First Sister and her family then moved in with Mother and the newlyweds occupied their Ngau Tau Kok flat. Over midafternoon tea with Sa-li, Mother explained to me that she had to part with First Son. When Mother finally had to give up First Son, she still would not accept the blame and characteristically shifted it to the modest and passive Sa-li. While Sa-li sipped tea without voicing opposition to her, Mother attributed the contentious feud to the inability of Sa-li and First Daughter-in-law to establish a close bond. Mother agreed to the realistic separation only after obtaining visiting rights with Elder Son.

"It will be tiring for Elder Son to commute to work from his new quarters. But he is always welcome to come to us from his hotel during his midafternoon break in order to rest. Sa-li never established a working relationship with First Daughter-in-law the two and a half years they lived here together. But what could I do about it? Sisters-in-law seldom get along together. Sa-li will be much happier now. You see, when First Daughter travels from Ngau Tau Kok with her baby to visit us, she must ride a bus for over an hour, and in summer the trip is sweltering for mother and child. So I've put First Daughter here with family, and I'm sure that Sa-li will be more comfortable next to her own flesh and blood."

Mother expended considerable effort over a period of 5 years to integrate First Daughter-in-law into a household strongly stamped by her personality. Mother's exertions made clear the high priority attached to patrilocal residence and the difficulties inherent in this prevailing mode. Mother's reluctance to give up her eldest son was grounded not only in sentiment but also family economics, because when he moved his family to a distant apartment, First Son's food, shelter, and transportation expenses no doubt doubled, and he could remit much less of his wage to Mother. This forced Mother to hire herself out as domestic help to a neighboring family on Haiphong Road.

The changing living arrangements in the Wong family are schematized in the following chronology. When I asked Sa-li in June, 1971, to enumerate the members of her household and to comment on how they got along with each other, she described a harmonious three-generational unit. Sa-li's conventional portrait differed greatly from the real conflicts coursing through the roots and branches of the Wong family. Mother sought a traditional Chinese matriarch role and attempted to surround herself with the families of her treasured sons and, if possible, those of her daughters, too. Over a 4-year period, beginning with Father's last months, I charted the changing living arrangement of the Wongs with Mother as a fixed pole and decision maker on Haiphong Road. During this time two marriages occurred in the younger generation, and I observed how Mother attempted at each stage to draw her sons closer but was forced by sentiment, in-law conflict, and financial constraints to adjust herself to the realignment of her household to what was, in her eyes, a second-best arrangement with her First Daughter and Second Son, and visits from First Son.

Domestic arrangements for the Wong family

May, 1971

A. Mother and Father Wong, who have lived in their Haiphong Road residence since 1970, occupy one-half of the subdivided tenement room with two of their five children. With them are Second Son (age 28 in 1971) and Sa-li (age 22).

B. Eldest Son (age 32), his wife, and their child occupy the other subdivision of the tenement room. Daughter-in-law cooks the joint family meals.

C. Eldest Daughter (age 24) lives with her husband in the Ngau Tau Tok Resettlement Estate room that is registered in Father's name.

D. The fifth Wong child has been raised since infancy by Mother's childless sister. This arrangement remains unchanged through 1974.

March, 1973

A. Father has died of cancer. Mother Wong lives in the same Haiphong Road tenement room with Sa-li and Second Son, who is now engaged.

B. Eldest Son and wife have a second child. Residence is unchanged, but their meals are no longer taken with Mother, Second Son, and Sa-li.

C. Eldest Daughter gives birth to her first child. She still lives in the resettlement estate room. She spends her days in the Haiphong Road tenement, where Mother assists her with child care.

September, 1973

A. Mother and Sa-li share the Haiphong Road tenement room. Mother works for a neighboring family watching their child and is absent from home during the day.

B. Eldest Son, his wife, and their two children move out of the tenement into an apartment some distance away. Eldest Son returns to the tenement for rest from work during the day.

C. Eldest Daughter, pregnant, moves with husband and child to the Haiphong Road tenement compartment previously occupied by Eldest Son.

D. Second Son marries, and he and his bride occupy the Ngau Tau Kok resettlement estate room.

December, 1974

A. Sa-li marries and moves to Singapore. No change in other housing arrangements.

Like all twenty-eight peers in my study, Sa-li conscientiously remitted over three-quarters of her wages to her family. Compared with those of her contemporaries and of Elder Sister, Sa-li's family obligations were light, and as the youngest at home Sa-li was herself supported by a cluster of elders. Although Elder Sister was permitted to receive only primary 6 schooling, Sa-li attended an Anglo-Chinese secondary school through form III. A younger daughter maturing today feels even fewer family demands.

Nevertheless, Sa-li's early years were difficult ones for the Wongs, as shown by the adoption of Twin Sister by Mother's sister. When Sa-li eventually entered the work force, the Wongs needed her income because First Son had already married and reduced his contribution, and they were saving for Second Brother's large wedding banquet. Sa-li was expected throughout to observe Mother's each commandment obediently and modestly, even to the extent of marrying the man Mother designated for her.

Work and friends

The Wong family expected that although the daughters would work hard to fill the family rice bowl, they would earn their wages in non-career occupations, and thus no effort was expended to train them for the hotel trade or related industries. After completing form III in 1965, the 16-year-old Sa-li left school to begin work in a small wig factory. She did not undertake further schooling until age 22, when she enrolled in part-time dress-making classes at a neighboring night school. First Sister, who was already employed at the wig factory, assisted Sa-li in obtaining this position and worked beside her. Sa-li struck up a warm friendship at the factory with a coworker named Ma-ci. Ma-ci was to become a friend of long standing who shared organized and casual recreational activities over the years with Sa-li.

The shopworkers constructed wigs by machine-sewing real or artificial hair onto cloth skull caps and were paid by the piece. The pace of these operations over a 9-hour day was intense and rapid, with only a 30-minute break for lunch. In early 1971, a frenzied rate of work was imposed by management to fulfill worldwide orders, and the girls netted a respectable wage of $5 per day. When the factory's order book shrunk in 1972, intermittent layoffs began and continued until the factory was eventually forced to close its doors in 1973. On slow days during fair weather Sa-li and Ma-ci brought their bathing suits to work, and when they had sewed their full orders, they were dismissed and they boarded a bus for the beach. Otherwise, they filled their afternoons by window-shopping along Nathan Road.

Sa-li and her family were gratified at her earnings, but since she was an even-tempered and rather reflective woman, Sa-li would have preferred more leisurely working conditions. Ma-ci was more highly strung and frenetic; for her a fast pace mainly meant the opportunity to wrestle for higher take-home pay. When the factory was shut down, Ma-ci, the second daughter in a family of five siblings of an impoverished hawker, immediately secured piecework employment at another garment factory. Sa-li's family did not pressure her to find another piecework job quickly, and Older Sister, who had meanwhile stopped work for marriage and childbearing, was unable to assist Sa-li in the job market. Sa-li took her time in the search for a position that suited her. She was troubled by the uncertain pay in piecework assembly and resolved under no condition to accept piecework employment.

Sa-li sized up the job market for several weeks, during which time she was uncomfortable and aimless and missed Ma-ci's companionship. While unemployed, Sa-li stayed at home, went strolling in the Kowloon shopping district with Elder Sister, and enjoyed looking after her infant nephew. Sa-li chafed about "sitting around without work while my friends are all on the job. I can't just play with my nephew all day long. Mother is not really after my money, but she doesn't like to see me hanging around with nothing to do."

"Can your mother help you find a job?" I queried.

"She doesn't really know anyone except her mahjong ladies."

Sa-li read the help-wanted columns for salesgirl positions and sought the assistance of employed friends. One of these, who was employed in the Apple Jeans factory, telephoned to report that there were piecework openings on its assembly line, a lead that Sa-li decided not to pursue. The alternative of dressmaking at home was considered, since Sa-li had completed over a year of dressmaking courses. But Sa-li lacked the entrepreneurial drive and support to succeed in a demanding endeavor of this kind. Finally, Mother realized that Sa-li was stymied by the recessionary economy in finding a new job, and after a 2-month period of grace instructed Second Brother, who was a dining room waiter at the Hong Kong Hotel, to secure a waitress position for Sa-li in the Hotel's street-level fast-food coffee shop. Both First and Second Brothers had obtained their choice rooftop banquet and dining room positions after years of table service in various smaller hotels, and despite their influence, no job could be found in the luxury dining room for an untrained woman like Sa-li. Sa-li earned $60 for each of her 3 months of probation, and when she qualified as a member of the permanent staff, her monthly wages increased to $100 and a small proportion (around $20 a month) of the service charge and tips. Sa-li found it difficult to communicate with her businessmen patrons because many of them spoke English with European or Japanese accents. Sa-li blushed when she told me that such customers had to repeat an order two or three times before she understood them, and even then she occasionally had to ask them to point out their selection on the menu. But since the menu was limited, she was after several months able to learn its pronunciation in all major international accents of English.

In order to encourage its public-service staff members, already presumed to be fluent in English, to further their communication skills in this cosmopolitan setting, the management of the Hong Kong Hotel met the tuition expenses of waitresses pursuing private evening courses in French or Japanese. After she completed a half-year of waitressing and had achieved the required mastery of English table conversation, Sa-li took advantage of this program to study French conversation in night school. However, since shifts in the Hong Kong hotel industry are rotated throughout the staff, Sa-li could not attend these French classes on a regular basis. Apart from variable shifts, Sa-li was reasonably content with the working conditions in the coffee shop. However, lacking hotel school training or patronage ties to any other big hotel in the colony, Sa-li could not move horizontally to another, better-paying hotel.

It was difficult at first for Sa-li to accept the coarse language and common habits of her fellow waitresses. "My workmates swear and raise their voices in the kitchen and the dressing room and gamble at cards during their free time. It also bothers me that most of them avoid really hard work. It has taken me three months to get used to this kind of life, but now I am finally able to make friends."

Sa-li and I had been sharing numerous casual hours at home and walking downtown since we had met 4 years earlier, and now we joined the excursions organized by the Hong Kong Hotel Coffee Shop waitresses. The timing and participants of these expeditions were minutely planned and work shifts and weekly holidays were informally traded among the girls so that companion groups could share the same outing. The itinerary typically consisted of long journeys to selected New Territories restaurants to sample local delicacies (seasonal shellfish from the New Territories or vegetable dumplings in a hillside Buddhist temple), excursions by launch to outlying beaches, and overnight stays at these and other recreational attractions.

I was invited by Sa-li and her companions to join them at a wharf in the Hong Kong Central District, where we boarded the ferry for an excursion to the outlying Cheung Chau Island, an hour's boat ride away. Our party of six chatted animatedly and set up a game of gin rummy on board. We spent the afternoon and evening on one of Cheung Chau's attractive beaches, and the merrymakers, who had become proficient swimmers on these outings, stroked confidently out to the raft, undeterred by the stings of miniature sea insects swarming on the water. After swimming, we collected driftwood, built a fire, and roasted our dinner on skewers: chicken wings and spare ribs marinated in soy sauce, vinegar, and peanut oil, frankfurters sandwiched between slices of bread, and strawberry preserves and oranges. The bread, butter, and jam had been conscientiously hoarded from the busing stations and pantry of the hotel coffee shop. This twilight repast was followed by another dip in the water and our return to sleeping quarters in a rented cabin, which one of the waitresses had sublet from her cousin. We splashed and chattered as we washed our hair and bodies, and several of the girls laundered all of our clothes in a large, cold-water tub. We then retired to our hard pallets on the floor of a balcony overlooking the cabin living room and began our pillow talk, which lasted half the night. This conversation consisted of a succession of individually recounted ghost stories from South China oral folklore. These stories were variants of well-known legends in the supernatural traditions (including Buddhist) of wandering ghosts and devils disguised as wily foxes and other predatory animals who seduced unwary travelers and maidens. Since early childhood the girls had listened to their mothers, grandmothers, and aunts recount these tales, and there in the cottage they huddled together in vaguely disguised apprehension.

The next morning a monsoon rain began to pour. While we prepared a breakfast of toast and jam, four university boys with drenched clothing and long, wet hair walked into the cabin. One of the four was the cousin of a girl in our group and the cottage was leased in the name of his club. The lads set up camp beside us and our combined parties endured the rainy weather over an extended poker game until we walked to the dock for the afternoon launch to the Central District and the night shift at the Hong Kong Hotel.

Sa-li and her friends made do on their group outings with little funds and equipment and enjoyed their confidential chats, energetic swims, and food fests. When young men came to be included in the outings, the group was maintained – couples rarely formed. Very much like these waitresses and their friends, eight of the ten women in this book organized outings with coworkers during days free from their sewing machines, electronics assembly lines, and sales counters. As with Sa-li, little direct opportunity was provided for male-female liaisons during their expeditions.

Dating: mother's choice

Sa-li's job in the wig factory afforded no direct contact with eligible young men, but she was pleased when Ma-ci and other workmates included her on outings with groups of their male friends and cousins. The coworkers dated in foursomes and larger units, which together visited the cinema, Chinese nightclubs, and beaches on Sundays. As the only single Wong offspring, Sa-li was expected to marry in good time. One afternoon over tea with Mother, she confirmed that, as her only unwed child, Sa-li was expected to cultivate her prospects, and I ventured to compliment Mother on her ability to marry off her children.

"Sa-li is my only worry now, and I can die with peace in my heart if she's married. I am the only one Sa-li can truly depend on. You may be very close to your brothers and sisters, but when trouble comes they can't help you. Parents are the most reliable people in the world."

Mother felt Sa-li needed to have her own family to assist her when Mother grew older and could no longer help.

"I haven't introduced any boys to Sa-li yet. I'll probably let her find her own. Actually, however, there was a man who lived on our same tenement floor who really liked Sa-li. He's a good clean fellow who doesn't smoke or drink and has a good skill, a goldsmith. But Sa-li ignored him and he became so frustrated that he left for Singapore two years ago. But he writes to her, and I think there may yet be hope."

Sa-li, listening, cocked her head and protested lightly, "I'm not sure if I care for him. I don't want to get married yet!" She expressed good-natured annoyance at Mother's discussion of marriage, and when she insisted "I don't like him!" she smiled demurely, showing her dimples. Sa-li then volunteered the information that the young goldsmith had indeed written to her twice from Singapore the previous summer, but that she had not replied. "It's not that I dislike him, but I just don't write many letters. I guess I'm lazy." Sa-li's reluctance was predictable, since the Chinese courtship ritual, like many others, requires the woman to neglect his advances for fear of being considered too forward.

Mother took Sa-li's cue and quickly added: "This man is not bad because he has a skill. When you choose a husband you should judge his ability and character more than his family origins. A person with a wealthy background but who knows no skill couldn't deal with hardship. But if the man comes from a poor family but has ability and knowledge, he can still find a way if he loses his fortune. It's the same thing for a woman. It doesn't matter if she comes from a rich family or not. The most important thing is her ability to endure hardship with her husband."

Sa-li seconded Mother: "Yes, I agree that ability and skill are most important." They were thus reaffirming a time-honored proposition of Chinese familism: Inherited wealth cannot be depended upon. It is far better for family members to pull together and make it possible for their youths to pursue useful careers.

Although many of Sa-li's workmates were still unmarried, they were more burdened with family obligations. In fact, when Second Brother married, Sa-li's economic responsibilities were eased, and marital prospects and status largely defined her identity. Once Sa-li and I happened upon a former schoolmate at an outdoor market. The woman's first question to Sa-li was "Have you gotten married yet?" Sa-li responded with the same question. Neither had taken the step, but marriage was uppermost in both of their minds.

In June, 1974, Sa-li accepted the goldsmith's invitation to visit him in Singapore. She paid for her own plane fare, and he met her accommodations and other staying expenses. "It was just a vacation," Sa-li told me after her return, but she did not disclose her destination to her workmates or to those at the class reunion she attended the next month. Sa-li affirmed to me that her host might be a suitable choice when she was ready to marry.

On a hot afternoon in July, 1974, Sa-li and seven alumni of my 1971 English evening class were chatting at a party in the small apartment of one of the male students. The talk gradually drifted to parental attempts at marriage arrangement. These efforts were considered a joking matter, and two young men regaled their listeners with humorous stories of awkward tea parties held by their mothers in an effort to speed up marriage. They recounted their experiences of being tricked into attending tea parties arranged by matchmakers under the guise of a birthday party, and of meeting there a mismatched prospect, too tall or too short, too young or too old for them. All present had participated in at least one such arranged meeting in order to please their mothers, all nodded in recognition of the problems entailed therein, and none would admit that partners introduced in this manner could be satisfactory. However, the possibility still existed that such an arrangement could be made fairly quickly, as Sa-li herself was aware.

When she was ready for marriage, Sa-li would not care for a large wedding banquet. Mother agreed that as the youngest child, Sa-li required no expensive social occasion: "Even if Sa-li has a travel wedding, it would be acceptable."

Sa-li enthused, "I love to travel. It would be nice to honeymoon in Japan." Sa-li felt that age 25 was "about right to marry" and explained that most Hong Kong youths marry so late for economic reasons, but that she was postponing marriage mainly to extend the period of a relatively carefree life.

"If you marry too young then you can't have a good time anymore. We like to go swimming, picnic, take tea together, and marriage makes that difficult because marriage brings babies. We Chinese don't postpone having babies after we marry like you Westerners do. My sister's case was like that. Before her first baby was born she could go out and do many things. But now she can't go out, and is tied to the home. So, people like me postpone marriage."

Sa-li married the young goldsmith in late 1974, and they established their home in Singapore. Toward the end of 1975, in the third trimester of her pregnancy, Sa-li returned to Hong Kong to bear her first child. Her family's support was helpful during her confinement, and she then brought the baby back to Singapore to take up family life.

Summary

Sa-li Wong, the family's youngest daughter, was compliant to her elders and hardworking at home and on the job. Being youngest and being raised in the 1950s and 1960s, a time of straitened circumstances for families like hers, required her to labor continuously on behalf of her family. Sa-li was given some latitude in choosing how she would contribute to the Wongs' family economy. When Sa-li and her coworker, Ma-ci, were laid off, Ma-ci as a major family income earner was at once compelled to take a new factory job, whereas Sa-li was allowed to search for a position that better suited her quiet personality and middle-school education. Sa-li nevertheless contributed over one-half of her earnings to the Wongs' purse during all of her working years. Sa-li supported Mother in the family quarrels, and after several years of hesitation Sa-li married the man of her mother's choice.

Although Sa-li, her deceased father, and her brothers served European and North American customers at the big Hong Kong tourist hotels, she was not too attracted by Western life-styles. Sali gradually became more accepting of the cosmopolitan outlooks and activities of her coworkers, but she fulfilled throughout her traditional family duties and obligations.

In the years I visited the family regularly, Mother spent considerably less time with her family and more time at the mahjong table. Nevertheless, her offspring and in-laws accorded Mother considerable respect and outwardly complied with Mother's requests. Sa-li's acceptance of maternal authority was as complete as that of the other working daughters.

Ci-li: from domestic servant to government service

Ci-li Chu worked as a daytime domestic servant (amah) for expatriate families. She wore used clothes bestowed upon her by these families, which suited her since she was large-boned and robust. In these double-knit outfits, one-piece dresses, and short, permed, matron-style hair, Ci-li appeared more mature than she was at 20 years of age in 1973.

Ci-li was the eldest of seven children. Father operated a small butcher shop. Mother was a hawker (street vendor) in Yue Wan resettlement estate on Hong Kong Island, near the Chus' home. The combined parental income enabled Ci-li to complete form V (grade 12) in an Anglo-Chinese mission school and thereby launch herself upon an upwardly mobile trajectory. The Chu family had broken out of the poverty cycle by dint of concerted investing and saving, and this development together with Ci-li's education and substantial parental encouragement whetted her aspirations to enter government service. Here was a woman who soberly planned to gain a middle-class way of life, not solely on her own behalf but for the betterment of her family.

Home

In the mid-1950s, shortly after emigrating from Chung Shan county to the colony, where they set up squatter diggings on a Shau Kei Wan hillside, the Chus were removed to a cottage area comprised of 100 tiny wood huts perched on a steep adjoining slope. These makeshift, substandard dwellings were built by the Hong Kong government and welfare missions as the earliest form of public housing to temporarily shelter a small portion of the big Chinese refugee influx. As has been common in similar makeshift slum settlements around the world, the authorities neglected the tenants of this suburban slum and charged them nominally for house and land rent and refuse collection. China Light and Power Company cables traversed the settlement, but in the absence of regular inspection by this utility, the Chu family and many other residents were regularly able to pirate this grid for their home power source. Each household was forced to haul its daily water supply from a standpipe several hundred meters distant, and they stored it in 50-gallon barrels on the walkway in front of the cottage. The postman refused to ascend the steep, canine-beset path leading from the entry road at the bottom of the hill to the settlement, and the residents were thus obliged to share a common mailbox down below. Ci-li voiced a common complaint when she told me that none of the letters I mailed to her at home was ever received.

Free rent was of course the basic advantage in squatter or cottage living, but the constant breeze, wide open spaces, and panoramic harbor view from the steep hillside were other benefits that the Chu family possessed that families with comparable income and occupations quartered in resettlement estates did not. During my 6 years of Hong Kong fieldwork (from 1971 to 1976) I spent the night in seven working- and lower-middle-class private and public quarters in Hong Kong, Kowloon, and the New Territories and visited another forty homes, but I preferred the Chu family hillside cottage above all others. The air was refreshing in the semitropical weather; the location provided rambling, panoramic walks over mountain paths and through rice fields to a secluded rocky beach. At home the multiplicity of rooms enabled me to close the door to rest or read quietly.

However, the Chus' poorly anchored cottage, unprotected from the elements, was vulnerable to the typhoon winds that regularly buffeted the colony during the tropical cyclone and winter monsoon seasons. This wet and exposed location was at a further disadvantage compared to concrete high-rise tenements and resettlement estates because the nearby sea and swampy agricultural grounds attracted swarms of mosquitos. The residents' only relief from the pests was to burn mosquito coils in the night. Excretion and sewage disposal were additional dilemmas for the Chu family. They passed solid waste in the trench toilets at the communal outhouses, where running water was lacking, but they preferred to urinate on the cement floor in the privacy of their kitchen. The family did what little it could to remedy this unfortunate despoiling of its domicile by washing the floor afterward with buckets of water, which flowed down the hillside below.

Ci-li told me that her family, like other hillside dwellers, dreaded most of all the outbreak of fires, which could destroy the wooden shacks along the narrow dirt roads, impassable to fire engines. I do not know if her community had personally experienced a big fire, but the press regularly reported the ruinous effects of hillside squatter fires. All Hong Kong residents have relatives and friends who were affected by conflagrations, such as the catastrophic Shek Kip Mei fire of 1953, which in one night rendered 50,000 squatters homeless and forced a reluctant Hong Kong laissez faire government to begin a large-scale program of construction of resettlement estates, which continues today. Vulnerability to disasters and the elements, relatively low density land use, and the structural dilapidation of the cottage area contributed to the Housing Authority's removal of the Chus and other cottage area neighbors to the nearby Chai Wan resettlement estate in mid-1976, in favor of new high-rise resettlement estate blocks planned for this acreage.

The Chus' cottage consisted of a timber frame covered with rough-sawn wooden planks. The windows were paned only with wire-mesh fly screens, temporarily boarded against the cold in January and February and typhoons in the summer. Father and Mother slept on a Western-style double bed in a curtained-off corner of the one-room cottage. An altar to Kwan-yin, Goddess of Mercy, stood upon a table, and a television set and large chest of drawers occupied a wall opposite. A 6-foot tall deep freezer, which took up much of the wall next to the altar, was loaded weekly with frozen uncooked and smoked meat fetched by Father and his sons in their old goods vehicle from a down-town wholesale meat depot. Across the narrow cement path fronting this cottage, the Chu family had erected a tiny two-room wood and tin shack. Ci-li, who worked 5 full weekdays as a domestic, and Mei-li, the lastborn, slept there on a narrow, metal-frame bunk bed; a gas burner, large and medium-size woks, an electric rice steamer, and other cooking pots and utensils filled the second cell. The kitchen also contained a set of matching stainless steel saucepans and an electric oven, in which white bread was toasted. Although their possessions would be considered sparse for a North American family of nine, the Chus were among the few Hong Kong households I knew to accumulate this many utensils. Ci-li used electrical conveniences at work and purchased some of them at below cost from homebound employers. The Chus shopped for their produce daily at the Yue Wan market and supplied their table with meat from the butchery.

An automatic washing machine stood outside the front door of the Chu cottage, and pedestrians were obliged to lower their heads when passing through the lines of clothes drying on bamboo rods overhanging the main path. Ci-li bought this machine for her family with cash she earned in her second year as an amah. Folding metal chairs and a detachable round tabletop were stored next to the washing machine for quick assembly on the infrequent occasions when the nine Chus dined together as a family.

The five sons at home slept on camp cots in the walkway during the summer nights and in the colder months pitched their cots in temporarily deserted nearby cottages. One of the first things I noticed on my visit to the Chus was a set of aerial dimensions tatooed in black next to their entrance way. These were the statutory limits to their cottage floor space. Construction of the Chus' tiny overflow shack therefore violated the housing regulation against exceeding allotted floor space. In practice, however, the hill families were relatively immune to inspection and prosecution by housing department inspectors, who were not expected to enforce the codes at this inaccessible, temporary location rigidly, so that illegal extensions were rarely detected and dismantled.

Mother had planted and daily pruned and watered with much care a cluster of red hibiscus and azalea on the shoulder of the Chus' slope in beds decorated by rings of inverted Tsingtao beer bottles, which formed a circular mosaic of green and brown glass. Mother also maintained throughout the year vases filled with fragrant flowers and foliage that were placed on Kwan-yin's altar and on the Earth God shrine outside the doorway. The Chus, like other market traders, believed their success in highly competitive and uncertain business depended strongly upon homage to the major Buddhist and Taoist dieties, and honored the principal Hong Kong religious ceremonies. Thus Mother refurbished her bouquets of flowers on the first and fifteenth days of every lunar month and propitiated gods with bowls of oranges on the dieties' birthdays.

A family store

Father presided over the family butcher store in a bustling ground-floor shopping center serving the Yue Wan resettlement estate in Chai Wan. This estate, which commands an imposing view from the north of picturesque Shau Kei Wan Bay, was built at the end of the 1950s and houses more than 80,000 tenants. Father was previously a counterman in this butcher store when his employer leased it from the Housing Authority. In the early 1970s Father bought the tenancy from the original owner.

Father enjoyed a monopoly of trade in fresh and prepared beef, pork, variety meats, and fowl for one large block in the estate. The pork was shipped by sea and rail from Kwangtung province, and the remainder of the larder was stocked with imports from Denmark, the United Kingdom, and New Zealand. Although the enterprise was busy from 8 a.m. to 7 p.m. daily, Ci-li denied that her family was in any sense prosperous. Ci-li pointed out in 1974 that Father was still repaying the loan and that Mother was only a part-time hawker, and hence the net family income could not be considered high. When I sketched what I could learn of the Chus' family finances to one of my colleagues, an experienced economic reporter for a Hong Kong English-language daily, he disagreed with Ci-li's reckoning and estimated the joint monthly net income of a resettlement estate storekeeper and part-time hawker at above $500. When Ci-li's earnings are included, the Chus' intake was probably 50% greater than the income earned by families of the other service women, Rainbow and Sa-li, in which there were more than three wage earners.

When he bought the tenancy of the butcher store, Father believed that the title could be passed on to his sons upon his retirement. But in the summer of 1974 the Housing Authority, in a move to reassert the crown's title to all resettlement estate property, proposed to bring the holders of resettlement shop tenancy cards into 3-year renewable agreements. Father was enraged at this regulation, because in his view no tradesman would build up his business if he doubted its future transferability to his sons or other heirs. Father and fellow shopkeepers rallied and marched that summer to protest the regulation, and due to the unexpected opposition the government proposal was withdrawn, and the customary "resettlement rights" to sell and will tenancies by private arrangement were restored.

The butcher shop drew upon the labor of four of the five sons. At 7 a.m. First and Third Sons pedaled their bicycles with a day's supply of meat and poultry from the living-room freezer down the hill to the shop, set up the viands on long wooden planks for displays, and left for the day. Second and Fourth Sons took turns helping carry on the cross-counter trade throughout the day, each of the two serving part-time while the other was at school. Together with Father, they closed the store for the night. Father clearly pinned his hopes for the family's future upon either Second or Fourth Son's inheritance of the butcher shop, but perhaps he was watching to assess which lad demonstrated the most aptitude and determination before he speculated on which would eventually don his white apron.

First Son was not slated to inherit the family store, because Mother and Father were ambitiously planning for his higher education and a white-collar career. This easygoing boy of 18 years, who lacked a taste for the cramming necessary for advancement in Hong Kong's examination-geared educational system, complicated these parental plans, and Ci-li and others who knew him felt he would do better in an upper-service occupation where his pleasant personality would stand him in good stead. Father, however, was impervious to Elder Daughter's oft-proffered advice on a better career for her brother. Fifth Son, who left school at age 13, resided some distance away at the tailor shop where he was apprenticed. With the exception of this lad, the boys were still attending secondary school.

In contrast to the education of the sons, Mother and Father failed to train Ci-li in a skill or career despite her abilities, and never viewed her as a possible carrier of the family heritage. On her own Ci-li learned by observation how to set up the butchery and display and market the meats, and she was pressed into assistance on her days off. On several occasions after passing the night at Ci-li's cottage, I walked down the hill with her and spent a couple of hours observing her adequate but unheralded management of this demanding role. Ci-li was not able, however, to select and purchase the meat at the godown, carve it in the shop, or barbeque the pork, and indeed could only have acquired these trade skills in the course of a somewhat formal apprenticeship.

Sometimes after observing at the store until 9 a.m., I strode with Father to the restaurant three doors down for his *dim sum* ("little hearts," small pastry snacks) tea. Teahouses in the resettlement estate are noisy, open restaurants where the fixtures scrape upon bare tile floors unadorned by rugs, quite unlike the carpeted and draped cafés on the outside, where better-dressed businessmen take their morning tea and coffee. This restaurant was furnished with plain, round marble-topped tables and hard, straightbacked folding chairs, some of which were set up on the pavement outside. Young waiters and waitresses plied the customers with bamboo trays of steamed delicacies suspended by a strap around their necks, and pushed their trolley carts from table to table, offering cakes, buns, puddings, and other "little hearts." Tea service, cups, and chopsticks are never sterilized, and it is customary for guests to douse the cups and chopsticks in a stream of boiling water from the teakettle, swirl the water around their bowls, and then empty it into the cuspidors under the table or on the exterior cement. Patrons sat wherever they could find a place, and diners were glad to share their table with strangers. Children of big families, initially split between several crowded tables, would from time to time mount vacant chairs closer to their mothers or grandmothers, and in this way unite the family around a single table. Young and old men alike read the morning paper, exchanged business intelligence, and chatted animatedly about yesterday's winners at the Happy Valley Racetrack.

Although courteous, Father was not an easy conversationalist at brunch, and his answers to my questions about home, family, and work were summary at best. Father began reading the morning paper as soon as the food arrived, and while I observed the shop and its patrons from my seat, he undertook occasional forays to chat with cronies and acquaintances at neighboring tables.

Meanwhile, at around 8 a.m., Mother, clad in gray rubber boots for protection from the puddles in the parking lot, set up her shop in the open market on the main lane at the bottom of the cottage hill. Mother conducted a brisk trade in frozen poultry and variety meats with the morning rush-hour shoppers from the estate some 200 yeards distant, with the aid of one or two sons. When Ci-li was at home from work, she pushed a four-wheeled flat dolly with the processed meat for sale from the butcher store to the hawker stand, clearing her pitch with the yell, "Watch out!" (in Chinese, *kuan-sui* – "boiling water"). Mother's mini-shop was a makeshift hawker's stall in a line of equally ramshackle unsturdy stalls; it consisted of planks of wood thrown across orange crates for a counter and an oil cloth roof as protection from the elements. Since her expenses were low, Mother could charge prices somewhat lower than those of established businesses. Customers jostled each other for an approach to the best-selling Danish hams, specialty sausages, and blocks of frozen chicken wings.

On sweltering June mornings I watched a press of customers so great that Mother, even with the continual assistance of three children, was unable to break away for a flask of tea. Marketing ended at noon, when the estate housewives and grandmothers returned home to prepare the midday meal for their family. Mother took down her roof shortly afterward and returned the unsold meat to Father's store, and then she assisted with sales in the store all afternoon while Father placed orders with the wholesaler and took his afternoon tea. At 5:30 Mother packed her shopping bag with assorted cuts of beef for dinner and walked home to prepare the evening meal.

The Chu family

At home Father and Ci-li spoke aggressively on a number of family and work issues about which they felt strongly. Father's gruff manner was augmented by a fierce temper, which he turned on Mother and the children. When he failed to gain his way, Father exited belligerently and stayed out until he thought that the others were ready to concede.

Despite his rough-and-ready demeanor, however, Father was at heart a generous person who offered traditional hospitality to a circle of his friends. Father preferred to maintain a comfortable distance from others, as he did at *dim sum* with me, and I did not see him accept a favor in return for his own benevolence. Father insisted on paying the checks at *dim sum,* and he hosted inexpensive banquets and home-cooked dinners annually for Ci-li's teachers and friends, but he refused to allow the guests to reciprocate. Father forbade his offspring to accept gifts, apparently for fear of appearing acquisitive and spoiling the family's reputation. When Ci-li was presented a modest Seiko watch as a token of thanks from a friend she had helped, Father insisted that she return it, even though her own watch was broken. I perceived that, to Father, one-way gift giving without reciprocation was a device for showing his respect or admiration and that this practice created long-term obligations that he might wish to redeem later.

Mother was a gentle, even-tempered woman, whose relaxed demeanor offset Father's rough stiffness. Ci-li pointed out that Mother was not completely dominated by her spouse and enjoyed a great deal of independence. Ci-li compared Mother with their close neighbor, Mrs. Lee, the mother of her best friend, Lin-ai Lee. Mrs. Lee was controlled by her husband, a small shopkeeper in the Shau Kei Wan market.

"Mrs. Lee must wait on her husband's every need," explained Ci-li. "Even though she does day work for a living, Mrs. Lee is expected to serve him at home. She doesn't even have time for herself on Chinese New Year. Last year Mrs. Lee wanted to go to the Wong Tai Sin Temple, and offered to prepare dinner in advance for her husband to warm up when he was hungry. However, her husband couldn't bear her absence, and wanted her to stay home, wait for him to return, and cook dinner for him, so she couldn't go. My mother is free to leave for the temple or any place when she's not working."

According to Ci-li, a good marriage was characterized by mutual respect. Mother's ability to work or pay visits without permission from Father was an example of Father's tolerance, in her view. Mother and Father thus had partially separated spheres of action, and Ci-li also commended the joint effort of her parents in the butcher store. Ci-li realized that Mother's inability to shape the rules of family discourse with Father and to control his outbursts of temper was unfortunate, but in Ci-li's opinion her parents had a good relationship. "My generation is going to set even higher standards," she believed. Starting with the freedom to work and pursue their own activities won by Mother's generation of women, Ci-li's cohort of husbands and wives would work together and plan for the family and leisure, thereby strengthening the marital bond.

The children's temperaments varied: Eldest Brother, the firstborn, and Second Sister, the lastborn, were quiet like Mother, and the other boys and Ci-li were boisterous and argumentative like Father. In June, 1974, I spent 3 weeks in the Chus' household. At least once a day I heard the Chus attempting to resolve their family differences in loud argument. Typically, two contending siblings stood at opposite ends of the patch that bisected their abode and directed shouts of grievance at one another. The complainant yelled out an accusation, which the accused attempted to ignore by turning his or her back or simply walking away. The turned back was a posture that cooled off arguments that might have led to fights if both parties had participated in an equally heated matter, and it was also a tactic to obtain privacy in close surroundings that provided no other means of escape.

Father and Mother had filled their present occupations since Ci-li's childhood, and when she entered secondary school Ci-li was responsible for watching her brothers and sister each afternoon and coaching them in their homework. During this period the chores of laundry, cooking, and house cleaning inevitably fell to Ci-li. She took the Eldest Daughter role to heart and insisted that the siblings comply with her directives. Ci-li maintained her claim to the obedience of the siblings even while they were entering their mid-teens, although they more strongly sought independence from her frequent commands. Brothers and sister saw Ci-li as humorless and overbearing and were ever reluctant to accept her discipline. Ci-li was perturbed every time her authority was called into question.

When Ci-li began working, the responsibility for all the household chores fell to the siblings. Mother and Father, however, were not prepared to insist that the boys work around the home. Thus Ci-li received little parental support when she tried to force classwork and household tasks on the six younger Chus, who evaded her imprecations by turning their backs on her.

At one time Eldest Brother bore the brunt of Big Sister's criticism because he was a poor student. Later, however, when he followed Ci-li's homework schedule, the two siblings became much closer.

Younger Sister's inattention to school and household tasks was Ci-li's next target. In the initial years of family formation, when the Chus were new immigrants to Hong Kong from Chung-shan county and the first off-spring were only just arriving, the family was poor. By 1974, when Younger Sister had entered her teens, the domestic economy had strength-ened considerably. This dreamy, quiet child was not required to work at the stalls. Younger Sister's studies had continued to fall in arrears, and by this time family finances and contacts allowed Father to place her in the home of her primary 6 schoolteacher. There she boarded and was expected to study long hours in preparation for the Secondary School Entrance Examination. Teacher's middle-class family assigned no domes-tic chores to Younger Sister, and she began, in Ci-li' view, to take their somewhat better living standard for granted. Ci-li reported to me angrily, "Sister even used perfumed soap there, and now she acts as if our plain laundry soap isn't fine enough for her body!" What little capacity Younger Sister ever had for housework had evaporated.

After only a few weeks back home, Younger Sister grew morose and despondent from Ci-li's insistent and perhaps harsh criticism of her style and manner. She performed her set chores only under Ci-li's personal supervision, and each afternoon and evening she sought consolation by daydreaming on her bed and reading comic books and popular magazines. Ci-li then condemned her outright: "Sister, all you know how to do around here is eat. Why don't you stop dreaming and start earning the food we're giving you?" Perhaps under Teacher's benign influence Sister's study habits had improved, but her level of application simply could not approach Ci-li's rigorous standards. On several occasions during my visit, when Mother's work schedule allowed her to be present in the home with the two daughters, I heard her calmly but firmly caution Ci-li to temper her severity with Sister and the other children.

Ci-li confided to me her frustration at the erosion of her authority, to which even Mother now contributed, and her apprehension that denigration of her leadership role would entail adverse consequences for family cohesion and achievement. Eldest Chinese daughters are expected to care for and discipline all younger siblings but are seldom accorded the undisputed authority that their personality, as in the case of Ci-li, might seek and require. Indeed, the literature provides examples of elder sisters imperiously commanded by parentally favored younger brothers (Wolf, 1970). Rooted in such structural features of Chinese family life, the heterogeneity of traits, abilities, and interpersonal styles among the Chu siblings seemed to balance, if not equalize, their adversary relationships.

Family religious observances

Market legend holds that families of small tradesmen and artisans are more superstitious than those who toil for a fixed wage. Father, Mother, and their fellow shopkeepers and hawkers at the Shau Kei Wan market, operating at small profit margins subject to negotiation and much uncertainty, were persuaded that their business fortunes depended upon the benevolence of hundreds of gods and lesser personages, organized into a vast bureaucracy to run the universe with all its heavens, hells, and living worlds. Since most of the gods are humans deified after death, they appreciate worldly offerings of precious objects and fine food and drink as do the living, and smile with favor upon earthly feasts and festivals in their honor. Traders were careful to observe the main Buddhist, Confucian, and Taoist ceremonies and festivals of worship.

I observed Mother's active participation in the Lunar New Year (when all the gods descend to earth on a tour of inspection); the Ch'ing Ming Festival, or Festival of Sweeping the Tombs (which occasions visits to family grave sites); and the Fifth Month (Dragon Boat) Festival, when Mother prepared *chung* (glutinous rice dumplings) for family and friends. During the August Yue Lan, the Festival of the August Moon (the seventh day of the seventh lunar month), she burned paper in honor of the frustrated romance of the Weaving Maid and Cowherd. Mother held membership in a neighborhood Seventh Daughter Club, whose monthly membership fees underwrote the ritual social celebration of the Double Seventh holiday. When a member married, she presented the club with a gift of barbecued pork, small sugar cakes, and fresh tropical fruit, and new mothers offered red-colored eggs to the celebrants. To further cement her ties with market women and to participate in enjoyable excursions to distant temples upon occasion, Mother joined other local chit funds (where celebration money is accumulated) to purchase food, paper wreaths, and other small offerings during the Festivals of Kuan-yin, Goddess of Mercy, and Tien Hou, Empress of Heaven.

Mother regularly sought counsel with the fortune tellers at the crowded, elaborate, and newly reconstructed Wong Tai Sin temple, over 1 hour by bus and cross-harbor ferry from the Chus' home. One Sunday afternoon, Mother returned from Wong Tai Sin worried and downcast. Ci-li explained: "Mother was warned about an unsettled family affair. If she does not attend to it at once, a misfortune is bound to occur. Mother visited the fortune teller again and was cautioned anew about a future mishap. Next time I'd better go and find out for myself."

The following Sunday afternoon Ci-li and her best friend, Lin-ai Lee, visited the Wong Tai Sin temple. The pair respectfully knelt to burn incense at an altar. Ci-li then emptied a lot (a long, flat, inscribed bamboo stick) from the lot container. Ci-li presented her stick to the guardian of the lots, who interpreted the omens. Ci-li told me in wonderment, "My forecast was pretty much the same as Mother's, even though the lot guardian did not know we were related. That's fate for you! A sixteen-year-old cousin of Mother's died ten years ago. The spirit is getting on in years and unless we arrange a marriage for the soul of the deceased cousin she will return to earth restless and cause trouble for the whole family."

With the assistance of the lot guardian diviner, a match was arranged for cousin's spirit and a wedding feast was enacted. The celebrants burned imitation currency, to facilitate the entry of funds into the nether regions where the newlyweds would be requiring it. The procession of Seven Sister's members, Ci-li and Younger Sister, and the family of the departed husband carried a set of umbrellas to deflect all evil ghosts, who are unable to bend around obstacles.

The proxy marriage embedded the other-worldly nuptials in a hierarchical set of family relations. Unmarried Chinese women are bereft of a lineage that would worship their souls after death. They can become honored ancestors by later generations only through marriage, when their soul tablet joins that of their husband and is worshipped with him by his family. By rectifying the imbalance in their family ancestral relations, the female Chus attempted to ward off the miseries foretold by the oracle.

Education

Father strongly insisted that each child receive an education, and thus Ci-li was able to complete secondary school. Lin-ai, however, was required to leave school at age 10, primarily because her labor was even more vital to the Lee family. Ci-li explained: "Father is enlightened [in Cantonese, *hoi-t'ung*, "open minded"], but unfortunately Mr. Lee is conservative and stubborn and thinks it is useless for a family to educate its daughters, and Lin-ai had to help with the housework and care for the younger children while Mrs. Lee worked as an amah. My parents tried to convince Father Lee that Lin-ai would qualify for a better job if she completed primary school, and I agreed with them. Now Lin-ai can't get a decent job at all. She followed her mother's footsteps and became a domestic servant, like me, but she can't speak enough English to work for those Europeans who pay higher wages to an English-speaking servant who can look after their children."

Because of the small number of university places, many Hong Kong secondary schools must slow down and narrow an already select population of entrants, and the repetition of grades is seen by most educators as an inevitable stage in a pupil's academic completion schedule. Those who proceed through form V have learned to prepare well for university entrance tests. A school's academic reputation relies on the consistent success of its candidates on the university entrance examinations, and the number of its pupils permitted to sit for the exam depends on the performance of their antecedent group. Most of the students above the age of 15 in Hong Kong's better secondary schools are potential university material, but since under 10% can actually be placed in the colony's postsecondary institutions, the remainder are unable to graduate at these schools.

After repeating primary 6, Ci-li entered a Methodist Anglo-Chinese secondary school, where as a student of average ability she was obliged to repeat one grade before matriculation, at age 17. She was unable, however, to obtain the English-language Secondary School Leaving Certificate, a necessity for positions in the civil service and white-collar sector. Ci-li's command of English was adequate for household work among expatriates, and she improved her conversational skills in their homes. While still an amah, Ci-li went on to complete several night school courses, and was finally able at age 24 to pass the civil service examination for a bottom-rung uniformed clerical position.

Academic training notwithstanding, Ci-li's obligations to her family paralleled those of all my less-educated working daughters. Although she entered the work force later, she maintained her economic contribution 2 or 3 years longer than the others, who married and transferred their family loyalties before age 25. Ci-li more than repaid the cost of her upbringing to her family and in all other respects fully justified Father's and Mother's patient confidence in her.

The Chus' aspirations for Eldest Brother were higher. In 1974 Eldest Brother was a form IV student at a well-regarded Roman Catholic Anglo-Chinese secondary school in Shau Kei Wan. Eldest Brother was not initially committed to his schooling, but after several years he became active in the youth social group at this school, joined the choir, and converted to Catholicism. On each of my Sunday morning visits with the Chus, Eldest Brother responded brightly to the tolling church bells and walked down the hill to sing for the morning choir service.

The enrollment squeeze in Hong Kong secondary schools caused the Shau Kei Wan school to restrict the number of students in its higher forms, and only one-third of the form IV students passed to form V in 1973–4 and 1974–5. This administrative practice maximized the school's chances of sending most of its last-year (form VI) pupils to the University of Hong Kong or the Chinese University. In the summer of 1974 Eldest Brother was instructed to re-enroll in form IV and to again sit for the form V entrance test in the spring of 1975. The Chus were dissatisfied with this retardation and began actively exploring alternative channels for Eldest Brother's advancement.

The first scheme they considered was enrollment in a Canadian high school. Eldest Brother applied to several Ontario schools, and when he received his first acceptance letter, Mother and Father sat down to take an accounting of the family's financial resources. They were dismayed to discover that their existing funds would support him only as far as high school graduation, not through university graduation. The family also wondered whether Eldest Brother could perhaps work his way through college. Aware of Canadian restrictions on work permits for student visa holders, the family decided these could be circumvented through unregistered employment in Chinatown in Toronto or Vancouver. Ci-li suggested that since all Westerners she knew enjoyed Chinese barbecue pork, Eldest Brother might learn the technique of producing this sweet, reddish brown meat over the summer and then be assured of a steady position in a Chinese butchery in Canada.

Ci-li preferred a vocational school in the tourist industries for him because she regarded Eldest Brother as sufficiently competent and personable to qualify as a restaurant maître d' hôtel in a good Hong Kong hotel. Although her suggestion seemed practical, it was regarded by Father and Mother as insufficiently promising academically and financially. Eldest Brother was reluctantly sent back to form IV, in the hope that he would do better in 1974–5 and be accepted into form V the following year, and finally form VI the year after that. Ultimately, Eldest Brother entered form V, but he was required to repeat form V as well. Most of his schoolmates had pursued the same course, and the standards of acceptance into the highest form had thereby become even more competitive. Despite diligent application, Eldest Brother could not attain the coveted place in the top one-third of the class.

Amahs, old and new

Traditionally domestic servants were fed and housed by their employers and were understood to be part of the family (Pruitt, 1967). A servant therefore spent relatively little cash on her personal upkeep and might even economize on expenditures for her own family members residing with her. The amah did not have much time of her own, was expected to live and toil around the clock for her masters, and could be summoned from bed to cook noodles or rice porridge for them. She would nevertheless be expected to arise the following dawn as usual to stoke the fire, prepare the kitchen, and begin household tasks. The traditional amah was released from duty only on the two or three annual Chinese holidays, and any additional free time remained at the discretion of the employer. In recent years, the availability of factory work has reduced the proportion of women desiring to enter domestic service, and the evening attractions of the peer culture have further undercut the few benefits of live-in employment. Therefore the established employment patterns of servants are changing greatly, and those young women who do become servants can bargain for wages and hours that approach or even exceed semi-skilled factory levels. English-speaking young women like Ci-li work for Western families whose demands might be less predictable than in Chinese households but who may agree to shorter workdays or weeks and more flexible working arrangements. Domestics in Western expatriate households are free to seek evening, weekend, and other part-time jobs, but they do forego pay when their employers take vacations or long leaves.

Ci-li insisted on delimiting her work week and maintaining a life independent of any employer, and she accomplished this by simultaneously holding three or four part-time housekeeping jobs, even though this often required her to hurry at midday between domiciles. Ci-li described her work system: "I do the necessary tasks, such as washing one day and ironing the next. When I finish the work, I leave early. If I can't get the work done in time, I stay later without charging overtime. If one day it rains and I can't hang out the wash, I leave it, and return on Saturday or Sunday afternoon when I'm free."

Ci-li hoped to remain in the family food-service line but to perform less arduous tasks than those shouldered by her parents. With the intention of qualifying as a chef in a large Hong Kong hotel, Ci-li enrolled in a course in continental cuisine at a 6-month fee of $100. Her class was taught dessert preparation two evenings per week. She pressed pink icing flowerettes from plastic tubing at home and was delighted when her cakes rose high. Although Ci-li could not afford to continue with lessons on main course cookery, she justified the time, energy, and expense of her baking class for its application to home entertaining and party giving, in which she took much pleasure.

Always keen to learn and work with groups of her peers, Ci-li was stimulated by the camaraderie of Sunday morning cake decoration lessons with her cooking schoolmates at a Chinese-owned bakery in Wan Chai. For Shana's first birthday party, which we celebrated with my combined English classes in our apartment, Ci-li contributed the surprise gift of the afternoon: a triple-layer vanilla cake decorated with icing rosettes. When it was served, all of the students drifted away from my vegetable salad platters and the patio barbeque, and with little of their usual social restraint gleefully devoured this treat.

Building steadily upon her secondary-level instruction, 2 years of evening courses in English grammar, and conversational practice in her employers' families, Ci-li was finally in late 1977 able to pass a civil service examination, which admitted her to employment with the Hong Kong Customs Department. Ci-li reported to me by letter that after a year on the job, she was assigned to a unit that scoured the holds of incoming ships in search of contraband narcotics. Ci-li praised the chief of her unit, who was willing to work with his staff in the hot engine room. This hard-working, spirited unit has won a good reputation for foiling would-be smugglers. Although Ci-li enthusiastically responded to its challenges, this job was difficult for a woman. Ci-li's hands had already been roughened by fuel oil and detergents, and she found it almost impossible to bear the heat under the holds in summer months. Ci-li wondered how long she would be able to keep up this demanding routine.

By a fortunate coincidence, Father stopped over in December, 1978, for 3 days in Toronto and Niagara Falls on a fortnight package tour of North America. I was expecting him after a letter from Ci-li, and I joined his tour party for their regular semiformal evening banquet at a Chinatown restaurant. I asked Father about Ci-li's work in Hong Kong customs, and he seemed pleased at Ci-li's prospects for advancement in government employment but somewhat impatient at her slow rise in income, which at that time had not reached $400 monthly. His comments indicated that the Chu family would continue to propel Ci-li upward in the job world.

Peers

Confined to her employer's immediate domicile and marketing chores, the traditional Chinese domestic worker was often more isolated than the housewives she served and was rarely able to form many friends and outside acquaintances (Pruitt, 1967). Although this is still the case for many Hong Kong amahs, Ci-li easily made friends among the domestic servants in the same apartment houses while they walked children to the nearby park or shopped. In addition, Ci-li pursued the friendships formed earlier at school and other work.

The bond between Ci-li and Lin-ai had grown stronger since their teens, and they tried to locate employers in the same neighborhood or even on the same street. The two girls would occasionally spend the night together in the tiny servant quarters allotted to one of them and when one was without work she assisted her partner with the laundry or cleaning and chatted to make the time pass more quickly. Upper-class Chinese employers would not have allowed this intimate sharing of work and experience, which transgresses the traditional proscription of an extensive personal life for servants. The non-Chinese families for whom Ci-li and Lin-ai worked were mostly unaware of the inherited master-servant norms, and this was a central reason why Ci-li preferred employment in the expatriate community.

Like many other working daughters in this study, Ci-li regularly visited the cinema with former school classmates. These friends also accompanied Ci-li to meet my English classes on Sunday and holiday outings at a small rocky beach cove in Shau Kei Wan. Ci-li threw herself into these outings with a whirl of energy, and she busied herself in her cooking shed hours beforehand, cooking large platters of fried noodles, mixed vegetables, and bean sprouts for the picnickers. Ci-li took pride in her skills as a hostess for these Shau Kei Wan beach parties and, taking after Father, would not permit anyone else to purchase or help prepare the food.

Ci-li formed close friendships when her secondary school class or other groups of pupils were hired to collate subscriber lists for the annual telephone directory and to count residents and collect household data for the Hong Kong Census of 1971. The census date was decreed a secondary school holiday, and the students were expected to walk between sometimes inhospitable dwellings completing pre-coded forms with vital demographic statistics. Afterward the pupils were assigned clerical tasks processing the census data for its eventual storage on cards. Ci-li recalled, "We worked under a lot of time pressure, and this forced us to cooperate closely. Sometimes we worked long into the night to tally all those numbers and so we sent out to a restaurant for dinner, which we ate in the census office. When the work was completed, a large picnic was organized to celebrate, and even now this same census group reunites for *dim sum* and dinner parties."

When I visited the Chus in the summer of 1974, Ci-li was dating a young electrician named Luke Lo. The couple had met 4 years earlier on the phone book project and then worked together on the census, where he was a team leader. Luke went on to complete a trade school apprenticeship, which enabled him to gain employment as a maintenance electrician at Kai Tak Airport. Ci-li and Luke visited inexpensive restaurants for coffee and tea after work and on weekends and chatted about their respective futures. They were also together at reunions of their census group during picnic parties and New Territories outings. Luke encouraged Ci-li's ambition to improve herself, and he supported her decision to better her job by upgrading her English. He criticized her for spending her spare time in frivolous pursuits, like cake baking and entertaining. Luke elicited in Ci-li the resolve to plan more carefully, so that she could make the decisive turn from domestic to government service.

Like other unmarried working daughters in my sample who were keen on bettering their class standing (Chin-yiu, Ming), Ci-li would not commit herself to marriage before she had achieved her plans. The friendship of Ci-li and Luke fostered their mutual aid for advances in the future. As Ci-li put it: "Luke says I have many things to learn, and he is always urging me to study. He earns a little more than I do, but I still like to pay my own way when we attend films, and last night I purchased his ticket, too. Sometimes when the cinema is crowded and we can't buy two adjacent seats at the boxoffice, we go in anyway and just sit apart."

Even though Ci-li eventually became a civil service official, she retained her respect for manual labor, and indeed regarded this as one of Luke's strong points: "Luke works hard at the airport, at an honest occupation. When I judge people, it's their character and not their income prospects that matters to me. I sincerely respect Luke. But I am somewhat uncomfortable at his increased attachment to me. I do not intend to marry for a number of years yet, so perhaps we should now temporarily see less of each other. If we keep on developing our relationship, his feelings will become even more serious. But I'm not sure whether I will share those emotions. But on the other hand, you don't have to be in love with someone to marry him. You can get to know him very well and approach work and life in common, and that will be and excellent basis for marriage. Maybe Luke and I someday might accomplish that, who knows?"

Ci-li found her attraction to Luke Lo growing stronger as they matured, and he allowed her sufficient space to pursue her career and peer-group interests. The couple became engaged in 1979 and Ci-li wrote me in December that their marriage was imminent.

Summary

Ci-li fully met the expectations placed upon her by the Chus as their eldest daughter. This shop-owning family possessed the financial resources to provide more education for Ci-li than was received by the working-class women of my sample. But Ci-li, like many other young women, was never trained in skills above low-paid office work. Two or three of her brothers were, on the other hand, given practical instruction, which led to skilled trades. Despite this shortcoming, Ci-li's home environment, together with her school and job experiences, enabled her eventually to undertake successful self-betterment efforts.

Ci-li chose for a time to become a relatively well-paid domestic servant. She used the practice in English conversation this calling afforded to help prepare herself for permanent civil service employment. Ci-li was supported in her initiative by her family, which sought advancement through her elevated job status and improved income. Ci-li was the only working daughter in my study to make the leap from menial employment to a white-collar position.

Ci-li's success required her to postpone consideration of marriage, and Luke offered timely encouragement that strengthened her resolve to take on extra study in order to change job categories. His support was the crucial test of the person Ci-li would marry when the proper time came, and now Ci-li and Luke are married and working together in the Hong Kong civil service.

Summary: a comparison

Rainbow, Sa-li, and Ci-li were employed in the tourist and expatriate service sector as waitresses and domestic worker. A regular experience of the work setting was contact with Westerners' life-styles and values. Despite proximity to the mass media and consumer goods culture, which is believed by others to weaken the social fabric and disrupt family relations, the three women demonstrated heightened senses of responsibility to their families.

Rainbow and Ci-li were eldest daughters, and they were expected as such to perform heavy household chores, including extensive child-care duties, before they began their employment. After entering the labor force, these women remitted more than 75% of their wages to their families. Sa-li, the youngest of four siblings, was spared house-work and child-care tasks when young, but Sa-li's wages as a factory girl and waitress likewise vitally augmented the family budget. In addition to family necessities, Sa-li's income was channeled to Second Brother's expensive wedding celebration and the first-month birthday banquet for the son of Eldest Sister.

All three women came from financially solvent working-class families, which educated their daughters through the intermediate or upper forms of secondary school. The three girls obtained more English-language training than the factory women, whose education generally ended with primary school. Consequently, Rainbow, Sa-li, and Ci-li entered lower-level service occupations that required some English fluency. They joined the labor force later than the factory daughters, and Sa-li and Ci-li remained there until their mid-20s, and married in their late 20s.

Rainbow was the sole respondent to leave work for marriage. Friction inevitably ensued between Rainbow and Father when she withdrew her substantial financial contribution. Rainbow deliberately calculated the specific financial claim she believed the family would require of her, and for the rest she argued that her wages, energy, and time as a minor had already more than repaid her debt for her upbringing. All other respondents dutifully accepted, even in the period between age 21 and their marriages, parental definitions.

In contrast, Ci-li adopted an upwardly mobile strategy and strove to better her family prosperity by achieving a sharp rise in job category. Sa-li and Ci-li both sustained long-term obligations to their families. Rainbow in her own way accepted her responsibility for a fair share of filial devotion. All three prided themselves on their obedience to the expectations that their family and society placed upon working daughters.

4. Two white-collar workers

Waiting for the Star Ferry at 8:30 a.m. and 5:00 p.m., white-collar workers form queues so long that they are roped off at intervals like cattle to prevent jostling for places on the ferry en masse. At noon they pack the coffee shops and hawker stalls in Kowloon's Tsim Sha Tsui and Hong Kong's Central District, their great numbers giving rise to the proliferation of Western-style quick-lunch counters, like Wimpy Burgers. As in other countries, white-collar workers, a sizable and increasing portion of the work force, are not evenly distributed, and in Hong Kong they are especially concentrated in the Hong Kong central business district, which adds to the peak hour intensity and volume of the movement of office and commercial personnel.

The assumption by women of clerical and sales positions is a recent phenomenon. These occupations are not stereotyped as female jobs as in contemporary European-American culture, and men are no less likely to be hired as bank clerks or telephone operators and are more likely than women to work as office clerks or at over-the-counter sales. In some positions clerical workers do not always earn higher wages than skilled industrial workers. However, the clerical workers and saleswomen enjoy more work stability than their sisters who are engaged in piecework machining, and because of what are regarded as higher-status job conditions, such jobs are popular with today's school graduates. Since the requirement of secondary-level Anglo-Chinese education has until recently demanded a considerable financial cushion, most white-collar working women come from a petit bourgeois or upper-working-class background. Such is the case for the two women described in this chapter.

Working in Hong Kong's Central District brings white-collar women into direct contact with Westerners. They not only sell articles to Western clientele, but they also enjoy close social relations with Western businessmen in established middle-rung occupations. Buyers, office managers, and visiting regional sales representatives call upon the offices and stores in which these women are stationed. On such occasions, these women enter into conversation with and may be included in evenings out to entertain the visiting Western dignitaries. Not surprisingly, the manner of the Western employers and coworkers influences these office workers. This is most visible in the young women's dress code of tailored dresses and suits, panty hose, and make-up, which replace the pleated skirts and T-shirts, worn blue jeans, bobby socks, and scrubbed faces of blue-collar women.

Are influences of such a work milieu more than skin deep? The following two cases evidence the ways social backgrounds and work routine affect white-collar daughters. Unlike waitresses, who hustle for their tips, not to mention factory girls, who frantically operate the assembly line for their piecework pay, sales and office workers predictably obtain not only a salary but a substantial New Year's bonus as well. Their higher education and stable, relatively routinized jobs give them a greater possibility to calculate their work in cause-and-effect terms. Longer work, if accompanied by proper planning, leads to savings and a better life, according to the white-collar worker. It is not unusual to find an office worker cherishing an identifiable plan for the future. This is consistent with her work setting, and planning as a way of life is known to occur in comparable strata in the West (Gissing, 1969). What is unique to the Hong Kong Chinese is the office worker's application of these precepts of planning to aid her family's livelihood. She hopes not only to elevate the standard of living of the small family that she will form but to contribute to and gratify the expectations of her natal family. This is another instance of the continual adaptation of the centripetal Chinese family to the urban industrial setting.

Chin-yiu: success in the office

The oldest of five children, Chin-yiu Lam was expected by her petit bourgeois family to attend secondary school, obtain a white-collar job, help the family with her earnings, and marry a white-collar man. Her family background instilled in Chin-yiu and her younger siblings a compelling desire to achieve upward social mobility. But when Father's small manufacturing business collapsed, the family could not ensure success of 13-year-old Chin-yiu in any concrete manner. Her dark prospects were over the years gradually dispelled by her determined struggle to secure independently the educational qualifications necessary to aid her family. Chin-yiu called herself a planner, and her life history illustrates how a highly motivated and capable working daughter overcomes adversity and helps restore the life chances of all other family members.

With quick, nervous mannerisms, stacatto speech, and short nods of agreement in conversation, Chin-yiu gave the impression that she was eager to please family and friends. Of medium height and proportions, Chin-yiu permed her short hair and was conventionally garbed in a tailored Western one-piece dress, nylons, and high-heeled pumps, and she ritualistically applied eye liner and mascara. Chin-yiu achieved the required office-girl look on a more slender clothing and cosmetics budget than most other secretarial employees. She owned two winter dresses and two for warm days, and she perfected a routine for maintaining this meager wardrobe, which included hand laundering her dress and hose every evening. Chin-yiu was saving her wages for the education of her two youngest siblings through secondary school, other family expenses, and her wedding trousseau.

Home and family

Chin-yiu lived with her parents and younger siblings in a four-story tenement block on Nathan Road in the Mong Kok district of Kowloon. This main artery bisects Tsim Sha Tsui, the downtown hub, and is thronged with residents and visitors engaged in buying, selling, and transmitting in this cosmopolitan bazaar. A myriad of curbside shops and large arcades, imposing neon signs, hotels, and offices keep Nathan Road perpetually bustling. The narrow stucco and plaster houses bordering the Mong Kok stretch of Nathan Road were constructed before World War I. With tall upper-level balconies fronting the street, the buildings were perhaps inspired by Macanese architects whose designs lent the area a Mediterranean patina before they were outnumbered by the modern concrete steel and glass high rises. In this thickly populated district these balconies are used as living space, and occupants suspend their laundry from bamboo poles wedged into the balcony rafters. Vegetables and herbs are put out for drying, and long tubes of Chinese sausages and other preserved foodstuffs hang from cords, lending a marketplace atmosphere to the streets.

The Lam tenement on the east side of Nathan Road was flanked by a brightly lit lamp and shade studio and by a high-fidelity stereo shop that emitted insistent rhythms and melodies during long business hours. Overseeing each floor of the tenement was the family of the "chief tenant," who rented it from the absentee landlord and sublet the individual cubicles and bed spaces to a mélange of individuals and families. Chin-yiu's father was the superintendent of the second floor and selected for the Lams the high-tiered balcony, two front rooms, and one adjoining cubicle at a monthly rent of only $75. In 1973 when I first made the family's acquaintance, I was interested to learn that the miniroom was being readied for occupancy by Chin-yiu and Heung-ng, her husband-to-be.

The spacious front rooms were the only two on this level that swung open to ventilate the interior and admit the afternoon sunlight. The other rooms had fixed postage-stamp size windows, and several of the residents slept in cubicles without natural lighting. All tenants shared the Lam's large kitchen, which was equipped with a sink, several hot plates with a bottled gas cooking source, and a refrigerator. Each housewife carried her wok and cooking ingredients to this space, where she stirfried and steamed her family's meals, and then returned to serve them in her own compartment. The single communal lavatory was located near the back porch.

Proud of her family home and anxious to accommodate my interest in visiting the quarters of working women, Chin-yiu several times invited me for dinner. On each occasion she attentively replenished my two-thirds-full rice bowl with steamed rice and a main dish of bean curd or steamed fish. Third Sister spoon-fed rice to Shana at my side in an easy chair while the two youngest sons quickly consumed their meal and began throwing the dice for Parcheesi on the linoleum floor beside us. Despite my satisfaction at these invitations and Mother's cooking, Chin-yiu's hovering began to ruffle me after dinner. When the table was cleared and folded, she from time to time lifted Shana from her chair, caressed her only briefly, and then put Shana down again. Chin-yiu's evident domestic awkwardness and unsteadiness with my infant contrasted with the polished nurturing of Ming, A-li, Shu-pui, and other working daughters who were forced by family circumstances to care for their young brothers and sisters and who relaxed me by their skill in delighting Shana over extended periods of time. Chin-yiu initiated several conversations with me about my family in California and my research assistant's life at the Chinese University, but she dropped these subjects after a few perfunctory interchanges. It seemed to me that Chin-yiu did not at this time allow herself sufficient ease in my presence to dispense with ritual gestures of politeness.

Chin-yiu was even more tense during my conversations with Mother. Even though Chin-yiu had apprised me that Mother was opinionated and spoke far more than Father in the domestic circle, I was unable to coax Mother into discussions of home and family. Mother preferred to remain in the kitchen. She had never worked for a wage and although she helped Father manage the tenement, her tasks of homemaking and child care seemed to occupy her fully. Mother's limited interaction with people outside the home contributed to her awkwardness with me: She had difficulty sustaining a conversation in standard Cantonese, and she did not fathom the interests I had in learning about her ordinary life.

Under such circumstances my other interviewees responded by including their mothers in the conversation, but Chin-yiu was unable to do so. When I spoke to Mother, Chin-yiu quickly answered in her stead, wishing to help me. Chin-yiu seemed to have felt a personal responsibility to occupy all of my time while I was in the home out of overweening politeness; she also acted as if I were a resource that ought not to be shared. Thus while I was a guest at the Lams, Chin-yiu concentrated more attention on her comportment and demeanor than on explaining her family history and dynamics.

Mother and Father were 1950 emigrants from Ch'ao-chou city (Ch'ao-an), located near Swatow. Mae's parents were also Ch'iu-chaonese, and both Mrs. Goh and Mrs. Lam kept house and were active members of women's groups (*hui*) that observed Buddhist holiday ceremonies. The main festivities in the Buddhist calendar are the birthdays of Kwan-yin, goddess of fecundity and mercy, and Yue Lan, the Festival of Hungry Souls, regarded with special affection by the Ch'iu-chao people throughout Southeast Asia.

The Feast of the Hungry Souls, or the Hungry Ghost Festival, is a Buddhist-inspired celebration observed on the fifteenth day of the seventh lunar month (late August). Believers conceive of souls as hungry and thirsty, restless and plagued with desire, who can bring misery to earthly beings if not placated. Observers therefore ask the priests of a Buddhist temple to read a mass for the dead, especially for those who were abandoned by their families and receive no sustenance. All "hungry souls" are invited to partake of a meal and to use paper replicas of houses, gardens, furniture, automobiles, airplanes, and heaps of "money" (Eberhard, 1972:107–9). During the festival, Taoist priests chant and Ch'iu-chao operas are staged in the playground space of re-settlement estates and adjoining empty lots, which are covered with tents to ward off rain and spirits.

Chin-yiu did not assist in Mother's preparation for the Hungry Ghost Festival, although Mae, more closely involved in parental concerns, did lend her presence. I was unable to attend with Chin-yiu's mother, but I am sure that like other mothers she fully enjoyed her experience with other worshippers and that her family supported the expenditure of time and money on such religious celebrations. The Hong Kong popu-lace considers the maintenance of folk festivities to bring good luck to the household and to ensure the happy marriage of daughters, the birth of sons to daughters-in-law, and the general well-being of the home. Chin-yiu would perform similar rituals when she married.

Like many Hong Kong refugees from newly liberated urban China who had once known rosier times as small, ambitious capitalists, Father had to abandon his possessions when he and Mother emigrated to the colony. He struggled to replicate his former substantial purchasing power in entrepreneurial Hong Kong, but it proved impossible for Father, as for many others, to attain a constantly rising income or even financial cushion. With another native from Ch'ao-an, who also was mobilizing new capital after his flight to Hong Kong, Father owned and operated a small workshop of fewer than ten employees where sweaters and outside wear were knitted. Neither Father nor his partner appeared to have been experts in the knitting trade. The business fell apart, and on the eve of the Lunar New Year, when all bills fall due, the partner suddenly and without warning absconded with the factory's working capital. Father attempted unsuccessfully to ascertain his whereabouts. Even with help from relatives and friends, he was unable to clear his debt, and the firm was bankrupt. During Father's ensuing 6 months of unemployment, Chin-yiu informed me, "He just sat idly around the home without lifting a finger to help Mother in her household chores. Father visited the teahouse every morning and then hung around the house like a fish out of water, a beaten man."

Teahouse conversation is comforting and serves a function for men of enforced leisure. Like other unemployed or self-employed fathers, Mr. Lam punctiliously followed a teahouse routine, which afforded him access to an assortment of convivial friends and acquaintances. Local city and village news, information, and employment leads were passed around the tables by those congregated. P'ui-ch'ing's father, an itinerant house painter, traded valuable job leads on contract letting every morning over small cups of bitter Ch'iu-chao tea and miniature stuffed dumplings. Ma-ci's father, an often unemployed hawker, similarly had a favorite teahouse retreat. Chin-yiu's father probably learned from his teahouse cronies that his past business experiences could qualify him as a bookkeeper in a small trading firm.

Father was likely advised by teahouse consensus that for such a post he needed no additional training or skills beyond his middle school education, which had provided instruction in the Chinese abacus. Moreover, he had accumulated ciphering and account maintenance skills in his knitting business. I surmised from family conversation that through the intercession of a well-placed friend or relative in the teahouse claque Father obtained an accounting position in a small Mong Kok firm. Father appeared satisfied in this occupation, but he was seldom able to return home before 9 p.m., and therefore my dinner visits were coming to a close when he greeted the family, hung his abacus from a nail on the wall, and sat down to his late meal.

The career of an office worker

At age 13, Chin-yiu looked forward to her first year of middle school in an atmosphere of family buoyancy. After the bankruptcy, however, even the earning power of an early teenager was required, and Chin-yiu's education was truncated. Chin-yiu was sent to work for 2½ years on the assembly line at the large Fairchild Semiconductor factory in the Kwun Tong district, side by side with hundreds of other teenage girls.

When Mae, Wai-gun, and Suyin were 12 and 13, they also began factory toil, but since they came from working-class families, they perceived their substantial burden as preordained and bore it with resignation. Chin-yiu's mind, however, was elaborating plans to recoup her educational losses and attain the white-collar position to which she had aspired even as her fingers were deftly assembling miniature semiconductor components. The Lams' tenacious striving to lift themselves from what they considered temporary adversity and to re-attain their rightful economic standing in the community affected Chin-yiu. Her parents articulated a clear desire for their children (First and Second Daughters above all) to aid them in promoting family recovery and they exhorted Chin-yiu to mobilize her personal ambitions and talents on the family's behalf.

The Lam family encouraged Chin-yiu to attend evening school. They shared with her the joint vision of success and inspired her whenever her interest flagged. "Mother and Father told me that I must find a way ahead and improve my job by education." At *dim sum* ("little hearts," small pastry snacks) lunches in Mong Kok teahouses and annual class reunion picnics on New Territories beaches, Chin-yiu's primary school classmates informed her of their job experiences. Chin-yiu learned that those with secondary education were able to enter white-collar positions, and she resolved to emulate their accomplishments. The upward pull of Chin-yiu's parental training and close peer group support thus helped her to improve by stages her position and salary. Totally absent in the Fairchild Semiconductor factory were apprenticeship or job upgrading programs, codes of advancement for the individual worker, and management concern for a stable work force. Under these circumstances, which were representative of factory employment in Hong Kong, and lacking Chin-yiu's parental endorsement, her working-class coworkers at Fairchild Semiconductor, when seeking escape from the widely disliked, closely monitored assembly-line routine, could only change factories and try piecework. At considerable cost, Mae and Wai-gun also attended evening school for several years, with the hope of bettering their status. But since they lacked guidance and direction, they selected courses on impulse and derived no concrete employment benefits from their studies. Chin-yiu, however, enrolled only in secretarial courses and channeled her energies in the narrow curriculum leading directly to job placement.

Although Chin-yiu presented her wages to Mother twice monthly for 3 years, she nonetheless managed to find time to complete evening school commercial and English courses and qualify for office employment. She was first hired by a Shanghainese businessman to run errands, make tea, and perform other menial services in his trading office. Chin-yiu tolerated her lack of status in this small firm because it offered her the opportunity to master the rudiments of each office task. After 6 months her employer entrusted her with typing of correspondence, filing, and telephone communication. She was then ready for advancement to the telex-based office of a medium-size Chinese factory in Kwun Tong. During the next 3 years Chin-yiu continued to perfect her secretarial skills until she obtained the position she held when we met: secretary in the sales office of General Electric, where she handled incoming phone calls, carried on the firm's exclusively English correspondence, and operated the telex.

In spring of 1973, Chin-yiu's monthly salary, which she continued to bestow upon her family, was $140, often augmented by overtime to $160. Because Chin-yiu had quit night school after form III in 1966, she received no formal instruction in electronic communication equipment. Now Chin-yiu aspired to gain on-the-job training in the global communication procedures of transnational enterprises.

In one of our conversations on her work and education, Chin-yiu recognized that she had lost considerable time in helping to reverse the Lam family fortunes. She articulated remorselessly the singular role of the female firstborn in devotion and dedication to the entire family prosperity: "It wasn't Father's fault, and we were all on hand to help rescue the family. And especially myself as an eldest daughter. Eldest daughters must serve the family. That's what elder daughters must do."

Chin-yiu's spadework cleared the way for Second Sister's easier entry into a white-collar career. Because of Chin-yiu's earnings, Wah-yiu was able to complete form III before the family required her to enter factory employment. Wah-yiu, too, signed on at Fairchild Semiconductor in Kwun Tong. Following Chin-yiu's lead, she simultaneously continued her technical education in a Mong Kok evening school. With this certified training she was hired by a British export-import firm at a salary exceeding Chin-yiu's highest expected earnings. Wah-yiu then advanced to an executive secretarial position in the firm.

Wah-yiu also contributed approximately three-quarters of her pay to the family purse until her marriage. In 1973, when I met the Lams, Wah-yiu was engaged and was saving her residual income for her forthcoming nuptials. Wah-yiu's intended was a sales representative for Jardine Matheson, Ltd., one of the colony's major long-standing China traders. The first son in a family with commercial background, his promising career with this influential house of Taipans was of supreme importance to his family.

Wah-yiu was more relaxed in conversation and more sophisticated in manner, dress, and makeup than Chin-yiu and seemed more self-confident. In other households to which I had been introduced by eldest daughters, the younger siblings were prepared and often eager to share their lives by participating in my interview conversations. Although Wah-yiu chatted politely and even smoothly with me, her unruffled exterior belied the Lams' struggle from the depths of poverty. She confessed to few of the financial and occupational problems that beset working daughters, and she was difficult to engage in frank discussion.

Not only Wah-yiu's manner and expectations from life but fashionable dress distinguished her from more modestly attired Chin-yiu. While Chin-yiu and I were chatting before dinner one evening, Wah-yiu sat at a corner dressing table confidently grooming herself for a dinner party with her future in-laws. She was donning an expensive, three-quarters length print dress that rustled as she deftly made up her face, curled her hair with an electric curling iron, and applied perfume. Her fiancé entered in a well-cut brown suit to greet the Lams, nodded to Shana and me, and the couple withdrew to the girls' bedroom where they playfully chose Wah-yiu's evening jewelry attire, and then ceremoniously exited for the restaurant meal.

Slightly bewildered by Second Sister's glitter and finery was Third Sister, Pao-yiu. Two years before she had also left school at age 13 to sign on at Fairchild, but unlike her two elder sisters Pao-yiu expressed no desire to enter an office. Pao-yiu was more comfortable in the company of family and friends than with continuing education. Seemingly content with Fairchild employment, she lacked the ambition to wrestle for a slightly higher hourly wage at a cut-and-sew piecework factory job. In one of our after-dinner conversations, I asked Pao-yiu whether she intended to upgrade her skills like her sisters. She shrugged her shoulders and commented, "The life of a working girl is the same on any job."

The emptiness of Pao-yiu's personal vision contrasted remarkably with the drive for individual and family betterment manifested by her elder sisters. The crisis in family fortunes occurred in Pao-yiu's infancy, and therefore the dashing of the family's high business expectations was not imprinted in her memory. The family had begun to recover during Pao-yiu's childhood. When Pao-yiu reached adolescence, Father had partially reestablished himself, and the employment of her older sisters substantially augmented the family purse. The family could then tolerate Pao-yiu's indifference to material values. Pao-yiu's tastes and dress were simple; she was a quiet and patient child who enjoyed playing games and who cleverly constructed Lego edifices for my daughter's amusement.

Between 1963 and 1972 (the primary 6 matriculation dates of

Chin-yiu and Pao-yiu), commercial and white-collar schooling and short-term certification courses for the technical and semiprofessional workers significantly increased in industry, service, and commerce. The requisite skills of English, filing, and bookkeeping were relatively easy for Chin-yiu's cohort to acquire on the job or in evening courses. The path from factory to office was quite narrow by the 1970s. After completing an English language-based academic or commercial course in lower-secondary school, most well-placed office and clerical workers had to obtain their more specialized office skills in technical and trade school. Today Chin-yiu would have much more difficulty in ascending the career ladder. This shed light on Pao-yiu's seeming lack of ambition.

"Plan, plan, plan!"

One of my 1971 English classes had been comprised of twenty outgoing young upper-working-class men and women who were beginning to circulate among Westerners and enjoy Hong Kong night life. Choi Nga-jing ("Angel"), one of the alumni, had in the interim befriended Chin-yiu at the Chinese factory office, where she operated the telephone switchboard, and she brought Chin-yiu to a class reunion in February, 1973, at my apartment. Chin-yiu was anxious to learn more English and improve her social skills through contact with Westerners, and she proposed an informal weekly conversation circle with me, to which Angel and Suyin were invited. At the circle we discussed how to complete a job history form and carry on a job interview in Cantonese and English, from which I learned much of their childhood family backgrounds and their likes and dislikes of their jobs.

Five years earlier in the same Chinese factory, Chin-yiu met a 21-year-old technician, Heung-ng, youngest son in a Ch'iu-chao family of four boys. Their courtship soon began. Because the marriages of Chin-yiu and Angel were imminent in 1973, they no longer budgeted much time for leisure activities with workmates or former classmates. Chin-yiu expected that upon marriage, contacts with her peers would lessen further.

Chin-yiu and I also discussed her home and work life in detail on Saturdays while visiting teahouses, boutiques, marketplaces, and strolling with Shana in a downtown park. On two or three of these occasions Heung-ng joined us to share a restaurant meal and afterward a promenade on Nathan Road in Mong Kok. Chin-yiu and Heung-ng were eager for me to sample other Ch'iu-chao delicacies in addition to the family fare at the Lams. The well-patronized Ch'iu-chao restaurant, the Red Mayflower on Nathan Road, overflowed with a crowd of expectant diners jostling one another on the evening we arrived, competing for the attention of the headwaiter and the next available table. Two-foot-long graceful garrupa swam to and fro in the aquarium, which served as the restaurant's front window, and when the waiter at last attended us he asked us to accompany him to the tank. He scooped up the fish to which we pointed and rapidly conveyed it to the kitchen for steaming. Complementing this main course were cold chicken slices with green onion and sesame oil, tiny boiled pigeon eggs, steamed chicken blood, an omelet cooked with steamed oysters, and hot *congee.* My interviewees and friends of various other dialects similarly delighted in exposing me to the uniqueness of the kitchen artistry of their group.

To reciprocate these warm-hearted invitations, I invited a number of the working daughters on different occasions to dinner at several of Hong Kong's well-appointed but reasonably priced foreign restaurants, such as La Traviata, Le Marseilles, and several Indian and Pakistani curry houses. Only there, away from their accustomed milieu, would their sense of hospitality permit me to act as hostess and meet the evening's expenses. Besides amiable dining, these dinners afforded me the opportunity to observe the individual and small-group responses of working-class Cantonese women to what for them were novel and exotic surroundings. Just as the factory girls seemed satisfied with pastries and much tea at Cantonese *dim sum* lunches, my tablemates selected from the Indian restaurant menus those unleavened, fried wheat flour products that resembled their native stuffed *won-tons.* The office girls partook more freely of *subji* (vegetables) and curries, and all exclaimed at the potency of the red pepper seasoning.

One evening in March, 1973, Chin-yiu and Heung-ng ventured forth with me to test the pungent fare of the Moghul, a Punjabi curry house. Despite a number of South Asian restaurants that dotted Tsim Sha Tsui and Hong Kong Island, neither Chin-yiu nor Heung-ng had sought to explore this large Asian cultural area through its culinary tradition. The cuisine of the subcontinent is enriched by the patient simmering of a treasure chest of spices and aromatics in clarified butter, and it was presented on heavy and expensive tableware in a softly lit and decorous atmosphere, with tape-recorded Punjabi melodies in the background. The Moghul in this respect contrasted with even the best Cantonese restaurants, which depend for their success on the rapid stir frying of the freshest possible, carefully chopped ingredients and a limited number of sauce constituents, and which carry the occasion with casual table service, plain wooden chopsticks, and low-cost crockery.

Chin-yiu and Heung-ng managed to consume most of what we ordered but, since they shunned the soothing yoghurt, suffered from the hot pepper flavor more than necessary. After tea with masala spices they engaged the Cantonese waiter in a lively conversation on the relative merits of Asian foods. The discussion turned then to the main regional Chinese dishes and their special characteristic ingredients, sauces, taste ranges, and cooking methods: spicy Szechuanese, Shanghai fish recipes, the classical Peking banquet fare, and the richly varied dishes of southeast China. Next my guests and the waiter congratulated themselves as Chinese on their openness to experiment with curry, but the preordained consensus was that in the end nothing could match the range, diversity, and flavor of the Chinese kitchen. This stylized ranking procedure is an affirmation of the larger Chinese tradition, in which Hong Kong residents identify themselves with a common historical and cultural legacy superior to that of their Asian neighbors. In the face of foreign claims to high culture, the southeastern Chinese pull together and temporarily ignore ethnolinguistic cleavages to celebrate their preeminence.

I interviewed my working-class daughters in classrooms offered by social welfare institutions, in their homes, at coffee shops and teahouses, at the beach, in my home, or while passing time in resettlement estates. In all of these person-to-person dialogues the working girls responded to my questioning frankly and informatively. My interactionist approach led me to supplement my interview-based analysis of working lives in the Hong Kong social structure with participant observation on the relationships of the women with their peers, their families of origin, and the families into which they would marry. I therefore expanded my knowledge of the women's situations by including in discussions and excursions all of the male partners they had introduced me to. I anticipated that the family and work lives of these men and their attitudes toward my respondents would become transparent through our two- or three-way conversations. Since I spoke Cantonese and was familiar with Hong Kong life, I also hoped that my presence would not inhibit the accustomed interaction of the couples.

However, the clear and confident definitions of my relationships with the working daughters were not preserved in the presence of their male partners. Some women acted restrained and proper and lost their conversational openness. Although Heung-ng was a good listener, whose presence encouraged Chin-yiu's volubility, all of her words became directed to him. When we visited Angel's fiancé, a travel bureau clerk, at a teahouse, he became the object of her energy and attention. Thus although Chin-yiu and Angel maintained a bright and airy banter, their social role changes prevented me from leading our talks into fields of substantive sociological interest. Although enjoyable in their own right, occasions with males present never evoked the frank sharing of personal experiences and sentiment that I had come to value.

Chin-yiu's account of Heung-ng's virtues helps explain the respect she had for him: "He's a quiet, sober, and hard-working person. He doesn't enjoy dancing parties, and he saves his money diligently. He's considerate and is willing to talk everything over with me."

Although Heung-ng's family converted to Roman Catholicism, both of the young people were born in the district of Shan-t'ou (Swatow). According to Chin-yiu, neither set of parents was opposed to the religious intermarriage. Her Buddhist-leaning elders were not especially critical because Chin-yiu was female and would leave the family line after marriage. Heung-ng's parents accepted Chin-yiu because his older brothers had already married, borne sons, and were successful in their careers. Chin-yiu explained that progeny was the most important consideration of Chinese. Once a family was assured of the future line, it could relax its standard for the spouse of the lastborn, like Heung-ng. She continued, "Heung-ng doesn't need to worry about meeting his obligations to his parents because his elder brothers have already fulfilled their hopes. The family line matters much more to us all than religion. Heung-ng's parents raised no objections when we told them that we are going to live in my home."

Apparently space was not available in Heung-ng's family dwelling to accommodate the couple, and thus, in a departure from tradition, the couple's room and board during the first few years of their marriage would be partly subsidized by the Lams. Matrilocal residence suggests to the patrilineal Chinese that the husband may not dispose of sufficient earning power to raise his new family, and it strengthens the wife's family loyalty. Hence it is a disfavored residence pattern in Hong Kong. However, Chin-yiu verbally made light of custom and opted for the most practical and business-like residential solution.

The couple's 5-year engagement was necessary to release Chin-yiu's salary for the education of the two younger Lam sons, and it also made it possible for Chin-yiu to advance as far as mid-career. If their marriage had occurred earlier, Chin-yiu would undoubtedly have forfeited the last increments of job training that led to her upper-secretarial post in favor of early childbearing. Chin-yiu planned at last to marry in January of 1974, at age 24, when the couple could afford to bear and nurture offspring. It was then expected that Chin-yiu would rank employment second to raising a family while her children were growing up.

Heung-ng was saving for a $4,000 wedding feast and Chin-yiu for her dowry. She reported: "Since our engagement we've put aside almost three thousand dollars, and even that's not enough! I should save much more. My parents would not stand for a travel wedding, for, after all, I'm the eldest."

Chin-yiu's savings during the engagement period underwrote a dowry that included a handsome set of bedroom furnishings. The couple's bunk bed already occupied their cubicle, and on the top level was placed the tuner-amplifier of their new stereo, whose speakers stood on the floor at the head and foot of the bed. A large chest of drawers against the wall that contained Chin-yiu's new clothes completed the bridal suite. Chin-yiu had begun fortnightly visits to a Ch'iu-chao tailor in Wan Chai, where her wedding wardrobe was being sewn. On social occasions Chin-yiu wore a jade necklace and a tiny diamond ring given to her by Father's younger brother upon her engagement, and she planned to don these accessories at her wedding.

Chin-yiu and Wah-yiu were favorites of their bachelor uncle, who returned to Hong Kong in early 1973 from a sojourn in Madagascar (where there are about 15,000 Chinese, mainly in retail trade and service industries), where he had founded a trading company. Chin-yiu explained: "Uncle rescued his capital just in time. Other Chinese merchants waited too long, and lost out. Uncle is now looking for a good investment here in Hong Kong. He considered investing in a sweater-knitting factory, but it looked like quite a shaky proposition, and he's just waiting for the right capital venture. Uncle's driving a taxi now. He has no other kin to spend his money on, and he's looking forward to the wedding."

Following Chinese tradition, Chin-yiu's marriage was scheduled ahead of Wah-yiu's by 3 months. The close proximity of the two daughters' weddings would not impose a financial burden on the Lams because in each case the groom's family was underwriting the gala expenses. Wah-yiu's fiancé was much better situated than Heung-ng, and this in addition to his sibling order explained her younger marriage age. Chin-yiu pointed out with a trace of envy, "He draws a good salary at Jardine's, and they pay him lots of commission, too. Wah-yiu won't have any financial worries." Chin-yiu stressed that her future brother-in-law was an eldest son and was under considerable pressure to squire male offspring.

On the evening of my third dinner invitation at the Lams, I discussed Wah-yiu's plans with her and Chin-yiu. Wah-yiu accepted Chin-yiu's judgment that she must leave home to move in with her fiancé's family, and in response to my suggestion that Wah-yiu might encounter domestic difficulties with her in-laws, she remarked, "Don't scare me! It's too early to think about such matters." I then asked Wah-yiu whether she expected her future mother-in-law to speak to her about her duties in the home. Wah-yiu shrugged, "I'll just watch to see how things are done over there, and since they are nice people, everything will work out." In a situation of restricted choices, denial was Wah-yiu's way of coping. Wah-yiu continued, however, "Chin-yiu's lucky that she will live here with Mother. Naturally, mothers and daughters get along well together."

Chin-yiu contrasted her views on marriage with those of her parents and the older generation: "Disputes will be settled in a different way by Heung-ng and me. Some of the older married people in our tenement quarrel with their partners every day. Although my parents do not battle with one another, they have their serious differences during which Father just sits there speechless. Mother does all the talking. In our own case when differences arise, we will certainly talk things over."

Like other working daughters, Chin-yiu also differed from the older generation in her determination that she and Heung-ng would contribute equally to family decision making. The makings of a dilemma were present, because Heung-ng seemed taciturn like Father. Chin-yiu's pointed inclusions of Heung-ng on our outings was both a statement that she and Heung-ng would henceforth relate to outsiders as a unit and an exercise in the achievement of this form. (Several of the affianced working-class interviewees hesitated or declined flatly to invite their fiancés along on social occasions with me. Thus, I was never introduced to the prospective husbands of Wai-gun, Rainbow, or Ci-li.)

The marriage date was settled by their parents for January. Garbed in her newly tailored beige linen suit, Chin-yiu planned to register her marriage with Heung-ng at the City Hall before noon, after which the wedding party would pose for group photographs in the plaza. After greeting a bevy of relatives at Heung-ng's family home, the wedding party would proceed to a large restaurant that had been reserved for the festive banquet. A flower-bedecked room adjoining the dining hall would be made available for the bride to don her heavily embroidered red marriage gown, patterned on a Ming Dynasty wedding costume, that Chin-yiu planned to rent for the occasion. Chin-yiu would receive assistance in dressing, in greeting well wishers, and the ceremonial bowing to elders from a middle-age bridesmaid, practiced and jocular, who earned her living by serving as mistress of ceremonies at wedding galas. The bride would again change her clothing into a rented white wedding gown for more photographs and the short walk across the impromptu restaurant podium to the strains of Western ballroom music, where the master of ceremonies would deliver a 5-minute eulogy on the groom's strength of character, the merits of the groom's family in the community, and the bride's moral and domestic virtues. Chin-yiu would then return to her chambers to don a silk and chiffon dinner dress. The banquet would begin with a birds' nest soup, and the guests, a good number of whom would have arrived early to play mahjong and consume appetizers, would prepare to enjoy the traditional twelve-course meal. The bride usually has time for only a few spoonfuls of the delicate soup. Accompanied by the groom and his parents, she must toast each table of guests in turn. The mistress of ceremonies would help Chin-yiu to maintain lighthearted conversation and absorb on her behalf the generous quantities of spirits the guests proffer. When the fried rice, long-life noodles, and orange quarters have at last been served, the feast ends. Chin-yiu, Heung-ng, and the two sets of parents, siblings, and close relatives would then head the reception line to shake hands with the departing guests. For this final event, Chin-yiu would again wear her white tailored suit.

The length of their engagement allowed Chin-yiu and Heung-ng ample time to formulate goals for child spacing and child rearing. Ten months before her wedding, Chin-yiu said to me in a teahouse: "Mother, other relatives and friends reared their children from one day to the next, but my generation must plan! plan! plan! Plan when to marry, plan when to have the first child, then the second. Think about family circumstances before you decide whether to have the third. Otherwise, we'll be short of money."

Chin-yiu elaborated upon her reference to those other relatives who did not plan. Wah-yiu's future brother-in-law, second son in the family, married his girlfriend at age 19 because she was pregnant. Chin-yiu and Wah-yiu agreed that early marriage was economically foolish and swore that their planning would be superior. Chin-yiu said, "Premarital sex is more common these days. But it's still risky because if a woman is pregnant too early, the couple won't be able to afford the wedding ceremony their family hoped for her. We are delaying my marriage until we are ready for children."

She desired to bear only two children. In her view, planning the timing of children is accomplished by marital postponement, and Chin-yiu did not intend to practice oral contraception until she had at least borne her first, and perhaps her second, child. "Marriage *means* raising the next generation. We don't want to delay childbearing artificially in case we interfere with the first birth; then when we want it, we might not be able to have it." (Like Wai-gun, Chin-yiu did not wish to upset the elders' dream of an early grandson.)

Chin-yiu's employment trajectory from factory to office illustrates concretely her success in personal forecasting. Her marriage delay was consistent with her long-term personal and family economic planning. She conceived her planning powers as integral to her entire approach of life. Chin-yiu thus postponed consumer spending and an early wedding in favor of a heavy burden of vocational education, office work, and determined frugality in order eventually to achieve a higher standard of living and social status for herself, the Lams, and her future family, which her upward vision would shape.

Syut-wa: a saleswoman

Syut-wa Lau, age 21 in 1973, was a sales clerk in the smoke shop in the main lobby of the Hong Kong Hilton Hotel, where she worked an 8½-hour shift selling magazines, smokes and accessories, and sundries to hotel guests. Father was a concessionaire, who for many years operated with an older brother a staff canteen in the basement of a district police station. Mother worked part-time as a door-to-door rent collector in a Kowloon tenement building owned by one of Father's paternal uncles. The combined income of the Laus enabled the family to enjoy many of the comforts of consumer society in Hong Kong.

Syut-wa was of medium height with a slender figure. Her wide eyes and open countenance were supported by a broad, expansive, dimpled smile, imparting to her a demure and innocent appearance. Syut-wa's hair was cut and curled in simple page-boy fashion. Behind the counter at the Hilton Syut-wa wore the hotel's red *cheong sam*-style dress (fitted sheath with Mandarin collar and an open seam at the hem) uniform. After working hours Syut-wa dressed modishly in a tailored outfit and pumps resembling the white-collar worker and office girls with whom she associated. I met Syut-wa for *dim sum* lunch on my return visit to Hong Kong in December, 1972, on her day off at the Oceania Restaurant in the Ocean Terminal. She wore a red velveteen maxi-length dress, with fitted matching coat, of Japanese manufacture. Syut-wa was carefully made up in the current Japanese-inspired couture popularized in fashion magazines addressed to her office-girl milieu: bright red polished nails, bow-shaped red lipsticked mouth, apple-rouged cheeks, and thickly mascaraed eyes.

At home

The Laus resided on Ching San Road, a large street in the Sham Shui Po district of Kowloon. Their home was in a crowded neighborhood of tenements and open-air street markets, where hawkers vended to the Chinese populace factory clothing seconds, household utensils, and fresh fruit and vegetables. For several years Syut-wa, together with other white-collar workers, traveled 2½ miles on Nathan Road by bus; the ride was slow and bumpy, the exhaust fumes were overpowering, and the bus stopped frequently on thickly populated streets, stretching the ride to 45 minutes. They then crossed the harbor to the Central District. Only in 1973 was a new double-decker express cross-harbor bus put into service for the white-collar commuters to Victoria Island.

Syut-wa had resided since birth in a fourth-floor cold-water walk-up in a narrow tenement building. The apartment above the Laus' housed a privately operated medical clinic, and below them was a crowded day-care center. The narrowness of the dwellings and the absence of pavement space precluded play activities for the dozen day-care youngsters. The fourth-floor railroad flat opposite the Laus' was subdivided by improvised wooden panels into ten or more bed-spaces, sublet by the chief tenant. The residents in this hostel were mainly single male transients, and Syut-wa disliked living so near these itinerants. One evening Syut-wa and I took the bus home from downtown to share dinner, and as Syut-wa preceded me up the steep and poorly lit stairway, she turned to apologize: "You see, all the better-off families have moved out of this building, and we, too, would like to find a new apartment. It's getting too complicated here now." By "complicated" Syut-wa meant the mixed social class milieu and possibilities for gambling and other shady activities.

The Laus' flat consisted of a small living room, four bedrooms situated on the side of a long front-back corridor, and the kitchen. The master bedroom was located at the end of the flat facing Ching San Road, and it was lit and ventilated by two wide corner windows. Syut-wa's three younger brothers and her maternal and paternal grandmothers slept on bunk beds situated along one side of the corridor. Off this corridor were two small bedrooms, separated by wooden partitions; one was rented to an aunt of the Laus and the other was for Syut-wa.

Syut-wa's 8′ by 8′ windowless cubicle was separated from the living room and Aunt's bedroom by thin wooden partitions. Syut-wa arranged her space as neatly as possible: a bed, wardrobe, dresser, and night table took up the entire floor space. Colored posters of Omar Sharif, Tom Jones, Alain Delon, and Bruce Lee, the Cantonese karate exponent, adorned two walls. The third wall displayed several calendar-type photos of nude women on the beach and a large likeness of a female apparition floating in the wind.

The only working daughter of this study to possess her own room, Syut-wa proudly gave me a tour: "I took these posters from *Mini Magazine* [a Hong Kong version of *Playboy*]. The dream woman was the publicity poster of a boutique downtown in which my friend sells clothes." Next to the reading lamp on Syut-wa's night table was her current reading matter: a Hong Kong *TV Programme Guide* and a popular romance novel from Taiwan, a gift from a fellow sales clerk.

The Laus' kitchen, located at the rear of the corridor, possessed only one narrow window and a light bulb suspended from the ceiling. Near the window stood a sturdy old wood-burning stove, upon which rested a large steel wok (frying pan with a rounded base), a set of earthenware pots, and a stack of nested bamboo steamers. Cleavers, used for all manners of cutting, a circular thick butcher block fashioned from an unfinished slice of tree trunk, and chopsticks completed the set of work tools. Water in Hong Kong must be boiled before consumption; the Laus drew their supply from a single tap in the kitchen. On a counter beside the sink stood jars of cooking staples: sugar, salt, corn starch, fermented black beans, soy sauce, and a 5-gallon can of peanut oil, which is the standard medium for stir frying in the wok. Peanut oil that had splattered from the wok streaked the adjacent walls. The Laus did not place a high value on a spotless kitchen. A 1 month's rice store and quantities of other, less-used staples, such as rock sugar, instant Japanese noodle soup, medicinal herbs, and jars of pickled vegetables, were purchased on sale and were stored on an upper shelf in the adult bedroom.

Crockery, cutlery, and eating utensils were placed in a long wooden commode adjacent to the living-room wall. The refrigerator, which was treated as an article of furniture, was located next to the television set in this room and contained soft drinks, a melon or other tropical fruits, and a dish or two of mealtime leftovers. A Japanese-made rice steamer, the only electrical cooking appliance I saw in most Hong Kong kitchens, stood on the living-room commode, next to the table.

When I first visited Hong Kong home kitchens, I was surprised that the mothers and grandmothers of my interviewees tolerated cramped cooking arrangements that were frequently even more rudimentary than were the Laus'. When adequate preparation of the main ingredients is carried out in advance, the flexible and economic Chinese cuisine lends itself to the rapid assembly of satisfying, nutritious family meals. I therefore came to understand how cooks like Syut-wa's paternal grandmother, Mae's mother (see Chapter 2), and many others entrusted with family meal preparation could put together balanced, palatable, and relatively inexpensive family meals with a minimum of utensils and clean-up chores. Syut-wa's forebears effectively utilized stir-frying cooking techniques, using only the wok and its accompanying tools (paddle, steamer, and lid) and few other kitchen accessories.

Except for the small kitchen, the combined floor space of this multi-room apartment exceeded that of most other working-class families of my study. Such a substantial family dwelling could only be occupied by pre-war middle-class inhabitants of Hong Kong, who obtained it before the housing crisis of the mid-1960s. In the subsequent decade and a half, rampant inflation with the absence of government controls on the rental or purchase price of free-market flats priced apartments like these out of reach of all but the upper-middle-class Hong Kong families.

The family at ease

As late teenagers in 1948, Mother and Father were each brought by their widowed mothers to Hong Kong from the same town in Nan-hai country, north of Hong Kong in Kwangtung province. The two were already acquainted and their marriage was contracted within a year of their arrival. The newlyweds occupied their railroad flat at the invitation of Father's uncle, who had arrived in the colony earlier and had amassed property.

It is customary for Chinese mothers to be supported in their old age by their mature sons. It was thus natural that Paternal Grandmother was given a room in the newlyweds' flat and took charge of shopping, cooking, and the household finances (or *tang chia,* "take charge of the household," which signifies manage the budget). Since there were no sons in Hong Kong who could care for Maternal Grandmother, she was also taken under the family roof.

Maternal Grandmother worked as an unskilled laborer in a blue-jeans factory. She pushed a trolly loaded with stitched goods from the machinists' area to the pressers and then transported pressed garments on the same bulky conveyance to the packing area. She had to toil at unskilled and very low-paying factory employment in order to pay her own way in the home because of her tenuous household status. She also performed all of the menial tasks in the Lau household. The differential treatment of Paternal and Maternal Grandmother illustrates the Chinese patriarchy. Father and his family were expected to honor his mother, the oldest living member of his lineage in the home. Maternal Grandmother, who was not a member of the Lau lineage, obtained no religiously inspired veneration.

Father's older brother, who emigrated from the family's Nan-hai county town to Hong Kong in 1938, obtained work in a small police station canteen, of which he later became proprietor. Father was taken into his enterprise shortly after he arrived in the colony a decade later, and the two men have continued to earn their living there ever since. Work at the canteen generally detained Father until after 9 p.m., and I rarely saw him on my afternoon and dinner visits to the Lau family.

Mother's unlined face and trim figure belied her age of 42 in 1973; many multiparous working-class housewife mothers in my sample who were approaching their middle years had a tendency toward obesity.

I attributed Mother's attractiveness in part to the Laus' economic solvency and her relatively comfortable and assured job, and to the fact that she had given birth only four times, whereas many of the mothers had undergone the strain of seven or eight births. Mother dressed in neat pantsuits, and I never saw her don a worn housedress in the home, unlike poorer women I knew. Mrs. Lau's large eyes, open smile, and demure, cheerful expression seemed to set the pattern for Syut-wa's countenance and imparted to both a refined, middle-class appearance.

As soon as she arrived in the colony, Mother took piecework employment on a sewing machine in a garment workshop. Father's paternal uncle, Grand Uncle Lau, who had arrived in the colony in the late 1930s and had amassed real estate, then offered Mother a job selling Chinese-style wedding buns and pastries behind the counter of the teahouse he owned adjoining the Laus' tenement. Mother said, "People don't want those buns filled with soy bean paste and lotus seeds anymore. Most families now buy Western-style layer cakes for their wedding guests, so the business isn't too good." After 9 or 10 years dispensing wedding pastries, Grand Uncle Lau promoted Mother to the position of rent collector in one of his five-story tenements. She undertook this door-to-door assignment for 10 days each month and was paid a fixed percentage of the rents she delivered. In her spare time she assembled one part of a mass-produced garment on her home sewing machine for a nearby clothing shop. Mother's income may have exceeded the sum Father brought home from the canteen, Syut-wa told me. Mother explained "I do old-fashioned jobs and most of the time I've worked for relatives. My children are working in better and more modern occupations. They really get to see a lot of people from different parts of the world."

Mother's relationship with Syut-wa was close, and she prided herself on her understanding of the younger generation's goals. Affirming Syut-wa's right, and that of her entire generation, to lead her own life, Mrs. Lau was the only mother in my sample to consciously shape and promote her daughter's peer-group activities. In response, Syut-wa shared her experiences with Mother and confided in her. Based on her understanding of the rights and requirements of adolescence, Mother respected Syut-wa's need for privacy. Approaching age 20 in 1971, Syut-wa, who slept on a bunk bed in the corridor, made clear to her parents her wish for a private bedroom. The Laus had taken in two roomers, who occupied a small room off the corridor, and when they decided in 1971 to vacate, Syut-wa insisted upon appropriating that space for herself. Mother and Father at first disagreed on economic grounds and sought to locate another set of tenants. Syut-wa told them bluntly that if they valued rents more than her happiness, then she was prepared to leave the apartment and move into a bachelor flat with another saleswoman. Mother was flexible enough to respect Syut-wa's needs and, relenting of her previous plan, awarded the room to Syut-wa.

On my first dinner visit with the Laus, I arrived before Syut-wa returned from the Hilton. Mother introduced herself to me on the landing of the flat, smiled at Shana, who was in the backpack, and motioned me inside for a chat. Unlike many members of her generation, Mother had some secondary school education, which perhaps helped her form and articulate an outlook and opinions on Hong Kong life. Mother's alertness and ease of speech, which she developed from conversing regularly with diverse people while collecting rents, made it possible for me at once to embark upon a lively conversation with her. We spoke of her experiences living in increasingly crowded Hong Kong over the decades, her bargain hunting, her forthcoming vacation with Grand Uncle Lau to Malaysia and Singapore, and her plans for the higher education of Third Son.

Mother's unstrained existence was based upon a household division of labor with the two grandmothers. Paternal Grandmother, who was readying the kitchen for the evening meal when I arrived, left after we exchanged pleasantries. Mother sent her to a nearby delicatessen with $10 (H.K.) to purchase one of the delicacies frequently offered to visitors: filets of barbeque pork. Syut-wa came home an hour later, followed just before dinner was served by Maternal Grandmother, attired in her factory apparel – a black pajama suit made of inexpensive, shiny cotton. Several months earlier I discussed with Syut-wa the composition of her household. My research assistant, who joined us on that occasion, noted that Syut-wa omitted Maternal Grandmother from her list of household members. It was only upon seeing this hard-working, wizened form that I fully realized the weakness of her position in the home.

While dinner was being consumed, Maternal Grandmother sat silently on the lowest stool at the table, which put her eyes below everyone else's line of vision. When dinner was over, Maternal Grandmother cleared the table while the others remained to continue their discussion. After Maternal Grandmother had finished washing the dishes in the dark kitchen, she timidly walked over and sat next to Syut-wa. During a pause in the conversation, with averted eyes she asked me several polite questions: "How old is your daughter?" "Do you like Hong Kong?" "Do you like Chinese food?"

After dinner Paternal Grandmother, who was better groomed and heavier than Maternal Grandmother and wore a good-quality serge pajama suit, sat near me on the living room sofa smoking cigarettes and offering authoritative comments to the assembly at large. She turned to me and queried, "How long have you been in Hong Kong?" "Where are you staying?" "Who gave your daughter a Chinese name?" Then she lifted Shana into her arms, walked around the room, and pointed out to her the fixtures, several small statues, and objets d'art. The tour brought them to a cupboard, where Shana was encouraged to finger the dishes and plastic fruit, teacups and mugs, and toothpick holder, whose contents she soon spilled onto the floor amid much laughter. This grandmother was free to sponsor Shana's minor disruption of the cupboard display, since she was the most venerated family member.

The Laus, like many other Hong Kong families, were woven into a network of family members. They brought several relatives under their roof, entered business relations with relatives, and maintained active visiting relations with their entire family circle. The Laus' ample living quarters facilitated such close bonds of kinship, and to some extent their economic ease must have aided their interchange with relatives.

The Lau family was economically solvent. They earned enough to aspire to being part of the Hong Kong lower middle class. Their flat was adequate for most of their physical needs, but not for these status aspirations. Syut-wa reminded me that her family had several times considered an apartment in a middle-class housing estate, but they could not afford the tripling or even quadrupling of rent that such a move would have entailed. On the whole, however, Mother expressed contentment with the family's mode of living, and one evening after dinner she voiced the family outlook: "Life in Hong Kong is pretty good. You can buy anything you want here. Compared to other places, it is one of the few remaining 'paradises.' "

Education of the Lau children

Most working-class parents select a secondary school for their eldest daughter that is near their home, because they wish her to return home in good time to keep house and mind the younger siblings. The Laus chose a secondary school for 12-year-old Syut-wa that was somewhat distant but well regarded academically: a private Anglo-Chinese secondary school operated by a Catholic sisterhood and subsidized by the government. Mrs. Lau wished her daughter to be reasonably well qualified academically and to broaden her job opportunities through the contacts made during attendance in this school. The Laus practiced folk Buddhism, but their high appraisal of Syut-wa's future employment possibilities overrode any ethical objections they might have had to a Catholic environment for their children. After the first year at the school it was only a short step for Syut-wa to convert to the Catholic faith. Syut-wa recalled, "I thought I would get better grades and have more friends if I became Catholic. Anyway, the more preaching you hear, the more you believe!"

In the summer after she matriculated form III, Syut-wa and two of her classmates took jobs as salesgirls in a large toy store for tourists on an upper floor of the Ocean Terminal, "just to see if we could earn some money on our own." While still attending classes, they worked part-time in the late afternoons and early evening and on weekends through the fall, and eventually left school altogether in favor of full-time work in the toy store. Syut-wa's parents felt that the purpose of the school had been accomplished and accepted the discontinuation of her studies.

Syut-wa had three younger brothers, ages 18, 16, and 14 in 1973, the youngest of whom attended secondary school; the older two had left school to take employment. First Brother, who had form V education, was a telephone installer for the Hong Kong Telephone Company. Second Brother, who had acquired electronics and radio skills in evening school after attending form III, was a skilled technician in a radio assembly plant. Mother spoke to me about her wishes and plans for Second and Third Brothers' education: "The length of my children's schooling has depended on their interests and on the family's financial condition. My middle son likes electronics and wants to work with radio sets in a factory, and that's why he left form three for radio school and his present job. He went to school at night at a place called Columbia Academy, which is advertised everywhere and is supposed to be good. Actually, Columbia's connections weren't too helpful, and even after the one-year course there he has to settle for the low-paying factory job he has now. I wanted him to learn air-conditioning maintenance, but so far he's stuck on the radio business. My youngest son can study for as long as he wishes. Last year he unfortunately failed the entrance examination for a good government secondary school. Right now he's attending form one in a private school, which is more expensive and inferior to a boy's Catholic school we know, and he has applied to transfer. Third Son's present school costs ten dollars a month, which increases to twelve dollars in the second form. The Catholic school costs nine dollars, and the cost won't rise because it's subsidized. But it's very competitive and many lads will be sitting the entrance exams at the same time. My husband went to the Catholic school to fetch application forms for him and he had to queue up for almost an hour. Hong Kong is like that, you know!"

The Laus had more resources to invest in education than the working-class families of Mae, Suyin, and Wai-gun (Chapter 2). They sought better and longer education for each offspring. They chose the schools according to a plan, starting at the earliest grades, in contrast to choice of a primary school based on location or unsophisticated hearsay.

My presence at the dining table one evening sparked a discussion of improving Third Brother's job prospects by sending him to a Canadian university. On behalf of her family, Syut-wa asked me, "Which provinces have the strictest immigration legislation?" "Is it true that in Alberta any student who applies for a work permit automatically receives one?" "How much would it cost to attend a Canadian university for 3 years?" In the end, however, the Lau children had to do without a university education. The expenses of a North American venture turned out to be prohibitive, and the competition for places in a Hong Kong postsecondary institution was too stiff.

Always pragmatic, Mother felt that, ultimately, her children had to make their own ways. If they did well, they should continue in postsecondary education. If not, they should go out to work. The Laus did not accept the intrinsic importance of a college education as a means to broaden the ideas and values of young people, and they applauded the immediately useful applied technical skills acquired by the boys, but Mother did not stress the importance of Syut-wa obtaining such skills.

Syut-wa's work and friends

Syut-wa became friendly with the assistant manager of the Ocean Terminal toy shop, a capable bachelor girl named Ruby, who was interested in fashion, parties, and an active social life. Ruby introduced Syut-wa to her life-style, and Syut-wa showed me a couple of photographs showing the two at banquets and nightclubs together with smart-looking businessmen. "Ruby and I were invited to a party given by the British fellow who managed the toy shop," she explained. "The men in this photo are American, Japanese, and South Korean toy salesmen who were invited to this affair. The American liked Ruby and dated her afterward. In the next picture you see us with some other salesgirls at a dinner party at the Miramar Hotel hosted by the American and his friends." Syut-wa next showed me a snapshot one of the toy salesmen had taken of her and Ruby on an outing to the Hong Kong Botanic Gardens. As in the party pictures, the two aspiring socialities looked happy and enchanting and were dressed in high heels, simple but attractive frocks, and broad-brimmed hats.

According to Syut-wa, Mother felt that Ruby's social life and dating patterns were a negative influence on her: "Mother insisted that I spend more time at home. She complained that I should do more housework, too. I tried to meet Mother's wishes by returning earlier from work and staying out less. But after all, Ruby was my superior and I was obliged to respond to her social invitations. Knowing of my dispute with Mother over my personal freedom, and the long bus ride to and from work, Ruby offered to share her Tsim Sha Tsui flat with me. That was the time when Mother finally offered me the small room as my personal bedroom and I decided to stay with my family. Mother asked me to apply to the head office of the toy shop for a transfer to its branch on the Hong Kong side, and I did so. But even after I was reassigned, there was no reason for Ruby and I to end our friendship, and we continued to see each other after work. Finally, in order to satisfy Mother, I applied for a job at the duty-free shop at Kai Tak Airport, where the commissions are quite high. While I was waiting for an answer from the airport, I managed to get a position selling magazines in the Smoke Shop at the Hilton Hotel. Two weeks later I heard from the airport people and I decided to look into their offer. I phoned the Hilton one morning saying that my grandmother was ill and I had to look after her, and put in a trial day's work at the duty-free shop. I wasn't comfortable there because the other salesgirls used profanity and raised their voices all the time. I suppose they were competing for customers. So I decided that the Hilton Hotel was a better spot for me, and that's where I stayed ever since. Mother is pleased at my new job and my new workmates and friends and no longer scolds me when I do remain out late. I guess you could say I live a carefree life now."

Syut-wa contributed most of her salary to her family, including the lump sum 2-week bonus that she received at Chinese New Year. The sum was important in the family budget and figured in the education of Third Brother. Syut-wa did not appear to have many household tasks, especially with two grandmothers in the house, and Mother was probably using the expression "You should return home early to do the household tasks" as a way of stating her concern that Syut-wa remain close to the family unit and maintain her duties to the family economy. Given Mother's obeisance to the new generation of women, Mother believed she felt what other mothers could not feel: genuine empathy with the younger generation. Mother always claimed to me that she never interfered in the jobs of her children. She always preferred to exercise indirect influence instead of issuing parental edicts. Mother had the time, the interest, and the understanding to acquaint herself with Syut-wa's peer group and social activities, and she could thereby influence Syut-wa's friendship choices effectively, albeit subtly. Mother enjoyed discussing her daughter's work experiences, outings, and dates, and (as in the case of Ruby) Mother exercised her veto right in a spirit of participation rather than that of more openly authoritarian control.

Mother spoke favorably of the generational changes that have occurred since Hong Kong began industrializing in the 1950s and she claimed to support them. One afternoon over tea, Mother started a discussion of the changes she witnessed in the relationship between generations. She believed that the generation gap was wider between Chinese mothers and daughters than that between Western youths and their parents. "We Chinese are changing fast, whereas Westerners have had several decades to work out the same changes. Nowadays Hong Kong daughters' ideas differ from those of the older generation, and that is how it should be."

Mother regarded her direction of Syut-wa's life as reasonable because, to her, interference meant the complete control exercised by traditional Chinese parents over every facet of their daughters' lives. Mrs. Lau's views extended to the all-important subject of marriage.

Marriage
Mother wished Syut-wa to marry a man with good economic and social prospects. She saw no contradiction between her ideology of free

choice for youths and her efforts to arrange such a match for Syut-wa. Even though Syut-wa at age 21 was clearly unprepared for marriage, Mother was willing to discuss prospective suitors with intermediaries and with Syut-wa herself. Mother explained to me in a personal conversation: "Recently, several Hong Kong men who have emigrated to North America approached me through their relatives about marrying Syut-wa. These contacts mean that my daughter might now be able to choose a more comfortable life with the chance of business success in the United States or Canada. One of the men said that he had a good civil service job with the U.S. government. He was 25 and had come back to Hong Kong to look for a wife. I asked his aunt to prove to us that he was really employed by the government. But Auntie had no convincing evidence, and I suppose she was relying on his word. The only way you can actually be sure of such things is through your own relatives in the States. I therefore told Auntie that Syut-wa may be ready in 3 years to consider marriage. One can't be too cautious in such cases. However, I don't see any harm in waiting for a better-placed suitor to come back from overseas."

Syut-wa corroborated, independently of Mother, the desirable qualities of her future spouse. She wished to obtain a companion who could advance her social position, and Syut-wa was willing to depend on a marriage partner for her future prosperity; she lacked the initiative to advance her position on her own.

"I would like to marry a man who has the ambition and strength of character to better his understanding in life and knowledge of the world. Even if he is not well educated, his will to go forward is the main thing. But it is important that he improve my situation at the same time. A year ago I met a fellow at a party whom I really liked. I was impressed at his brightness, but he looked down on me and my friends, and we had a hard time communicating. I felt uncomfortable that I couldn't keep up with him."

Syut-wa and her friends had various opportunities to meet eligible men: "We attend parties and sometimes we date men we meet there. But if I meet someone special at a party, I would have to find out more about him before I took him very seriously. My parents would have to approve also."

At age 23, when Syut-wa did not yet have a beau, she affirmed: "I'm still too young to contemplate marriage. Marriage would be too troublesome." By "troublesome" she meant that her family needed her income for some time to come and also that she personally would find marriage less interesting than the station of a sheltered working girl in Hong Kong's cosmopolitan central district. Mother appeared to agree: "She should not give all this up lightly. I cook, keep house, wash Syut-wa's clothes. Her responsibilities are not great. Why should she marry so soon and lose all this comfort?"

Mother contrasted her own truncated adolescence to her daughter's ability to put off marriage in order to attain some of the benefits in life. In remaining single until age 20, Mother regarded herself as fortunate, because "an unmarried 18-year-old was practically an old maid back in my village. But nowadays, it's even possible for many 30-year-old women to make good marriages in Hong Kong!"

After marriage, Syut-wa did not intend to reside with her husband's family, no matter how agreeable her mother-in-law might be. Syut-wa's objection to patrilocal residence was grounded upon her supposition that her values and ideas would be markedly different from those held by her in-laws and her wish to retain and act upon her views. As Mother pointed out, "Syut-wa won't live with a mother-in-law because she's afraid that the younger generation's ideas are too different from those of the elders. That's true in my opinion. Syut-wa is eager to go the way of the contemporary younger generation in matters of dating, courtship, and marriage."

Summary

Syut-wa led a protected and reasonably comfortable existence in an extended family of upper-working-class economic standing. Starting from the time that Mother and Father emigrated from China, property-owning relatives in the colony had aided the Laus with jobs and accommodations, which shielded the family from much of the prevalent economic uncertainty. Syut-wa knew neither the extreme poverty and tragic family illness of Wai-gun's family nor the bankruptcy and economic ruin of Chin-yiu's family. She was a party neither to the cultural deprivation of Wai-gun nor the thirst for organized knowledge experienced by Ming. The Lau family was satisfied with its economic cushion and at ease in the consumer society of Hong Kong.

As eldest daughter, Syut-wa was assigned major economic responsibilities to the household. Mother was a woman who stressed an egalitarian partnership with her daughter, and Syut-wa did not regard these responsibilities as onerous tasks. Instead, Mother presented them as opportunities that enabled Syut-wa to explore the wider extrafamily worlds of work and friendship.

Summary: a comparison

Chin-yiu Lam and Syut-wa Lau originated in petit bourgeois and affluent working-class families, respectively. The enterprise of Chin-yiu's father floundered, whereas Syut-wa's father succeeded in stabilizing his small family partnership. When the two families advanced along their earning cycle and their incomes were expanded by the addition of the children's reasonably well-paid white-collar and service incomes to the family accounts, however, the resources of both exceeded those available to any of the working-class families I knew.

Reared in relatively comfortable environments, the two white-collar daughters were expected to carry forward their family status in their education, friendships, jobs, and marriages. Father Lam's business failure, however, disrupted the Lam family's plans to open broader vistas for Chin-yiu, and she was required to work exceptionally hard to upgrade her family income and her qualifications to the level originally envisaged. Syut-wa had no such overwhelming ambition, and she attained the acceptable educational level of lower-middle school and white-collar sales job as a matter of course. The different fortunes of the Lam and Lau families determined the outlook of the daughters: Chin-yiu, a secretary and planner, and Syut-wa, a salesgirl moving with the tide of family well-being. Eventually, both women attained the jobs appropriate to their stations in life.

Mothers were ambitious for their daughters. The specific economic circumstances of the two families differed, and the mothers' roles varied accordingly. Mother Lam prodded Chin-yiu to upgrade her economic status in the hope of recovering the family's past higher social position and attaining the job she might have had if Father had not gone bankrupt. Mother Lau was more concerned that her daughter select friends and beaux of the proper social standing and deportment. Chin-yiu and Syut-wa both complied with their families' economic and social aspirations for them.

Both eldest daughters were proud of their abilities to bear the full share of the family economic burden and advance their families' positions. The higher education of their younger brothers to levels beyond their own was attained in significant measure through their economic input. The Laus were uncomfortable with their tenement home and with Syut-wa's help were saving for an apartment in a more respectable neighborhood. Dining well in restaurants, teahouses, and at home and tasteful dress were high on the list of the Laus' current pleasures, and these extras were made possible by Syut-wa's wages.

The two white-collar women spent more for their own needs than did the blue-collar daughters. Their working environment in Hong Kong's financial and tourist centers widened their horizons of what could be purchased for a fee. Chin-yiu concentrated on budgeting her money for her splendid wedding, and Syut-wa saved for clothing purchases. Despite their abilities to advance their own consumer goals, both women were proud of their capabilities to aid their families.

5. Two women in the semiprofessions

The proportion of Hong Kong working women occupying the positions of nurse, teacher, and social worker was an estimated 6% of the total female labor force in 1971. In the past a secondary school graduation certificate qualified a young woman for such semiprofessions, but in the 1970s a college degree or equivalent academic certification became essential for appointment to and advancement in these positions. Relative to their cross-sectional cohort, which entered manufacturing occupations after primary school, the semiprofessionals, with their relatively high levels of education, wages, and security of employment, are select members of the Hong Kong working population.

One of the two women college graduates I introduce here taught in a postsecondary school and the second taught primary school for a short period and then became a social worker at a Christian welfare agency. According to the disjunctivist tenet that work-force commitment shatters family allegiances, the ideology of such educational and community service organizations binds their employees to overarching norms and values in conflict with centripetal family precepts. Therefore the two semiprofessional women ought to have been the least dutiful daughters in my sample.

Although it is true that the bureaucratic educational and welfare structures demanded ideological conformity from their employees, neither organization challenged centripetal familistic loyalties or provided alternatives to the familist way of life. Welfare agencies did not require local staff members to embrace agency dogma, because they were more visibly concerned with carrying out much-needed work among the poor than with recruiting converts in the short term.

A more important source of conformity to centripetal norms is the political nature of welfare funding. Although part of agency budgets derives from Western parental and oversight bodies, an increasing share is provided by the Hong Kong government's Council of Social Service. Agencies are at the mercy of the Hong Kong authorities, whom they choose not to alienate. Moreover, functionaries of the Lutheran, Catholic, and other Christian persuasions exercise considerable informal power in Hong Kong and actually share in the formulation and implementation of a political-ideological stance acceptable to the business community and government decision makers. In other settings, the denominational organizations are more radically activist, as the split between social reform and status quo orientations within the Catholic Church in Latin America demonstrates. In Hong Kong, however, the missionary welfare organizations have not articulated a consistent moral line favoring the oppressed, and as the case of Ming reveals, they may consciously repress spontaneous efforts for social justice.

It is often expected that large-scale professional bureaucracies, which expect their staff members to function as much more than paid hands, will give rise to a professional work or service ethic. Organizational commitment is fostered to a much greater extent among semiprofessionals than among blue-collar workers (Bendix, 1957; Kanter, 1977; Papanek, 1973). However, in another Chinese setting, Silin (1976) found that the managers of a Taiwanese factory, although they did not foster loyalty to the organization, did promote loyalty to themselves. Management personnel competed with one another to gain the favor of the company leader, and the consequent emergence of cliques prevented employee allegiance to a dominant value system of professional expertise or work ethic. The same was true for Ju-chen's school in Hong Kong, where the teachers' allegiance to the principal was stressed more than the goals of education. The consequent clique formation undermined adherence to a set of abstractly valued norms of service, which weakened the basis for any professional work ethic that might compete with the hold of the family over the teaching staff. In sum, the two cases that follow describe white-collar, large-scale, privately managed bureaucratic work settings in Hong Kong that exert no centrifugal pressures upon their employees and do not pull them away from their family norms and values.

Ju-chen: a teacher

The Leung family aspired to maintain a comfortable standard of living and provide sufficient education to enable each of its five offspring to obtain well-paid white-collar employment. Indeed, one of the two eldest sons attended a university, the youngest daughters aspired to follow in his footsteps, and Ju-chen was a teacher in the extension program of a Hong Kong college. It fell to Ju-chen, firstborn and economic leader of the family, to compensate for the permanent absence of her petit-bourgeois father, whose business ventures caused him to emigrate to Singapore, and she sought to perform her role well. Ju-chen was most comfortable at the center of her family (brothers and sisters, mother, and grandmother), and sought their esteem most of all. Ju-chen was saddened that her wish for recognition and power in the family went essentially unfulfilled.

Family and home

When the Leungs emigrated from Canton to Hong Kong in 1951, they left behind Father's sizable family dwelling, now sublet to tenants. Father's prosperous family background enabled him to send the children to school in Hong Kong. After only a few years in the colony, however, Father reemigrated to Singapore. Originally he had hoped to strike it rich and send for his family, but after a number of business failures, Father was forced to accept subsistence wages as a clerk in a small watch store, after which he was able to remit only small sums of money to his Hong Kong family. Like many Chinese businessmen in the South Seas, Father accepted his permanent isolation from wife and children and, in spite of his poor economic condition, remarried. He was wed to his Singapore wife according to customary ceremony, and in Singapore she was accorded primary wife status.

Father informed only Ju-chen and Fat-choi, his eldest son, about his second family and they, fearing that Mother would collapse psychologically if she learned the truth, did not disclose that he had remarried and that his former modest level of remittances had dwindled to nothing. The news was withheld not only to shelter Mother but to save Ju-chen's face in her circle of friends and colleagues. Better-educated Hong Kong youths, like Ju-chen and her siblings, considered Father's act in remarrying unfortunate both for him and for the family, but they never communicated this view of him.

The absence of Father's support and Mother's wish to spend lavishly on such events as First Son's wedding forced Ju-chen into a highly demanding provider role. Mother was not fully cognizant of the great size of her children's contribution, because of the pretense that Father was responsible for the family allowance. If Ju-chen had told Mother about

Father's new family, Mother might have realistically revised her assessment of the Leungs' economic potential and lowered the household living standard.

First Brother was a counter clerk at a travel agency in the Hong Kong Central District, and Second Brother held a desk job in an office of a large Western trading firm. The youngest child, age 16, was enrolled in a secretarial course and a 17-year-old sister attended secondary school.

Paternal Grandmother was supported by a daughter in New York, who remitted $100 every month for her living expenses. Ju-chen commented, "This is a tidy sum. It more than covers her rice and keeps her in fruit and other extras as well. We don't even need to save for her funeral, because Auntie in New York has started a fund for Grandmother's burial expenses." Chinese tradition by no means obliges a married daughter to support her elderly mother, but Auntie's generous pension made life tolerable in the home of the Leungs, who apparently appropriated for themselves a percentage of Grandmother's allowance.

During their first 15 years in Hong Kong, the Leung family occupied one and a half rooms in a Tsim Sha Tsui tenement, within commuting distance of the offices where the two brothers worked. Ju-chen rode a bus to her college and the two younger sisters took a bus to their schools. Thus the tenement's downtown location afforded the Leungs quick transportation to work and school as well as a wide selection of restaurants and teahouses and several open-air produce markets. On hot and humid evenings after supper, the children took refuge on the rooftop, where they studied or chatted and upon occasion brought their rice bowl and chopsticks to complete their supper.

The Leungs' cramped accommodations permitted only a bare minimum of household furnishings, each of which served multiple purposes. The sisters and Mother and Grandmother occupied adjoining bunk beds and the boys slept on a platform suspended from the ceiling (a cockloft), but on summer evenings they set up cots in the hall. Mother cooked on a single gas burner and nearby brazier. The Leungs' dining table, a circular slab of metal, rested atop their card table, which was folded and placed under one of the bunk beds after meals. There was a small refrigerator, a television, a telephone, and a high-fidelity console in a cupboard. The Leungs' housing conditions were similar to the cramped quarters of their working-class neighbors.

The Leungs' tenement was purchased by a land development firm, which tore it down to clear the plot for a high-rise apartment house in

1974. Ju-chen realized that Mother was delaying making the alternative housing arrangements until their home of nearly 15 years was destroyed from under them, so she took charge and, after studying the housing ads in the papers for weeks, purchased a flat in a new private housing estate, Mei Foo Sun Chuen. Ju-chen ordered the new furniture and commandeered the move.

The afternoon of my first visit to the Leungs' home, Typhoon Elsie was raging, but the families of Mei Foo Sun Chuen were strolling in the refreshing autumn air along their sheltered brick walkways, oblivious to the winds blowing around them. This self-contained apartment house complex is one of the largest privately financed condominiums in the world. It is financed partly by Mobil Gas and sits on reclaimed waterfront land edging Hong Kong's New Territories factory district of Sham Shui Po. The community is largely Chinese, but contains a sprinkling of British and Indian families and is uniformly middle and lower-middle class. A concrete island amid crowded industrial streets, Mei Foo Sun Chuen offers its self-contained amenities and services to residents; meat, fish, and vegetable markets; furniture and appliance shops; a Chicken Delight take-out villa; a Western coffee bar; Chinese teahouses and restaurants; and nurseries and primary schools. The Mei Foo Sun Chuen bus service transports residents along heavily trafficked Nathan Road to their workplaces in industrial and government offices, schools, and army barracks, and a private ferry takes other residents to the Vehicular Ferry Pier in Hong Kong's Central District. Housing in this middle-income settlement symbolizes the separation of family life from the world of work.

The Leungs' former tenement quarters, located in an area mixed with residences, stores, and workshops, did not distinguish them from working-class families, but the Mei Foo Sun Chuen housing complex was separated from the neighboring working-class factory area by concrete walls. These served partly to protect residents from crime and partly to demonstrate the higher status of the complex than that of the surrounding neighborhood. Robbery was a growing problem in the area, and numerous rapes were reported. The dormitory community, quiet and isolated during the day, became a setting in which muggings, thefts, and other violent crimes took place in desolated elevators and corridors, where passersby could not hear a call for help.

The Leungs' new flat was considerably larger than their previous apartment. Instead of the multipurpose one and a half tenement rooms, subdivided and with cocklofts, any of which could be used for sleeping and eating, and without a separate entrance, private kitchen, or bath of its own, the new apartment had several small rooms. There were two bedrooms, a living room, a dining area, a small kitchen, and a bathroom. Each room had its own function and had been furnished accordingly.

The living room became the display area of the house. The old serviceable but undecorative furniture, which was now considered out of place, was given away or sold and replaced by new matching furniture purchased on installment. The living room contained a rocker, several padded chairs, a plastic imitation teak dinner table, which did not fold up and hence occupied much space, several small tea tables, folding stools, a stuffed sofa covered in velour, and a large commode in which was displayed the hi-fi set and records, knicknacks of glass, pottery, peacock feathers, a teacup set, an empty but decorative 10-pound box of Swiss chocolates, and an unopened, 2-foot high bottle of VSOP brandy. The television was given a separate stand in the corner. The other rooms had new furniture as well: bunk beds, desks, and chairs. The kitchen was still organized in a practical fashion, but a matching set of porcelain pots replaced the assorted and more cumbersome earthenware vessels. A new washing machine stood in the corner.

The selection and upkeep of the more expensive furnishings and larger accommodations in Mei Foo Sun Chuen required more care than had the utilitarian and serviceable furniture in the older tenement, and the Leung family shifted its concern from survival to appearance. The more substantial of the Leungs' purchases included a secondhand car, ostensibly for transportation to and from work, but more frequently used for the sons' courtships. Mother and Grandmother were driven back to the older residential area with which they were familiar and preferred to shop for groceries, "where they know us."

Although only a small minority in Hong Kong can afford the status symbol of home as retreat, this goal is diffused through the media in their projection of the consumer-oriented family. Advertisements and Nathan Road shop windows and stores in Mei Foo Sun Chuen display the furnishings that the apartment dwellers are urged to purchase. For the newly established middle class, housing and furnishings are becoming a symbol of prosperity and well-being.

As a chief breadwinner, Ju-chen selected the Leungs' housing and furnishings and committed her salary to pay for them. She made most of the arrangements to purchase the flat. Ju-chen attributed her centrality in the family move to her position as eldest child in a family whose father was absent and mother unemployed and inexperienced in commercial negotiations.

Despite this, however, Ju-chen felt she would like more say in family budgeting. There were many areas of family disagreement, and most revolved around money. The family purchased the car against her expressed wishes. Ju-chen's brothers drove to work, but because they could not find an inexpensive car park near their offices, they had to park midway and take a bus or taxi the rest of the way. "A taxi would have been cheaper from the start!" Ju-chen complained. The battery went dead shortly after the car was purchased, and the replacement was expensive. "Naturally, I had to pay for the battery," she said. "When I heard the cost, I blew up in anger, walked out of our home and slammed the door!"

The Leungs occasionally discussed their major expenditures, but Ju-chen did not often have her way. When such was the case, she nonetheless had to accept the family's decision, which she did with barely suppressed resentment. Ju-chen tried to talk Mother out of certain "unwise" extravagances, but she was hampered in her arguments by her inability to reveal the father's noncontributory role. Ju-chen illustrated this dilemma by the large wedding banquet to be held for Fat-choi, her eldest brother: "I told Fat-choi to have a tea party with Western cakes, then go to Taiwan for a honeymoon. I also informed him about the package tour organized by Malaysian Airlines and the Hong Kong Hilton. The hotel sponsors a group wedding ceremony and everyone goes to Singapore for the honeymoon. The total cost is four hundred dollars instead of the four-thousand-dollar cost of the banquet here in Hong Kong. But Fat-choi didn't say a word. Anyway, Mother wouldn't be too happy if her eldest son had a travel wedding." Ju-chen resented being overruled. She explained to Mother that if such a substantial sum was spent on Fat-choi's wedding, less would be available for Second Sister's education abroad. Moreover, Ju-chen added, in a scarcely veiled threat, the money would have to come out of the savings for Mother's old age.

"I told Mother that we would do what we could for her, but she should not dip into the money saved for her old age. Mother replied, 'Never mind, we can always get money from Father for the wedding ceremony.' I didn't say anything, just grimaced. She doesn't have a realistic assessment of what Father will give to the family, and so I can't talk openly to Mother about these issues."

Ju-chen complained with feeling about the onesided demands on her income. She confessed to following the conventional mores, which dictated that she put the interests of her family ahead of her own. The Leung family, despite its financial dependence on her, took issue with Ju-chen's initial choice of apartment (they eventually accepted her second choice) and did not heed her views on her younger sisters' education, the purchase of an automobile, and the wedding ceremony for Fat-choi.

"Couldn't you sit down and discuss the various family needs, including your own, and work out a plan with your family?" I asked her.

"No, they'd think I was selfish. They won't listen to me," she replied.

"In other words, you lack the right to determine how the family's money is spent?"

"I've no real power in such situations at all!"

As Ju-chen saw it, her brothers were treated as the important figures in the home because of their sex. The sons took the place of Father and also represented the continuation of the family line, Mother's overriding concern. The daughters were accorded less voice, although their material importance was considerable. Ju-chen continued: "The men in our family are 'weak in earnings but strong in personality.' They have the real power in the family. Mother also has the power to keep control over the family budget. As long as decisions do not counter the family's perceived interests, I can decide because of my experience, but I can't decide in terms of my own interests alone."

The personalities of Ju-chen and her siblings contrasted sharply. Wo-chen, the second daughter and fourthborn, displayed far less responsibility to her family – the input of her three elder siblings obviated her own. Ju-chen invented for Wo-chen the motto: "Let tomorrow take care of itself." Fat-meng, the second son in the family, lived also for the present. Ju-chen therefore played the stabilizing role in the family. Ju-chen illustrated her mediating influence to me: "Wo-chen is enamored of a salesman who is very irresponsible and earns little. The payments on his car are exactly equal to his monthly income, leaving him without any money for gasoline. His mother is displeased with him too! She owns a shoe factory but has written off this boy as a loss, although he still lives at home. She has doubts whether to continue lending him money. And now, Wo-chen tells me, they want to get married. On what? Our mother is very upset. When Mother talks to Wo-chen, Sister and Mother end up fighting, so Mother asks me to reason with her. I try, but I can't order Wo-chen around. I only say, 'Please think this over very deeply before you do it, or in the future you will blame me for withholding my advice when you needed it.' I can't directly tell Wo-chen that she is dumb for marrying! Sister only says to me, 'Ju-chen, you are too serious!' Wo-chen won't come out and say, 'You are jealous because you don't have a boyfriend,' but that is what she is thinking.

"My brother Fat-choi sympathizes with Wo-chen because, after all, he is in the same boat. We disapprove of his girlfriend, too. So Fat-choi just says, 'Leave Sister alone!' He also says to Wo-chen, 'I'll introduce you to a young doctor. If you want to marry now, you might like him.' Fat-choi has lots of friends, and might actually do this.

"Wo-chen's boyfriend always eats with us. This angers Mother. She says it's a disgrace even for a potential son-in-law to eat his wife's family's food, and everyone will come to resent it. Anyway, Mother says she can't afford to support him and Sister too."

Thus, Mother, whose allegiance and partiality to her sons was clearly much greater than her bond to the daughters, was forced to ask Ju-chen to intercede. After listening to Ju-chen complain about the subsequent rejection of her advice, I asked Ju-chen directly why she did not move away from home. She answered: "I could leave home, but that means money to rent a room. I'd have to cook, clean, and live all by myself, and I'd be very lonely when I returned home after work. I've become used to having people around to talk with. It would also be very troublesome and it would be going against the family, too, so I don't think it's the solution."

"It would give you the opportunity to plan your life, though," I pointed out.

"Perhaps, but it would make my family short of money and they wouldn't be able to make ends meet," she countered.

Thus Ju-chen was ambivalent about obtaining a separate residence for herself. Her deep involvement with her family was as much a reality as her straining to be an individual in face of the family demands on her. Yet the intriguing possibility of living alone reflected her positive desire to demand something new of herself in changing Hong Kong.

Ju-chen expressed the wish to study in France and was attending evening French classes at the Alliance Francaise. She confessed, however, that she was really "afraid" to go to France by herself. Moreover, Ju-chen was circumscribed by the family's expectations that she would meet their economic requirements as they set them, and she had no idea how many demands would be made on her future wages. Ju-chen and her brothers purchased their new apartment for $12,000. She breathed a sigh of relief. "In three years more the flat will be paid off. But that's a long way off and I'll be old by then," she shrugged resignedly. Ju-chen also wanted her two sisters to study further and preferably abroad. "With these financial demands taken into account, what hope do I really have myself? I can only save twenty dollars a month from my job for myself and I only have four hundred dollars in the bank. I'll never get to France on that amount."

Work

Ju-chen sat on the edge of her desk as she conducted drills in Cantonese vocabulary with her students, her head cocked to one side, showing her attractive profile to advantage. She wore an Indian shirt of embroidered muslin and jangly bracelets. She was making a statement through her dress to her European and North American male and female students that she wished to be distinguished from the other, more conventional two- or three-piece-suited schoolteachers.

Ju-chen was a good teacher because she was a good storyteller. Her approach to life was best characterized by her comment, "In this world you can find every kind of person!" Ju-chen enjoyed describing the various people in the papers and on television or those she learned about through colleagues and friends. She used incidents of idiosyncratic responses or unusual situations to illustrate grammatical points or simply as conversational gambits. This not only made Ju-chen a lively conversationalist but a worthwhile informant. Her evaluation of what makes people tick in Hong Kong was conveyed in her remark, "In Hong Kong respectability or 'face' is everything," a characterization that naturally applied to Ju-chen herself. She clearly perceived her own preoccupation with status, although she was unable or unwilling to transcend this concern. Ju-chen's storytelling habit seemed to help her distance herself from discomforting conventions of family, work group, and peers.

The school where she taught had been founded by the Divinity School of Yale University, although the ties had been attenuated. It was run by the firm hand of the principal, who was an immigrant from Taiwan. The principal governed the school at the apex of a broad-based pyramid consisting of many teachers with no competing authority. His power was reinforced by the school's reliance on the uncertainties of outside funding and fee-paying students. Lecturers were enjoined to leave all decisions to the principal, a custom strengthened by the absence of tenure because of the short-term and market-dependent nature of the college's funding. The principal had many opportunities to dispense favors, such as extra hours of paid tutoring to the teachers, which further expanded his power.

Cliques formed to compete for status and influence around the principal and his close aides, as has been described for Taiwanese organizations (Silin, 1976). The shortage of classrooms and consequent limited office space for teachers permitted no physical escape from cliques and their incessant backbiting. With little chance to rise in the hierarchy, some of the more enterprising and quite competent teachers started private tutorial lessons on their own, using many of the teaching aids and techniques of the school. This was inevitable and might have been taken as a compliment by the principal, but he deeply resented the ensuing competition for the fees of the expatriate students. The principal was suspicious of all attempts at innovation and independence by his faculty.

Another source of contention in the staff was that between Mandarin-speaking Chinese emigrants and Cantonese-speaking native Hong Kong teachers. For its Mandarin-speaking lecturers, the school drew mainly from recent Chinese emigrants, most of whom had taught in the People's Republic of China. They brought with them an antipathy for Cantonese speakers, reciprocated by the Hong Kong teachers, who felt the disdain of the Northerners. More problematic was the substantially different political style to which the teachers trained in the People's Republic were accustomed. They had their own perceptions of the broader democratic possibilities in organizational life and found the hierarchical Taiwanese style of the school objectionable. One told me, "In Peking we used to analyze and evaluate school problems critically. Here all we can do is listen to what the principal says. There is no democracy. The principal has a comfortable office with a couch, and we sit two at a desk. But much worse, only he can call a meeting. In China any one of us was able to call a staff meeting at any time. We just posted a notice on the board. Or we staff could raise any topic we wanted at the regular academic meeting. But here the principal calls a meeting only when he wants us to rubber stamp his decisions. He issues orders, then it is a fait accompli. Once I got so mad, I just had to say something about it."

"How did the local staff respond?" I asked.

"They just sat there. They have all given up. If they ever had the nerve to contradict or even think contrary thoughts, they don't anymore."

Ju-chen was not much involved in such infighting. She was not an ideologue, nor had she "given up," because she had never clung to a set of principles. Ju-chen observed and even enjoyed the conflicts and used them as grist for her storytelling mill. In her view, there were several cliques of teachers (which she delighted in describing) and all stood to lose face if they openly challenged the principal or each other. Because they could not be open about their different views or interests, they engaged in indirect intrigue, manipulation, and gossip. And so Ju-chen concluded, "You just can't say anything. It does no good. You might as well enjoy life!"

Ju-chen did not expect to build a career of teaching, and her lack of commitment to the job in all likelihood contributed to her resigned acceptance of the unpleasant internal quarreling. Despite her almost 10 years of service to the school, Ju-chen had formed no collegial base, and did not wish to, because she was wedded to contemporary views of the woman's place as the helpmate of her husband.

Peers and marriage

Ju-chen did not look her age, which was about 29 in 1973; she was coyly reluctant to state precisely how old she was. The reason she looked young to me may have been my assumption that a woman of 30 or so years in Hong Kong must already have married and had several children. Dating, marriage, and her advancing age were important to Ju-chen, and they often arose in our conversations.

Ju-chen gave me several examples of the problems today's young Hong Kong people face in dating and marriage. Her own friends served as illustrations of the two main pitfalls: nonchalance and overreaction. Both dilemmas revealed insecurity in male-female relations. When her friends felt themselves under great pressure to marry, they responded either as if they did not care or as if they cared too much.

"Most of my friends are *fa*. This means they do not care deeply about things which they should. If things are strange, they do not feel they are so. If things are happy, they do not feel happy. Perhaps it's because they have seen too much whereas I have not seen enough. Take the friend we met for tea the other day. She is *fa*. She doesn't consider anything seriously. If she hears of something unusual, she says, 'Well, I've seen things like that before.' If somone is happy, she says, 'Well, it's not so important.' Many of my friends are like that.''

Ju-chen gave another example of such a jaded attitude: "Two of my friends who were studying at different universities in Canada just returned home to Hong Kong after five years. They were acquainted only slightly before they went. On their return to Hong Kong they met again and one week later decided to marry. I said, 'You hardly know each other.' They said, 'So what? What's the problem?' I think this is *fa;* they don't see the problems in marriage after superficial acquaintance.''

Another friend responded so deeply that it proved totally inadequate to the situation: "This girl, Ly-lok, about twenty-five, is very active in her church where she is the leader of the youth group. The best-educated person there, Ly-lok is looked up to by all the church members. One fellow, about twenty-one, looked up to her with respect. Ly-lok mistook his admiration for romance and treated him too affectionately. This embarrassed him and he stopped going to church. Ly-lok used to go out with church people after services, to tea and on picnics, and now either she can't go or he can't go, and the situation is embarrassing. Ly-lok asked my advice, and I told her frankly that she had erred a bit. She got angry at me then and we had a falling out.

"This girl desperately wants to get married. She doesn't get along with her parents and wants the chance to move from home. Ly-lok is clever but is homely and looks old for her age, so she turned to church groups for boyfriends. She probably looks to the church setting for friends because in church it is possible for people to know her as a person, whereas in school people didn't get to know her as an individual, only her exterior, which is ugly. And so Ly-lok had no boyfriends in college.

"I tried to fix her up with a former neighbor. He is a government teacher and a good boy. But he is short and bald at age twenty-eight. Ly-lok has much pride and said, 'No!' Then her aunt tried to introduce her to an eligible doctor, but she replied, 'No, he would know too much about me.' The pastor tried to match her to a waiter, but she looked down on his low status. You can see how 'face' is really problematic. Pride is so important!''

Ju-chen also criticized those of her friends who passively waited for men to come to them as blasé, or *fa:* "I have a friend, Yin-lai, from college who is conservative. She dresses like a man. She cuts her hair short-like women in China – and her dress is sloppy. I told Yin-lai to curl her hair and wear different clothes, but she didn't do it. I told her, 'If you don't fix yourself up you won't find a man.' Yin-lai went to a girls' school, and doesn't know how to mix with boys. Although she went to college, she didn't learn to mix there, and now that she's back teaching at a girls' school, she may never learn. Yin-lai is not interested in trying new things. She's basically very attractive, with nice round eyes. Chinese have slanted eyes, and girls with round eyes are very attractive to Hong Kong men, you know. But Yin-lai said, 'Never mind, I won't marry!' I replied, 'Your sisters will all be grown up and your mother too old, your friends will be married and unwilling to go out with you. Now you can join them for tea, but later on you won't have their company!''

"What do you mean by 'later'?" I asked Ju-chen.

"Now!" she exclaimed. "It's starting right now! My friends are all getting married and they won't go out with me anymore."

Thus, like her friends, Ju-chen was under great pressure to get married. She knew that to rush into marriage was a mistake, but she faced social sanctions on all sides: "People always ask me, 'Why aren't you married?' Everyone pressures me – my students, my colleagues. Once it was a hot day and I bought a watermelon to share with the teachers in my office. One of them said, 'We don't want watermelon, we want to be invited to eat [wedding] cakes!' I just smile and pretend it doesn't matter, but I think such pressure is unnecessary. After all, you need a boyfriend you think is special before you can get married.''

I said she could always have someone arrange her marriage.

"Some people might not care if the fellow is special or not. But if you do get a boyfriend that way, then you feel you are not worth anything. You get an 'inferiority complex.' " (She used the English term to make her point.)

Although Ju-chen counseled others to accept an arranged match, she was reluctant to accept a match herself because she considered it superficial and face-losing.

Ju-chen's goal was a proper marriage. "I agree with the saying, 'Men fear entering wrong [the wrong line of work], women fear marrying wrong!' " The "right kind of man" would support her economically after marriage in the style to which she aspired. He would have a higher education and better social status than she and have good feelings toward her. Ju-chen continued. "We Chinese don't believe in divorce, so it is rather important to find the right man. Men can have other girl friends and even wives, but women cannot. It's hard to know the right man because sometimes they change after marriage. They become stubborn and angry, and their faces turn red. The only way to know ahead of time what a man is really like is to ask his friends and relatives. An example is Fat-choi's girlfriend. We tell her about my brother's bad points so she'll know them. It doesn't bother him."

I wished to learn Ju-chen's reaction to a widespread North American middle-class dilemma: the "double day" — homemaking plus a career for women. I described to her an autobiography of a woman who decided to stop serving her husband and four children at home and to devote herself to her continued education and career. She reorganized the entire household routine so that everyone participated in its operation. The chores were divided up equitably and rotated weekly. Everyone was responsible for his or her personal effects, and anything that cluttered the house was in danger of being tossed out. (The book was titled *I'm Running Away from Home, but I'm Not Allowed to Cross the Street.*)

Ju-chen listened and quickly responded in turn with a story of her Hong Kong friend who married a professor of chemistry at Stanford University who spent most of his time in his laboratory. His wife decided to change things. "Her friends all said to her, 'Your life is good. You don't need to worry about money. You have two children, you have no material wants, so your life must be complete!' She replied, 'I have experienced nothing. All my life I've traveled this same road, and I want to try new things.' She left her husband and went off to San Francisco and met a fellow who knew how to enjoy life. They lived together for a while. Meanwhile, her husband thought the whole affair was wasteful. He had given his wife everything she wanted, and he could not understand her need for a fling. The house was messy, the children ill cared for, and so on. Everyone criticized her. Finally, she left San Francisco and returned home, and everyone said it was the right decision. So you see," Ju-chen concluded, "it's no use to rebel!"

Ju-chen decided that she must subordinate her personal aspirations to the kinship groups of which she was a member: her family, in which she grew up, and the family that she would form after marriage. Although her search for personal identity was important, it could only be carried out within, not outside, the confines of these groups.

I have often wondered whether Ju-chen might not concede to an arranged marriage after she fulfilled the demands placed by her family on her income. Ju-chen maintained that such arrangements were not "modern," but she nevertheless advised her friends and her sister to enter them. Ju-chen was looking for "meaning" in life, and to her such meaning would be manifested in a love marriage. However, a loving relationship need not exclude money and status. Thus I suspect that she would consider an arranged match with a refined person, although she would wait until mutual feelings of respect and affection had developed.

Ming: social worker and activist

At an early age Ming Yao, the eldest in a line of eight children, was forced by severe family crises to become a family mainstay. Ming was educated in a reputable Anglo-Chinese secondary school, as befitted the daughter of a small businessman. Father passed away suddenly when Ming was approaching adolescence, leaving the family financially bereft. Ming completely fulfilled every obligation then devolving upon the firstborn, but she never allowed her major family duties to detract from her principal concern of serving the wider community.

Ming was critical when centripetal families husbanded their energies and income without concern for the needs of other hard-pressed Hong Kong families, who were inevitably beset by similar and even worse tragedies. She believed that the families of the laboring poor could take joint social action to overcome their grievous misfortunes and to relieve the social and economic pressures that severely oppress thousands of Hong Kong families. In her student activism in the Chinese University during the mid-1970s, Ming was able in part to realize this creed by bringing the students from campus to the working neighborhoods. Ming's mission of protecting and advancing her family's well-being while successfully pursuing a fast-changing career in community-oriented social work was her peculiar charisma.

Family background

Ming's mother was born in Canton around 1930. Her family operated a small button and comb production business that employed two workmen. Mother attended middle school, learned how to keep accounts, and helped at the workshop. In addition, she was taught sewing and embroidery, probably as a preparation for marriage.

During the anti-Japanese war (1937–45), Mother's father was able to relocate the family to his native village in Nan-hai county, Kwangtung province, where his kin cultivated the paddy. At the conclusion of the war, the family resumed its life in Canton, but in the late 1940s Mother again found herself in the village, where she won distinction by actively participating in a campaign to save the crops during a particularly bad drought. Her collective interest and spirit were much praised by the village cadres after Liberation, in spite of her merchant-class background, which prompted many of her family and friends with similar bourgeois status to refuse to cooperate with the village poor.

After Mother's marriage to the scion of a petit merchant family, the couple bequeathed their relatives the small button and comb establishment, which had in the meantime fallen to them. Since the entrepreneurial future did not look bright under the People's Republic, the Yaos took advantage of lax emigration control and, with the newly born Ming, left for Hong Kong in 1952, bringing all possible securities and valuables. Father was reunited there with an older brother and they pooled their refugee capital to establish a small garment factory. Throughout, Elder Brother never provided Father with a full balance of factory accounts or with a statement of his equity share in the firm.

Ming's rapidly growing family was forced by Father's subordination to his brother and generally poor business acumen to accept a highly uncertain fate. The family rented a subdivision of a large tenement room, which became ever more crowded with the births of three more daughters and at last a son. Father was overjoyed that the final three children were also boys, but he doted on the eldest in traditional fashion. Ming recalled that this active youngster found the small cubicle too constricting, and it was her task to pull him back from the grill that separated theirs from an adjacent tenant quarter. The family feared that if the child was too noisy, the neighbors would complain to the head tenant and cause their eviction. Father hoped to obtain a better station in life for the family by keeping his narrow bank roll tied up in the business and persevering until its prospects greatly improved.

With no apparent warning, Father died of a heart attack not long after the eighth child was born. Uncle contributed irregular small sums to Mother's budget, and in return Ming was sent to work as a secretary and girl Friday in the factory office. Mother suspected that much more was due them from Father's founding participation in the enterprise. Although her contact with the company as an unpaid family worker did not give her access to the financial accounts, Ming also got the impression that business was doing better than Uncle admitted. All of Father's debts and obligations fell on the shoulders of Mother, who wished to lift this burden by favorably liquidating Father's assets in the factory.

In any society lacking social insurance, the loss of the family breadwinner is devastating. At Father's death there was no way to keep the family together. Despite emotional anguish, Mother temporarily placed Eldest Son in a Christian orphanage in the distant New Territories, where it was understood that his schooling would be advanced, and one of Father's sisters was willing to take in Fourth Daughter. The other six children moved with their mother onto the roof of a five-story tenement, where they constructed a shack of wood planks, corrugated iron, cardboard, and chicken wire. Rooftop dwellers lacked even the few amenities enjoyed in the government-tolerated squatter areas and were forced to haul their water manually from below and to lower their refuse in buckets for disposal. A typhoon swept away their shed, and the family had no alternative but to camp in a few square feet of flat space on an upper stairwell of the building. But even this miserable perch was taken from them by the landlord's summary eviction. Ultimately, after hard bargaining with the police and housing administrators and payment of gratuities, Mother obtained one and a half 10' by 12' rooms in a resettlement estate and was able to call back First Son and Fourth Daughter.

The forced dispersal of the family was a sore blow to Mother, and it would have destroyed the morale of a weaker person. Mother in desperation set up a business based upon her adolescent training. She took in piecework sewing at the small resettlement estate room. Eventually, she was able to build up a sizable clientele and required more space for additional machinery. This need led her to set up shop illegally on empty land near the apartment and build there a corrugated iron shed for her sewing machines and worktables. Soon other squatters converged on neighboring plots to form a small community around Mrs. Yao. After she learned that her workshed might be tolerated by the police, Mother further transgressed land ordinances by establishing a second hut across the makeshift path. In these minuscule, improvised workshops, Second and Fourth Daughters helped her with sewing tasks, and at times their brothers made button holes and hawked the garments.

Mother effected this miraculous family industry by a combination of innate personal skills, dynamism, and the occasional contributions from relatives and Father's former business contacts and personal acquaintances. Stabilization of the family income met the food, shelter, and clothing budget and allowed the children to remain near Mother instead of signing on at child labor sweatshops.

In her struggle to stave off economic catastrophe, Mother refused to sacrifice the futures of her children. Starting a business from nothing with no capital and nine mouths to feed is a fearsome venture, but Mother was fortified by her vision of each one's future.

I found over my 6 years of interviewing Hong Kong working-class families that in the ubiquitous economic crises that beset these people, the able-bodied daughters were usually propelled into the work force. However, Mother responded to her misfortunes in a vastly different manner. Flexible and open minded, Mother grappled with thorny economic and bureaucratic obstacles in the path of eight educational careers. Her homemade curriculum tenaciously matched the individual skills of each child to the educational opportunities available. The ability to recognize and exploit the siblings' individual talents is a precondition for mobility of centripetal families. Mother fully appreciated the intellectual capacities and quick wit of Ming, the eldest, and Feng-yun, the third daughter, and annually scraped together the $500 to $600 to see them both through form VI of Anglo-Chinese secondary school. Judging that Second and Fourth Daughters lacked comparable academic aptitude, Mother budgeted equivalent annual sums for 1- to 2-year courses in vocational schools, where they learned stitching and dressmaking. She imparted her tailoring trade skills to them and integrated their much-needed labor into the shop.

Ming performed adequately in her Anglo-Chinese secondary school and went with her classmates to the City Hall Library to cram for annual examinations. Her increasing curiosity about social problems led Ming to reduce her study time so that she could delve into the library's English-language collection of critical history, economics, and psychology tracts. She passed the ordinary-level examinations in several liberal arts subjects, scoring highest in English. Circumstances at this time did not permit Ming to enroll in the advanced-level course, and she temporarily took work as a teacher.

Feng-yun told me during my third year of acquaintance with the Yaos, "I have recently decided to become a doctor." Indirectly appealing for the assistance she thought one in my position might be able to provide, she continued, "I want to secure a place in the Hong Kong University Medical School. Do you know any teachers there?" Aware that medical school entrance was restricted, Mother nevertheless endorsed Feng-yun's ambition.

"People say one can use black money in order to win a place at the university," Mother commented to my research assistant about the bribing of bent school officials.

"This indicated that Mother was ready to pay any price to get a real education for her daughter," my assistant wrote in her notebook.

Feng-yun had just completed form V at an Anglo-Chinese secondary school and she then re-enrolled there to obtain the necessary biology and chemistry subjects to pursue her new premedical bent. Mother appointed her the family's housekeeper, and while Feng-yun continued her demanding academic course, she managed to accomplish most of the marketing, cooking, cleaning, and laundry chores. Homemaking detracted substantially from her schoolwork, but Ming was already employed as a teacher and thereby excused from most household tasks, whereas the less academically inclined Second Daughter was fully occupied at Mother's right hand in the shop; neither of the elder sisters could therefore ease Feng-yun's homemaking burden.

Eldest Brother was unable to accept school discipline and was repeatedly expelled for mischievous, unruly classroom behavior – first from an Anglo-Chinese secondary school, then from two other Chinese institutions, and finally from a missionary vocational school, where he was as a last resort enrolled in a shop course. Ming confided to me that Elder Brother was unable to settle down because he, more than any other, was troubled by Father's untimely passing. After losing Father's special affection, Elder Brother underwent the trauma of removal to the orphanage, and this shock greatly deepened his insecurity and rendered him incorrigible at school. His psychological problems were never acknowledged or treated by teachers, who felt threatened by the boy's repeated challenges to their authority.

Like Ming and Feng-yun, Second and Third Brothers were the bene-ficiaries of Mother's respect for higher learning as the portal of entry to careers. They also reached secondary school, and during my third interviewing visit to Hong Kong Second Son confessed to me that he had again been obliged by the principal to repeat his form. Third Brother stated proudly that despite his rather abject failure in three subjects, he had just been permitted to advance to the next year. The youngest son was a quick learner and hoped to study mathematics.

The boys' erratic education shows that even when poverty-stricken families sincerely attempt to educate all of their members, a combina-tion of financial, administrative, and personality problems will fre-quently make this impossible. This perhaps explains why most other working-class families I knew limited their expectations and planning for their children's education.

Home

The Yao family resided for over 10 years in the Luk Fu resettlement estate, a community for over 30,000 persons built in the early 1960s on a hill not far from Kai Tak Airport. Neighboring estates were Wang Tau Hom, a conglomeration of 57,000, and Wong Tai Sin, one of Hong Kong's largest at close to 97,000.

The family's cubicle was bisected by a full-length sliding curtain of gray fabric. In the windowless sleeping area demarcated by the curtain and lit at night by an overhead fluorescent lamp were a chest of drawers, one family-size double bunk bed, and a waist-high old electric refrigerator, recently presented to the family by Mother's sister. Mother and Youngest Brother slept on the bottom bunk, and a dozen bolts of out-of-season cloth awaiting tailoring were stored in the upper bunk – wool in the summer and lightweight polyester in the winter. When family members wished to wash or bathe, they carried water from the cistern on the balcony and placed their plastic wash basin on the floor next to the refrigerator. Water for Mother's bath was heated in an electric teakettle.

Across the curtain was the living area, which contained two multi-shelf Chinese wooden cabinets, one of which was crowned by the family's altar to Kwan-yin, the goddess of fertility and mercy. Mother and the older children burned joss sticks in this altar on the major folk holidays of the year. Two solid workbenches, each equipped with a Japanese commercial electric sewing machine, a small wicker sofa, and several folding chairs completed the furnishings. Illumination was provided by a second overhead fluorescent lamp and the long barred windows fronting the balcony and the exit way.

The second 10′ by 12′ room, which was allocated to the family in their fourth year of tenancy when its occupants finally vacated, contained a single bunk bed accommodating the four daughters, a desk, and a set of bookshelves. After a time, Ming installed a tiny washing machine, which was filled and emptied manually. Space was miraculously found in this room and its doorway for a folding cot when my 9-month-old daughter and I were asked to stay overnight in the spring of 1973, and I was just able to squeeze Shana's car crib between the cot and the bunk bed. The room was so small that I was politely requested to substitute a Chinese-style cloth infant carrier for my larger, noncollapsible, metal-frame backpack, because this bulky conveyance claimed precious living space.

During my calls upon the Yao family domestic quarters in 1971 and 1973, I gained on overall impression of transience and indifference, compared to the fastidious interiors of some other poor and crowded estate dwellers whose homes I regularly visited. In other living rooms there was a semblance of decor and a show of fancy. The Yao family could not budget the time and energy for the much-needed whitewashing of the concrete walls or covering of the forever-soiled cement floor with linoleum. Neither could they pick up and organize the personal and family effects strewn about the crowded flat. In 1971, while I resided in these quarters, I purchased a 50¢ straw hat as protection against the summer sun and carelessly left it on the top bunk bed when I departed for Canada in the autumn. I was amazed to find it apparently unmoved on the same perch 20 months later.

Since they stemmed from educated business people, the Yaos had somewhat higher expectations than their equally poor next-door neighbors. On one side lived a middle-age widow and her three grown sons, none of whom appeared gainfully employed. Mother and Ming suspected that this foursome lived on the earnings of a secret society and forbade Eldest Brother, already a discipline problem, to visit them. After a nasty fight, the boys next door spitefully polluted the Yaos' cistern with the droppings of their pet German shepherd, and relations between the two families were frozen.

In the other adjoining compartment there resided a grandmother, her 25-year-old daughter, and two grandchildren, a girl age 6 and a 5-year-old son. (I never learned the whereabouts of the father.) Grandmother cared for the young brother and sister while their mother labored long hours in a factory and even minded them after the mother returned home from work. The rambunctious 6-year-old eluded Grandmother's attempts at discipline and frequently skipped down the three flights of stairs to the estate courtyard, where she sought the excitement of playmates and explored the vicinity. The sedentary grandmother could not discover the routes she took on her explorations. The child one day overtaxed Grandmother's patience by remaining downstairs until midnight. Upon her return, the anxious grandmother beat her severely with a bamboo switch, and the next morning she leashed one of her errant ankles to the heavy wooden leg of the family kitchen table.

At nine o'clock the next morning I saw this forlorn child seated on the floor next to the table leg eating rice from a small bowl with a spoon. It was clear that the distraught grandmother thought that only this form of corporal punishment could prevent the child from yet another midnight odyssey. That afternoon, seeing that the child remained fettered, Ming's mother intervened to remind Grandmother that the youngster meant no harm and that this form of confinement would not train her to return earlier from play. The 6-year-old was released several hours later, and from then on thankfully turned to Ming and Mother for protection. The solution finally adopted by the frustrated grandmother and the nonchalant mother was a charitable convent boarding school on an outlying island in the New Territories, recommended by a *kaifong* (street association) counselor, where the child was kept under the stern eyes of the sisterhood.

Workplace

Enjoying only one or two annual holidays, the Yao family commenced its daily routine in the small dry-goods stall, where cloth was tailored and sold and many of the family's meals were cooked. To protect this life-giving shack, two of the sons unrolled their bedding and slept on the cutting tables behind the entrance way, padlocked every evening by Mother from the outside before she headed homeward. Every morning at eight, Mother and Second Daughter roused the boys from their plank beds and unfurled bolts of cloth and their cutting implements on the tables. They consumed their hurried breakfast of paper-wrapped flavored broad noodles carried in from a cooked food stall while organizing the day's activities. Later in the morning, if time permitted, these women would take a more substantial bowl of rice gruel at the *congee* stall. Second Daughter tended the store with Mother all morning while the younger children went to school. In the afternoon, when the others returned from school for lunch, another child joined Mother in the stall. The younger siblings had not yet learned how to measure and cut the cloth and were therefore confined to customer sales.

Mother subcontracted to tenement neighbors various sewing operations, such as buttonholing, covering cloth buttons, and hemming, and hired a young seamstress part-time. However, Mrs. Yao believed that hired hands were less reliable than her own family labor. At rush peaks, such as the spring and autumn festivals and New Year period, when the populace orders new clothing and the family desperately needed help, the workers were likely to demand higher wages and they often failed to meet delivery deadlines. The entire family worked under the same roof only during these seasonal holidays, when they labored around the clock.

With her 10 months of vocational training, Second Daughter bore the main tailoring burden and when, by dint of unstinting toil, the family's business began to break even, Second Daughter again attended form IV. She continued to work the morning shift in the stall, went to school from 1:30 p.m. to 6:30 p.m., returned to help her family close down the stall, and did her homework in the evening. Despite her expertise in the tailoring business, Second Sister dreamed of using her minimal education to escape this arduous routine. She confided in me that, like her friends, she envisioned an office or clerical position, a sentiment common to her peer group, which preferred a dignified and orderly work environment to hawker business. Nor was any child committed to a full-scale expansion of the tailoring trade. Despite the overall preoccupation with tailoring, all the Yao children regarded the business as a necessary but stagnant and tedious cul-de-sac, and each cultivated an aspiration for alternative occupations.

The Hong Kong government has long been intent on reducing the hawker population and centralizing it in more readily controllable concession plots. This policy is integral to government attempts to boost the industrial labor force by delimiting and ultimately reducing the volume of the petty tertiary activities of hawkers, peddlers, pirate taxi cabs, and all street and lane vendors and mobile tradesmen. Although the Yaos were cognizant of this antihawker stance and its stringent enforcement by the licensing authorities and police, they were stunned when in 1974 the authorities decided to clear their squatter sheds and scores of others in their lane. One morning, having given perfunctory notice, a gang of wreckers arrived and summarily demolished the product of 12 years of backbreaking toil and patient cultivation of customer and client relationships. The whole hawker community was indiscriminately broken apart and burned, and not a single squatter hut or fixture remained in the lanes. The government compensation assistance included the right of the squatters to bid first on commercial property in large and newly built, but distant, resettlement estates.

This second near-fatal blow to the Yaos revived the protective instincts of all its members, who closed ranks to assist Mother in the removal. Mother bid for a premium site in a new resettlement estate some 6 to 8 miles distant. When she was able to demonstrate to the Government Housing Authority the family's competence to manage a high-turnover garment stall and its ability to capitalize such a venture, Mother was granted a new ground floor shop. The children pooled their accumulated New Year's gifts and other petty cash with Mother's meager savings. The family barely managed to scrape together from all of its sources the sizable sum required by the licensing authorities as downpayment for a 3-year lease on the shop. The steep expenses for the shop fixtures, fluorescent lighting, shelves, linoleum, whitewashing, and locked door grilles were discouraging. In Mother's view, it would take many years to attract a volume of customers equivalent to her former trade at the crossroads of three major resettlement estates.

The family's new accommodations consisted of a more modern linoleum-floored apartment at the rear of the shop. While erecting shelves for cloth in the shop, the family was also able to attach a number of useful shelves around the freshly whitewashed apartment walls. Again, the core of the apartment was one large living room and bedroom, but this apartment was equipped with an interior closed kitchenette, a cold-water tap, and a seatless trench toilet. Clearly, the rent for this new dwelling was substantially higher. With the predictably small initial clientele, the family's finances were severely straitened.

To overcome this second crisis, the three younger daughters were forced to abandon their education and career plans. Although Second Daughter still dreamed of secretarial work, she was now rooted to the shop. Third Daughter, who had just repeated form V and whose sights had still been trained on medical school, was likewise deeply disappointed by the turn of events. Next to Ming's, her aspirations were the most ambitious, and therefore the abrupt change in plans affected her greatly. Lacking a marketable skill, she set up a rickety borrowed typewriter in the rear of the shop each afternoon and practiced to attain 40–50 words per minute so that she could apply for a secretarial position in an import-export firm. Fourth Daughter, who entered adolescence at this unpropitious moment, was compelled to drop out of form II in a Chinese middle school to work full time in the store with Second Daughter. Like her, Fourth Daughter enrolled in night school tailoring courses. The sons were not directly brought into shop work and were permitted to continue their unsteady quest for a modicum of education.

Just as in the period following Father's death, over a decade earlier, the family worked shoulder to shoulder to resolve their debts. This time, however, the maturing daughters were poised for self-standing occupations. Their relatively brief experiences with independent, promising, secondary school peer-group relations were suddenly truncated and, in Ming's opinion, their subordination to the family in its misfortune necessarily stifled the creativity of each daughter.

Ming's position in the family

The depths of the allegiance called forth by the centripetal Chinese family in Hong Kong are measured by the fact that Ming's principled struggle against Mother's lifelong determination to maintain her ties to the wider Yao family never led to even a temporary break from the family. Ming believed that the sums Uncle sporadically remitted to Mother for family maintenance should have been contractually regulated within an overall settlement of Father's estate and that despite his protestations to the contrary, Uncle could well afford a salaried replacement. She therefore felt that Uncle's ready use of her after-school office labor was highly exploitative, and she resented Mother's continued connivance at this paternalistic arrangement.

Tradition-bound Mother defended her attitude, however, arguing that one's reputation and success in small business depended upon the goodwill and trust engendered in family, neighbors, and clients; she considered a show of propriety essential at all times. Ming criticized her mother's acquiescence to Uncle as a misapplication of the principle of true reciprocity, which is based on noncoercive and mutually beneficial aid. The deference extended to Uncle as Father's elder brother and a propertied member, although probably appropriate to the traditional mode, further increased the Yaos' long-term uncertainties and aggravated their financial predicament.

When Ming completed lower form VI, she successfully prevailed upon Mother to challenge Uncle by allowing her to leave his employ for a teaching position that was available. Every fortnight for the next 2 years she contributed most of her entire salary of approximately $100 to the family purse. With the help of a law student acquaintance, Ming later initiated a round of negotiations between Mother and Uncle, in which she played an invisible role as Mother's adviser. The Yaos thereby obtained an informal settlement with Uncle, in which they abandoned all further claim upon him in return for a lump-sum payment. Although Ming's side never gained access to the accounts and was unable to calculate the amount due them from Father's share in the factory, this victory confirmed to Mother that Ming and her "modern ways" of confronting respected elders had merit.

In addition to providing financial support, Ming attempted to shape the education and values of her siblings and undertook to reeducate Mother. She was inspired in this difficult project by standards of altruistic service to the common people, which she had assimilated from the literature of the Chinese political campaigns of the Cultural Revolution. Ming wanted to raise her family's true concerns to a higher ethical plane than economic subsistence and the acquisition of material goods, the twin aims of the centripetal family in colonial Hong Kong.

Ming's intense self-directed study and her ability to see objective reality optimistically and as a whole made possible her persistent efforts to explain politics to her family. She underscored to them that working people constituted a class, that Hong Kong was rent by inequality and employers' exploitation of the working class and that the Chinese masses were deprived of their social, economic, and cultural birth rights and ought to struggle against colonialism. She viewed her family's problems, and especially the relocation crisis, as a byproduct of undemocratic Hong Kong politics and colonial greed. Ming explained to me that after the recession of 1975, large companies were profiting at the expense of the petty business sector, and she showed me her files of clippings from the vernacular Chinese establishment press that she believed substantiated this assertion. She had an unerring sense of the significant trends of the time and read between the lines of the newspaper reports. Short paragraphs on factory disputes and closures were elaborated with Ming's realistic interpretation of the development and inevitable clash of the major capitalistic forces in contemporary Hong Kong. Ming strove to help her family realize their vision of a brighter future by aiding them in an exemplary day-to-day struggle against the corruption and callousness of the colonial bureaucracy.

Ming approached her family in the same straightforward manner she used successfully in her peer groups of teachers, social workers, and Chinese University students. Her long-standing efforts to sensitize the Yao family to the dynamics of capitalist exploitation were also integral to Ming's appeal for support for her own goal of mass mobilization. However, the family crises and household upheavals sapped Ming's energies no less than the others. Ming was almost overwhelmed by the protracted internecine conflicts in winning a compromise settlement from Uncle and by Elder Brother's scholastic incorrigibility. These problems were further entangled by her own difficulties in re-entering the academic stream and the sudden deleterious effects of the uprooting of the family store on the family economy and her hopes for higher studies. Since the rest of her family was not politically minded, they did not wish to have their everyday behavior scrutinized or shaped along her lines. Ming's family was unprepared to abandon the quest for status and face that was characteristic of personal relationships in contemporary Hong Kong. But Ming compassionately took into account all of her family's hesitations, their lack of comprehension of her political approach, and their preoccupation with the day-to-day struggle for existence. She continued to strive for the integration of the respective needs of each member into a superior family whole.

Ming was aggrieved by Mother's occasional financial profligacies. Guests at Hong Kong weddings customarily present small, red envelopes to the groom's family containing generous sums of cash *(licee)*, and Mother adhered firmly to this practice at the weddings to which she was regularly invited by fellow market people. Ming urged her instead to save the family's money. Mother spurned Ming's imprecations, but I imagine that had she yielded and remained at home, she would nevertheless have bestowed the *licee* on the celebrants on another occasion. Mother clearly feared being labeled stingy, unsociable, and (in the new location) an outsider, and insisted upon the proper conventional response, an expensive investment that may well have benefited her business. I do not know how Ming responded to Mother's belief that good neighbors are a trading asset, but she frowned on the etiquette and compromise from which Mother obtained a modicum of enjoyment. Mother, however, became increasingly disturbed at what she regarded as Ming's elevation of a priori principles above the sensibilities and expectations within the family's circle of acquaintances and business contacts.

In Ming's view, not even the monumental shop relocation justified Mother's demands on the time and creative energies of her siblings. Ming argued from her ideological persuasion that the children should all mature as physically and socially active and independent-minded young adults, unencumbered by the daily tedium of a small shop. Pressured like many of her generation by powerful dilemmas of survival, Mother mistrusted nonutilitarian pursuits and hobbies that did not result in tangible family benefits. Ming clashed with Mother when Eldest Brother began to play basketball after school in the estate courtyard during the homework period Mother had compulsorily assigned to him. Although Ming looked with alarm upon the playground rowdiness that accompanied the sport, she nevertheless endorsed Eldest Brother's desire for vigorous recreation and convinced Mother that the family could budget time for Eldest Brother to complete his homework in the evening. "I suppose you know the modern way of doing things," murmured Mother resignedly.

Ming closely observed the life patterns and personal habits of her siblings and constantly strove to discover meaningful education and employment for them. She struggled to lessen their dependence on family institutions and control and to propel them into new social experiences. Ming was thus dismayed when she saw teenage gangs springing up in the recreational courtyard where Eldest Brother played basketball. Her solution was to send First Brother away from the estate and its surroundings into the patriotic Chinese educational system. The schools in this system would, in her view, find positive mechanisms, short of expulsion, for resolving the discipline problems of its students, and in particular would be able to reform Eldest Brother. However, although Ming knew many students, recent graduates, and teachers in this system socially, Mother had no personal contact with the patriotic sector. None of the Yaos' neighbors and friends from the estate enrolled their children in a patriotic school, and Mother therefore did not envision such a course for First Brother. Mother argued against such schools on the grounds that they would not prepare him for white-collar employment in Hong Kong enterprises.

Ming took exception to Mother's education of the boys for petty clerical positions and retorted that Hong Kong was at the mercy of international economic fluctuations and not even the commercial stream in a more orthodox vocational school would guarantee a secure position as government clerk, bank teller, or draughtsman's assistant. In effect, Ming opposed narrow occupational training, which short-circuited the broader critical and humanistic learning that she was convinced her siblings needed. Setting her sights to the future, she said, "Since no one can predict the future of Hong Kong, my brothers and sisters need to learn how to think in spite of their education. They should go to a school that will teach them to learn by themselves."

The second crisis affected the sisters' education much more than that of the four youngest boys, two of whom were pre-teenagers when they relocated. Ming's advice was disregarded when she vocally opposed Mother's reassignment of her submissive sisters to functions in the home and shop. Ming conceded that Second Sister, from her work-bench in the shop, could no longer realistically entertain visions of more desirable nonfamilial office employment. Ming tried to convince Mother that Fourth Sister, then entering an unstructured and person-ally precarious adolescence, should not be pressed into similar voca-tional training and a future in the shop.

Ming told me that she could not properly screen the influence of pop radio, Hollywood cinema, and other mass media she regarded as decadent on impressionable Fourth Sister. Ming's task was lightened by Mother's deliberate abstention from purchasing radio and television sets, on the grounds that these would disturb the children's concentra-tion on homework lessons. Nevertheless, I noticed Fourth Sister strum-ming her guitar to "top of the rock" tunes she had heard outside the home on Radio Hong Kong. Mother and Ming agreed that derivative colonial culture was harmful to youths, although Ming's prospective solution involved more personalized alternatives than Mother's preference for formal academic and vocational training. Ming hoped that whatever the ensuing job prospects, an arts and sciences education would promote the sisters' development as cultured, critical Chinese. Rote learning, frequent examinations, and a wooden treatment of sociopolitical reality are well-known characteristics of secondary and even university education in the colony (Ross, 1976). Ming nevertheless felt that liberal arts schooling would provide more educational, cultural, and perhaps also political alternatives for her sisters than would a technical vocational course of study, sprinkled with units on English and social studies.

Some time before I met her, Ming developed the desire to move away from home, and she continually harbored this hope for detachment. She said, "I get tied up in family affairs and cannot find a quiet place to study in our apartment. I want to help solve my family's problems but they seem never ending. That's less the way it is in Hong Kong. [She was referring to First Brother's academic delinquency, Fourth Sister's attraction to teenage drifters, and crises in the family business.] I need a quiet room of my own where I can read, invite friends for discussion on social problems in Hong Kong, and complete some of my personal projects." Mother claimed to me that her opposition to Ming's departure from the home was based on the added expense. "Why should my daughter pay rent for a second flat when we already have this apartment?" she said, gesturing around the four walls of the flat. But in Ming's opinion, Mother also feared that a bachelor apartment for her, although the other daughters might not want to follow suit, was nevertheless tantamount to family collapse. A daughter who left home before marriage was, in the view of Mother's generation, rejecting her familial and ancestral obligations.

The opportunity for Ming's partial escape from home was afforded by a group of Western postgraduate students and other reformers, mainly female, whom she met at a City Hall Library reading table. After discovering they had much in common, the Westerners invited her to share a two-room communal flat in Mong Kok, where they were organizing anit-Vietnam war activities directed at the thousands of U.S. servicemen sent to the colony from Vietnam for rest and recreation. Ming assisted this small agitprop commune in the preparation and distribution of leaflets directed at the servicemen, which invited them to visit the flat for a film presentation, discussion, and refreshments. She was one of only two Chinese youths in my study who were attracted to the activities of this small antiwar outpost in politically inhospitable Hong Kong.

Ming spent several nights a week in Mong Kok, departing in the morning to teach school and returning again later. On those evenings when she slept with her family, her brothers eagerly asked her what was said and done at the communal flat, which films were shown, and how the servicemen dressed. Ming occasionally brought her flatmates and others from their circle to her own home, where Mother welcomed and befriended them. Mother was genuinely curious about the ways of life of the Australian, North American, and British young adults abroad. Like other Chinese, who are certain that non-Chinese cannot fathom the ways of the Central Kingdom, she was bemused by their intent to learn Cantonese, and ultimately amazed at the facility with which one graduate student used written Chinese. Mother never ceased recounting to me that this American student and English language tutor in the Chinese University had once even corrected her miswriting of a complex character, and for several years afterward Mother followed the events in the student's family of spouse and young daughter.

Many of Ming's flatmates worked as teachers and tutors of Chinese youths, and they knew how difficult it was for Ming to struggle for her independence. The communards therefore respected and admired her efforts to establish herself and encouraged her to persist on this chosen path. After several intense months, Ming could no longer budget the rent required to room part time in the commune, which was experiencing its own financial tribulations, and she returned to spend almost all of her nights with her family.

Ming was ready for a renewed effort to build trust with her kin. She had always intended, through regular home visiting, to show that her striving for an independent existence could encompass a continual caring attention for Mother and her siblings. By doing so she reassured Mother of her continued commitment and concern. When Ming later enrolled at Chung Chi College, she traveled home from its dormitory on weekends to help her brothers with their lessons and wash the family's clothes.

Ming's eagerness to engage her family in dialogue reminded me of what she proudly mentioned on an earlier occasion about Mother's collective leadership in a Kwangtung harvesting campaign at Liberation. Ming clearly had taken on Mother's social concerns and skills in implementing them in an atmosphere of grinding poverty. Ming adapted a conflict-resolution technique initiated by cadres in China when implementing the Communist Party's family policies. After Liberation, communist policy toward the centripetal family undermined one of its bases, the filial inheritance of ancestral and productive property, and sought to integrate the family work efforts into a planned economy to meet the collective's long-term requirements of increased agricultural and industrial production.

To implement these family policies, discussions were initiated in which all members had an equal say in resolving problems where family needs appeared to conflict with those of the collective. The Chinese press reported that the case-by-case reforms fostered by this technique have raised agricultural production (Tsao, 1970), although the majority of foreign scholars hold that family political struggle appears in the short run to impede production. In any case, no study has yet shown the demise of the centripetal family in China.

Ming adopted conflict resolution techniques and frequently organized discussions for the amicable settlement of some of the main family disputes. The difference between the techniques Ming used for family reform and those she was adapting from the mainland resided in the contrasting value structure of the respective societies. Ming could never persuade Mother that a cause might exist that should take priority over the needs of the family. Even if Ming were to agree in some measure with Mother on the goals of the family, the two women would part company on their accomplishment. Although unresponsive to communist-led campaigns in Hong Kong, Mother was skillful at mediation and reconciliation of opposing views of workmates and neighbors. Fortunately, therefore, both she and Ming were ready for constructive discussion, and the wide divergence in their views never caused acrimonious confrontation. This relatively harmonious relationship set a constructive tone for all interfamily transactions, including those between the siblings themselves.

Mother was far more receptive to her daughter's ideology of self-realization and struggle than any other parent I met. Most other parents in my sample feared the demise of cherished family patterns and revolution in the home if they relinquished their decision-making authority, but Mother remained open to wide-ranging discussions. Ming likewise patiently focused her powers of compassion and understanding upon the specific needs and problems of all those in the home; and I never heard her lose her temper or even raise her voice above conversational level. She elected never to separate herself completely from the home and persisted in her ongoing, energy-consuming effort to raise the family's social consciousness.

Career and college

Ming strove continually to achieve her occupational goal: a professional position from which she could organize young people and instill in them her socialist ideals. She began semiprofessional employment (at age 18 until age 19) as a primary-level teacher in the elementary school of Elsie Elliot, a well-known and respected British missionary reformer in Hong Kong. She then (from age 20 to 22) became a community organizer with Caritas, the international Catholic charity headquartered in the Vatican. After 4 years at a university, Ming became an organizer at the YMCA branch in a medium-size working-class population center at age 26. Caritas and the YMCA figure prominently in the Annual Report of the Hong Kong Council of Social Service, of which both are members.

Ming undertook teaching because of her love for children and her quest for experience in imparting the ethic of cooperation and community in youth. She expected that the Christian activism of Elliot and her several dedicated collaborators would mesh with her own secular aim of sowing the seeds of a new society. Even under Elliot's direction, however, the primary school was constrained to prepare its pupils for junior high school entrance and a succession of other rote examinations. Although Ming was granted some leeway in selection of instructional units, she was stymied by the anxiety of the pupils and their parents over mastering the set text and syllabus. She reluctantly realized that her introduction of individualistic curricular material would decrease the pupils' swotting time and hence their chances of scoring high on the all-important Secondary School Entrance Examination.

Retreating after several months to the standard lesson plan, Ming sought nevertheless to vitalize certain auxiliary aspects of the instructional process. It was, for example, the school custom for the class to stage a restaurant lunch for its mistress at the conclusion of the academic year. Ming at first considered declining this invitation because banquets were costly for working-class families and were part of the reciprocity pattern she disliked. But she did attend, and she saw that the collective meal offered interesting pedagogical possibilities: the joint celebration of the end of the school year, the creation of an intense final experience for pupils who would then remain lifetime chums, and the pupils' organization of a complex social activity.

As her year of teaching drew to a close, Ming saw that her personal objectives would not be realized in the school and sought a post with more scope and dynamism. She joined the nearly 2,000-member social work staff of Caritas, the social service agency of the Roman Catholic Church in Hong Kong, which assigned her to a one-room, four-person field office on the ground floor of a large resettlement estate. Her tasks included organization of young people up to age 16 for singing, games, athletics, weekend outings, and cookouts. In addition to these more or less conventional services, Caritas was prepared at this stage to organize the poor under its organizational credo: "To better individual and collective standards of living in order to achieve physical, socio-cultural and spiritual fulfillment of the human person within the framework of the community."

Community organization was novel in Hong Kong and Ming was at first granted broad leeway to pursue her tasks. Ming carried out her new mandate by systematically walking from door to door, notebook and credential in hand, to converse with the inhabitants through their locked iron grilles and learn their main needs and grievances. The rule in Hong Kong's mass occupancy dwellings is "Never open your gate to strangers," and acquaintances of mine employed by the Census and Statistics Department recalled the countless doors that were slammed in their faces. I therefore found it difficult to believe that the wary, preoccupied residents in a crime-ridden tenement block would unburden themselves in discussion with a strange young woman, but soft-spoken Ming gained their ear. Some of their numerous complaints were amenable to the elementary group action suggested: petitions, letters, and delegations to the Management Office for replacement of light bulbs, repairs to the elevator, more study spaces for children, installation of doors on toilet stalls, and the removal of garbage from the walkways. Some of these minor amenities were reluctantly granted by the Department of Resettlement. Ming was happy for these small gains but conscious that the deeper concerns of the residents, which she identified to me as crime, the financial and psychological burdens of the school system, insufficient cultural and recreational facilities, and general inferior quality of life, were not being articulated.

Six months after she joined Caritas, Ming learned that the Department of Resettlement had issued eviction notices to all residents of a small village adjoining a main New Territories artery so that the road could be rerouted through the center of the village. The government had promised alternative housing elsewhere in the New Territories, but its delay in fulfilling this commitment multiplied the anguish of the already distraught villagers. Although forced resettlement of entire populations is common in Hong Kong and had taken its toll on the Yao family itself, normal procedures in the New Territories entailed extended negotiations, lasting sometimes for years, during which the lineage leadership demanded adequate compensation for the destruction of their native places and institutions: homes, temples, orchards, and, above all, the rice paddies. On this occasion, however, the government appeared to dispense with the final stages of such negotiations and, under pressure possibly from the Public Works Department, moved unilaterally to destroy the village.

One morning a fleet of bulldozers and wrecking cranes from nearby highway construction entered the village periphery. The militant resistance displayed by several hundred villagers was reported in the colony's press. Upon reading a sympathetic article about the villagers in the patriotic Chinese daily *Ta Kung Pao,* Ming immediately assessed the significance of this unprecedented dispute. Acting under the Caritas guideline of "promptly assisting those who are victims of calamities and disasters," and possibly with the assent of her immediate superiors, Ming visited this village and at once made plans to join the protesters. Caritas permitted Ming to tutor the villagers in drafting a petition to the Department of Resettlement. She was delighted to encounter among the farmers former indigenous anti-Japanese World War II activists, and together they led a band of approximately fifty protesters to the Tsim Sha Tsui office of the Resettlement Department, carrying bedclothes and food for an overnight stay. The demonstrators, Ming included, demanded to see the director, and when he did not appear, they sat down in the doorway. Soon police vans drove up and carted the sitters to prison. When the black Marias (official vans for transporting prisoners) appeared, Ming had to decide on the spot whether to preserve her unsullied reputation in Caritas by exiting quickly or to risk her job and suffer incarceration with the villagers. She took the leap, hoping that her presence would dramatize the issue for the mass media and lend authority to the villagers' petition campaign. After spending the night in prison, the villagers were sent back home and the Resettlement Department found it politic to make available the long-awaited new homes immediately.

The press reported the clash extensively and spotlighted the Caritas affiliation of Ming, for whom the repercussions were immediate. Ming's forthright confrontation with the police irritated the charity's leaders, and she was chastised for allowing her identification with the villagers to spill over into the public domain. Ming retorted that community organizers should not undermine the cause of their needy constituents by parting company with them in the thick of their struggle. Caritas promptly tightened its vertical chain of command binding grass-roots organizers to the main body of the organization and eliminated independent decision making among its community-level staff.

Although Ming and the villagers won concessions, it was impossible for Ming's career at Caritas to flourish. After consultations with her family, which was proud of her public role, Ming reactivated her plans, dormant for over 3 years, to resume formal studies. She reasoned that with a university degree she could obtain much-needed status and leverage in the organization where she would eventually work and would be less likely to incur the wrath of its officials. She was anxious to continue her program of self-betterment and to study the history and politics of British colonial rule in order to find a model for its twilight phase in Hong Kong. Ming told me that she sought an academic framework in which to comprehend the colonial government policy of manipulating the beleaguered social welfare sector to intensify social control and deflect and attenuate all popular criticism. She hoped to locate other fledgling revolutionaries to join her in this task.

The Chinese University is a product of this late colonial phase. Intellectual refugees from Canton's Ling Nan University founded Chung Chi College in a New Territories market village in the mid-1960s. The North American and other missionary bodies that subsidized Ling Nan University continued their patronage of its principals when they emigrated with a portion of their staff to Hong Kong after Liberation, and their evangelical influence today sets the tone of student-faculty relations at Chung Chi (literally, the "Worship Christ" College). The student body is required to acknowledge the gospel through a compulsory weekly morning chapel service and enroll in a first-year civilization course framed according to Protestant doctrine.

In response to the pressing need for postsecondary places for sons and daughters of the colony's growing bourgeoisie, the Chinese University was created and its two other constituent colleges, United and New Asia, moved from Kowloon and Victoria in the early 1970s to join Chung Chi at its strikingly picturesque Tolo Harbor site adjoining the market town of Shatin. Chinese was the preferred language of instruction at Chung Chi from its inception, but because of an influential minority of mainland Chinese speakers, the Cantonese student body, and even some Hong Kong-bred staff members, found it difficult to establish complete linguistic rapport with all of the faculty. Only when the second generation of teachers, born and brought up in the colony, received their advanced degrees and were recruited to the university did standard Cantonese take deeper root.

The department heads at Chung Chi made academic and personal alliances with a variety of North American and British parent educational institutions and, in the absence of indigenous social science, they quickly became dominated by overseas exporters of educational patronage and ideology. The positivistic, survey data–based sociology curriculum, for example, was planned at the University of Pittsburgh, where the sociology department has for a number of years been guided by the noted Cantonese scholar C. K. Yang. The Chung Chi dons considered the critical theory of the Frankfurt School, the Max Weber–C. Wright Mills continuum, and other highly respected sociological approaches as irrelevant.

Ming needed to score highly on its competitive examination in order to win a place in the Chinese University. However, more than 3 years had elapsed since she left form VI, and when she was at school she pursued her mental development independently (extensive reading of library books and periodicals, frequent discussion groups in Chinese and English), to the detriment of rote memorization of examination techniques. Ming's solution was the tactical declaration of an intended major in English literature at Chung Chi, candidates for which underwent an oral examination after their written paper. She hoped her independent, well-rounded accomplishments over the years in English would compensate for not having the superior secondary school background and training, tutorial, and special test preparation sessions that the 17- and 18-year-old form VI examinees had. After the written papers were marked, Ming saw her tactic bear fruit as she was one of the first candidates called to Shatin for the departmental interview.

At the interview Ming ably defended herself. She spoke widely and knowledgeably of the books she had read and impressed the British faculty examiner with her clarity of mind and presence and maturity. At the close of the interview, he said as an afterthought, "I do hope you are going to remain in our faculty. It's very common for student entrants nowadays to come in on English and then switch over to our oversubscribed economics and sociology faculties." He bemoaned the smaller pool of students competing for a literature or language degree and attributed the low student demand for humanities to the pulling power of a social science degree in the wider world of Hong Kong employment.

When the formalities of registration were completed, Ming indeed squeezed through the procedural loophole and applied to the sociology department to which, after another series of interviews, she was accepted. Ming's hope of deepening her knowledge of the society in which she and her family lived and struggled fell short of realization at Chung Chi. The major analytical social scientific studies were not introduced in the first-year texts, although volumes by Marx, Marcuse, Bottomore, and David Gordon could be found in the library. Nevertheless, while revealing of major trends in Western social thought, such works were not specific to her local needs, and Ming in particular became aware of the gross deficiency of critical studies on British colonialism in China. Contemporary Hong Kong students have no corpus of critical or analytical writing on which to base perceptive critiques of industrial colonialism.

Ming struck up a rapport with several younger faculty members who were intellectually curious about political economy outside of Hong Kong, and she also located literature on the New China and the role of women before and after Liberation. However, she was dissatisfied with the overall shallowness of Chinese missionary education and the inappropriateness of the corpus of elite study material produced by those known as "China-watchers" to social struggle in Hong Kong.

Ming more and more devoted herself to student politics, and during her freshman year she led an activist party of students to victory in college elections. This group organized orientation sessions for all incoming students in September of Ming's sophomore year, at which students learned how they could participate in community activities through their representatives and how to join in the political and social science activities being launched at the college. Functioning deliberately through the administration-sanctioned channels of student government, Ming's group established liaison with trade union and community movements. In the rather open political climate of the early and mid-1970s, students for the first time in the Chinese University engaged in discussions with representatives of patriotic trade unions and donated their weekend labor to working-class neighborhood-betterment schemes. Thus, when in October 1975 Typhoon Elsie struck the colony, uprooting homes and flooding entire squatter compounds, Ming and other students pitched in to aid the rebuilding of homes and neighborhood facilities.

Ming's student group published articles about its community organizing in the Chinese University student paper, which attracted wide notice. Students in Ming's group who had recently visited the People's Republic reported in this periodical on the reform movements they witnessed and their personal experiences in town and country. Ming's group regarded this information as essential for all students, especially because earlier generations of Hong Kong youths had passed through the college gate with no exposure to developments on the mainland and in the patriotic Hong Kong sector.

Chinese University sociology graduates were sent mainly into secondary school teaching and social welfare positions, and when Ming matriculated in 1978 she was delighted to be one of the first females hired by the YMCA to oversee youth work in one of its branches. The Yao family beamed with pride when they learned that Ming's years of toil and application had led to a responsible and visibly respected junior administrative position.

Among the missionary settlements, the Hong Kong YMCA is regarded as one of the most accessible and forward looking. Like its active predecessors in Shanghai and other Chinese treaty ports in the 1920s and 1930s (Garrett, 1970), the Hong Kong YMCA was a meeting place for large numbers of youths and students and strove for a high degree of community outreach and consciousness-raising in such politically noncontroversial areas as adult literacy programs, public health improvement, sports, and Chinese culture. Ming's responsibilities as branch Youth Director included physical education, leadership of games and excursions, and supervision of culture and leisure-time clubs.

Ming has over the years strengthened her deep personal commitment to the radical betterment of Hong Kong society. She has acquired considerable experience in winning gains by employing the hierarchical status quo community organizations (charity and missionary groups, secondary and university school systems), to realize much-needed, if short-term, improvements. She is now amply appraised of the vast difficulties in effecting longer-range reforms, but I do not imagine that Ming will lightly abandon her questioning of all ideas and institutions, and I shall follow from afar her fascinating political odyssey.

Friendships

Ming drew her friends from among Chinese intellectuals and unionists, overseas graduate students and teachers, student political leaders, and fellow social workers and teachers. Whereas my other interviewees and their peers questioned outsiders only on such mundane topics as family matters, fashion, and the cinema, Ming quizzed her anti-war communards and other overseas friends and acquaintances about the politics and economics of Hong Kong colonial rule and on prospects for social change in the colony. Her passionately engaged discussions raised many profound and disquieting issues that were difficult to answer. "Have you noticed," Ming said to me, "that the government is utilizing the social work section to increase its control of every aspect of the lives of the common folk? Look at the recent authoritarian block organization under the guise of an anti-crime campaign. Have you ever read anything on other mature colonial governments towards the end of their rule that will shed light on such repressive practices?" At the time, when I relayed Ming's perplexing questions to a Harvard doctoral candidate in sociology, he replied, "Even though I cannot answer her tough questions, I never run out of things to discuss with Ming." Some years later, he added: "I always seek out Ming to continue our discussions on my annual visits to Hong Kong."

When she was with her Chinese friends, most of Ming's activities were aimed at amelioration of social injustice and the exploration of their common cultural heritage. Ming and Chinese University student activists of vaguely "New Left" persuasion mounted a modest but well-publicized demonstration against the rising cost of living, which decimated workers' incomes. The demonstration was significant because, until the 1970s, university students had long despaired of changing the rigid Hong Kong society and rarely took their politically circumscribed causes to the streets. The bonds that the activist student community began to forge led to the community organization in which Ming participated as a student in 1975–8. She attended a folk-singing club, to which Wai-gun also belonged. The club rehearsed and sang Cantonese and Mandarin folk songs and lent their voices to the anti-inflation rally.

Beginning in the early 1970s, China welcomed visits from compatriots in Hong Kong and Macau, and Ming took advantage of this outward turn to visit the mainland on a number of occasions, both alone and in company. Mother, for her part, paid for family visits to Father's native village in Nan-hai county. For Mother, renewed contact with the Yaos' village strengthened her identification with land and family. She enjoyed reactivating her relationships with paternal relatives and she fulfilled her obligations to ancestors by visits to their well-kept graves. Mother carried with her costly gifts, such as Japanese synthetic fabrics from her stall, herbal medicines exported from China but unavailable in Nan-hai, and ginseng from Korea, fulfilling the still strong traditional expectation that higher-status clansmen should bestow gifts on the poorer kin. Mother was unable to visit as often as she would have liked, because she could afford neither the time nor the gift-bearing role.

Ming's visits had a completely different purpose. They were intended to bring her closer, through the vehicles of family and village, to an appreciation for the quality of life in the new China and an understanding of peasant receptiveness to putting the collective interest above that of the individual and the family. (Wai-gun's motives for visiting her ancestral village were similar.) When Ming made her only pilgrimage to Father's native place, she chose not to bear commodity gifts, reasoning that by Hong Kong standards her family was too poor to donate the expected elaborate ritual offerings. Mother was predictably annoyed at Ming's abstemiousness, and their difference over gift bearing was a prototypical dispute that widened their divergence over the necessity of family frugality.

On a subsequent visit to her homeland, Ming and a group of three or four friends traveled through a number of provinces, staying overnight in dormitories and low-cost hotels, dining in proletarian canteens, and otherwise attempting to share the life of the common people. Ming's small travel party encountered formidable administrative obstacles: long queues for travel documents, tickets, public accommodations, and scarce ration coupons for canteen meals. These hindrances inhibited most other Hong Kong Chinese from ever taking such expeditions.

Ming's team, through uncommon patience and youthful persistence, won the opportunity to spend several fruitful days establishing personal rapport with young Chinese in schools, playgrounds, at markets, and at other public places. Ming was deeply impressed by the responses of several children to her questions about their tasks in the Chinese revolution. For instance, Ming asked a group of children, "What do you want to be when you grow up?"

"We want to serve the people!" they replied in chorus.

"But what does this mean to you?"

"It means going where I am needed," said one child.

"Have you already begun to serve the people?"

"Last year we helped the peasants bring in the crops at harvest time," answered another.

When she related these conversations to me shortly after her return, Ming pointedly compared the willing, eager responses to the attitudes of Hong Kong elementary school pupils, who have no wider reference community than the family economy and factional society and whose career choices barely exceed colonial administration and the industrial-commercial sector. Ming hoped on a follow-up visit to learn more about education for service and the life for which mainland youth are being trained by observing instruction in elementary classrooms in Canton and other Kwangtung province centers.

More firmly established in her social change commitment after returning from her exciting visit north of the border, Ming intensified her altruistic commitment and further turned her back on the common-place vying for status and material goods that characterized her contemporaries under commercial media influence. These compelling qualities, which had by now firmly won the grudging respect of Mother and the rest of her family, also drew to her a circle of alert friends and supporters who reciprocated her affections. Ming was an open, understanding person who readily responded to all human difficulties. In Ming's apartment on stifling summer evenings my daughter Shana chafed and fretted and I seemed unable to calm her. Ming gently overcame Shana's uneasiness by singing to her as she walked with Shana in her arms back and forth along the balcony.

Ming was indifferent to fashion and cosmetics and did not approach conventional beauty standards derived from traditional Chinese stereotypes of an attractive woman, expressed by some as seductive, "catlike" beauty. I attribute Ming's undoubted personal charm and attractiveness to the opposite sex substantially to her separation of physical and psychological intimacy from preparation for marriage. Serious young men were drawn to Ming's indifference to dating rituals and conventions and took the opportunities this presented to explore their ideas and feelings in conversation with her. Even the more worldly males in Ming's circle appeared to require the psychological security afforded by safe, because familiar, home ties. Ming's suitors were unable to exploit the possibilities inherent in a collegial relationship with her, because they were moved by the family-building ethos to seek early engagement. Ming said to me about more than one of them: "Our relationship is at an end now, but he is only slowly becoming aware of it." Marriage-oriented dating would most likely have diverted Ming's energy from her chosen path of professional work, political activity, and cultivation of her own abilities and those of her family.

Summary

Ming exercised First Daughter charisma by shouldering with Mother all of the enormous burdens of her young, fatherless family. Her ideology of service to the common people contrasted with the familial or sectional approach of other working-daughter respondents. Ming's efforts to organize for change were encumbered by the retrograde aspects of the centripetal family, which she regarded as a historical throwback. Ming never slighted her necessary household tasks and constantly struggled to resolve, or at least manage, the tensions between survival and service to society.

Ming could only succeed by gaining allies in all of her struggles, although her dedication drew forth more support from her peer group than from her kin. The Yaos did not share Ming's ideological premises and instead attributed their economic and social difficulties to an unfortunate concatenation of particular problems and dilemmas that was best met internally by the relentless dawn-to-dusk toil of a tightly co-ordinated family unit. Influenced by China's family reform campaigns, socialist-minded Ming strove to teach Mother and her siblings that the family's dirt poverty and the foreshortening of the youngsters' career opportunities was caused by the inequities of the Hong Kong capitalist system. Ming viewed cooperation as extending far wider than family, relatives, patrons, and clients. She envisaged the process of community-wide cooperation as a stage in class struggle that could ultimately overthrow the dominance of the rich in Hong Kong.

Ming's fundamentally political attitude toward life demarcated her from all but one of the twenty-eight working women in this study. I am looking forward to learning more about the turbulent and demanding course Ming Yao has chosen.

Summary: a comparison

The life histories of Ju-chen and Ming closely resemble each other. These two women had been matriculated in a university, in contrast to white-collar service peers who went no farther than secondary school. The Leungs and Yaos supported their eldest daughters' career aspirations and fully underwrote the Anglo-Chinese secondary school education, which was a prerequisite to ascending the professional ladder. This process prolonged the period of the involuntary dependence of both women upon the family.

Their jobs in large organizations did not compete with their roles in the family and, indeed, the bureaucratic structure and ideology of these institutions gave rise to employee behavior entirely consistent with the factional competition of the Hong Kong order. The centripetal family, as I have stressed, is a response to the demands of such a society. The status strivings of her colleagues and students paralleled the efforts of Ju-chen to better her family standard of living and upgrade its environment. She shunned the cliques and sectarian skirmishes of her workplace and hence did not envisage a career of lifetime teaching. Instead, Ju-chen looked forward to marriage, raising a family, and part-time work.

In contrast, Ming could endorse the reformist bent of the primary school and the then-stated community betterment aims of Caritas. Each time Ming ignored the expectations of the organization that its cadres contribute to the Hong Kong status quo and strove to exploit the zone of ambiguity inherent in all efforts to serve the Hong Kong poor, she effectively limited her duration of employment. It was true that Caritas had been momentarily amenable to her activism, but its overriding concern was to maintain its power base in Hong Kong, and when Ming singlehandedly brought these goals into collision, centrifugal-oriented social change was subsumed under centripetal politics.

The two women had different responses to their work settings, but both kept their family needs foremost. They balanced the strenuous efforts needed to realize their ambitious personal goals with the necessities of filial piety and expanded their positions as key providers as they matured. Ju-chen's and Ming's earnings far exceeded the wages of other women interviewed, and for several years after completing college, the families of these two women were especially dependent upon their higher wages. Both women were determined to aid their families with their incomes as well as with their wider experiences.

Their contributions to the family budget and broad educational experiences reinforced their already substantial voices in family councils. The families' acceptance of their leadership roles was further conditioned by the daughters' resolve to exercise leadership, as well as the families' own acceptance or determination of this leadership. The Leung family disregarded Ju-chen's pleas for more say in family decision making. Because she was female, they granted her sway mainly in the realm of purchases but otherwise excluded her from the central family goals of marriage plans for the sons and daughters. Although frustrated by her family's aspirations to elevate its living standards, Ju-chen was nonetheless drawn into its economic plan. Because she strove for status like the other family members, Ju-chen, unlike Ming, could not demarcate herself from the everyday trials and tribulations at home. She did not attain greater leadership position at home.

Mrs. Yao could not comprehend Ming's efforts to abandon those areas of the family economy that were concerned with higher status. As her history reveals, Ming forcefully opposed time-consuming and expensive efforts to train her brothers for petty white-collar jobs. Apart from Ming, the other family members feared that the family's economy would fall behind other Hong Kong families who were making similar plans. Ming also devalued ritual exchanges with relatives and neighbors. The Yaos interpreted Ming's low social posture as motivated by a self-seeking individualism inappropriate to their understanding of what was required in commercial Hong Kong. Ming resisted the compulsion of her family to tie itself to relatives and various personal and business acquaintances in order to hold its own and compete with like-acting families. Although Ming's family was by no means responsive to her anticentripetal ideology (Mother's persistence in wedding plans, gift-bearing role to the mainland, education of the sons, and tying Second and Fourth Daughters to the store), they did at least allow her to persuade them in several key matters (termination of her employment with Uncle, her return to school when the family finances were at a nadir. These examples illustrate my fundamental contention that working daughters may well win difficulties and disputes where their own interests alone are at stake, but they seldom win when the future of other family members and that of the family itself is involved.

To summarize, the two women responded differently to Hong Kong's society and settings, and they defined their roles in the family and society in fundamentally contrasting ways. Nevertheless, Ju-chen and Ming nicely balanced and integrated their personal goals with a direction chosen by their families and maintained throughout the expected role of key counselors and providers, as was expected of dutiful daughters.

Conclusion

The Hong Kong working women of this study were typically raised in densely settled housing estates and educated in overcrowded primary schools, the first step in the colonywide competitive educational hierarchy. They worked on factory assembly lines, which confronted them with the impersonal, rapidly changing market economy. During their 10-year (or longer) factory term, which commenced at about age 13, these women voluntarily changed posts a number of times and because of the transient and cyclical nature of international consumer demand, perpetually anticipated layoffs and firings. Hong Kong's commodity economy effectively terminated home production for domestic needs and the girls shopped for most of their personal requirements with their own wages. They joined disparate nonfamilial social groups, which were necessary for successful job force integration and whose definition was beyond the capabilities and scope of their families. The families relied on the schools and community youth centers and informal groups of peers to socialize their daughters in mores appropriate to industrializing Hong Kong. In short, the circumstances of the daughters' lives changed greatly from those of their mothers. Their parents have been unable to train them, as was the case in rural Kwangtung several generations ago, and they therefore control a smaller portion of their daughters' lives today.

Clearly, major differences developed as the contemporary Hong Kong family evolved from its southern Chinese forerunner. Hong Kong has become an industrial city-state whose colonial regime drives an economy based on an impersonal division of labor. Hong Kong society is composed in the main of complex, bureaucratic, and nonfamilial organizations, but it is also penetrated by a dense network of allegiances between individuals and families. All industrial states are characterized by impersonal social structures, but the retention of earlier networks and ideologies demands explanation in the case of Hong Kong today.

257

Certainly Hong Kong's personalistic bonds are looser than those forged over centuries of China's rural past, and families need not duplicate the earlier, wider-ranging reciprocal social alliances constructed for production and physical protection. In Hong Kong's low-wage economy the family of each working daughter studied depended upon her wages to survive and advance. No individual proletarian wage earner can bring home enough to fill the family rice bowls. Moreover, the laissez faire economy, based on exports and commercialism, is subject to the vicissitudes of its global markets and forces families to compete for scarce jobs and educational opportunities, thereby preventing emergence of alternatives to the purposive family economy. Families have greatly reduced the scope and intensity of traditional reciprocal alliances with friends, kinsmen, and colleagues, only to form more loosely organized street and neighborhood associations, benevolent fraternities and fellowships, officialiy sanctioned pressure groups, and individually struck patron-client and colleague relationships. More fluid than those of the past, these subjective bonds are easily entered and altered to suit immediate family needs.

Shaped by the blend of traditional and modern influences, the compact and delimited Hong Kong family of today is peculiarly appropriate for the attainment of its main goals and raisons d'être. These are, first, economic cooperation and pooling of members' earnings to advance the family economy and second, the pride of place of all sons who continue the religious-cultural focus on the patriliny as the hallmark of the ancestral tradition. Generalized reciprocity within an ongoing circle of friends, colleagues, relatives, and patrons is valued to meet family economic needs, and sons are the main recipients of family benefits. The unmarried daughter, like other family members, abides by these strictures, which demand her loyalty to her family of origin before marriage and devotion to her husband's family thereafter. I refer to the Hong Kong family unit formed to fulfill these twin goals as the *modified centripetal family.*

The labor force participation of Hong Kong working daughters is invariably harnessed to realize these family objectives. Despite the importance of their work experiences, the daughters' poorly paid jobs lend insufficient economic security and status in the family and society to free them from their families. Moreover, factory, service, and semi-professional jobs and the peer and leisure time opportunities they create provide too few allegiances to compete effectively for young women's energy or attention. Therefore, the ability of the working daughter to sell her labor power for a price does not attenuate the bonds of familism. Ironically, wage labor-force participation has enabled close-knit families to reintegrate their daughters of toil by incorporating their earnings and experiences as a promising means of attaining primary family goals.

The central player on my stage is the Hong Kong working daughter, whose position in family and society directly depends upon: 1) the economic history and other socioeconomic attributes of her family; 2) the daughter's birth order, the size of the completed family and its generational composition, and the ages of her parents and their physical condition; and 3) the position of females in the Chinese patriarchy, which limits changes in daughters' lives. An analysis and comparison of my twenty-eight interviewees in light of these criteria will show how the modified centripetal family molds women's status and circumscribes their opportunities in contemporary Hong Kong.

Family status in the socioeconomy

Each of my twenty-eight working daughters (and apparently most of their siblings as well) had been trained early to contribute her talents and energies unstintingly to the kin group and to identify herself totally with its survival and aspirations. Because of their mothers' busy involvement with toddlers and infants, domestic and other family tasks were assigned to the daughters long before they reached adolescence. All of the mothers were occupied by a demanding round of child care and homemaking. The burden on the daughters was considerably heavier when outside employment was added to their mothers' domestic tasks (in about one-third of my sample). Performing assembly tasks at home was also popular among the working daughters (plastic flower making, transistor assembly, bead work). Home industry served as a convenient bridge to actual work, and it added income to the family budget. Little individual recognition was accorded this form of toil, which conformed to the existing home-based handicraft pattern of Hong Kong artisan workers and familywide enterprises. Thus much followed tradition, as reflected in the bridal lament (p. *v*).

Family economic circumstances determined the training of the daughters and the age at which they undertook employment. Working-class daughters entered primary school directly from the home without the benefit of even one preschool or kindergarten year. All respondents completed primary school and were in most cases the first in their families to achieve this. (Because of economic pressures and the more restricted educational opportunities some years back, their elder siblings had been unable to continue their schooling past primary 4.) My working-class respondents entered the labor force between the ages of 12 and 14, whereas the upper-working- and lower-middle-class subjects were matriculated in lower secondary school, and they became wage earners around age 16.

Educational level and scope of family connections mostly determined the level at which women joined the employment hierarchy. Working-class girls studied in government Chinese-language primary schools and, with their imperfect skill in English (which can only be improved with difficult-to-obtain supplementary educational experiences), fell short of the proper certification and demeanor to qualify for posts like receptionist, secretary, or teacher. Formal apprenticeships in technical training programs were (and still are) scarce in the colony, and working-class women were consigned to the semi-skilled, mass process, assembling occupational bracket.

Upper-working- and middle-class daughters received more English-language training, although they, too, lacked the opportunity to cultivate special job skills. Their English background and panache enabled service girls and certain semiprofessionals to interact with the international tourist and foreign business set they encountered through white-collar activities. Their introductions to these more elevated positions derived from relatives, friends, or schoolmates.

Although the parents of some working-class families attempted to chart a course out of poverty, only a few of the daughters formulated individual achievement plans. Extensive overtime and wrestling for slightly better piecework wages could increase their pay packets only temporarily, and these women lacked the means and opportunities to ascend the ladder of job categories. They were bereft of even the few hundred dollars needed to embark on petty trades and concessions, as some of their male counterparts did. Many of these women diligently pursued their education through evening courses or English-language clubs, but these efforts rarely led directly to job promotion and enhancement.

The families of white-collar women, whose economic circumstances are more predictable than working-class households, were able initially to locate their daughters in such steady, preferred positions. These positions, however, offered limited opportunities for advancement. The clerical and semiprofessional daughters could selectively change posts horizontally to improve job position marginally, but to gain significantly better paying positions, additional schooling was required. Those women intent on long-term social mobility had a much greater chance of accomplishing this than did their blue-collar counterparts, because their families continued to supply material aid and moral encouragement.

All families suffered from fluctuating income, and several middle-income households experienced downward mobility. Daughters were taught to anticipate middle-school education and then entry into white-collar jobs, but a father's bankruptcy could annul these bright expectations. The burden of restoring their families' economic prospects and their own economic advancement would then fall to the daughters. The daughters from these downwardly mobile petit bourgeois families were strongly motivated to attain the higher level of occupations that were once expected of them and thereby to overcome the domestic crises of their youth.

The structure and cycle of the family

The Hong Kong industrial wage does not enable fathers to support their families unaided. Therefore, blue-collar households especially seek to increase the ratio of wage earners to dependents. At the outset of the family cycle, when the household consists of numerous young children and few wage earners, the budget is not large enough to permit much schooling for the eldest children. The first working-class daughters to reach puberty are immediately sent to work and their entire earnings are remitted home. Middle-income families whose fathers earn the larger business wage are not in such straitened circumstances, and as long as Father retains his post, all daughters have a chance at secondary schooling.

The next stage of the family cycle begins when the eldest children have joined the labor force and the wage-earning ratio increases until the young-adult wage earners marry and form families of their own. The withdrawal of the income of older daughters through marriage, if not accompanied by simultaneous entry into the labor force by their teenage siblings, decreases the wage-earning ratio (the third stage of the family cycle).

Table 4. *Ratio of wage earners to family dependents, 1960–74*

Respondents	1960	1965	1970	1973	1974
Working class					
A-li	1:8	3:7	3:7	4:6	4:6
I-ling	1:4	2:4	3:3	3:3	3:3
Mae	1:7	3:5	4:3	4:3	3:3
Wai-gun	1:7	3:6	3:6	4:5	5:4
Upper working class					
Ming	1:6	1:8	3:6	3:6	4:5
Middle class					
Ju-chen	1:9	2:7	3:7	4:6	3:6

Table 4 displays wage-earning ratios for representative selected families of my sample, which are shown graphically in Figure 1. This ratio increased from 1960, after which the increase continued in two cases and was reversed in two cases. Around 1960 a parent was the sole family wage earner. By the mid-1960s, the eldest children had entered the labor force, but since more children had been born, it was not until the turn of the decade that the wage-earning ratio approached its maximum. In 1974, family income was at a 10-year high in all but two families (Mae, Ju-chen), who lost income from a sibling who married.

Figure 2 reveals the considerable proportion of the household income contributed by several young women at two points in the second stage of their family, when mature children enter the labor force and wage-earning ratio approaches its maximum. In those cases where the father provided little due to unemployment or reduced work time, illness, residence elsewhere, or his demise, the family income was particularly low and the daughters' early income was most important. Education of the daughters suffered, which meant that family income could not be improved through job upgrading from these offspring, thereby perpetuating a downward economic spiral.

The ratio of income earners to dependents determined the uses to which the daughters' earnings were put. When the ratio of the family income to its size was small, as around 1965 in the beginning of the second stage of the family cycle, the daughters' wages were earmarked for rent and food and other necessities. Outlays for medical care followed, and after necessities like these were accounted for, education for younger children took up a larger part of the budget. When the number of earners and the total size of the budget expanded, families purchased more consumer goods. During the late 1960s and early

1970s, all twenty-eight families acquired telephones, twenty-seven purchased small electric refrigerators, and twenty-seven purchased television sets. Several families purchased sewing machines. The economically better off families in my sample could afford small Japanese-made washing machines. Some of these upper-working- and lower-middle-class families were preparing moves to new apartments. Whereas the working-class families hoped to transfer from resettlement estates to low-income housing units, middle-income families expected to move from tenements to private apartments in newly built quarters. This whole complex of expenditures was undertaken only because the working daughters augmented the family budget from 30% to 70%.

The deployment of the family income for children's education was of central importance in all twenty-eight families. When the family reached its more affluent second stage, more resources were invariably

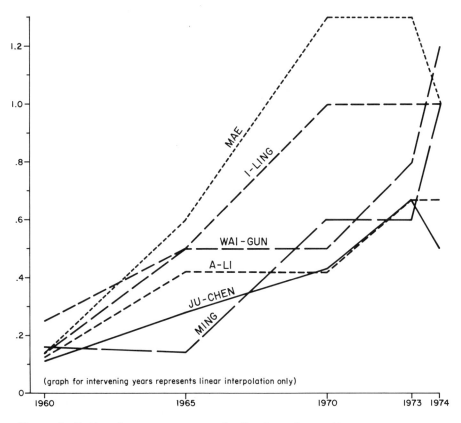

Figure 1. Ratio of wage earners to family dependents, 1960–74. Figure 1 is a graphic representation of Table 4.

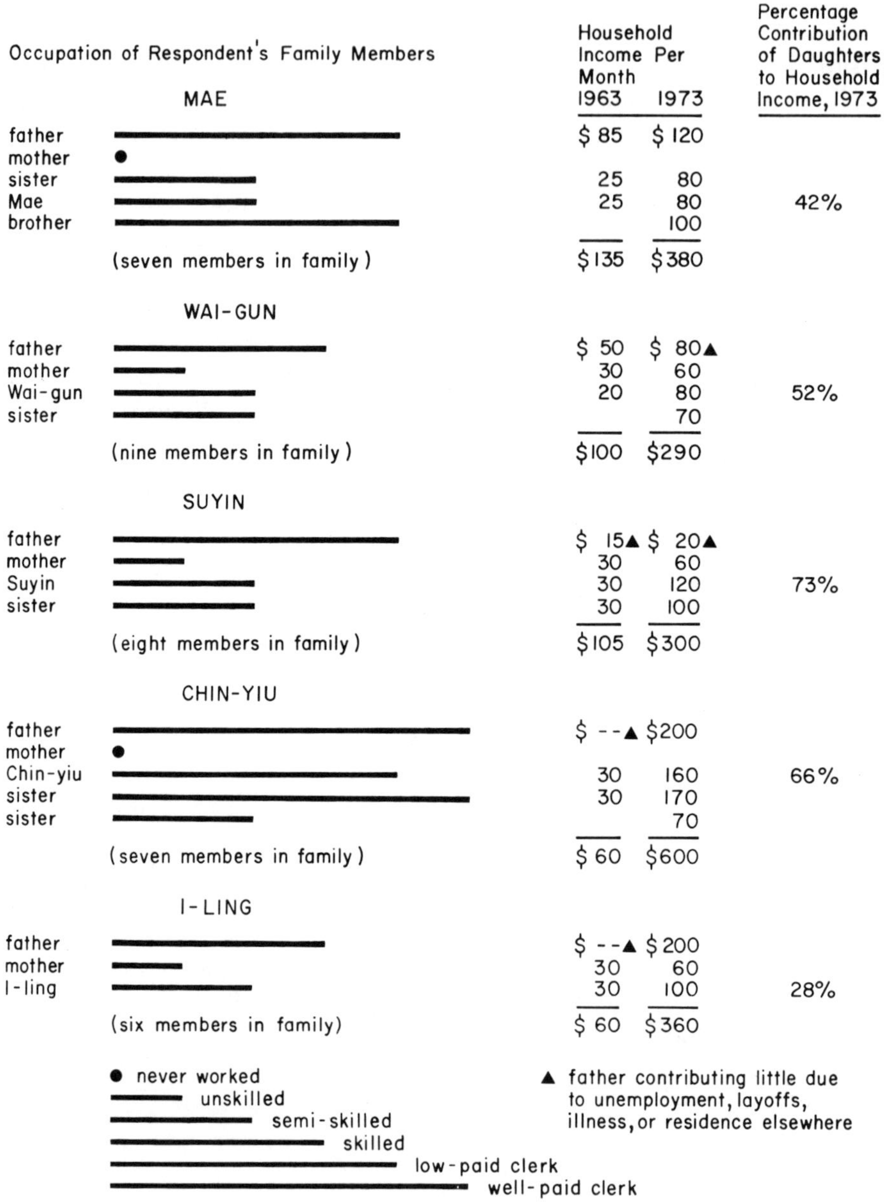

Occupation of Respondent's Family Members	Household Income Per Month		Percentage Contribution of Daughters to Household Income, 1973
	1963	1973	
MAE			
father	$ 85	$ 120	
mother			
sister	25	80	
Mae	25	80	42%
brother		100	
(seven members in family)	$135	$380	
WAI-GUN			
father	$ 50	$ 80▲	
mother	30	60	
Wai-gun	20	80	52%
sister		70	
(nine members in family)	$100	$290	
SUYIN			
father	$ 15▲	$ 20▲	
mother	30	60	
Suyin	30	120	73%
sister	30	100	
(eight members in family)	$105	$300	
CHIN-YIU			
father	$ --▲	$200	
mother			
Chin-yiu	30	160	66%
sister	30	170	
sister		70	
(seven members in family)	$ 60	$600	
I-LING			
father	$ --▲	$ 200	
mother	30	60	
I-ling	30	100	28%
(six members in family)	$ 60	$360	

● never worked
unskilled
semi-skilled
skilled
low-paid clerk
well-paid clerk

▲ father contributing little due to unemployment, layoffs, illness, or residence elsewhere

Figure 2. Occupational profiles and income of family members.

channeled into the education of its younger sons and daughters. There were greater sex differences in educational opportunities within poorer families. Sons of families in stage two were always encouraged to continue to secondary school even if their exam scores did not merit government financial support, whereas stricter conditions were imposed on the daughters' advancement. There were four blue-collar families in which younger sisters of the respondents did not continue in school past primary level because they performed poorly on the Secondary School Entrance Examination, and they undertook factory employment after resigning from the educational stream. No younger sons were similarly handicapped.

Sexual distinctions were not pronounced in decisions concerning secondary-level education of offspring in middle-income families; all the younger sisters of my respondents in this economically more comfortable category had the opportunity to enter secondary school. The attainment of secondary-level education ultimately determined the job level the daughters could obtain. Because of their parents' ability to sponsor their secondary education, the daughters had the assurance of continuing in the families' white-collar bracket.

As the family cycle advanced, blue-collar daughters' earnings were spent on personal and family recreation and family festivities (ritual events, life-cycle ceremonies of kin and friends). When a financial cushion was provided by a working daughter, her family could, often for the first time, sponsor and enjoy birthday and wedding banquets. This gave the families opportunities to strengthen links with their relatives, patrons, and friends. In 1973, four families arranged gala (eight to ten restaurant tables) events for grandsons and elderly parents and one family had a less pretentious home birthday celebration. At the same time, families were expectantly planning expensive weddings for their sons, who were around ages 25 to 30.

Each family thus aspired to improve its position in life by means of combining the incomes of wage-earning members. One middle-class respondent referred to the sudden tragic death of her 19-year-old male cousin as the loss of a boy who was in his "golden years," the point at which he would have begun to make the substantial input to his family's budget that they expected.

Sibling order, and particularly educational and employment opportunities, were other determinants of the blue-collar girls' life histories. Older daughters in a line of brothers and sisters began to help out at home and care for their siblings long before adolescence and the commencement of their regular wage-earning cycle. Eldest daughters thus matured when their family wage-earning ratio was near its minimum, and for many years all daughters' factory wage packets were dutifully deposited in the family purse. Less onerous were the burdens borne by the younger siblings of the respondents, who matured when the family wage-earning ratio was on the rise. Their crucial early adolescent years, when secondary school entry was weighed against factory toil, coincided with the attainment of the peak maximum wage-earning ratios.

Hong Kong's economic development also shaped the daughters' opportunity structure. When these 28 women were being raised in the 1950s and early 1960s, the economy was still struggling to establish and reap the fruits of its newfound export orientation. Their younger siblings, in contrast, matured when the economy had entered a relatively more economically prosperous stage (early 1970s). These younger sisters and brothers consequently enjoyed far more freedom to spend their own money on peer activities, and the percentage of earnings devolving to their families was much smaller.

Social class dictated the uses to which the women's wages were applied, but without exception all families drew upon their daughters' wages; invariably, three-quarters of their income went to their families. The family wage economy is one primary manifestation of the modified centripetal family in Hong Kong today.

Limits to daughters' independence and change in their lives

Marriage choices

Women have gained little in the core areas of the family's concern, but the families have retained selective, rather than comprehensive, control over their lives. Industrialization and the expansion of female labor that accompanied it enabled Hong Kong women to loosen the tight family bonds and widen marriage choices, consumer spending habits, and peer-group activities. In addition, however, the daughters enriched their filial roles in the family itself.

Most marriages are no longer arranged. Thirteen women in my sample had steady male companions, or fiancés (and toward the end of my study, husbands), and only one became a bride in a fashion remotely resembling former parentally arranged liaisons. This was Sa-li, who at Mother's urging became close to a young goldsmith from a neighboring tenement flat and corresponded with him when he emigrated to Singapore to seek better employment. Sa-li's mother continually referred approvingly in my presence to the many virtues of the goldsmith, and Sa-li for her part said that she would never marry a man unless her mother endorsed him. Three of four elder sisters of my interviewees who married during my visits to their families did, however, have an arrangement, thereby attesting to the novelty of the gain in marital freedom in Hong Kong.

My interviewees met their partners primarily through peer-group activities; however, the extent of heterosexual mixing and dating should not be overemphasized. These working daughters rarely dated workmates and the conventions for striking up steady relationships were not well defined. The confining structure of the women's work setting and restraints imposed by home residence complicated the initiation of free associations leading to love marriages. The semiprofessionals dated colleagues and clients with little hesitation, as did several white-collar employees and the waitresses, but only two factory workers were approached at their workplace and courted by job mates. The remainder met young men who worked elsewhere during picnics and excursions organized by social work agencies and colleagues or else at social gatherings at relatives' homes. The first man dated by a woman generally became her fiancé. If for some reason, such as parental opposition, this primary relationship foundered, a woman experienced considerable difficulty in resuming personal contact with other potential mates. Courtships usually lasted several years, during which the couple accumulated funds for the nuptial banquet and their future household and gradually became better acquainted in a fashion that the women came to desire through their peer-group socialization.

Two of my respondents and five of their siblings became pregnant before their marriages. The mothers, in most of these seven cases, were actually pleased at their daughters' pregnancy because the value of children is so strong in Hong Kong society. Several of these mothers smiled as they folded their arms and simulated their expected grandchild's cradle and said, "Never mind the timing. We'll be so happy to take the new baby in our arms." In only one case, when the couple had insufficient time to accumulate wedding funds, was a mother distraught over her eldest daughter's pregnancy before wedlock. All of these bridal pregnancies ultimately ended in marriage, which effectively demonstrates that the measure of premarital sexual opportunities that become available to women when they participate in wage labor in no way disrupts parental control in the key decisions of their lives.

Parents halfheartedly sought to influence the marriage of their daughters. Ten mothers attempted to act as matchmakers and all were rebuffed, after which each gracefully retreated with the attitude of "youths will be youths." Parents did scrutinize the cultural background of each potential spouse, however, and successfully insisted that their children marry within their own ethnolinguistic group. More than once a daughter lost a potential husband because he was of the wrong dialect group. Parents were aware that common ethnolinguistic background will strengthen bonds between agnates and affines, whereas crossing of language backgrounds will deprive the family of a potentially wider circle of reliable helpmates.

The public celebration of marriage remained central to ordinary family strategies of long-term social obligations because, through it, families sustained their reputations for generosity, reliability, and willingness to affirm social bonds, and they established particular relationships of exchange with others. The wedding banquet was planned by the families jointly, whereas the major alternative, the travel wedding, where the couple goes off alone, excludes the family. The families of eight of the daughters and their siblings whose marriages I witnessed staged a traditional banquet. The sole exception was a family that had recently launched such a ceremony for an eldest brother.

Even more important was the timing of marriage, which signals the close of the daughter's financial contribution to the family, and families were of one voice that the daughters should delay their nuptials through their mid-20s. Fifteen of the twenty-eight women in this study told me that they postponed active consideration of marriage in deference to their parents, and this was especially true of several elder sisters whom I met in the respondents' homes. The betrothed women also benefited personally from this abstention by putting aside close to 10% of their earnings for their marital abode. This aided them in equipping their new homes with such appliances as rice cooker, electric fan, and stereo; a double-tiered bed, dresser, and wardrobe might also be included in the bride's dowry. In six cases, daughters told me that they were delaying marriage while their fiancés saved at an even greater rate for a lavish banquet (Salaff, 1976a).

Although women of Hong Kong can now exercise freer choice of marriage partner, most are expected by their families to seek a mate from within their own subcultural group and stage a costly wedding banquet (especially if early-born). The parents generally choose the year and even month of the marriage. This parental concession to a love marriage does not reduce parental control, and parents may still extend their ties with the wider family and its periphery and forge new bonds with kinsmen through daughters' marriages. In all these ways the new marriage comes to strengthen the core of the modified centripetal family.

Spending money

Respondents retained from their salary packets a small, regular amount that was mutually agreed upon at home. These allowances increased with the ratio of wage earners to dependents. Women thus obtained pocket money for leisure time, peer-group activities like outings, night school, cultural activities, and personal effects like clothing. Their parents allowed them to use whatever spending money they could muster for strictly personal acquisitions. Thus, the workplace made enhanced leisure time activities with a wider circle composed of workmates financially possible.

Peers

In exchange for their economic input, the working daughters were exempted from their earlier household tasks, such as cooking and child care, and their mothers or female siblings were even prepared to wash and iron the employed daughters' clothes. Mothers employed outside the home reapportioned most of the home chores among younger siblings in order to lighten the working daughters' domestic burdens.

The early 20s are years of relative domestic freedom and outward extension of working daughters' talents and interests. Because most respondents entered the labor force directly from school, they could not enjoy even several months of toil-free adolescence. They won only belatedly a modicum of leisure time, funds, and companionship to help them pursue their youthful ambitions. Working daughters' numerous formal and informal clubs and the wide variety of workplace-derived peer activities they organized and enjoy today contrast with the knowledge and experience gained by their younger siblings from longer schooling and more extensive mass media exposure. The peers of my respondents sought new or alternative employment opportunities in common, exchanged skills and techniques needed for factory or wait-ressing work, and were a primary source of enjoyable moments. Peers provided a unique opportunity for women to learn nonfamilial social roles. Their intense and at times frenetic whirl of female peer-group pursuits continued only until marriage, when they settled down to a life centered on their new husband and family obligations.

Filial roles in the family

As children who entered the labor force and were the first in their fam-ilies to obtain formal schooling, my interviewees and their elder and younger siblings thereby obtained valuable wider experiences and per-sonal contacts, which were drawn upon eagerly by their parents. Em-ployed daughters help their families choose appropriate schools and streams of education for younger children in the family (Rose, 1976). Working daughters sometimes directed younger siblings' careers, but their opinions were ignored if they countered the parents' versions of family needs. Daughters aided parents in meeting long-standing obliga-tions: Thus their labor was donated by some families to the shops and offices of various relatives. Often the eldest working daughter found that her economic achievements, and especially monetary input to the func-tion at hand, enhanced the deference accorded to her at family gather-ings like wedding banquets, where she might represent her family. My interviewees were proud of their families' improving status and power to stage ceremonial events.

Daughters were permitted to make decisions concerning matters that heralded little for the family future. My respondents could often decide the quality and type of household purchase but never the level and dur-ation of sibling education or the scale of extravagant family banquets. Ten of the fathers, who were authoritarian, successfully abrogated com-modity purchases, but in the remaining eighteen families the daughters were granted privileges in performing the larger-scale shopping tasks (Salaff, 1976b).

The opportunities for females have unquestionably widened over the generations, as seen in women's family formation, the use of their own money, peer relations, and their enlarged role in family decision mak-ing. Mothers and daughters welcome the new, enlarged options for young women in the contemporary industrial configuration, but while exercising the autonomy that their work and wages grant them, employed daughters are expected at all times to keep family prerogatives in full view. Chinese families in Hong Kong still work as economic entities to accomplish their goals and, as in the past, daughters' contributions to the ongoing family unit are unquestioned and critical.

Female rights in the Chinese patriarchy: a look forward

Peripheral family goals have been distinguished from those at its core in an effort to apprehend the individual and social dynamics of industrial Hong Kong. The core features of the kinship institution are deeply rooted historically in Chinese social structure and have enabled the family and its organized kin groups to gather in its forces and compete with other families for scarce resources. Peripheral adjustments have been made to accommodate to the effects of industrialization and transnational penetration. The modified centripetal family has defended and advanced its interests (the continuity of the patriliny) by employing a mix of strategies. In the life histories presented here, these adjustments never weakened the family's constant mode of using family energies in the struggle for scarce economic and political goods.

The active industrial service and semiprofessional work-force participation of Hong Kong daughters actually reinforced a centripetal structure, even though it forced the family to offer peripheral compromises and adjustments that partially freed the laboring daughters from family oversight of their personal lives. Women carved significantly larger areas of opportunity for themselves within the confines of family prescriptions and obligations, but I found that change occurred mainly in spheres that did not affect core centripetal family institutions (Rainbow ultimately was permitted to attend secondary school, but was never trained as an ivory craftsman to inherit her father's artisan establishment). Women could not invest their increased resources from work to enlarge their material assets. Daughters' contributions to the family budget in no case merited a permanent seat on family councils, and indeed the phenomenon of continuity beside change marks family process in Hong Kong society today.

It is evident that before equality can be achieved, the centripetal family's existing limits on the structurally based exercise of authority of women must be annulled. From time immemorial the centripetal family and its associated demands on family energies were grounded in economic and political features: the competition of a vast population for scarce resources, economic security and protection, the inability of the authoritarian political regime to penetrate deeply into local politics at times far removed from the center, and a slow-moving state apparatus that seldom mobilized the social sections of China's polity.

The China-born families of Hong Kong have brought their family-based protective concerns to the colony, where they have encountered a setting whose history has given rise to its own wellsprings of competition for status and goods. The ceiling on the opportunities for economic advancement for today's Hong Kong populace imposed by Hong Kong's complete dependence on the transnational capitalist economic system has given rise to intense vying for school admission, which since industrialization has become the principal means by which youths can qualify for more remunerative and prestigious posts. Because the colonial administration makes the direct redress of grievances difficult, a network of government-sanctioned, self-appointed sectional community leaders, underpinned by the family alliance system and negotiated exchanges with informal groups, monopolizes all movements for social betterment. (The exception is the patriotic center, which for its own reasons mutes its considerable political potential.)

The family that revolves around a father-son axis is thought to provide the most continuity and protection against the considerable economic hardships and uncertainties that characterize a pre-industrial economy (Paige, 1973). By keeping males together, the patrilineal family prescribes clear-cut lines of authority, resources, loyalty, and a coordinated work group. When patrilineal kinship was further linked with patrilocal residence, it provided the solid manpower required for masculine defense in strife-torn early modern China and pre-industrial Hong Kong (Freedman, 1958, 1966). Even today, the exigencies of the early industrial, laissez faire market economy in Hong Kong, with its deficient social security system, seemingly demand the modicum of continuity promised by patrilineal descent, whereby the men in the family can operate as an interest group and protect and promote family interests.

The prevailing institution of patrilineality truncates Chinese daughters from their families of origin, and thus less education, attention, affection, and family pride is bestowed upon the girls in their formative years. Although the considerable financial input of working daughters is greatly welcomed by their families, my case studies show that they

are not accorded privileges and power commensurate with their contributions.

Better-balanced family forms are conceivable in which parents would
mobilize and permanently reward labor and energies of daughters as
well as sons. Such a symmetrical family has never evolved, perhaps because the material and political bases are lacking in Hong Kong. The
bilateral form risks an uncoordinated, relatively defenseless family
economy. The prescribed ancestral religious rites and emotional and
psychological deference to males from infancy reinforce the material
structure of the patriarchy in Hong Kong today.

In order to suggest how Chinese societies like that of Hong Kong
might equalize women's rights and opportunities, it is useful to consider Farber's (1975) concept of *communal society.* I find this concept especially useful in understanding societies in which special family
interests are subordinated to and realized under universal programs of
growth and development. A communal society is one in which state-
controlled structures and institutions establish a popular and universal
base to channel commitment of individuals and their families to the
goals of the total polity. The important examples of such broadly encompassing structures of such modern communal societies are compulsory primary and secondary school systems, the church in Roman
Catholic societies, the welfare state, and the military in an age of con-
scription.

The Tilly and Scott (1978) model of the family consumer economy
that exists in the contemporary welfare state emphasizes the impact of
a wage sufficient to support the entire family by the male household
head in attenuating the economic hold of the parents over their offspring. Whereas poverty, unemployment, and economic uncertainty in
early industrial society give rise to the centripetal family-wage economy
as a collective response, an improved level of living, the extension of
education, and a comprehensive social security system have, by decreasing the importance of children as old-age insurance, obviated the
centralized family economy in certain Western nations (Schorr, 1960;
Stearn et al., 1975:108–109). According to the Rosser and Harris
(1965) study of pre-war Swansea, Wales, families, the depressed economy, low levels of state welfare services, large family size, wives whose
lives were centered on their homes and families, and the absence of an
ideology justifying the sharing of tasks between husband and wife or
close marital communication gave rise to the family that expected

children to subordinate themselves and work in concert toward family goals. With the postwar higher levels of urban employment and the penetration of the British state and social services more deeply into the Welsh society, a secular decline in family size, entry of married women into the labor force, and dissemination of an ideology of equality, the decline of the tight family wage economy was ensured.

In addition to a modicum of economic prosperity, institutional conditions that have been referred to here as "communal" were thus historically prerequisite to the termination of the family wage economy. A universally applicable social security system was one such structure. Another was the school system. Covello (1967) recorded Italian immigrant parents' complaints that their children no longer obliged them with their wages or complied obediently with restrictions of their peer activities once they came into contact with an American school. As a communal structure designed to assimilate immigrant children into the American nation-state, the school deliberately sought to wean children from close identifications with their ethnic groups and families.

Some modern polities fall under Farber's (1975) heading of democratic communal governments (the United States and other advanced capitalist societies), whereas the mobilization form of communal society has become important with the victory of socialist revolutions (the Soviet Union, China, Cuba). The mobilization polity that was brought into being and developed by mass public participation in communal elements (Soviets, Liberation Armed Forces) supports and further develops mass-based participation in the major decisions affecting the lives of the populace (Fagen, 1969; Nettl, 1967).

Major communal forces martial energies for the realization of national objectives by undercutting familism and cleavages along racial, linguistic, and national lines. The communal state attacks conservative family ties and cliques based upon land ownership and the means of production and mobilizes young family members out of the family grip into a wider occupational hierarchy, and even into campaigns for the attainment of national objectives. Under industrial capitalism, institutionalized forms of capital accumulation (banks and trust companies) preponderate over family compacts, networks, alliances, and family capital mobilization (Berkowitz, 1975).

Communalism thereby gives rise to the centrifugal family, counterposed to the centripetal kinship unit of factional orders. In the centripetal framework, individuals advance in rank and status only when they receive substantial personal introductions and recommendations for education and especially employment, which for the most part are derived from the family and its carefully cultivated satellites. If the more or less egalitarian, large-scale education, job training, and social insurance provisions of the communal regime render family control of inherited opportunities superfluous and create alternative authority patterns to kinship, the traditional patrilineal prescriptions for equality of women in Chinese society will be formed. Therefore, the transformation of the Chinese modified centripetal family to some form of a centrifugal family rests upon implementation of far-reaching social, political, and ideological advances.

The Chinese kinship structure has a socially sanctioned inner reality of its own, and its members are intensely attached to it emotionally, psychologically, and intellectually. In a recent study of marriage reform in the Peoples Republic in the early 1950s, Johnson (1976) acknowledged the importance of economic and political reforms for the betterment of women's positions in the family and society but stressed that restructuring and reform of the tenacious centripetal family was organizationally neglected. Johnson found that the Communist Party of China's leadership was aware of the deleterious effect that the traditional rural family had economically on the party's campaign to liberate Chinese women, but it chose not to launch a struggle against its major aspects: arranged or semi-arranged marriage, patrilineal descent, patrilocal residence, masculine leadership in family decision making, and male-dominated village and commune leadership. A study by Parish and Whyte (1978) reinforced this conclusion through an in-depth survey of refugees from Kwangtung province. The bequeathing of dowries increased substantially in the 1960s, the long-standing family division of labor still prevailed in the Kwangtung villages, and child care and the domestic economy were still the preserve solely of women, who nevertheless tilled the paddies while men monopolized political and administrative tasks.[1] Moreover, sons were still heavily favored in the allocation of scarce education and job training resources, which perpetuates the unbalanced patrimony (Diamond, 1975).

Johnson (1976:261–2) concluded that despite China's ongoing mobilizational politics, "this revolutionizing process failed in many ways to penetrate and transform the cultural underpinnings of some of the most basic human relationships – the relationship of women of men and of women to the traditional family unit." As long as the core centripetal family norms legitimately define family action, women will be dependent upon the family and their labor-force participation will expand their opportunities largely to the extent deemed necessary by their parents, acting consistently with long-standing family norms.

Clearly, however, the communal society and its accompanying centrifugal family is no automatic panacea for equality. In major industrial societies, the centrifugal family is now characterized by relatively increased isolation from its kindred and subsequent intensification of the household chores borne by women, and unequal husband-wife division of labor, community, household, and family tasks (Meissner et al., 1975; Willmott, 1973). Marxists freely concede that the advent of socialism does not bring about equality of the sexes.[2] But from the vantage point of the centripetal Chinese family, a movement away from the demand for youths' labor to support the patriliny toward more symmetrical forms could be the first step to equality.

Appendix

Hong Kong: a photographic essay

by Fred Salaff

Seaming sleeves in a factory producing fashionable garments

Knitting in a factory producing fashionable garments
Attaching pockets in a blue jeans factory

Garment assembly in a blue jeans factory

Teaching the trade in a small electronics company that is a subcontractor for a Japanese firm
A family rattan ware business

An ivory carver
A family tailoring business

Dusk in a resettlement estate

Dinner preparations in a resettlement estate

Main bedroom of a working-class apartment

The storage area in the living quarters of a family's resettlement estate apartment

A cottage area, soon to be demolished

A working-class woman in the main room of a cottage

Mei Foo Sun Chuen, a middle-class housing estate

At ease in a Mei Foo Sun Chuen home

Shopping in a hawker's bazaar at a resettlement estate

Buying a snack for younger sisters

A rendezvous at the Star Ferry concourse

Notes

Introduction

1 The three historical modes of economic activity distinguished by Tilly and Scott (1978) for eighteenth to mid-nineteenth century Britain and France are: "the family economy" (1700 to ca. 1875), in which the family manufactured at home many of the goods it used, exchanged, and sold in the market, and children and adults contributed their energies to the family income without individual recognition; the "family wage economy" (late-nineteenth to early-twentieth centuries), in which no single wage earner could support an entire family, and the wages of several employed sons and daughters were pooled with those of their parents; and the "family consumer economy" (ca. 1930s through today), in which the adult male wage earner obtains wages sufficient to support his family members. Children are withdrawn from their direct contributory role in the economy to attend school for longer periods, and wives may choose to withdraw from the labor force to raise their young children.

2 The findings of Tilly and Scott (1978) that family control over wage contributions of the youthful members continues through the early stages of industrial capitalism is borne out by Katz and Davey (1978) for a Canadian city. Katz and Davey found that the ties between parents and children became stronger in the early stages of industrialization. Other research on working-class families that stresses the importance of the family wage economy in the early stages of industrialization includes Anderson (1971), Bossard (1956), Braun (1966), Collier (1965), Dublin (1975), Ets (1970), Less (1969), Roberts (1976), Rowntree (1901), and Walkowitz (1971).

3 See Belloni and Beller (1978) for analyses of factionalism in political parties in China and elsewhere.

4 Examples of groups with overlapping bonds that provoked conflict are the secret societies established by southeastern Chinese immigrants to North America, each of which was grounded in a discrete, recognized heritage of surname and place of origin. The societies provided the immigrants with substitute kin, economic aid, and a political voice. They built hotels and clubhouses where the immigrants lived and passed their time in companionship with members of their own groups. The different associations often argued, and the sharpest of their conflicts led to violent altercations ("tong wars") (Lyman, 1979:48–9).

Chapter 1. Modern times in a colonialized Chinese city

1 Women comprised only 21% of the registered labor force in 1931, whereas they comprised 34% in 1971 (although it is not known whether outworkers were excluded in 1931 and whether they were as numerous as in 1971). The labor force is young: In 1971 close to half of the occupied female workers were 25 years or less. In 1971, 10% of all females ages 10 to 14, 56% of those ages 15 to 19, and 70% of those ages 20 to 24 worked. The labor-force participation was especially high for unmarried women: 88% of

294

the single women ages 20 to 24 were in the labor force full time in 1971. In the category of ever-married (married, widowed, divorced) women, 30% ages 20 to 24 were in the labor force in 1971 (Census and Statistics Department, 1971, unpublished tabulations for 1931, 1971).

2 Registration of industry with the Department of Labour is voluntary for business. Although all sizable firms register their labor force, economists suspect that workers in smaller firms are underregistered by half and may account for 18% of the labor force (Dwyer and Lai, 1967; England, 1971:223).

3 In 1967 I interviewed the manager of Fairchild Semiconductor, Ltd., a Stanford University Business School graduate, and he emphasized the programmatic, superior-imposed constraint on his ability to recognize a union in this Hong Kong firm.

4 In market prices U.S. dollars. Henceforth all money is expressed in the U.S. dollar equivalent in 1973, approximately $5 H.K. = $1 U.S.

5 The labor statutes that had been passed at the midpoint of interviewing (1973-4) were workers' compensation for industrial accidents; 4 days off per month for factory and office workers (but not shop workers); a 48-hour work week for women, excluding overtime, which was permitted to reach 240 hours a year (a statute passed in 1969, before which hours and days off were not regulated); no hiring of children under 14 in industry (however, they may be hired in teahouses where alcoholic beverages are not consumed); unpaid maternity leave (Ma, 1972; Social Welfare Department, 1967, 1973a,b; Stanford Research Institute, 1971). Recent coverage for public assistance is described in social welfare publications (Social Welfare Department, 1978, 1979).

6 In 1971 older female factory workers (craftsmen, production workers, and laborers), ages 25 to 39, had attained the following educational levels: no education, 30%; some primary, 58%; some secondary, 11%. The younger women, ages 15 to 24, had some primary, 75%; some secondary education, 20%. The same rise in educational level was apparent by age group for female clerical and sales workers. Males also improved their educational level over time (Census and Statistics Department, 1971b:Table 26). J. R. Scholtz (1971), Chairman of the Vocational Training Committee, Hong Kong Council of Social Service, and Supervisor, Caritas St. Francis Prevocational School, stated that a student today acquires an "unrealistic pretence" that he will be able to get a job in an office "if only he learns hard enough." Yet "the majority of school leavers will find their way into semi-skilled or unskilled operative jobs in industry, whether they like it or not."

7 Estimated by Dr. Christopher Parker (1974), who taught for 2 years at Hong Kong University. Even 20 years ago, American workers ages 35 and 54 whose education ended with high school earned 80% of what college graduates earned. In Britain, those around 40 years of age in 1966 with higher national certification earned an average of £1,800; those with university degrees earned over $3,000 annually (Little, 1972:112-13; see also Freeman, 1976).

8 For further discussion of the Ch'ing and republican Chinese political systems see Buck (1978), Ch'ien (1970), Chow (1953), Ch'ü (1962), Folsom (1968), Hsiao (1967), Kuhn (1970, 1975), Nathan (1976), Sheridan (1975), Tien (1972), Van Der Sprenkel (1962), and Wakeman (1966, 1975). Studies that describe the effects of republican reforms upon village and market-town life include Gamble (1968:125-65), Kulp (1966:ch. 5), Lin (1947), Pepper (1978), Treudley (1974:ch. 12), C. K. Yang (1959:ch. 7), and M. C. Yang (1945). Hofheinz (1977), Hsieh (1972, 1974), Rhoads (1975), and Yang (1975) analyze southeast China's resistance to central government political control.

9 Buck's 1929-31 study of 202,617 peasants found that 1 in 1,000 Chinese women and 3 in 1,000 Chinese men had never married (Barclay et al., 1976:610, 617). Taeuber (1970:64-5) suggested that the sample drawn for Buck's study was from relatively pros-

perous and accessible villages during a period of comparative peace and stability. Not all men married young, however, according to Gamble's (1968) sample of 5,255 married families of roughly the same period in Ting county, Hopei province. He found that not until they were 39 years of age were 90% of the males married, and 5% married when over 50 years of age (pp. 39–40). There is scattered evidence from studies of more impoverished and remote villages during the wartime blockade and early post-civil war years that men were unable to marry (Crook and Crook, 1959, 1979). However, such studies did not provide precise demographic evidence, and it is possible that the men reported as unmarried in their early adulthood did contract marriages years later. Nevertheless, marriage age was inversely related to social class according to these demographic and village studies.

10 Of the 360 arranged marriages in 170 villages in North China, Fukien, and Kiangsu provinces studied by Lang (1946:123), only once did the parents ask the consent of their son in his marriage, and he was a college student. See also Burgess (1933:404), Ch'en (1979), Fei (1962:40), Gamble (1968:379), Treudley (1974:155), and Yang (1959: 82–4).

11 Cohen (1976) found in a Taiwan Hakka village that women did not obtain a piece of the land, but they were able to use their dowry to invest in farm animals or lend out at interest, thereby reducing their complete economic dependence upon their husbands. Writing on Kwangtung, however, Kulp (1966:150) found that a woman's husband could take her dowry, unless prevented by social pressure.

12 Women comprised the following percentages of the Taiwan industrial labor force in 1973: textiles, 79%; apparel, 86%; electrical equipment and supplies, 66%; food processing, 59% (Taiwan Provincial Labor Force Survey and Research Institute, 1973:17).

Chapter 2. Introducing three factory workers

1 Missionary groups provided many recreational activities for young workers in London, England, at the turn of the century (Gillis, 1974:169–70; Platt, 1969).

Chapter 3. Women in the service sector

1 In 1978 the number of tourists topped the two-million mark (equivalent to an excess of one-third of the colony's population) (Hong Kong Tourist Association, personal communication).

Conclusion

1 Parish and Whyte unfortunately did not seek the centripetal essence of the Chinese family, but their nice dissection of family and village rituals (life-cycle ceremonies, peasant agriculture calendar, and associated festivities) adds a further dimension to our analysis of the centripetal family and its persisting effects.

2 The work of Lapidus (1978) is characterized by a perceptive effort to determine the historically rooted problems and prospects of women in the Soviet Union. See the extensive review of literature by Soviet sociologists on issues of equality cited therein.

See also Jancar's (1978) comparative survey of the structural and attitudinal constraints on women's positions in several contemporary socialist societies.

References

Ahern, E. 1973. *The Cult of the Dead in a Chinese Village.* Stanford: Stanford University Press.

Allen, C. 1970. *Communication Patterns in Hong Kong.* Hong Kong: The Chinese University of Hong Kong.

AMPO. 1977. "Free trade zones and industrialization of Asia." *AMPO: Japan-Asia Quarterly Review* 8(4), 9(1–2).

Anderson, M. 1971. *Family Structure in Nineteenth Century Lancashire.* Cambridge: Cambridge University Press.

Aries, P. 1965. *Centuries of Childhood: A Social History of Family Life.* New York: Doubleday.

Arrigo, L. G. "More working women." In M. Sheridan and J. Salaff (eds.), *Lives: Chinese Working Women.* In preparation.

Baker, H. 1968. *A Chinese Lineage Village: Sheung Shui.* London: Frank Cass.

Barclay, G. W., A. J. Coale, M. A. Stoto, and T. J. Trussell. 1976. "A reassessment of the demography of traditional rural China." *Population Index* 42:606–35.

Barry, H., M. K. Bacon, and I. L. Child. 1959. "Relation of child training to subsistence economy." *American Anthropologist* 61:51–63.

Belden, J. 1970. *China Shakes the World.* New York: Monthly Review Press.

Belloni, F. P., and D. C. Beller 1978. *Faction Politics: Political Parties in Comparative Perspective.* Santa Barbara, Calif.: ABC-Clio Press.

Belshaw, C. S. 1965. *Traditional Exchange and Modern Markets.* Englewood Cliffs, N.J.: Prentice-Hall.

Bendix, R. 1957. *Work and Authority in Industry.* New York: Wiley.

Berger, J. 1972. *Ways of Seeing: A Book Made by John Berger [and others].* London: British Broadcasting Corp.

Berkner, L. K. 1972. "Rural family organization in Europe: A problem in comparative history." *Peasant Studies Newsletter* 1(4):145–56.

Berkowitz, M. 1969. *Folk Religion in an Urban Setting: A Study of Hakka Villagers in Transition.* Hong Kong: Christian Study Centre on Chinese Religion and Culture.

Berkowitz, S. D. 1975. "The dynamics of elite structure: A critique of C. W. Mills' 'power elite' model." Doctoral dissertation. Brandeis, Mass.: Brandeis University, Department of Sociology.

Blake, C. F. 1978. "Death and abuse in marriage laments: The curse of Chinese brides." *Asian Folklore Studies* 37(1):13–33.

Ethnic Groups and Social Change in a Chinese Market Town. Honolulu: University of Hawaii Press. In press.

Blood, R. O., and D. Wolf. 1960. *Husbands and Wives.* Glencoe, Ill.: Free Press.

Boserup, E. 1970. *Woman's Role in Economic Development.* London: George Allen & Unwin.

Bossard, H. H. S. 1956. *The Large Family System.* Philadelphia: University of Pennsylvania Press.

Boxer, B. 1961. *Ocean Shipping in the Evolution of Hong Kong.* Research Paper No. 72. Chicago: The University of Chicago, Department of Geography.

Braun, R. 1966. "The impact of cottage industry on an agricultural population." In D. S. Landes (ed.), *The Rise of Capitalism*, pp. 53–64. New York: Macmillan.

Buck, D. D. 1978. *Urban Change in China: Politics and Development in Tsinan Shantung, 1890–1949*. Madison: University of Wisconsin Press.

Buck, J. L. 1968. *Land Utilization in China*. New York: Paragon Book Reprint.

Burgess, J. S. 1933. "Some observations on Chinese village life." *Social Forces 11*(3):401–9.
　　1945. "Community organization in China." *Far Eastern Survey 14*(25):371–3.

Census and Statistics Department (Hong Kong). 1931. *Population and Housing Census*. Unpublished tables. (Typescript.)
　　1961. *Hong Kong Population and Housing Census*. 3 vols. Hong Kong: Government Printer.
　　1966. *Report of the By-Census, 1966*. 2 vols. Hong Kong: Government Printer.
　　1969. *Hong Kong Statistics, 1947–1967*. Hong Kong: Hong Kong Government Census and Statistics Department.
　　1970–2. Marriage registration data. Unpublished tables. (Computer printout.)
　　1971a. *Population and Housing Census, 1971, Hong Kong: Main Report*. Hong Kong: Government Printer.
　　1971b. *Population and Housing Census, Basic Tables, 1971*. Hong Kong: Government Printer.
　　1973. *Estimates of Gross Domestic Product, 1966–71*. Hong Kong: Census and Statistics Department.

Chaney, D. C. 1971. "Job satisfaction and unionization: The case of shopworkers." In K. Hopkins (ed.) *Hong Kong: The Industrial Colony*, pp. 261–70. Hong Kong: Oxford University Press.

Chaney, D. C., D. Podmore, and A. Lu. 1973. *Young Adults in Hong Kong*. Hong Kong: University of Hong Kong, Centre of Asian Studies.

Chen, F. M. C., and R. H. Myers. 1976. "Customary law and the economic growth of China during the Ch'ing period." *Ch'ing-shih Wen-t'i 3* (November):1–32.
　　1978. "Customary law and the economic growth of China during the Ch'ing period." *Ch'ing-shih Wen-t'i 3* (November):4–27.

Ch'en, J. 1979. *China and the West – Society and Culture –1815–1937*. London: Hutchinson.

Ch'en, T. H. 1920. "Shang-hai sheng-sha-ch'ang Hu-nan ün-kung wen-t'i" ["The problem of female workers from Hunan in a Shanghai cotton mill."] *Hsin Ch'ing Nien [New Youth]* 36(May):1–47.

Cheong, G. S. C. 1969. "Education as enterprise in Hong Kong." *School and Society* (October): 395–8.

Ch'ien, T. S. 1970. *The Government and Politics of China: 1912–1949*. Stanford: Stanford University Press.

Chodorow, N. 1978. *The Reproduction of Mothering: Psychoanalysis and the Sociology of Gender*. Berkeley and Los Angeles: University of California Press.

Chou, K. R. 1966. *The Hong Kong Economy*. Hong Kong: Academic Publications.

Chow, Y. T. 1953. "Life histories." In H. T. Fei (ed.), *China's Gentry: Essays on Rural-Urban Relations*, pp. 145–87. Chicago: The University of Chicago Press.

Ch'u, T. T. 1962. *Local Government in China under the Ch'ing*. Cambridge, Mass.: Harvard University Press.

Cohen, M. 1968. "The Hakka or 'guest people': Dialect as a sociocultural variable in Southern China." *Ethnohistory 15*(3):237–92.
　　1970. "Developmental process in the Chinese domestic group." In M. Freedman (ed.), *Family and Kinship in Chinese Society*, pp. 21–36. Stanford: Stanford University Press.
　　1976. *House United, House Divided*. New York: Columbia University Press.

Cole, J. W. 1973. "Social process in the Italian Alps." *American Anthropologist 75*:765–86.

Collier, F. 1965. *The Family-Economy of the Working Classes in the Cotton Industry, 1784–1833*. Manchester: Manchester University Press.

Cooper, E. 1980. *The Wood-Carvers of Hong Kong: Craft Production in the World Capitalist Periphery.* Cambridge: Cambridge University Press.

Coser, L. A. 1966. *The Functions of Social Conflict.* Glencoe, Ill.: Free Press.

Covello, L. 1967. *The Social Background of the Italo-American School Child.* Leiden: E. J. Brill.

Croll, E. 1978. *Feminism and Socialism in China.* London: Routledge & Kegan Paul.

Crook, I., and D. Crook. 1959. *Revolution in a Chinese Village: 10 Mile Inn.* London: Routledge & Kegan Paul.

1979. *Ten Mile Inn: Mass Movement in a Chinese Village.* New York: Pantheon.

Davin, D. 1976. *Woman-Work: Women and the Party in Revolutionary China.* London:Oxford University Press.

Davis, K. 1940. "The sociology of parent-youth conflict." *American Sociological Review* 5 (August):523–35.

Department of Labour (Hong Kong). 1967. "Report by the Hong Kong textile and industrial committee." In *The Manpower of the Textile Industry, 1967.* Hong Kong: Department of Labour, Textile and Industrial Committee. (Mimeographed.)

1969, 1972, 1973, 1977, 1978, 1979. *Annual Report.* Hong Kong: Government Printer.

1970. *Second Manpower Survey of the Electronics Industry, 1970.* Hong Kong: Department of Labour, Electronics Industrial Committee. (Mimeographed.)

Diamond, N. 1969. *K'un Shen.* New York: Holt, Rinehart & Winston.

1975. "Collectivization, kinship and the status of women." *Bulletin of Concerned Asian Scholars* 7(January–March):25–32.

1976. "Taiwan factory women." Paper presented at the annual meeting of the Association of Asian Studies, Toronto, March.

Dixon, R. B. 1976. "The roles of rural women: Female seclusion, economic production and reproductive choice." In R. G. Ridker (ed.), *Population and Development, the Search for Selective Interventions,* pp. 290–321. Baltimore: Johns Hopkins Press.

Djau, A. 1976. "Social control in a colonial society: A case study of working-class consciousness in Hong Kong." Doctoral dissertation. Toronto: University of Toronto, Department of Sociology.

Dublin, T. 1975. "Women at work: The transformation of work and community in Lowell, Massachusetts, 1826–1860." Doctoral dissertation. New York: Columbia University, Department of History.

Dwyer, D. J. 1971. "Housing provision in Hong Kong." In D. J. Dwyer (ed.), *Asian Urbanization: A Case Book,* pp. 33–47. Hong Kong: University of Hong Kong.

Dwyer, D. J., and C. Y. Lai. 1967. *The Small Industrial Unit in Hong Kong: Patterns and Politics.* Hull, Quebec: University of Hull.

Eberhard, W. 1972. *Chinese Festivals.* Taipei: Asian Folklore and Social Life Monographs.

Emerson, R. 1937. *Malaysia: A Study in Direct and Indirect Rule.* Cambridge, Mass.: Harvard University Press.

Endacott, G. D. 1964. *Government and People of Hong Kong.* Hong Kong: Hong Kong University Press.

Engels, F. 1973. *The Condition of the Working-Class in England.* New York: International Publishers. (First published in 1843.)

England, J. 1971. "Industrial relations in Hong Kong." In K. Hopkins (ed.), *Hong Kong: The Industrial Economy,* pp. 207–59. Hong Kong: Oxford University Press.

England, J., and J. Rear. 1975. *Chinese Labour under British Rule.* Hong Kong: Oxford University Press.

Epstein, A. L. 1958. *Politics in an Urban African Community.* Manchester:Manchester University Press.

Ets, M. H. 1970. *Rosa: The Life of an Italian Immigrant.* Minneapolis: University of Minnesota Press.

Evans, D. M. E. 1973. "The new law of succession in Hong Kong." *Hong Kong Law Journal* 3(1):7–50.

Ewen, S. 1976. *Captains of Consciousness: Advertising and the Social Roots of the Consumer Culture.* Toronto: McGraw-Hill.

Fagan, R. R. 1969. *The Transformation of Political Culture in Cuba.* Stanford: Stanford University Press.

Farber, B. 1975. "Bilateral kinship: Centripetal and centrifugal types of organization." *Journal of Marriage and the Family* 37(November):871–89.

Fei, H. T. 1962. *Peasant Life in China: A Field Study of Country Life in the Yangtse Valley.* London: Routledge & Kegan Paul.

1975. *Earthbound China: A Study of Rural Economy in Yunnan.* Chicago: The University of Chicago Press.

Folsom, K. E. 1968. *Friends, Guests and Colleagues: The Mu-Fu System in the Late Ch'ing Period.* Berkeley and Los Angeles: University of California Press.

Foner, A., and D. Kertzer. 1978. "Transitions over the life course: Lessons from age-set societies." *American Journal of Sociology* 83(March):1081–104.

Freedman, M. 1958. *Lineage Organization in Southeast China.* London: Athlone Press.

1966. "Shifts of power in the Hong Kong New Territories." *Journal of Asian and African Studies* 1(1):3–12.

Freeman, R. B. 1976. *The Overeducated American.* New York: Academic Press.

Fried, M. 1953. *The Fabric of Chinese Society.* New York: Octagon Press.

Friedman, D. D. "Old lady Chang." In M. Sheridan and J. Salaff (eds.), *Lives: Chinese Working Women.* In preparation.

Gamble, S. D. 1968. *Ting Hsien: A North China Rural Community.* Stanford: Stanford University Press.

Garrett, S. 1970. *Social Reformers in Urban China: The Chinese YMCA 1895-1926.* Cambridge, Mass.: Harvard University Press.

Gillis, J. 1974. *Youth and History.* New York: Academic Books.

Gissing, G. 1969. *The Odd Women.* New York: AMS Press.

Goode, W. 1959. "The theoretical importance of love." *American Sociological Review* 24 (February):38–47.

1963. *World Revolution and Family Patterns.* Glencoe, Ill.: Free Press.

Gutman, H. G. 1977. "Work, culture and society in industrializing America, 1815-1919." In H. G. Gutman, *Work, Culture and Society in Industrializing America,* pp. 3–78. New York: Vintage Books.

Hambro, E. I. 1955. *The Problems of Chinese Refugees in Hong Kong.* Leiden: A. W. Sijthoff.

Hammond, J., and B. Hammond. 1966. *The Town Labourer.* London: Longmans.

Ho, P. T. 1966. *Chung-küo Hui-kuan Shih [History of the Chinese Landsmannschaften].* Taipei: Hsüeh-sheng Shu-chu.

Hoadley, J. S. 1970. "Hong Kong is the lifeboat: Notes on political culture and socialization." *Journal of Oriental Studies* 8(January):208–18.

1974. "Political participation of Hong Kong Chinese: Patterns and trends." *Asian Survey* 13(June):604–16.

Hofheinz, R., Jr. 1977. *The Broken Wave: The Chinese Communist Peasant Movement, 1922-28.* Cambridge, Mass.: Harvard University Press.

Hong Kong Council of Social Service. 1967. *Chai Wan Social Needs Study.* Hong Kong: Hong Kong Council of Social Service.

Hong Kong Family Planning Association. Various years. *Annual Report.* Hong Kong: Hong Kong Family Planning Association.

Hong Kong Government. Various years. Hong Kong Annual Report. Hong Kong: Government Printer.

Hopkins, K. 1969. "Public housing policy in Hong Kong: An inaugural lecture from the chair of sociology." *University of Hong Kong Supplement to the Gazette 16*(May 21).

(ed.). 1971. *Hong Kong: The Industrial Colony.* Hong Kong: Oxford University Press.

Howard, C. W., and K. P. Buswell. 1925. "A survey of the silk industry of South China." *Agricultural Bulletin 12*(January) (Ling Nan Agricultural College).

Howard, L. L. 1974. "Industrialization and community in Chotanagpur." Doctoral dissertation. Cambridge, Mass.: Harvard University, Department of Sociology.

Hsiao, K. C. 1967. *Rural China: Imperial Control in the Nineteenth Century.* Seattle: University of Washington Press.

Hsieh, W. 1972. "Triads, salt smugglers and local uprising: Observations on the social and economic background of the Waichow Revolution of 1911." In J. Chesneaux (ed.), *Popular Movements and Secret Societies in China 1840-1950,* pp. 145-64. Stanford: Stanford University Press.

1974. "Peasant insurrection and the marketing hierarchy in the Canton delta, 1911." In M. Elvin and G. W. Skinner (eds.), *The Chinese City between Two Worlds,* pp. 119-42. Stanford: Stanford University Press.

Hsü, F. L. K. 1967. *Under the Ancestor's Shadow.* New York: Doubleday.

Hu, H. C. 1944. "The Chinese concept of face." *American Anthropologist 46*:45-64.

ILO (International Labor Organization). 1966. *Conventions and Recommendations Adopted by the ILO 1919-1966.* Geneva: ILO.

Ingham, G. K. 1970. *Size of Industrial Organization and Worker Behaviour.* Cambridge: Cambridge University Press.

Inkeles, A. 1960. "Industrial man: The relation of status to experience, perception and value." *American Journal of Sociology 66*(1):1-31.

Inkeles, A., and D. H. Smith. 1974. *Becoming Modern.* Cambridge, Mass.: Harvard University Press.

Jacobs, J. B. 1979. "A preliminary model of particularistic ties in Chinese political alliances: Kan-ch'ing and kuan-hsi in a rural Taiwanese township." *The China Quarterly 78*(June): 237-73.

Jamieson, G. 1970. *Chinese Family and Commercial Law.* Hong Kong: Vetch & Lee.

Jancar, B. 1978. *Women under Communism: A Cross-National Analysis of Women in Communist Societies.* Baltimore: Johns Hopkins Press.

Johnson, E. 1975. "Women and childbearing in Kwun Mun Hau village: A study in social change." In M. Wolf and R. Witke (eds.), *Women in Chinese Society,* pp. 215-42. Stanford: Stanford University Press.

"Great-Aunt Yeung: A Hakka wage-laborer." In M. Sheridan and J. Salaff (eds.). *Lives: Chinese Working Women.* In preparation.

Johnson, K. 1976. "The politics of women's rights and family reform." Doctoral dissertation. Madison: University of Wisconsin, Department of Political Science.

Jones, S. M. 1972. "Finance in Ningpo: The chien-chuang, 1750-1880." In W. E. Willmott (ed.), *Economic Organization in Chinese Society,* pp. 47-77. Stanford: Stanford University Press.

Kanter, R. M. 1977. *Men and Women of the Corporation.* New York: Harper-Colophon Books.

Katz, E., and P. Lazarsfeld. 1964. *Personal Influence.* Glencoe, Ill.: Free Press.

Katz, M., and I. Davey. 1978. "Youth and early industrialization in a Canadian city." In J. Demos and S. S. Boocock (eds.), *Turning Points: Sociological Essays on the Family,* pp. S81-119. Chicago: The University of Chicago Press.

"Ke-ming chia-chang ti kuang-jung tse-jen: Sung-tzu wu nung-shih chi-hsüan" ["The glorious duty of revolutionary parents: Selected accounts of young people engaged in agriculture"]. Shanghai: People's Press. Translated in *Chinese Sociology and Anthropology* (Winter), 1978-9.

Kemper, T. D. 1968. "Reference groups, socialization and achievement." *American Sociological Review 33*(February):31–45.

Kerr, C., J. T. Kunlop, F. H. Harbison, and C. H. Myers. 1960. *Industrialism and Industrial Man.* Cambridge, Mass.: Harvard University Press.

Kett, J. E. 1978. *Rites of Passage: Adolescence in America, 1790 to the Present.* New York: Basic Books.

King, A. C. 1975. "Administrative absorption of politics in Hong Kong, emphasis on the grass roots level." *Asian Survey 15*(May):422–39.

Klapper, H. 1960. *The Effects of Mass Communication.* Glencoe, Ill.: Free Press.

Kohl, S.B. 1976. *Working Together: Women and Family in Southwestern Saskatchewan.* Toronto: Holt, Rinehart & Winston.

Kuhn, P. A. 1970. *Rebellion and Its Enemies in Late Imperial China: Militarization and Social Structure, 1796–1864.* Cambridge, Mass.: Harvard University Press.

———. 1975. "Local self-government under the Republic." In F. Wakeman and C. Grant (eds.), *Conflict and Control in Imperial China,* pp. 287–95. Berkeley and Los Angeles: University of California Press.

Kulp, D. H. 1966. *Country Life in South China: The Sociology of Familism,* Vol. 1: *Phenix Village, Kwangtung, China.* Taipei: Ch'eng-wen.

Kung, L. 1976. "Factory work and women in Taiwan: Changes in self-image and status." *Signs 2*(Autumn):35–58.

———. "Factory women." In M. Sheridan and J. Salaff (eds.), *Lives: Chinese Working Women.* In preparation.

Lam, W. "Lives: Hong Kong emigrant families." In M. Sheridan and J. Salaff (eds.), *Lives: Chinese Working Women.* In preparation.

Lamson, H. D. 1930. "The standard of living of factory workers." *Chinese Economic Journal* 7:1240–56.

———. 1931. "The effect of industrialization upon village livelihood." *Chinese Economic Journal* 9:1027–77.

Lang, O. 1946. *Chinese Family and Society.* New Haven, Conn.: Yale University Press.

Langer, E. 1972. "Inside the New York Telephone Company." In W. O'Neill (ed.), *Women at Work,* pp. 307–60. Chicago: Quadrangle Books.

Lapidus, G. W. 1978. *Women in Soviet Society: Equality, Development and Social Change.* Berkeley and Los Angeles: University of California Press.

Lazarsfeld, P. F. 1968. *The People's Choice.* Glencoe, Ill.: Free Press.

Lee, W. Y. 1969. *Youth and the Media.* Hong Kong: Lutheran World Federation Broadcasting Service.

Leeming, F. 1977. *Street Studies in Hong Kong.* Hong Kong: Oxford University Press.

Lees, L. H. 1969. "Patterns of lower-class life: Irish slum communities in nineteenth century London." In S. Thernstrom and R. Sennett (eds.), *Nineteenth Century Cities,* pp. 359–85. New Haven, Conn.: Yale University Press.

Lerner, D. 1958. *The Passing of Traditional Society: Modernizing the Middle East.* New York: Free Press.

———. 1967. "Comparative analysis of processes of modernization." In H. Miner (ed.), *The City in Modern Africa,* pp. 21–38. New York: Praeger.

Lethbridge, H. J. 1978. *Hong Kong: Stability and Change, Collection of Essays.* Hong Kong: Oxford University Press.

Leung, J. 1973. "Production lines damage young minds." *South China Morning Post,* September 23, Hong Kong.

Levenson, J. 1957. "The amateur ideal in Ming and early Ch'ing society: Evidence from painting." In J. K. Fairbank (ed.), *Chinese Thought and Institutions,* pp. 320–41. Chicago: The University of Chicago Press.

Levy, M. J. 1949. *The Family Revolution in China*. Cambridge, Mass.: Harvard University Press.
 1970. "Some hypotheses about the family." *Journal of Comparative Family Studies* 1(1):
 119–31.
Li, C. H. 1929. *Pei-p'ing Chiao-wai Chih Hsiang-ts'un Chia-t'ing [Rural Families in Suburban Peiping]*. Shanghai: Shang-wu yin-shu-kuan.
Lin, Y. H. 1947. *The Golden Wing: A Sociological Study of Chinese Familism.* London: Kegan Paul, French & Treuber.
Little, A. 1972. "Education." In P. Barker (ed.), *A Sociological Portrait*, pp. 112–25. London: Penguin.
Liu, T. C., and K. C. Yeh. 1965. *The Economy of the Chinese Mainland, National Income and Economic Development*. Princeton, N.J.: Princeton University Press.
Lutz, H., and B. Snow. 1971. "Hard labour for life." *Far Eastern Economic Review* 86(January 16):17–19.
Lyman, S. 1979. *The Asian in North America*. Santa Barbara, Calif.: Clio Books.
Ma, N. 1972. "Welfare in the cheap." *Far Eastern Economic Review* 87(2):15.
McLuhan, M. 1966. *Understanding Media*. New York: Signet.
Man, T. Y. 1972. *I Ko Nü-küng Ti Pi-chi [The Biography of a Factory Girl]*. Hong Kong: Wan Chiao.
Mander, J. 1978. *Four Arguments for the Elimination of Television*. New York: Morrow.
Mann, M. 1970. "The social cohesion of liberal democracy." *American Sociological Review* 35(3):423–39.
Marsh, R. M. 1968. "The Taiwanese of Taipei." *Journal of Asian Studies* 27(May):571–84.
McElderry, A. L. 1976. *Shanghai Old-Style Banks (Ch'ien-Chuang) 1800–1835*. Michigan Papers in Chinese Studies No. 25. Ann Arbor: The University of Michigan, Center for Chinese Studies.
McGee, T. 1970. *Hawkers in Selected Asian Cities: A Preliminary Investigation*. Hong Kong: University of Hong Kong, Centre of Asian Studies.
Meissner, M., E. Humphreys, S. Meis, and W. Scheu. 1975. "No exit for wives: Sexual division of labour and the cumulation of household demands." *Canadian Journal of Sociology and Anthropology* 12:424–39.
Miller, K. 1976. "Modern experience, the family and fertility in six nations." Doctoral dissertation. Stanford: Stanford University.
Mills, L. 1942. *British Rule in East Asia*. London: Oxford University Press.
Miners, N. J. 1975. *The Government and Politics of Hong Kong*. Hong Kong: Oxford University Press.
Mintz, B. 1977. "Interviews with young working women in Seoul." In S. Mattielli (ed.), *Virtues in Conflict: Tradition and the Korean Woman Today*, pp. 169–89. Seoul: Royal Asiatic Society, Korea Branch.
Mitchell, R. M. 1972a. *Family Life in Urban Hong Kong*. 2 vols. Taipei: Asian Folklore and Social Life Monographs.
 1972b. "Residential patterns and family networks, II." *International Journal of Sociology of the Family* 3:23–41.
Mitchell, R. M., and I. Lo. 1968. "Implications of changes in family authority relations for the development of independence and assertiveness in Hong Kong children." *Asian Survey* 8(April):309–22.
Myers, R. H. 1975. "Cooperation in traditional agriculture and its implications for team farming the People's Republic of China." In D. H. Perkins (ed.), *China's Modern Economy in Historical Perspective*, pp. 261–77. Stanford: Stanford University Press.
Nathan, A. 1976. *Peking Politics 1918–1923: Factionalism and the Failure of Constitutionalism*. Berkeley and Los Angeles: University of California Press.
Nettl, J. P. 1967. *Political Mobilization*. London: Faber.

Nisbet, R. 1970. *The Sociological Tradition.* New York: Free Press.

Olsen, S. 1973. "Family structure and independence training in a Taiwanese village." *Journal of Marriage and the Family* 35(August):512–19.

Osgood, C. 1975. *The Chinese: A Study of a Hong Kong Community.* 3 vols. Tucson: University of Arizona Press.

Owen, N. 1971. "Economic policy." In K. Hopkins (ed.), *Hong Kong: The Industrial Colony,* pp. 141–206. Hong Kong: Oxford University Press.

Paige, J. M. 1973. "Kinship and polity in stateless societies." *American Journal of Sociology* 80(2):301–21.

Papanek, H. 1973. "Men, women and work: reflections on a two-person career." *American Journal of Sociology* 78(January):852–72.

Parish, W. L., and M. K. Whyte. 1978. *Village and Family in Contemporary China.* Chicago: The University of Chicago Press.

Parker, C. 1974. "Hong Kong students are pressured to make the grade, says Professor." *Daily Aztec,* November 7. San Diego, Calif.: San Diego State University.

Parsons, T. 1951. *The Social System.* Glencoe, Ill.: Free Press.

Pasternak, B. 1972. *Kinship and Community in Two Chinese Villages.* Stanford: Stanford University Press.

Pepper, S. 1978. *Civil War in China: The Political Struggle, 1945–1949.* Berkeley and Los Angeles: University of California Press.

Pinchbeck, I. 1969. *Women Workers in the Industrial Revolution, 1750–1850.* New York: Augustus M. Kelley.

Platt, A. 1969. *The Child Savers.* Chicago: The University of Chicago Press.

Pleck, J. 1977. "The work-family role system." *Social Problems* 24(April):417–27.

Podmore, D. 1971. "The population of Hong Kong." In K. Hopkins (ed.), *Hong Kong: The Industrial Colony,* pp. 21–54. Hong Kong: Oxford University Press.

Polanyi, K. 1957. *The Great Transformation.* Boston: Beacon Press.

Porter, R. 1975. "Child labour in Hong Kong in the 1970s and related problems: A brief review." *International Labour Review* 111:427–39.

Powell, J. D. 1970. "Peasant society and clientelist politics." *The American Political Science Review* 64:411–25.

Pruitt, I. 1967. *A Daughter of Han: The Autobiography of a Chinese Working Woman.* Stanford: Stanford University Press.

Rear, J. 1971. "One brand of politics." In K. Hopkins (ed.), *Hong Kong: The Industrial Colony,* pp. 55–139. Hong Kong: Oxford University Press.

Registrar of Trade Unions. 1975. *Annual Department Report.* Hong Kong: Government Printer.

Rhoads, E. J. M. 1975. *China's Republican Revolution: The Case of Kwangtung, 1895–1913.* Cambridge, Mass.: Harvard University Press.

Richardson, D. 1972. "The long day: A study of a New York working girl." In W. O. O'Neill (ed.), *Women at Work,* pp. 1–303. Chicago: Quadrangle Books.

Roberts, W. 1976. *Honest Womanhood: Feminism, Femininity and Class Consciousness among Toronto Working Women, 1893–1914.* Toronto: New Hogtown Press.

Rosen, S. 1978. "Sibling and in-law relationships in Hong Kong: The emergent role of Chinese wives." *Journal of Marriage and the Family* 40(August):621–8.

Ross, M. 1976. "Competition for education in Hong Kong: The schools, the entrance examination, and the strategies of Chinese families." Doctoral dissertation. Austin: University of Texas.

Rosser, C., and C. Harris. 1965. *Family and Social Change.* London: Routledge & Kegan Paul.

Rowe, E. 1966. *Failure in School.* Hong Kong: Hong Kong University, Hong Kong Council for Educational Research, No. 3 (February).

Rowntree, B. S. 1901. *Poverty: A Study of Town Life,* London: Nelson.

Runciman, W. G. 1972. *Relative Deprivation and Social Justice.* Middlesex: Penguin.

Safa, H. 1978. "Women, production and reproduction in industrial capitalism." Paper presented at the Conference on the Continuing Subordination of Women and the Development Process, Institute of Development Studies, Sussex.

Safilios-Rothschild, C. 1972. "Methodological problems involved in the cross-cultural examination of indicators related to the status of women." Paper presented at the annual meeting of the Population Association of America, Toronto, April 13–15.

Sahlins, M. D. 1965. "On the sociology of primitive exchange." In M. Banton (ed.), *The Relevance of Models for Social Anthropology,* pp. 139–236. London: Tavistock.

Salaff, J. W. 1972. "Institutionalized motivation for fertility limitation in the People's Republic of China." *Population Studies 26*(July):233–61.

1976a. "The status of unmarried Hong Kong women and the social factors contributing to their delayed marriage." *Population Studies 30*(3):391–412.

1976b. "Working daughters in the Hong Kong Chinese family: Female filial piety or a transformation in the family power structure?" *Journal of Social History 9*:439–65.

The Structuring of a Modern Society: Class, Social Policy, and Family Plan in Singapore. In preparation.

Salaff, J. W., and A. K. Wong. 1977. "Chinese women at work: Work commitment and fertility in the Asian setting." In S. Kupinsky (ed.), *The Fertility of Working Women: An International Synthesis of Research,* pp. 81–145. New York: Praeger.

Sankar, A. "Spinster sisterhoods." In M. Sheridan and J. Salaff (eds.), *Lives: Chinese Working Women.* In preparation.

Schak, D. C. 1974. *Dating and Mate Selection in Modern Taiwan.* Taipei: Asian Folklore and Social Life Monographs.

Scholtz, J. R. 1971. "Careers today: Are youngsters getting a fair go?" *South China Morning Post,* July 12, p. 16, Hong Kong.

Schorr, A. 1960. *Filial Responsibility in the Modern American Family: An Evaluation of Current Practice of Filial Responsibility in the United States and the Relation to It of Social Security Programs.* Washington, D.C.: U.S. Social Security Administration, Department of Health, Education and Welfare.

Scott, J. C. 1972. "Patron-client politics and political changes in Southeast Asia." *American Political Science Review 66*:99–113.

Seccombe, W. 1974. "The housewife and her labour under capitalism." *New Left Review* (January):3–24.

Selznick, P. 1952. "Cooptation: A mechanism for organizational stability." In R. K. Merton (ed.), *Reader in Bureaucracy,* pp. 135–9. Glencoe, Ill.: Free Press.

Sheridan, J. E. 1975. *China in Disintegration.* New York: Free Press.

Sheridan, M. "Women in revolution" In M. Sheridan and J. Salaff (eds.), *Lives: Chinese Working Women.* In preparation.

Shiga, S. 1978. "Family property and the law of inheritance in traditional China." In D. C. Buxbaum (ed.), *Chinese Family Law and Social Change in Historical and Comparative Perspective,* pp. 109–50. Seattle: University of Washington Press.

Shorter, E. 1972. "Capitalism, culture and sexuality: Some competing models." *Social Science Quarterly 53*:338–56.

1975. *The Making of the Modern Family.* New York: Basic Books.

Silin, R. H. 1976. *Leadership and Values: The Organization of Large-scale Taiwanese Enterprises.* Cambridge, Mass.: Harvard University Press.

Simpson, R. F. 1967. *Priorities for Educational Development in Hong Kong.* Hong Kong: Hong Kong University, Hong Kong Council for Educational Research.

Skinner, G. W. 1966. "Filial sons and their sisters: Configuration and culture in Chinese families." Paper prepared for the conference "Kinship in Chinese Society," SSRC and ACLS, Riverdale, New York, September 15–18.

Slater, P. 1968. *The Glory of Hera: Greek Mythology and the Greek Family.* Boston: Beacon Press.

Smedley, A. 1978. "Silk workers." In A. Smedley, *Portrait of Chinese Women in Revolution,* pp. 103–10. Old Westbury, N.Y.: Feminist Press.

Smelser, N. J. 1959. *Social Change in the Industrial Revolution.* Chicago: The University of Chicago Press.

Snow, R. 1977. "Dependent development and the new industrial worker. The case of the export processing zones in the Philippines." Doctoral dissertation. Cambridge, Mass.: Harvard University, Department of Sociology.

Social Welfare Department. 1967. *Report of the Working Party on Social Security.* Hong Kong: Government Printer.

   1973a. *Social Welfare in Hong Kong: The Way Ahead.* Hong Kong: Government Printer.

   1973b. *The Five Year Plan for Social Welfare Development in Hong Kong. 1973-1978.* Hong Kong: Government Printer.

   1978. *The Public Assistance Scheme.* 7th ed. Hong Kong: Social Welfare Department.

   1979. *Social Welfare in the 1980's.* Hong Kong: Social Welfare Department.

   n.d. "Community centres in Hong Kong." Hong Kong: Social Welfare Department. (Mimeographed.)

Sparks, D. 1976. "Interethnic interaction - a matter of definition in a housing estate in Hong Kong." *Journal of the Hong Kong Branch of the Royal Asiatic Society 16*:55–80.

Stanford Research Institute. 1971. *Comparative Labor Costs, Korea, Taiwan, Hong Kong, Singapore.* Palo Alto, Calif.: Stanford Research Institute.

Stearn, D., S. Smith, and F. Doolittle. 1975. "How children used to work." *Law and Contemporary Problems 39*(Summer): 93–117.

Szczpanik, E. F. 1958. *The Economic Growth of Hong Kong.* London: Oxford University Press.

Taeuber, I. B. 1970. "The families of Chinese farmers." In M. Freedman (ed.), *Family and Kinship in Chinese Society,* pp. 73–85. Stanford: Stanford University Press.

Taiwan Provincial Labor Force Survey and Research Institute. 1973. *Establishment Survey on Employment, Hours, Earnings, and Labor Turnover in Secondary Industries in Taiwan Area, Republic of China.* Taiwan: Taiwan Research Institute.

Tavuchis, N. 1968. "An exploratory study of kinship and mobility among second generation Greek Americans." Doctoral dissertation. New York: Columbia University.

Tien, H. M. 1972. *Government and Politics in Kuomintang China: 1927-1937.* Stanford: Stanford University Press.

T'ien, J. K. 1968. "Female labor in a cotton mill." In K. H. Shih (ed.), *China Enters the Machine Age: A Study of Labor in Chinese War Industry,* pp. 178–95. New York: Greenwood Press.

Tilly, L., and J. Scott. 1978 *Women, Work, and the Family.* New York: Holt, Rinehart & Winston.

Topley, M. 1969. "The role of savings and wealth among Hong Kong Chinese." In I. C. Jarvie and J. Agassi (eds.), *Hong Kong: A Society in Transition,* pp. 156-86, London: Routledge & Kegan Paul.

   1975. "Marriage resistance in rural Kwangtung." In M. Wolf and R. Witke (eds.), *Women in Chinese Society,* pp. 67–88. Stanford: Stanford University Press.

Treudley, M. B. 1974. *The Men and Women of Chung Ho Ch'ang.* Taipei: Asian Folklore and Social Life Monographs.

Tsao, H. M. 1970. "Using materialistic dialectics to revolutionize the family." *Peking Review* (November):10–12.

UMELCO (Unofficial Members of the Executive and Legislative Councils). 1974. *Report* (February). Hong Kong: UMELCO. (Mimeographed.)

Van Der Sprenkel, S. 1962. *Legal Institutions in Manchu China. A Sociological Analysis.* London: Athlone Press.

Wakeman, F. 1966. *Strangers at the Gate: Social Disorder in South China.* Berkeley and Los Angeles: University of California Press.

—— 1972. "The secret societies of Kuangtung, 1800–1856." In J. Chesneaux (ed.), *Popular Movements and Secret Societies in China, 1840–1950*, pp. 49–62. Stanford: Stanford University Press.

—— 1975. *The Fall of Imperial China.* New York: Free Press.

Wales, N. 1951. *The Chinese Labor Movement.* New York: John Day.

Walkowitz, D. 1971. "Working-class women in the gilded age: Factory, community, and family life among Cohoes, New York cotton workers." *Journal of Social History* 5:465–90.

Watson, J. L. 1975. *Emigration and the Chinese Lineage: The Mans in Hong Kong and London.* Berkeley and Los Angeles: University of California Press.

Weiner, M. (ed.). 1976. *Modernization: The Dynamics of Growth.* Chicago: The University of Chicago Press.

Weinstein, F., and G. Platt. 1969. *The Wish to Be Free: Society, Psyche and Value Change.* Berkeley and Los Angeles: University of California Press.

Wertheim, W. F. 1965. *East-West Parallels.* Chicago: Quadrangle Press.

"Wig factory-girls win $8670 [H.K.] in damages." 1971. *South China Morning Post*, July 20, Hong Kong.

Wolf, A. 1974. "Gods, ghosts and ancestors." In A. Wolf (ed.), *Religion and Ritual in Chinese Society*, pp. 131–82. Stanford: Stanford University Press.

Wolf, M. 1970. *House of Lim.* New York: Appleton-Century-Crofts.

—— 1972. *Women and the Family in Rural Taiwan.* Stanford: Stanford University Press.

Wong, A. K. 1970–1. "Political apathy and the political system in Hong Kong." *United College Journal* 8:1–20.

—— 1972. *The Kaifong Associations and the Society of Hong Kong.* Taipei: Asian Folklore and Social Life Monographs.

—— 1973a. *Job Satisfaction among Higher Non-expatriate Civil Service in Hong Kong.* Working Paper No. 9. Singapore: University of Singapore, Department of Sociology. (Mimeographed.)

—— 1973b. "Rising social status and economic participation of women in Hong Kong – Review of a decade." *Southeast Asian Journal of Social Sciences* 1(2):11–27.

Yang, C. K. 1959. *A Chinese Village in Early Communist Transition.* Cambridge, Mass.: The MIT Press.

—— 1967. *Religion in Chinese Society.* Berkeley and Los Angeles: University of California Press.

—— 1975. "Some preliminary statistical patterns of mass action in nineteenth-century China." In F. Wakeman, Jr., and C. Grant (eds.), *Conflict and Control in Late Imperial China*, pp. 174–210. Berkeley and Los Angeles: University of California Press.

Yang, M. C. 1945. *A Chinese Village: Taitou, Shantung Province.* New York: Columbia University Press.

Yeung, M. 1973. "They call it the hot bowl. . . and adults don't like it." *Standard*, June 23, Hong Kong.

Young, J. A. 1974. *Business and Sentiment in a Chinese Market Town.* Taipei: Asian Folklore and Social Life Monographs.

Young, M., and P. Willmott. 1973. *The Symmetrical Family.* London: Routledge & Kegan Paul.

Index